DATE DUE

DEMCO 38-296

Peter Maxwell Davies

Sir Peter Maxwell Davies at Edinburgh Castle.
(Photograph courtesy of Judy Arnold)

Peter Maxwell Davies

A Bio-Bibliography

CAROLYN J. SMITH

Bio-Bibliographies in Music, Number 57
Donald L. Hixon, Series Adviser

Greenwood Press
Westport, Connecticut • London

Library of Congress Cataloging-in-Publication Data

Smith, Carolyn J.
    Peter Maxwell Davies : a bio-bibliography / Carolyn J. Smith.
       p.   cm.—(Bio-bibliographies in music, ISSN 0742–6968 ; no.
57)
    Includes bibliographical references, discography, filmography, and
index.
    ISBN 0–313–26831–2 (alk. paper)
    1. Davies, Peter Maxwell, 1934– —Bibliography. 2. Davies, Peter
Maxwell, 1934– —Discography. I. Title. II. Series.
ML134.D25S65   1995
780'.92—dc20
[B]   95–21757

British Library Cataloguing in Publication Data is available.

Library of Congress Catalog Card Number: 95–21757
ISBN: 0–313–26831–2
ISSN: 0742–6968

First published in 1995

Greenwood Press, 88 Post Road West, Westport, CT 06881
An imprint of Greenwood Publishing Group, Inc.

Printed in the United States of America

To Robin

Contents

Preface

In keeping with the intent of the series *Bio-Bibliographies in Music*, this book is intended as a guide to resources for those wishing to do further research. I make no claim to comprehensiveness: even unannotated citations of all the reviews, interviews, and articles on Peter Maxwell Davies would produce too long a volume.

This volume is arranged in the following manner:

(1)   A very brief biography of Sir Peter Maxwell Davies. This is intended merely to give a broad outline of the composer's life. A full-length biography by Mike Seabrook has just been published: *MAX: The Life and Music of Peter Maxwell Davies* (London: Victor Gollanz, 1994). Those wishing more information on his life and the history of individual compositions will find much of value there. Analytical discussions of his compositions through the early 1980s may be found in Paul Griffiths, *Peter Maxwell Davies*, and in the *New Grove's* article by Steven Walsh, among other sources.

(2)   A list of works, arranged alphabetically by composition title, with a description of each work and information on publication and first performance(s), including location, date and performers, manuscript location, and recordings, to the extent that I know them. Where I have no information about premiere, manuscript, or recording, I have simply omitted this part of the entry rather than listing them as 'unknown' when all I can really say is that *I* do not know. Derived works and arrangements of original composition follow the original work, retaining that number with the addition of a subsidiary letter to distinguish them from the original work. All works with references in the Bibliography are then followed by the relevant bibliography citation numbers.

For works listed in the catalog maintained by Judy Arnold, I have given the 'J' number after the title. I have tried to make my list as complete as possible, but it obviously cannot include works not yet written (and with Peter Maxwell

Davies, there are likely to be a large number of those). Another consequence of his astonishing productivity is that occasionally works turn up which he had forgotten about writing. I have therefore arranged my catalog alphabetically rather than chronologically, since I regard my work as provisional, not definitive. Its purpose is to provide access to sources concerning the works, and an alphabetical list is easier to use. (A chronological list, with 'J' numbers, appears near the end of the book.)

(3) A Discography, including sound recordings in all formats (i.e., LP, cassette, CD) of Maxwell Davies's recorded works. My entries are based on a number of sources, especially database information which is available to anyone who has access to the relevant systems. One of the most important sources, however, has again been Mrs. Judy Arnold, who has generously kept me informed of not only older recordings but the newest available and those forthcoming. The arrangement is alphabetical by work and includes the work number, followed by a listing of the recordings in chronological order. Each entry includes the recording company, number, date, and format and, where possible, re-releases. Performer(s) follow, as does the album title if it is unique rather than just a listing of the album contents. The couplings are last, including the full names(s) of the composer(s) as well as the selections. The appropriate citation reference numbers follow.

(4) A Bibliography arranged alphabetically by author; articles and reviews are listed first, then books, theses, and dissertations. It is intended for use with the list of Works and First Performances: for articles concerning a particular work, consult the *SEE* listings in each entry. My summaries are only intended to provide information about the scope and content of an item, though I sometimes give an indication of the general tone of a review. In a few obvious cases (e.g., the *New Grove's* article) I have dispensed with annotation.

Essays and articles by Peter Maxwell Davies are included in the Bibliography in their normal alphabetical location.

(5) A brief Filmography listing several videotape and film sources concerning the composer, as well as the two films for which he wrote scores. Much additional recorded material, including radio programs and interviews, is available at the National Sound Archive (many are listed in Bayliss: see B914).

(6) A Chronological Listing arranged, so far as possible, by date of *composition*, which is occasionally several years earlier than first performance. Premiere dates are given when I know them. Some works have had long or complex compositional histories (e.g., *Ecce Manus Tradentis*, *Taverner*); in these cases, I have chosen a date that seemed reasonable.

(7) An Index of references to persons, places, and organizations (works are referenced through the List of Works and Performances).

Since September 1993, the great majority of the manuscripts have been in the British Library. The Library's excellent catalog of these holdings has been invaluable to me. It should be noted that this collection includes some sketches by the composer's students at Cirencester Grammar School. In the few cases in which I have been able to determine that an item is definitely not one of his compositions, I have not listed it here.

The 'J' numbers (so designated, at the composer's suggestion, after Judy Arnold's given name) first appeared in Colin Bayliss, *The Music of Sir Peter Maxwell Davies* (see B914), which indexed the works through 1990. However, Mrs. Arnold has since made some adjustments in the numbers to reflect more accurately the chronological order of compositions (and of course many new works have been composed in the meantime). The 'J' numbers I give are in accordance with her latest revisions and sometimes differ from those in Bayliss.

Mrs. Arnold's catalogs are the obvious source to consult for up-to-date information on published works. Among those available to date are:

Peter Maxwell Davies: The Complete Catalogue of Published Works. Compiled and edited by Judy Arnold, with Rechard Emsley, Stephen Pruslin, and Ruth Thackeray. 1981. With *Supplement: Works of January 1981 to February 1982*; *Supplementary List No. 2* (through 1985).

Peter Maxwell Davies: The Published Works. Judy Arnold, with editorial consultant Stephen Pruslin. 1989.

Peter Maxwell Davies: A Guide to the Dramatic Works. With Introduction and Notes (in German and English) by Paul Griffiths. c. 1987.

Peter Maxwell Davies: A Guide to the Orchestral Works. With Introduction and Notes (German and English) by Paul Griffiths. c. 1985, supplement c. 1989.

Peter Maxwell Davies: A Guide to the Works for 1–17 Instruments. With notes by Paul Griffiths. 1987.

Peter Maxwell Davies: A Guide to the Works for Young Performers. Introduction and Notes by Paul Griffiths. c. 1985

For these and more recent catalogs, contact Mrs. Judy Arnold, 50 Hogarth Road, London, SW5 0PU.

I am indebted to a number of people for their generous assistance with this book: Andrew Cross, Archivist of the Salford Archive; I. C. Cunningham, Keeper of Manuscripts, Maps and Music, National Library of Scotland; Robert K. Leslie, A. L. A., Chief Librarian of the Orkney Library, Kirkwall; Mrs. C. A. Banks, Assistant Music Librarian, and Timothy Day, Curator of Western Art and Music, both of the British Library; Northwestern University Music Library; The Library of Congress; Graham Melville, Cataloguer, National Film and Television Archive, London; Ann McKay and the staff of the Scottish Music Information Center, Glasgow; Anne Sinclair, Arts Council Films, Arts Councils of England; Schott & Co.; David Lea, Manager, Copyright Dept., Longman Group; several persons at Boosey & Hawkes, including R. A. Fell, Managing Director, Group Publishing; Sally Cox, Publishing Editor; Elaine C. Carroll, Promotion; and Emma Kerr, Promotion Assistant; James Rushton, Managing

Director, Chester Music; Archie Bevan, Eva Bergh, John Carewe, Sir William Glock, Hilary Groves, Sylvia Junge, Ian Kellam, Gerard McBurney, Charles Thompson, and Timothy Walker (for information about the location of manuscripts); Ann and John Flett, for their hospitality and assistance; Nelda Elder, John Vander Velde, and the staff of the Collection Development Department, Kansas State University Library.   Kansas State University supported my research with several grants for travel and the acquisition of materials; I am also grateful to Dr. Stephen Atkins, Head of Collection Development, Sterling C. Evans Library, Texas A&M University, for his support.

But above all, I owe an enormous debt of gratitude to Mrs. Judy Arnold, the composer's agent since 1975.   She and her husband Michael allowed me to rummage freely through their enormous files of reviews, supplied me with endless faxes in response to my queries, provided me with invaluable information about performances, recordings, and other matters that I should never otherwise have been able to obtain, and generally saved me from hosts of errors.   (Those that remain are, of course, my responsibility alone.)

And finally, my thanks to my always patient family.   To Robin especially, for his technical help with formatting, translating, and proofreading.

Biography

Peter Maxwell Davies was born September 8, 1934, in Salford, near Manchester, Lancashire. He was the son of Thomas Davies, factory foreman and skilled maker of precision instruments, and Hilda, a talented amateur painter. His musical precocity was evident from his earliest years. An amateur performance of Gilbert and Sullivan's *The Gondoliers* at the Salford Central Mission, which he attended at the age of four, was like an epiphany for him, a vision of another magical world on stage. By the age of eight, he already knew that he would be a composer. His formal education began at age 5 at the Moorside Council School, which he has described more than once as "brutal." From there, he went on early to the Leigh Boys Grammar School, where the Headmaster's strict discipline and bullying tactics made life still more gruelling. Despite this inhospitable environment, he began composing works as early as 1942; one of his pieces, *The Cloud* (for piano), was performed on the BBC Children's Hour in 1948.

In 1952, with no assistance at all from the Headmaster of Leigh School, he received a Lancashire County scholarship to the Royal Manchester College of Music (now the Royal Northern College of Music) and Manchester University, to read in music. He received little help in composition there, being effectively thrown out of class because he took seriously the 'wrong' music; therefore, he wrote his thesis on Indian music. However, he did become acquainted with a group of extremely talented men who would be effective in changing the direction of British music (which was heavily dominated at the time by Britten and Vaughan Williams). These five, known later as the 'Manchester School,' also included composers Harrison Birtwistle and Alexander Goehr, trumpeter Elgar Howarth (who was later to become a prominent conductor), and pianist John Ogdon. While at Manchester, he wrote the *Sonata for Trumpet and Piano* (1955) for Ogdon and Howarth, *Five Pieces for Piano* (1956) for Ogdon, and

Sonata for Clarinet and Piano (1956) for Birtwistle.

In 1957, Davies applied for and received a scholarship from the Italian government to study with Goffredo Petrassi in Rome. His eighteen months there left him with an enduring love for Italy and (with his natural gift for languages) a fluent command of Italian. During this period, he composed two major works: *St. Michael Sonata* (1957) and *Prolation* (1958), for which he won the Olivetti Prize. Both works show his exploitation of compositional devices and materials from the renaissance and middle ages, though transformed enormously. *St. Michael Sonata*, for 17 wind instruments, uses chants from the Requiem Mass and, in its antiphonal grouping of the ensemble into a wind band and a brass octet, recalls Gabrieli. In *Prolation*, his first work for full orchestra (which Paul Griffiths describes as "a quite extraordinary feat of musical engineering"), he employs medieval/renaissance techniques for proportional relations of time but extends them to extraordinary complexity and development.

Upon his return to England in 1959, he took a post as Director of Music at Cirencester Grammar School, a position he held until 1962. This was a very significant time for Maxwell Davies: he recognized the need for imaginative, challenging, and original music for children to perform, and the sad lack of anything of that sort in the existing repertoire. Accordingly, he began composing works himself to fill this need and producing arrangements of the works of other composers, including J. S. Bach, Byrd, Monteverdi, Giovanni Gabrieli, Satie, Stravinsky, Poulenc, and Milhaud. Moreover, he encouraged his students to compose as well. In an interview with Robert Cockroft in 1984, he remarked:

> What I was about was unblocking natural musicality in nine out of ten children...I found there was in the school a tremendous musicality which would find its way out.[1]

His method of teaching children music by encouraging them to write and perform themselves soon attracted national attention. The commitment to composing works for young performers which he acquired at Cirencester has never diminished. In addition, the Cirencester experience also important effects on his compositional style. Arranging other works to suit the performers available led to an increased concern with the needs of performance and to an increasing use of borrowed and parodied material in his own compositions.

Among the works he wrote for his students were three major compositions: *O Magnum Mysterium* (1960), *Five Klee Pictures* (1959), and *Te Lucis Ante*

---

[1]Robert Cockroft, "Time to Tear Down the Ivory Tower." *Yorkshire Post*, Nov. 12 1984, p. 5.

Terminum (1960).   Other works of this period include the small carol *Ave Maria, Hail Blessed Flower*; *Five Motets*; a *String Quartet* (1960-61); *Leopardi Fragments* (1961-62); and the chamber-orchestra work *Sinfonia* (1962). These displayed his increasing interest in medieval and renaissance material and compositional techniques, such as prolation, isorhythm, and parody (though transformed through the lens of his own twentieth-century style).

In 1962, at the urging of Aaron Copland and the support of Benjamin Britten, he was awarded a Harkness Foundation Fellowship to support two years of study at the Graduate School of Princeton University. There, he worked with such figures as Roger Sessions and Earl Kim.   His status among students at Princeton was quite unusual, since he was already an established composer in Britain.   During his Princeton residence, he travelled in the United States and became acquainted for the first time, at first hand, with modern commercialism and the consumer society.   This aspect of American life repelled and horrified him, and that revulsion later found expression in many of his compositions in the later 1960s.   Its strongest depiction is in the opera *Resurrection*, which he began planning as early as 1963, though it would not reach the stage for another quarter of a century.

While at Princeton, his use of renaissance and medieval material and compositional devices expanded. *Veni Sancte Spiritus* (1963), for instance, was based on a work of John Dunstable.   More significantly, he became deeply immersed in the life and music of sixteenth-century English composer John Taverner and composed the major part of the central work of his younger life, the opera *Taverner*. This took Taverner's religious and artistic betrayal as a metaphor for all crises of conscience: it is the tragedy of a man who prefers dogma to internal experience.   *Taverner* would not see its first performance until 1972, but work on it led to several other compositions from the Princeton period, including *First Fantasia on an 'In Nomine' of John Taverner* (1962), *Second Fantasia on John Taverner's 'In Nomine'* (1964), and *Seven In Nomine* (1965).

Following his stay at Princeton, he returned to England for a short stay and then departed again for Australia to participate in a UNESCO conference on music education and to tour the country.   Upon his return to England in 1964, he joined with Harrison Birtwistle and Alexander Goehr to found a summer school of music at Wardour Castle.

In May 1967, he and Birtwistle organized the Pierrot Players, taking the name of the group from the title of Schoenberg's *Pierrot Lunaire* since the instrumentalists represented the instrumentation of that piece (with the addition of percussion).   For the next twenty years, he would write most of his compositions for this group and its successor, the Fires of London (sometimes with the addition of singers, especially mezzo-soprano Mary Thomas).   These have taken a variety of forms: instrumental ensembles, music-theatre pieces (a genre he has virtually come to define), and solo instrumental works for members of the group such as *The Door of the Sun* (1975) for viola, *The Seven Brightnesses* (1975) for clarinet, and *Sonata for Piano* (1980).

The compositions of the later 1960s, usually described as Davies's 'expressionist' period, have an explosive and revolutionary quality which was part both of his thinking and of the political climate of the time. Many are marked by a powerful, deliberately shocking style, often employing a huge variety of percussion and even unconventional instruments such as whistles, plungers, Klaxon horns, and biscuit tins. Noteworthy are *Revelation and Fall* (1965-66), *Antechrist* (1967), *Missa Super L'homme Armé* (1968).

The most remarkable year of this period was certainly 1969, which included the premieres of four major compositions. First performed on April 22 was what was to become the most famous of the theatre pieces: *Eight Songs for a Mad King*. The inspiration for the work was a small mechanical organ, which Sir Steven Runciman had shown to Davies in 1966, that had once been the property of George III. The king had evidently used it, during the time of his madness, in an attempt to teach birds to sing; the image of the mad king, with his birds and his mechanical organ, "left a peculiar and disturbing impression" on the composer. He composed the *Eight Songs* using as libretto a series of eight poems by Australian poet Randolph Stow that include some of George III's own phrases. A baritone portrays the mad King George (or perhaps the madman who thinks he is King George), with instrumentalists on stage in bird cages; the extraordinarily demanding vocal part takes him through a struggle with madness which ends with his final and terrifying acceptance of his insanity.

Vesalii Icones, premiered on Dec. 9 of the same year, was inspired by a reproduction of Vesalius' famous anatomical treatise *De Humani Corporis Fabrica* that Davies had acquired. This powerful piece for male dancer, solo cello, and ensemble is structured around a series of fourteen plates of dissected cadavers in Vesalius' text. Each of its scenes is a representation of one of these illustrations and, at the same time, a parody representation of one of the fourteen Stations of the Cross. The work ends with the resurrection, not of Christ, but of Antichrist.

Completing the major premieres of 1969 were two large orchestral works. The first, *St. Thomas Wake: Foxtrot for Orchestra*, transforms a pavan of John Bull's into 1930s dance-band foxtrots while an orchestra deveolps the same material symphonically. The second, premiered on August 29 at a Proms Concert, was *Worldes Blis*, a 'motet for orchestra' based on the thirteenth-century monody of the same title. A composition of extraordinary complexity and rich texture, requiring a very large orchestra, this piece was something of a summation of the composer's views at the time. Unfortunately, its premiere, at a Proms Concert of the BBC Symphony, overtaxed somewhat the capacities of its audience, many of whom walked out on what was to become one of

Davies's most celebrated works, since acclaimed as "one of the most monumental musical achievements of the post-war period."

The year 1970 was transitional in more than one way. First, Harrison Birtwistle left the Pierrot Players. The group reorganized and continued under the name 'The Fires of London,' suggested by Steven Pruslin. Second, Davies completed the opera *Taverner*, having been forced to reconstruct large portions of it that were lost in a fire at his cottage in Dorset in 1969. Thus, this work, which embodied so much of his viewpoint on music and much else, was at last finished. Third, during July, he visited the Orkney Islands while on holiday and made the acquaintance of the Orcadian poet George Mackay Brown during a visit to the island of Hoy: poet and island would play central roles in his life from then on. He soon decided that Hoy would provide the peace and isolation he needed for his composing. In 1972, he arranged to lease and restore a derelict croft perched on the edge of a cliff on Hoy, overlooking the incessantly violent waters of Pentland Firth, and in 1974 he moved in.

In 1971, he used Mackay Brown's *Fishermen with Plows* as the basis for a composition, *From Stone to Thorn*; this would be the first of over twenty works drawing on the Orkney poet, including *Dark Angels* (1974), motivated by a tragic drowning in his own valley; *Westerlings* (1977), *Solstice of Light* (1979), and *The Martyrdom of St. Magnus* (1976), drawn from Orkney history; *Lullabye for Lucy* (1981), celebrating the birth of Lucy Rendall, the first child born in 32 years in the village of Rackwick on Hoy; and depictions of Orcadian life such as *Fiddlers at the Wedding* (1973), *An Orkney Wedding, with Sunrise* (1985), and *The Blind Fiddler* (1976). Describing these years, Mrs. Judy Arnold, his manager from 1975, says: "It is here that he has lived and worked and where the place and its landscape and seascape and people have permeated his music ever since. The move to Orkney brought a calm, more reflective Max, more at peace but no less original." The composer describes the importance of Hoy to him in his *"Pax Orcadiensis."*

In 1971, Davies wrote two film scores on commission from director Ken Russell. They could hardly be more different. The first was for *The Devils*, a portrayal of sexual hysteria, political repression and insanity masquerading as demonic possession based on Aldous Huxley's *The Devils of Loudun*; Davies's score is appropriately violent and brooding. The second was for *The Boyfriend* (which starred Twiggy, Christopher Gable, and Tommy Tune), a film that took Sandy Wilson's musical, a gentle pastiche of the 1920s, and enlarged it by making the original story a film within a film. Davies's score includes outrageous foxtrots, dance sequences, and Hollywood fantasies. He subsequently extracted a suite from each score, and these were premiered together by the Fires in December 1971.

After its lengthy gestation, *Taverner* was premiered by the Royal Opera, Covent Garden, on July 12, 1972. This complex work presents a reading of

Taverner's life (or what might have been Taverner's life) with artistic and religious betrayal at its center. The reviewers' receptions were various, but it was heavily reviewed: at once, it became the subject of articles and even dissertations. Despite this, the opera still remains unrecorded and has seen relatively few productions: one is forced to confront the score 'head on.'

Among the other compositions of the early 1970s are *Blind Man's Buff*, a 'Masque for Soprano, Mezzo-Soprano, mime and small orchestra,' commissioned by the BBC; *Hymn to St. Magnus*, for instrumental ensemble and mezzo-soprano, premiered by the Fires in October 1972; the *Tenebrae super Gesualdo*, for mezzo-soprano, guitar, and instrumental ensemble; and a large composition for mezzo-soprano and orchestra, *Stone Litany*, commissioned by the Scottish National Orchestra and the University of Edinburgh.

The seven years from 1972 to 1979 were especially fruitful ones. In 1974, what was to become the companion piece to *Eight Songs for a Mad King* was composed and premiered: *Miss Donnithorne's Maggot*. Responding to a commission from the Adelaide Arts Council, the composer again chose a mad figure from history, this time an Australian woman who had served as the model for Miss Havisham in Dickens's *Great Expectations*. Like the *Eight Songs*, the work is performed by a solo singer with instrumental accompaniment.

Commissions became increasingly frequent during this time. *The Blind Fiddler* (1976), a song cycle for mezzo-soprano and ensemble, was commissioned by the Newtown Concert Society of Edinburgh. In the same year, Davies wrote his first Symphony, on commission from the Philharmonia Orchestra (it was premiered in February 1978).

A work of special importance for several reasons was the chamber opera *The Martyrdom of St. Magnus*, commissioned by the BBC and completed in 1976. This took its story from George Mackay Brown's novel *Magnus* about St. Magnus, the patron of Kirkwall's magnificent twelfth-century cathedral, who, in order to bring an end to civil war in the islands, allowed himself to be murdered at the hands of his cousin Haakon. But the composer (and Mackay Brown) had more in mind than Orkney history. As a man who undergoes martyrdom for his inner convictions, Magnus represents an antithesis of Taverner.

Its premiere, in June 1977, was also of importance because it was at St. Magnus Cathedral, Kirkwall, during the first St. Magnus Festival. This annual Festival, taking place around the summer solstice in the Orkneys, was founded by the composer and has continued to be of major importance to him. He was its artistic director from its inception until 1986, when he became its President (a post he still holds).

The Festival became a new opportunity for compositions for children, and beginning with *The Two Fiddlers* (1978), Davies has written something for children for almost every festival: the song cycles *Kirkwall Shopping Songs*

(1979) and *Songs of Hoy* (1981), the children's opera *Cinderella* (1980), the pantomime drama *The Great Bank Robbery* (1989), and many other smaller works, premiered by children from the Stromness Academy, the Papdale Elementary School, or the Kirkwall Grammar School.

Turning again to medieval legend for a source, the 1978 theatre piece *Le Jongleur de Notre Dame* tells the tale of a juggler who performs before a statue of the Virgin and is rewarded for his homage when the statue comes to life and wipes the sweat from his brow with her robe. In Maxwell Davies's version, the juggler is cast with a genuine juggler, who performs the role in mime while instrumentalists double as disapproving monks. A children's band forms part of the accompaniment. The ballet *Salome* also draws on religious sources for its story, but its premiere in Copenhagen by the Royal Danish Ballet in 1978 was far more sensational because of the extended scene danced in the nude by Vivi Flindt. *The Lighthouse*, a chamber opera for three singers premiered in 1979 at the Edinburgh International Festival, took its story line instead from a genuine unsolved mystery: the disappearance of three lighthouse-keepers from Flannan Isles lighthouse in the Hebrides in 1900. The composer offers us no solution to the mystery, only a portrait of the three lighthouse-keepers in their suffocating isolation and a deliberately ambiguous ending. Many other shorter compositions, primarily for the Fires of London, also date from these years.

In 1979, Maxwell Davies became Director of Music at the Dartington Hall Summer School, a post he retained until 1983.

Awards, commissions, and compositions of every sort came at an increasing pace during the 1980s. A full-scale pantomime opera for children, *Cinderella*, was produced in 1980, joining the children's opera *The Two Fiddlers* of 1978. After its premiere at the 1980 St. Magnus Festival, the composer took the production of *Cinderella* on tour to Italy.

As noted above, *Symphony No. 1* was premiered in 1978. *Symphony No. 2* was commissioned by the Boston Symphony in 1980 and premiered by them under the baton of Seiji Ozawa in 1981 as part of the Orchestra's commemoration of its centennial. The *Sinfonia Concertante*, commissioned by the Academy of St. Martin-in-the-Fields, followed in 1983; the appropriately titled *Sinfonietta Accademica*, commissioned by the University of Edinburgh, was premiered in 1983; and Edward Downes conducted the BBC Philharmonic in the first performance of *Symphony No. 3*, commissioned for that orchestra, in February 1984.

On May 10, 1985, the Boston Pops Orchestra gave the first performance of *An Orkney Wedding, with Sunrise*, a work commissioned for them. This delightful work, inspired by the wedding of Jack Rendall, from whom he leased his croft on Hoy, was the first that orchestra had performed which included Scottish bagpipes. It has since become one of Maxwell Davies's most widely performed pieces. Another major orchestral work of the 1980s was the

Concerto for Violin and Orchestra, premiered by Isaac Stern and the Royal Philharmonic (which had commissioned it) at the 1986 St. Magnus Festival. Premiered at the same Festival was a work of a much different scale and character, the choral song cycle *House of Winter* (receiving its initial performance by the King's Singers). Later in the decade, the *Concerto for Trumpet and Orchestra* (another commission by the Philharmonia) was premiered in September 1988 in Hiroshima, Japan, and *Symphony No. 4* at a Proms Concert in September 1989.

Writing these large orchestral works did nothing to slow the stream of chamber pieces for the Fires and other ensembles, which continued apace during the 1980s: *Little Quartet No. 1* (1980); *The Medium*, a monodrama premiered by Mary Thomas in 1981; the *Piano Sonata* (1981) for Stephen Pruslin; and the conductorless *Image, Reflection, Shadow* (1982), a companion piece to the 1975 *Ave Maris Stella*. *The No. 11 Bus* (1984), a theatre piece depicting a motley assortment of characters on an infernal bus ride, follows in the tradition of *Eight Songs* by making the instrumentalists part of the stage action. *Into The Labyrinth*, a larger-scale work for tenor and chamber orchestra commissioned by the Scottish Chamber Orchestra, was premiered with tenor Neil Mackie at the 1983 St. Magnus Festival. *Winterfold*, a song cycle for mezzo-soprano and ensemble, was written in 1986 and premiered in January 1987. Other small ensembles commissioning works included the King's Singers, for whom the composer wrote *Sea Runes* (premiered November 1986) as well as *House of Winter* (noted above). Max's political activism came to the forefront in pieces provoked by the threat of uranium mining to the peace and environmental integrity of the Orkneys: *Solstice of Light* (1979), *Yellow Cake Revue* (1980), *Black Pentecost* (1982).

As these many commissions testify, Davies was increasingly being recognized as Britain's leading composer and honored accordingly. In 1981, he was awarded a CBE on Queen Elizabeth's Birthday Honours List. The following year, he became President of the Schools Music Association (a post which he used to campaign for increased support of school music programs, and which prompted him to write a *Schools Music Association Grace*). In 1987, he was awarded the title of Knight Batchelor in the 1987 New Years Honours. Despite his reluctance, he eventually accepted the honor and became Sir Peter Maxwell Davies. In that same year, the Fires of London was dissolved. This group gave its farewell concert on January 20, 1987, at the Queen Elizabeth Hall. A third event of 1987 was the commission from the Strathclyde Regional Council of the Strathclyde Project. This was to be a series of ten concertos for the Scottish Chamber Orchestra, each featuring a different soloist or combination of soloists from that group. Such a commission is quite remarkable in this century and may well have seemed, at the time, a rash undertaking. The first *Strathclyde Concerto*, however, saw its premiere in April 1988. This was a concerto for oboe and orchestra. *Strathclyde Concerto No. 2* for cello and orchestra followed in February 1989; *No. 3,* for horn, trumpet and orchestra, in January 1990 and *No. 4,* for clarinet and orchestra, in November of that year; *No. 5,* for violin, viola and string orchestra, and *No. 6,* for flute and orchestra, jointly in March 1992; *No. 7,* for double bass and orchestra, in November 1992; *No. 8,* for bassoon and orchestra, in November 1993; and *No. 9,* for six wind instruments, in February 1995. At this writing, only *No. 10* remains to be composed. Even by Maxwell Davies standards, nine concertos in seven years (intermingled with an opera, two more symphonies, and scores of other compositions) is an exceptional feat.

In September 1988 the opera *Resurrection*, originally conceived during the Princeton years, was performed for the first time. This savage black comedy portrays the destruction of an individual's soul by modern consumer society with the shock and bite of the Maxwell Davies of the 1970s: the instrumentation includes a rock band, the music incorporates television commercials and announcements. The central character is a literal dummy. During the main scene, he is 'cured' of various 'anti-social' (i.e., individualistic) attitudes by a grotesque parody of psychosurgery in which his brain, heart and genitals—all that makes him human—are removed and replaced with sanitized substitutes. All this takes part on the lower part of the stage; above it, television commercials periodically comment on passing events. At the end, the dummy undergoes his 'resurrection': he turns to the audience and rises, as does his penis, in the form of a machine-gun which fires fiery streamers over their heads. *"Resurrection is, above all, a comic opera, and even when the comedy is black, the touch should be light,"* writes the composer. Much of this humor, unfortunately, failed to come through in its first performance in Darmdstadt on September 18, 1988. The composer was excluded from preparations until the very last stages, leading to major divergences from his conception of the work, and many elements of the production (for instance the rock band) were badly unprepared. The composer's intentions for the music are much better realized in the concert performance (under his direction) recently released on compact disc, but as of this writing *Resurrection* still awaits its first true realization on the stage.

In March and April 1990, the South Bank Centre in London presented a series of concerts of his works under the title 'Maxfest'. Inevitably, Max contributed new works for the occasion: *Jupiter Landing*, a theatre work for children (other works for children in that year included *Dinosaur at Large* in July and *Dangerous Errand* at the St. Magnus Festival in June). 1991 saw the premiere of a second ballet choreographed, like *Salome*, by Flemming Flindt: *Caroline Mathilde*. This was based on the short life of King George III's younger sister, who married Denmark's King Christian VII and, as a result of an affair with a court physician, was banished from the court to die alone at the age of 23.

The 1990s have seen increasing ties with major orchestras: in 1992, the post of Associate Conductor/Composer of the Royal Philharmonic and a similar post with the BBC Philharmonic in Manchester.   Though neither conducting nor composing works for orchestra were new to Davies, these associations have led to many compositions as well as an increasing recognition of his abilities as conductor, in which capacity he has divided his efforts between his own compositions and the older repertory, such as Beethoven and Mozart.

Peter Maxwell Davies continues at his almost Mozartean pace, with a list of compositions now approaching three hundred.   He has shown himself competent in virtually every conceivable genre of composition and has, in fact, developed genres of his own.   His compositions range from works for very young children such as *Six Songs for St. Andrew's* to symphonic masterpieces like *Worldes Blis* that challenge the greatest orchestras.   His style can be extraordinarily simple, as in *Lullabye for Lucy* or *Farewell to Stromness*, or dauntingly complex, as in *Prolation*; abrasive and dissonant, as in *Eight Songs for a Mad King*, or quiet and reflective, as in *Sir Charles his Pavan*.   He can produce a frightening picture of political terror in *The Martyrdom of St. Magnus* as well as the gentle humour of *Le Jongleur de Notre Dame* or the combination of terror and humor in *St. Thomas Wake*.   The *Times* has put it well: "To hear a living composer speak through his art as vividly and as variedly as does Sir Peter Maxwell Davies cheers the heart."   With his devotion to music at every level, his extraordinary versatility, and his limitless productivity, he is Britain's leading practicioner of the musical art as the twentieth century becomes the twenty-first.

Works and First Performances

W1. Agnus Dei. (J197)
Motet for two solo sopranos, viola and cello.
Composed: 1984
Publication: Chester Music SAS01954 (Score and Parts), 1984.
Premiere: Union Chapel, Islington, London, June 23, 1986; Members of the Almeida Festival Players conducted by Oliver Knussen.
Manuscript: British Library nos. 71343, 71415 (item 2) vol. 164.
SEE: B563.

All Sons of Adam. *SEE* **Four Instrumental Motets, W84**

W2. Allegretto, con Moto. (J11)
For two pianos.
Composed: 1952
Publication: Unpublished.
Premiere: Unknown.
Manuscript: British Library no. 71435, vol. 184, item 10.

W3. Alma Redemptoris Mater. (J22)
For flute, oboe, two clarinets, horn and bassoon.
Composed: 1957.
Publication: Schott 10802 (miniature score), c. 1965; conductor's score and parts, rental.

Premiere: Dartington Hall Summer School, Devon, May 7, 1957; New
Music Ensemble conducted by John Carewe.
Manuscript: British Library no. 71376, vol. 25.
SEE: B72, B97, B177, B339, B831, B923, B926, B941, B944, B958,
B962, B964.

W4.   Alma Redemptoris Mater. (J222A)
For mezzo-soprano and oboe. Written for Jan deGaetani.
Composed: 1989.
Publication: unpublished.
Premiere: unknown.
Manuscript: Philip West, Rochester, New York.

Alma Redemptoris Mater. *SEE* **Four Carols.**

W5.   'Also Hat Gott Die Welt Geliebet' by Dietrich Buxtehude. (J95)
Arranged for soprano, flute, violin, cello and harpsichord/celeste.
Composed: 1970.
Publication: Chester Music no. 55227 (score), 1980.
Premiere: Dartington Summer School, Devon, August 10, 1970; Mary
Thomas, soprano and the Pierrot Players conducted by the composer.
SEE: B83, B498.

W6.   Amor Jesu.
For SATB choir.
Composed: c. 1959–1961.
Publication: unpublished.
Premiere: Pupils of Cirencester Grammar School (date unknown).
Manuscript: British Library no. 71437, vol. 186, item 12.

W7.   Anakreontika. (J140)
For soprano, alto flute, cello, harpsichord, and percussion. Text, late
ancient Greek.
Composed: 1976.
Publication: Chester Music no. JWC 55315 (score), 1981. Parts for
sale.
Premiere: Queen Elizabeth Hall, London, September 17, 1976; Mary
Thomas and the Fires of London conducted by the composer.
Manuscript: British Library no. 71413, vol. 147.
SEE: B395, B498, B561, B678.

W8.   Andante in E Major. (J10)
For solo piano.
Composed: c. 1950.
Publication: Unpublished.
Premiere: Unknown.
Manuscript: British Library no. 71435, vol. 184 item 9.

W9.   Andantino and Allegro from 'Les Cinq Doigts' by Igor Stravinsky, arranged by Peter Maxwell Davies.
Format unknown.
Composed: c. 1959–1961.
Publication: Unpublished.
Premiere: Pupils of Cirencester Grammar School (date unknown).
Manuscript: British Library 71437, vol. 186, item 9.

W10.   Antechrist. (J72)
For piccolo, bass clarinet, percussion (3 players), violin and cello.
Composed: 1967.
Publication: Boosey & Hawkes, B & H 19738 (score), no. 3736, 1969, 1994; conductor's score and parts, rental.
Premiere: Queen Elizabeth Hall, London, May 30, 1967; Pierrot Players conducted by the composer.
Manuscript: British Library 71382, vol. 31.
RECORDINGS: D1, D2
SEE: B62, B75, B97, B192, B258, B570, B603, B650, B704, B793, B833, B916, B924, B926, B931, B941, B956, B962, B964.

W11.   Apple Basket, Apple Blossom. (J238)
For unaccompanied choir SATB. Words by George Mackay Brown.
Composed: 1990.
Publication: Chester Music CH 59618 (score), 1992.
Premiere: St. Alban's Church, Birmingham; BBC Singers conducted by Simon Jolly.
Manuscript: British Library 71434, vol. 183, item 3.

W12.   Ave Maria, Hail Blessed Flower. (J45)
For SATB chorus unaccompanied.
Composed: 1961.
Publication: Novello, 1961; included in *Treasury of English Church Music, vol. 5: 1900–1965* (London: Blandford Press, Ltd., 1965) pp. 196–199.
Premiere: Pupils of Cirencester Grammar School (date unknown).

RECORDINGS: D3, D4
SEE: B25, B747.

W13. Ave Maris Stella. (J131)
For flute, clarinet, marimba, piano, viola and cello.
Composed: 1975.
Publication: Boosey & Hawkes B&H 20594, HPS 1264 (9533) (miniature score); B&H 3737 (score), 1976; conductor's score and parts, rental.
Premiere: Theatre Royal, Bath, during the Bath Festival, May 27, 1975; Fires of London.
Manuscript: British Library no. 71328, vol. 78, item 1; no. 71385, vol. 134.
RECORDINGS: D5, D6.
SEE: B111, B127, B128, B169, B181, B192, B293, B303, B310, B501, B536, B565, B588, B658, B679, B680, B693, B789, B839, B840, B903, B923, B924, B936, B944, B945, B948, B966.

W14. Ave Plena Gracia. (J60)
For SAT soli and SATB chorus and optional organ.
Composed: 1964.
Publication: Oxford University Press,1965; Included in *Carols of Today* (Oxford University Press, 1965), pp. 24–30; Also included in *100 Carols for Choirs*, edited by David Willcocks and John Rutter, Oxford University Press, 1987, pp. 54–60.
Premiere: Pupils of Cirencester Grammar School (?).
Manuscript: British Library no. 71252, vol. 1 item 2, sketches; no. 71424, vol. 173 item 1.
RECORDINGS: D7.

W15. Ave Rex Angelorum. (J150)
For SATB chorus unaccompanied.
Composed: 1976.
Publication: Boosey & Hawkes B&H 20562 (CCS11) (6087) (score), 1982.
Premiere: St. Magnus Cathedral, Kirkwall, Orkney, December 18, 1976; pupils from the Kirkwall Grammar School conducted by Norman Mitchell.
RECORDINGS: D8.

W16. The Bairns of Brugh. (J176)
> For piccolo, bass clarinet, piano, marimba, viola, and cello. In memory of Sverre Bergh.
> *Composed:* 1981.
> *Publication:* Boosey & Hawkes 20626 (score), 1983; conductor's score and parts, rental.
> *Premiere:* Bergen International Festival, May 30, 1981; Fires of London.
> *Manuscript:* Mrs. Eva Bergh, Bergen, Norway.
> *RECORDINGS:* D9, D10.
> SEE: B400.

W17. The Beltane Fire: Choreographic Poem for Orchestra.
> *Composed:* 1995.
> *Publication:* (in preparation).
> *Premiere:* Symphony Hall, Boston, April 3, 1995; BBC Philharmonic conducted by the composer.

W18. 'Benedicam Dominum' by Johnson from the *Mulliner Book*. (J38)
> Arranged for wind band.
> *Composed:* 1960.
> *Publication:* Unpublished.
> *Premiere:* Pupils of Cirencester Grammar School (date unknown).
> *Manuscript:* British Library 71437 vol. 186 item 3.

W19. Bessie Millie's Wind Shop. (J183A)
> For violin, piano, oboe and flute. Incidental music for a play for children by George Mackay Brown.
> *Composed:* 1982.
> *Publication:* Unpublished.
> *Premiere:* Orkney Arts Theatre, Kirkwall, Okrney, during the St. Magnus Festival, June 19, 1982; pupils of the Stromness Academy.
> *Manuscript:* Mr. Archie Bevan.

W20. Birds. (J3)
> For voice and instruments. Words by Moira O'Neill.
> *Composed:* December, 1947.
> *Publication:* Unpublished.
> *Premiere:* Unknown.
> *Manuscript:* British Library no. 71435, vol. 184, item 3.

W21. Birthday Greeting. (J270)

For orchestra. Composed for the 60th birthday of the BBC Symphony Orchestra.

Composed: 1994.

Publication: Unpublished.

Premiere: October 1, 1994; BBC Symphony Orchestra conducted by Yan Pascal Tortelier.

Manuscript: Mrs Judy Arnold.

W22. Birthday Music for John. (J193)

For flute, viola and cello. Composed for the birthday of John Carewe.

Composed: 1983.

Publication: Chester Music JWC 55685 (miniature score), 1985. Parts for sale.

Premiere: St. Mary's Church, Swansea, during the Swansea Festival, October 13, 1983.

Manuscript: Mr. John Carewe.

SEE: B474.

W23. Black Furrow, Gray Furrow. (J127)

For voice, alto flute and marimba. Words by George Mackay Brown.

Composed: April, 1974.

Publication: Unpublished.

Premiere: Unknown.

Manuscript: British Library no. 71411, vol. 160, item 1.

W24. Black Pentecost. (J158)

For mezzo-soprano, baritone and orchestra. Text from the novel *Greenvoe* by George Mackay Brown.

Composed: 1979.

Publication: Chester Music JWC 55386 (score) 1983; conductor's score and parts rental.

Premiere: Royal Festival Hall, London, May 11, 1982; Jan deGaetani, Michael Rippon and the Philharmonia Orchestra conducted by Simon Rattle.

Manuscript: British Library nos. 71331–71333, vols. 80–82.

RECORDINGS: D11, D12.

SEE: B137, B237, B314, B480, B552, B809, B822, B855, B870, B944.

W25. The Blind Fiddler. (J141)

For mezzo-soprano and instrumental ensemble. Text from *A Spell For Green Corn* by George Mackay Brown.

Composed: 1976.

Publication: Boosey & Hawkes B & F 2538 (score) 1978, 1981; conductor's score and parts, rental.

Premiere: Freemason's Hall, Edinburgh, February 16, 1976; Mary Thomas and the Fires of London conducted by the composer.

Manuscript: British Library no. 71414, vol. 169.

SEE: B127, B310, B822.

W26. Blind Man's Buff. (J106)

For boy treble (or high soprano), mezzo-soprano, dancer, mime and chamber ensemble. Text by Peter Maxwell Davies, taken fron Büchner's *Leonce und Lena* and some other sources.

Composed: 1972.

Publication: Chester Music JWC 55333 (score), 1981; conductor's score and parts, rental.

Premiere: Roundhouse, London, May 29, 1972; Josephine Barstow, Mary Thomas, Mark Furneaux and the BBC Symphony Orchestra conducted by Pierre Boulez.

Manuscript: British Library 71267, vol. 16.

SEE: B74, B100, B300, B301, B304, B569, B647, B747, B754, B923, B942, B943.

W27. The Boyfriend. (J99)

Score for a film by Ken Russell.

Composed: 1971.

Publication: Unpublished.

Premiere: Film premiere 1971.

Manuscript: Unknown (but see **Pussycat**).

SEE: B363.

W28. Concert Suite from 'The Boyfriend.' (J99A)

Suite from the score for the Ken Russell film.

Composed: 1971.

Publication: Chester Music; conductor's score and parts, rental.

Premiere: Queen Elizabeth Hall, London, December 11, 1971; Fires of London, conducted by the composer.

Manuscript: British Library 71265–71266, vols. 14–15.

RECORDINGS: D13, D14, D15.

SEE: B20, B318, B356, B501, B538, B706, B713, B747, B792, B928.

W29. Brass Quintet. (J180)
For two trumpets, horn, trombone and tuba.
Composed: 1981.
Publication: Chester Music JWC 55497 (miniature score), 1984; parts, 1981.
Premiere: Private: Morse Auditorium, Boston, March 19, 1982; Empire Brass Quintet; Public: Town Hall, New York City, March 20, 1982; Empire Brass Quintet.
Manuscript: British Library nos. 71394–71395, vols. 143–144; no. 71396, vol. 145.
SEE: B38, B356, B463, B510, B534, B724, B814, B844, B945.

W30. Burchiello. (J17)
For instruments of percussion.
Composed: Bayliss says 1955; Ian Kellam says 1960s.
Publication: Unpublished.
Premiere: Unknown.
Manuscript: Ian Kellam.

W31. Canon ad Honorem Igor Stravinsky. (J71)
For SATBBB. Part of *Homage to Stravinsky*, a set of 12 pieces, each by a different young composer, in honor of Stravinsky.
Composed: 1967.
Publication: Facsimile published in *Tempo* no. 81 (1967).
Premiere: Cheltenham, July 15, 1967 (at the Cheltenham Festival).
Manuscript: British Library 71318, vol. 67, item 3 (pencil draft); no. 71424, vol. 173, item 5.
SEE: B833.

W32. Canon in Memoriam Igor Stravinsky. (J111)
Puzzle canon. (The title is given in B170 as *Canon in Memoriam I. S., 1971.*)
Composed: 1971.
Publication: Reproduced in *Tempo* 97 (1971) pp. 24-25.
Premiere: Westminster Festival, June 17, 1972; members of the London Sinfonietta.
SEE: B170, B712.

W33. Cantata Profunda op. 2002. (J152)
For 'Heldentenor und übergroßes Hammercembalo.'
Composed: 1977.
Publication: Unpublished.

Premiere: Unknown.
Manuscript: Ian Kellam.

W34. Canzona by Giovanni Gabrieli. (J83)
Arranged for chamber ensemble.
Composed: 1969.
Publication: Chester Music JWC 55268 (score), 1980; conductor's
  score and parts, rental.
Premiere: Queen Elizabeth Hall, London, April 11, 1969; Orchestra
  Nova conducted by the composer.
Manuscript: British Library no. 71437, vol. 186 item 8.

W35. Canzona 14 from Canzone e Sonate, 1615 (Giovanni Gabrieli).
For school ensemble.
Composed: c. 1959–1961.
Publication: Unpublished.
Premiere: Pupils of Cirencester Grammar School (date unknown).
Manuscript: British Library no. 71437, vol. 186 item 8.

W36. Carol at Christmastime '58 for Julian. (J26)
For voice and guitar. Dedicated to Julian Bream.
Composed: 1958.
Publication: Unpublished.
Premiere: Unknown.
Manuscript: British Library 71378, vol. 127, item 2.

Carol on St. Steven *SEE* **Four Carols.**

W37. Caroline Mathilde: Ballet in Two Acts. (J234)
Scenario and choreography by Flemming Flindt.
Composed: 1990.
Publication: Chester Music CH 60893 (score), 1993; conductor's score
  and parts, rental.
Premiere: Royal Theatre, Copenhagen, Denmark, March 14, 1991;
  orchestra conducted by Markus Lehtinen.
Manuscript: British Library nos. 71295–71299, vols. 44–48.
SEE: B605.

W38. Caroline Mathilde: Concert Suite from Act I of the Ballet. (J244)
For orchestra.
Composed: 1990–1991.

Publication: Chester Music CH 60949 (score); conductor's score and parts, rental.

Premiere: Cheltenham Festival, July 12, 1991; BBC Philharmonic conducted by the composer.

RECORDINGS: D16, D17, D18, D19.

SEE: B22, B81, B276, B457, B468, B469, B621, B775.

W39. Caroline Mathilde: Concert Suite II. (J249)
For SA soloists or small chorus and orchestra.
Composed: 1991.
Publication: Chester Music; score in preparation; conductor's score and parts, rental.
Premiere: Royal Festival Hall, London, October 5, 1992; Royal Philharmonic conducted by the composer.
SEE: B253, B276, B868.

W40. Caroline Mathilde: Two Dances From Caroline Mathilde. (J259)
Arranged for flute and harp.
Composed: 1993.
Publication: Chester Music (in preparation).
Premiere: City Hall, Thurso, Scotland, September 24, 1993; David Nicholson, flute and Iluned Pierce, harp.

W41. Carolísima – Serenade. (J269)
For instrumental ensemble. Commissioned by Jens Högel for his wife Carol's 50th birthday.
Composed: 1994.
Publication: Schott and Co., score (in preparation); conductor's score and parts, rental.
Premiere: Prestonfield House Hotel, Edinburgh, August 30, 1994; Scottish Chamber Orchestra conducted by the composer.
Manuscript: Carol Högel, Edingurgh.

W42. Cauda Pavonis. (J81)
Piano solo.
Composed: 1969.
Publication: Unpublished.
Premiere: Purcell Room, London, January 3, 1970; Stephen Pruslin, piano.
SEE: B240.

W43. Chat Moss. (J264)
For school orchestra.
Composed: 1994.
Publication: Chester Music, score (in preparation); conductor's score and parts, rental.
Premiere: St. Edward's College, Liverpool, March 15, 1994; St. Edward's College Chamber Orchestra conducted by John Moseley.
RECORDINGS: D20.

W44. Christmas Card for Judith and Roger. (J129)
For flute and bassoon.
Composed: c. 1974.
Publication: Unpublished.
Premiere: Unknown.
Manuscript: British Library 71411, vol. 160, item 3.

W45. Cinderella. (J164)
Opera in two acts for children to play and sing. Scored for recorders, trumpet, percussion, piano and strings. Libretto by Peter Maxwell Davies.
Composed: 1980.
Publication: Chester Music JWC 55311 (vocal score) 1980; conductor's score and parts, rental; libretto for sale.
Premiere: St. Magnus Festival, Kirkwall, Orkney, June 21, 1980; pupils of the Papdale School and Kirkwell Grammar School conducted by Glenys Hughes.
Manuscript: British Library 71279-71280, vols. 27-29.
SEE: B43, B46, B136, B142, B234, B236, B268, B362, B419, B489, B537, B592, B608, B617, B662, B671, B744, B826, B877, B945.

W46. The Cloud. (J4)
For solo piano.
Composed: 1943-44.
Publication: Unpublished.
Premiere: May 20, 1948: Peter Maxwell Davies.
Manuscript: Peter Maxwell Davies.

W47. Coleran's Currant. (J274)
For piano. Composed for the 65th birthday of Bill Coleran, November 25, 1994.
Composed: 1994.
Publication: Unpublished.

Premiere: Unknown.

W48. Concerto for Trumpet and Orchestra. (J219)
Composed: 1988.
Publication: Boosey & Hawkes HPS 1174 (study score) 1989; 8254 (reduction for piano and trumpet) 1990; conductor's score and parts, rental.
Premiere: Yubin-Chokin Kaikan Hall, Hiroshima, September 21, 1988; John Wallace and the Philharmonia Orchestra conducted by Giuseppe Sinopoli.
Manuscript: British Library nos. 71356–71357, vols. 105–106.
RECORDINGS: D21, D22.
SEE: B3, B73, B89, B109, B270, B279, B459, B477, B532, B816.

W49. Concerto for Violin and Orchestra. (J208)
Composed: 1985.
Publication: Chester Music CH 55780 (miniature score), 1990; CH 55915 (violin and piano reduction), 1990; conductor's score and parts, rental.
Premiere: St. Magnus Cathedral, Kirkwall, Orkney, during the St. Magnus Festival, June 21, 1986; Isaac Stern with the Royal Philharmonic Orchestra conducted by André Previn.
Manuscript: British Library nos. 71348–71349, vol. 97–98.
RECORDINGS: D23, D24.
SEE: B13, B34, B106, B166, B191, B316, B393, B412, B434, B456, B479, B506, B523, B529, B548, B563, B625, B758, B766, B769, B774, B779, B783, B825, B874, B949, B951.

W50. Concerto No. 27. (J236)
For partypopper and orchestra, arranged for piano.
Composed: 1990.
Publication: Unpublished.
Premiere: Unknown.

W51. Corpus Christi, with Cat and Mouse. (J260)
For unaccompanied choir, SATB. Text from *Richard Hill: Commonplace Books*. Commissioned by Balliol College, Oxford, to commemorate the death of Benjamin Jowett.
Composed: 1993.
Publication: Chester Music CH 60956 (in preparation).
Premiere: Balliol College, Oxford, November 30, 1993; Chapel Choir of Balliol College conducted by Mark Dawes.

W52. Cross Lane Fair. (J267)
> For solo Northumbrian pipes, Boodhran, and Orchestra. Commissioned by the St. Magnus Festival, Orkney, and the BBC Philharmonic Orchestra.
> *Composed:* 1994.
> *Publication:* Chester Music (in preparation): conductor's score and parts rental.
> *Premiere:* St. Magnus Cathedral, Kirkwall, Orkney, during the St. Magnus Festival, June 18, 1994; Mark Jordan, Northumbrian pipes, Rob Lea, Bodhran with the BBC Philharmonic conducted by the composer.
> *RECORDINGS:* D25.

W53. Dangerous Errand. (J232)
> Music theatre work for young children to sing and play. For melody instruments, percussion and piano. Libretto by Peter Maxwell Davies.
> *Composed:* 1990.
> *Publication:* Longman, 1991; Chester, 1994 (score, teacher's book, libretto, parts and piano reduction).
> *Premiere:* Papdale Primary School, Kirkwall, Orkney, during the St. Magnus Festival, June 25, 1990; pupils of the Papdale Primary School conducted by Glenys Hughes.
> *Manuscript:* British Library 71294, vol. 43.
> SEE: B819.

W54. Dark Angels. (J120)
> For voice and guitar. Text by George Mackay Brown.
> *Composed:* 1973–1974.
> *Publication:* Boosey & Hawkes B&H 20296 (score), 1977.
> *Premiere:* Dartington Summer School, Devon, July 31, 1974; Mary Thomas, soprano, and Timothy Walker, guitar.
> *Manuscript:* British Library no. 71324, vol. 73, item 3; no. 71410, vol. 159.
> *RECORDINGS:* D26.
> SEE: B51, B111, B127, B257, B302, B366, B438, B665, B700, B796, B918, B944.

W55. The Devils. (J98)
> Score for the Ken Russell film *The Devils.*
> *Composed:* 1971.
> *Publication:* Unpublished.

Premiere: Film premiere 1971.
SEE: B158, B928, B937.

W56. Suite from 'The Devils.' (J98A)
Suite from the score for the Ken Russell film *The Devils*. For instrumental ensemble with soprano obbligato.
Composed: 1971.
Publication: Chester Music: conductor's score and parts, rental.
Premiere: Queen Elizabeth Hall, London, December 11, 1971; Fires of London, conducted by the composer.
Manuscript: British Library 71263–71264, vols. 12–13.
RECORDINGS: D27.
SEE: B318, B352, B501, B713, B747, B792.

W57. Dinosaur at Large. (J228)
Music theatre work for children to play and sing. Scored for voices, bugle, trumpet, melody instruments, percussion. Libretto by Peter Maxwell Davies.
Composed: 1989.
Publication: Longman, 1991 (score and teacher's book, libretto, parts and piano reduction); Chester, 1994.
Premiere: Leeds Grammar School, July 4, 1990; Pupils of Pudsey Bolton Royds Junior School conducted by Rose Hudson.
Manuscript: British Library no. 71293, vol. 42.
SEE: B200.

W58. The Door of the Sun. (J132)
For solo viola.
Composed: 1975.
Publication: Boosey & Hawkes B&H 20419 (3742) (score), 1978.
Premiere: University of Surrey, Guilford, March 9, 1976; Duncan Druce, viola.
Manuscript: British Library no. 71386, vol. 135, item 1; no. 71387, vol. 136, item 1.
RECORDINGS: D28.
SEE: B498.

W59. Drummond's Dumpe. (J273)
For piano. Composed for the 60th birthday of John Drummond, November 24, 1994.
Composed: 1994.
Publication: Unpublished.

Premiere: Unknown.

W60. Ecce Manus Tradentis. (J84, J64)
Motet for instrumental ensemble with SATB soloists and SATB Chorus.
Composed: Movement 1. **Eram Quasi Agnus**, 1969 (J84); Movement 2. **In Illo Tempore**, 1964 (J64).
Publication: Boosey & Hawkes B&H 20574 (3743) (score), 1978, 1980, 1982; conductor's score and parts, rental.
Premiere: Movement 1: Queen Elizabeth Hall, London, June 19, 1969; English Bach Festival Ensemble conducted by the composer; Movement 2: Wardour Castle Summer School, August 20, 1965; Summer School Choir and the Melos Ensemble conducted by the composer.
Manuscript: British Library no. 71378, vol. 127, item 5; no. 71423, vol. 172.
SEE: B97, B570, B923.

W61. Eight Songs for a Mad King. (J80)
Music theatre work for male voice, flute, clarinet, piano/harpsichord, violin, cello and percussion. Texts by Randolph Stowe and King George III.
Composed: 1969.
Publication: Boosey & Hawkes 8085 (score), 1971, 1987; conductor's score and parts, rental.
Premiere: Queen Elizabeth Hall, April 22, 1969; Roy Hart and the Pierrot Players conducted by the composer.
Manuscript: British Library nos. 71256–71257, vols 5–6.
RECORDINGS: D29, D30, D31, D32, D33, D34.
SEE: B4, B5, B12, B41, B56, B72, B76, B97, B98, B100, B112, B134, B137, B187, B194, B198, B213, B263, B266, B272, B286, B290, B304, B307, B312, B313, B314, B329, B333, B337, B373, B386, B423, B430, B438, B465, B558, B569, B573, B580, B605, B629, B647, B651, B669, B690, B709, B722, B747, B787, B794, B846, B850, B864, B866, B881, B904, B912, B913, B919, B923, B940, B941, B942, B945, B946, B948, B950, B956, B958, B961, B962, B964, B965, B966.

W62. Epistrophe. (J74)
For two pianos.
Composed: c. 1968.
Publication: Unpublished.
Premiere: Unknown.

Manuscript: British Library no. 71382, vol. 131, item 5.

W63. Eram Quasi Agnus. (J84) *SEE* **Ecce Manus Tradentis**
For nine instrumentalists. Revised version of Section I of **Ecce Manus Tradentis**.
Composed: 1969.
Publication: *SEE* **Ecce Manus Tradentis**.
Premiere: Queen Elizabeth Hall, London, June 19, 1969; English Bach Festival Ensemble, conducted by the composer.

W64. Excuse Me. (J212)
For mezzo-soprano, flute (doubling alto flute), clarinet in B flat (doubling clarinet in A), violin (doubling viola), cello, percussion and piano. Parody songs after Charles Dibdin.
Composed: 1986.
Publication: Chester Music CH 55868 (score), 1987; conductor's score and parts, rental.
Premiere: Queen Elizabeth Hall, London, February 26, 1986; Mary Thomas and the Fires of London conducted by Nicholas Cleobury.
Manuscript: British Library 71416, vol. 165, item 1.
SEE: B129, B352.

W65. Fantasia and Two Pavans after Henry Purcell. (J77)
For piccolo (doubling flute), clarinet in B♭, harpsichord (doubling out-of-tune piano), violin, cello, and percussion. Optional vocal part in the second Pavan.
Composed: 1968.
Publication: Boosey & Hawkes B&H 20475 (3745) (score), 1969, 1978, 1980; conductor's score and parts, rental.
Premiere: BBC Concert Hall, Broadcasting House, London, January 13, 1969; Pierrot Players conducted by the composer.
Manuscript: British Library no. 71382, vol. 131, item 4.
RECORDINGS: D35.
SEE: B97, B140, B229, B266, B286, B303, B945.

W66. Fantasia Upon One Note. (J118)
Free transcription of a work by Henry Purcell. For alto flute, bass clarinet, violin, cello, percussion and harpsichord.
Composed: 1973.
Publication: Chester Music JWC 55259 (score), 1980; conductor's score and parts, rental.

Premiere: Royal Albert Hall, London, BBC Promenade Concert, July 24, 1973; Fires of London conducted by the composer.
Manuscript: British Library no. 71383, vol. 132, item 7.
RECORDINGS: D36.
SEE: B714.

W67. Farewell—a Fancye. (J214A)
For flute, bass clarinet, marimba, piano, viola and cello. After John Dowland. Composed for the Fires of London Farewell Concert.
Composed: 1986.
Publication: Boosey & Hawkes 7934 (score), 1987, 1989; conductor's score and parts, rental.
Premiere: Queen Elizabeth Hall, London, January 20, 1987; Fires of London conducted by the composer.
Manuscript: British Library no. 71403, vol. 152, no. 2.
SEE: B112, B140, B266, B353, B508, B847, B881.

W68. Farewell to Stromness. (J166)
Piano interlude from **Yellow Cake Revue**.
Composed: 1980.
Publication: Boosey & Hawkes B&H 20521 (3747), 1980, score. Published with **Yesnaby Ground**.
Premiere: St. Magnus Festival, Orkney, June 21, 1980; Peter Maxwell Davies, piano.
Manuscript: British Library no. 71415, vol. 164, item 1.
RECORDINGS: D153, D154, D155, D156, D157.
SEE: B665, B935.

W69. Fiddlers at the Wedding. (J119)
For mezzo-soprano, alto flute, percussion, mandolin and guitar. Text by George Mackay Brown.
Composed: 1973.
Publication: Boosey & Hawkes B&H 20537 (3748) (score), 1978, 1981; conductor's score and parts, rental.
Premiere: Salle Pleyel, Paris, May 3, 1974; Jane Manning and the Ensemble conducted by Daniel Chabrun.
Manuscript: British Library nos. 71408–71409, vols. 157–158.
SEE: B111, B127, B449, B725.

W70. First Fantasia on an 'In Nomine' of John Taverner. (J51)
For orchestra.
Composed: 1962.

Publication: Schott & Co. 10818 (miniature score), 1966; conductor's score and parts, rental.

Premiere: Royal Albert Hall, London, September 13, 1962 (BBC Promenade Concert); BBC Symphony Orchestra conducted by the composer.

Manuscript: British Library no. 71315, vol. 64.

SEE: B101, B106, B348, B365, B437, B495, B540, B830, B831, B923, B941, B943, B958, B964.

W71. First Ferry to Hoy. (J206)

For instrumental ensemble, youth choir, and children's recorders and percussion group. Text by Peter Maxwell Davies.

Composed: 1985.

Publication: Boosey & Hawkes, B&H 20831 (7767) (score), 1985, 1988; B&H 7520 (vocal score), 1985, 1987; conductor's score and parts, rental.

Premiere: Queen Elizabeth Hall, London, November 12, 1985; London Sinfonietta, ILEA Youth Choir and Children's Band conducted by Elgar Howarth.

Manuscript: British Library no. 71432, vol 181, item 2.

SEE: B113, B265, B507, B594, B698, B727.

W72. First Grace of Light. (J248)

For solo oboe.

Composed: 1991.

Publication: Boosey & Hawkes, in preparation.

Premiere: BBC Radio 3, November 7, 1991; Nicholas Daniel, oboist.

Manuscript: British Library no. 71403, vol. 152, item 4.

W73. Five Carols. (J70)

For unaccompanied women's voices.

Composed: 1966.

Publication: Boosey & Hawkes B&H 19592 (3749) (score), 1967.

Premiere: All Saint's Church, London, December 11, 1966; Finchley Children's Music Group conducted by John Andrewes.

Manuscript: British Library no. 71424, vol. 173, item 4.

RECORDINGS: D37.

W74. Five Klee Pictures. (J30)

For school, youth or professional orchestra.

Composed: Originally composed 1959, Cirencester Grammar School; then lost. Revised version, 1976.

Publication: Boosey & Hawkes School Series HSS300; no. 301, B&H 20360 (score and parts).

Premiere: St. John's, Smith Square, London, October 16, 1976; Young Musicians Symphony Orchestra conducted by James Blair.

Manuscript: British Library no. 71436, vol. 185 item 1.

RECORDINGS: D38.

SEE: B90, B155, B190, B309, B413, B698, B826, B935, B948.

W75. Five Little Pieces. (J61)

For solo piano.

Composed: 1960–1964.

Publication: Boosey & Hawkes, B&H 19737, (3750), (score), 1968.

Premiere: Wardour Castle Summer School, August 1964; Peter Maxwell Davies.

Manuscript: British Library no. 71378, vol. 127, item 6.

W76. Five Motets. (J29)

For soloists (SATB) and chorus (SSAATTBB) with orchestra.

Composed: c. 1959; 1964; 1965.

Publication: Boosey & Hawkes B&H 19288 (score), 1966; HPS 770 (3751) (miniature score), 1966; B&H 19277 (3752) (vocal score), 1965; conductor's score and parts, rental.

Premiere: Macnaghten concert, Friends House, Euston, St. Pancras Festival, March 1, 1965; Ambrosian Singers and the English Chamber Orchestra conducted by Norman Del Mar.

Manuscript: British Library nos.71417–71418.

SEE: B67, B102, B545, B601, B948.

W77. Five Pieces for Piano. (J19)

For solo piano.

Composed: 1956.

Publication: Schott & Co. 10051 Schott (score), 1958.

Premiere: Liverpool, December, 1956; John Ogdon, piano.

Manuscript: British Library nos. 71373, vol. 122, and vol. 71374, vol. 123, item 2.

RECORDINGS: D39.

SEE: B496.

W78. Five Songs. (J9)

For voices and instruments. Text by Morgenstern.

Composed: c. 1950 (?).

Publication: Unpublished.

Premiere: Unknown.
Manuscript: British Library no. 71435, vol. 184, item 8.

W79. Five Voluntaries. (J41)
Arranged for school orchestra (or amateur orchestra).
Composed: 1960.
Publication: Schott & Co, Edition Schott 10994 (score) c. 1969; parts
for sale.
Premiere: Cirencester Grammar School, 1960; Cirencester Grammar
School Orchestra conducted by the composer.
Manuscript: British Library no. 71437, vol. 186, item 5.
SEE: B935.

W80. Fool's Fanfare. (J107)
For speaker and chamber orchestra.   Texts taken from speeches of
Shakespearian fools and clowns.
Composed: 1972.
Publication: Chester Music JWC 55228 (score), 1980; conductor's
score and parts, rental.
Premiere: Southwark Cathedral, London, April 23, 1972; Ron Moody,
speaker and the London Sinfonietta conducted by the composer.
Manuscript: British Library no. 71406, vol. 155, item 2.
SEE: B319.

W81. Four Canons. (J32)
For junior orchestra.
Composed: 1959.
Publication: Unpublished.
Premiere: Cirencester Grammar School, February 3, 1960.
Manuscript: British Library no. 71436, vol. 185, item 2.
SEE: B157.

W82. Four Carols. (J52)
**Alma Redemptoris Mater, Jesus Autem Hodie, Carol on St. Steven,
Nowell**. For SATB chorus unaccompanied.
Composed: 1961.
Publication: Schott & Co. 6481 (**Alma Redemptoris Mater**), 6482
(**Jesus Autem Hodie**), 6483 (**Carol on St. Steven**), 6484 (**Nowell**),
scores, 1962.
Premiere: St. Pancras Town Hall, London, November 26, 1962; New
Music Singers conducted by Graham Treacher.

Manuscript: **Alma Redemptoris Mater, Jesus Autem Hodie, Carol on St. Steven**: British Library no. 71419. vol. 168, item 4; **Nowell**: Unknown.
RECORDINGS: D40, D41, D42.
SEE: B495, B600, B841.

W83. **Four Instrumental Motets, from early Scottish originals: Si Quis Diligit Me. (J117)**
Motet for six instruments arranged after David Peebles and Francis Heagy.
Composed: c 1973.
Publication: Boosey & Hawkes B&H 10430 (3753) (score), 1978; conductor's score and parts, rental.
Premiere: Dartington Summer School, Devon, July 29, 1973; Fires of London conducted by the composer.
RECORDINGS: D43.
SEE: B294, B303.

W84. **Four Instrumental Motets, from early Scottish Originals: All Sons of Adam. (J122)**
Motet for seven instrumentalists arranged after an anonymous Scottish 16th century original.
Composed: c 1973.
Publication: Boosey & Hawkes B&H 20430 (3753) (score), 1978; conductor's score and parts, rental.
Premiere: Queen Elizabeth Hall, London, February 20, 1974; Fires of London conducted by the composer.
RECORDINGS: D44.
SEE: B303, B306.

W85. **Four Instrumental Motets, from early Scottish originals: Our Father Whiche in Heaven Art. (J151)**
Motet for six instrumentalists arranged after John Angus.
Composed: 1977.
Publication: Boosey & Hawkes B&H 20430 (3753) (score), 1978; conductor's score and parts, rental.
Premiere: Dartington Hall Summer School, Devon, August 18, 1977; Fires of London conducted by the composer.
Manuscript: British Library no. 71391, vol 140, item 1 item 6; no. 71391.

RECORDINGS: D45.
SEE: B303.

W86. Four Instrumental Motets, from early Scottish originals: Psalm 124. (J123)
Motet for seven instrumentalists arranged after David Peebles, John Fethy, and an anonymous source.
Composed: 1974.
Publication: Boosey & Hawkes B&H 20430 (3753) (score), 1978; conductor's score and parts, rental.
Premiere: Dartington Summer School, Devon, July 28, 1974; Fires of London conducted by the composer.
Manuscript: British Library 71384, vol. 133, item 3.
RECORDINGS: D46.
SEE: B303, B310.

W87. Four Lessons for Two Keyboards. (J157)
Originally titled **Four Lessons for 2 Clavichords**. Published title as above.
Composed: 1978.
Publication: Boosey & Hawkes B&H 20598 (3789) (two keyboard score), 1978.
Premiere: Dartington Summer School, Devon, August 23, 1978; Sylvia Junge and Bernard Roberts, clavichords.
Manuscript: British Library no. 71391, vol. 140, item 3; Mrs. Sylvia Junge.

W88. Four Movements from 'Vespers of 1610' by Monteverdi. (J50)
Arranged for school orchestra and SATB choir.
Composed: 1962.
Publication: Unpublished.
Premiere: Pupils of Cirencester Grammar School, no date.
Manuscript: British Library no. 71438, vol. 187, items 3–4; no. 71439, vol.188, item 3.
SEE: (NONE: but see B834).

W89. Four Quartets: Incidental Music. (J89)
Incidental music to a reading by Alec Guinness of T.S. Eliot's *Four Quartets* for the BBC. Composed for the Fires of London.
Composed: c. 1970.
Publication: Unpublished.

Premiere: Unknown.

Manuscript: Apparently lost.

W90. Four Voluntaries by Thomas Tallis. (J187)

Arranged for brass quintet.

Composed: 1982–1983.

Publication: Chester Music JWC 55650 (score), c. 1984; Five parts on sale.

Premiere: The Cloisters, New York (City), U.S.A., December 9, 1983: Empire Brass Quintet.

Manuscript: British Library nos. 71399–71400, vols. 148–149,.

W91. From Stone to Thorn. (J96)

For mezzo-soprano, clarinet, percussion, guitar, and harpsichord. Based on *Fishermen with Plows* by George Mackay Brown.

Composed: 1971.

Publication: Boosey & Hawkes B&H 20484 (3754) (score), 1978.

Premiere: Holywell Music Room, Oxford, June 30, 1971; Mary Thomas, mezzo-soprano, Alan Hacker, clarinet, Timothy Walker, guitar, and Barry Quinn, percussion, conducted by the composer.

Manuscript: Mrs. Sylvia Junge.

RECORDINGS: D47.

SEE: B75, B131, B158, B294, B586, B704, B793, B932, B966.

W92. Funeral March in B Major (for a Pig). (J7)

For piano solo.

Composed: late 1940s.

Publication: Unpublished

Premiere: Leigh Grammar School, c. 1950; Peter Maxwell Davies (see Seabrooke's biography, p. 21).

W93. The Great Bank Robbery. (J222)

Music-theatre work for children to play and sing.   Text by Peter Maxwell Davies.

Composed: 1989.

Publication: Longman, 1990; Chester Music (score, teacher's book, libretto, piano reduction and parts), 1994.

Premiere: Kirkwall Arts Theatre, Kirkwall, Orkney, during the St. Magnus Festival, June 16, 1989; pupils of the Kirkwall Grammar School conducted by Glenys Hughes.

Manuscript: British Library nos. 71289–71290, vols 38–39.

SEE: B200, B484, B617, B698.

W94. Hallelujah! The Lord God Almichtie. (J225)

For SATB chorus, SA semichorus, or soli, and organ. Text is early Scottish.

Composed: 1989.

Publication: Chester Music CH59881 (score), 1992.

Premiere: St. Giles Church, Edinburgh, June 11, 1989; Choir of St. Paul's Old Church, Edinburgh conducted by Leslie Shankland.

W95. Der Heiße Ofen.

Comic Opera in five acts and three Entr'actes. Collaborative project, under the general coordination of Hans Werner Henze, with music by Richard Blackford, Henning Brauel, Peter Maxwell Davies, Michael Dennhoff, Hans Werner Henze, Niels Frédéric Hoffman, Thomas Jahn, Geoffrey King, and Francis Pinto.

Composed: c. 1975.

Publication: Hans Sikorski Internationale Musikverlag (rental only).

Premiere: March 18, 1989, Staatstheater Kassel, Opera Chorus and Orchestra of the Staatstheater Kassel, members of the Rock'N'Roll Club of Kassell.

Manuscript: Hans Sikorski Internationale Musikverlag.

SEE: B743, B930.

W96. Highbury Fling. (J235)

For piano solo.

Composed: 1990.

Publication: Unpublished.

Premiere: Unknown.

Manuscript: Sheila McCrindle.

W97. Hill Runes. (J175)

For solo guitar.

Composed: 1981.

Publication: Boosey & Hawkes B&H 20652 (6243) (score), 1983.

Premiere: Dartington Summer School, Devon, July 25, 1981; Julian Bream, guitar.

Manuscript: British Library no. 71391, vol. 140 item 4.

RECORDINGS: D48, D49.

SEE: B19, B104, B332, B417, B700, B918.

W98. Hircus Quando Bibit. (J223)

For voice and piano.

Composed: 1989.

Publication: Unpublished.
Premiere: Old Brewery, Mere, Wiltshire, June 20, 1989; Linda Hirst, mezzo-soprano and John Lenehan, piano.
Manuscript: British Library no. 71416, vol. 165, item 2.

W99. Hodie Christus Natus Est.
For SATB chorus.
Composed: c.1959–1961.
Publication: Unpublished.
Premiere: Pupils of Cirencester Grammar School (date unknown).
Manuscript: British Library no. 71437, vol. 186 item 15.

W100. 'Hoquetus David' by Machaut. (J101)
Arranged for soprano and ensemble. Written for the Fires of London.
Composed: 1971.
Publication: Unpublished.
Premiere: Unknown (but see B837).
Manuscript: Lost.
SEE: B837.

W101. House of Winter. (J210)
For unaccompanied choir AATBBB or SATBBB. Text by George Mackay Brown.
Composed: 1986.
Publication: Chester Music CH55856 (score), 1987.
Premiere: East Church, Kirkwall, Orkney during the St. Magnus Festival, June 23, 1986; King's Singers.
Manuscript: British Library no. 71433, vol. 182.
SEE: B78, B191, B291, B407, B506, B572, B594, B766, B783, B798, B894.

W102. A Hoy Calendar. (J265)
For unaccompanied choir, SATB. Text by George Mackay Brown.
Composed: 1994.
Publication: Chester Music (in preparation).
Premiere: St. Edward's College, Liverpool, March 15, 1994; St. Edward's College Chamber Choir conducted by Terrence Duffy.

W103. Hymn to St. Magnus. (J108)
For mezzo soprano, flute, clarinet, percussion, keyboard instruments, viola and cello.
Composed: 1972.

Publication: Boosey & Hawkes B&H 20457 (3755) (score), 1978, 1980; conductor's score and parts, rental.

Premiere: Queen Elizabeth Hall, London, October 13, 1972; Mary Thomas and the Fires of London conducted by the composer.

Manuscript: British Library no. 71407, vol. 156.

RECORDINGS: D50.

SEE: B62, B131, B158, B294, B301, B324, B858, B932, B962, B966.

W104. Hymn to the Word of God.   (J239)

For two tenor soloists and SATB chorus, unaccompanied. Byzantine text.   Composed for the 500th anniversary of King's College, Cambridge.

Composed: 1990.

Publication: Chester Music CHW 59626 (score), 1992.

Premiere: King's College Chapel, Cambridge University, March 6, 1991; Choir of King's College conducted by Stephen Cleobury.

Manuscript: British Library no. 71434, vol. 183, item 4.

RECORDINGS: D51.

W105. Hymnos.   (J73)

For clarinet and piano.

Title in Greek: Ὕμνος Ἑσπερῖνος (*Evening Hymn*).

Composed: 1967.

Publication: Boosey & Hawkes B&H 19924 (3756) (2 scores), 1970.

Premiere: Cheltenham Town Hall, Cheltenham, Gloucestershire, during the Cheltenham Festival, July 17, 1967; Alan Hacker, clarinet and Stephen Pruslin, piano.

Manuscript: British Library no. 71382, vol. 131, item 2.

RECORDINGS: D52.

SEE: B361, B557, B657, B704, B793, B833, B932, B966.

W106. I Can't Compose Today.   (J67)

Three part canon.

Composed: c. 1965.

Publication: Unpublished.

Premiere: Unknown.

Manuscript: British Library no. 71421, vol. 178, item 2.

W107. Ice Walk in Sheldon's [Borrowed] Boots.

For piano solo.

Composed: c. 1977.

Publication: Unpublished.

Premiere: Unknown.
Manuscript: British Library no. 71425, vol. 174.

W108. Illa Autem Arbor. (J15)
For SSAA chorus unaccompanied.
Composed: c. 1955.
Publication: Unpublished.
Premiere: Unknown.
Manuscript: British Library no. 71419, vol. 168, item 1.

W109. Illuxit Leticia.
For 2 voices (SA or TB).
Composed: c. 1966.
Publication: Unknown.
Premiere: Unknown.
Manuscript: British Library no. 71320, vol. 69, item 1. With the
autograph of *Worldes Blis*.

W110. Image, Reflection, Shadow. (J184)
For flute, piccolo, alto flute, clarinet, bass clarinet, violin, cello,
cimbalon, and piano.
Composed: 1982.
Publication: Chester Music JWC 55476 (miniature score), 1984;
conductor's score and parts, rental.
Premiere: First complete performance: Memorial Theatre, Lucerne,
Lucerne International Festival, August 22, 1982; Gregory Knowles,
cimbalon, with the Fires of London.
Manuscript: British Library no. 71394, vol. 143, vol. 1; nos. 71396--
71397, vols. 145-146.
RECORDINGS: D53, D54.
SEE: B151, B182, B184, B192, B223, B267, B293, B400, B474,
B501, B726, B751, B804, B817, B854, B882, B945.

W111. Incantations. (J2)
For solo piano.
Composed: 1947.
Publication: Unpublished.
Premiere: Unknown.
Manuscript: British Library, no. 71435, vol. 184, item 2.

W112. Into the Labyrinth. (J194)

> For tenor and orchestra (two flutes, two oboes, two clarinets, two bassoons, two horns, two trumpets and strings). Text from *The Well* by George Mackay Brown.
>
> *Composed:* 1983.
>
> *Publication:*   Chester Music JWC 55669 (miniature score), 1986; conductor's score and parts, rental.
>
> *Premiere:*   St. Magnus Cathedral, Kirkwall, Orkney, during the St. Magnus Festival, June 22, 1983; Neil Mackie, tenor, and the Scottish Chamber Orchestra conducted by James Conlon.
>
> *Manuscript:* British Library nos. 71339–71340, vol. 88–89.
>
> *RECORDINGS:* D55.
>
> **SEE:** B37, B145, B187, B286, B295, B314, B335, B340, B419, B424, B435, B445, B493, B494, B503, B514, B581, B616, B620, B663, B789, B799, B811, B822, B848, B855, B879, B885, B893.

W113. Island of the Saints – Incidental Music. (J230)

> For flute, oboe, clarinet, horn, cello, and piano. Incidental music for a play by George Mackay Brown.
>
> *Composed:* 1983.
>
> *Publication:* Unpublished.
>
> *Premiere:*   Orkney Arts Theatre, Kirkwall, during the St. Magnus Festival, June 18, 1983.
>
> *Manuscript:* Glenys Hughes.

Jesus Autem Hodie. *SEE* **Four Carols.**

W114. Jimmack the Postie. (J209)

> Overture for orchestra.
>
> *Composed:* 1986.
>
> *Publication:*   Chester Music JWC 55790 (miniature score), 1987; conductor's score and parts, rental.
>
> *Premiere:*   Phoenix Cinema, Kirkwall, Orkney, during the St. Magnus Festival, June 22, 1986; Royal Philharmonic Orchestra conducted by the composer.
>
> *Manuscript:* British Library no. 71350, vol. 99.
>
> *RECORDINGS:* D56.
>
> **SEE:** B36, B173, B191, B284, B434, B506, B594, B625, B766, B773, B781, B782, B813, B883, B891.

W115. Le Jongleur de Notre Dame. (J155)

Masque for baritone, mime/juggler, chamber ensemble and children's band. Text by Peter Maxwell Davies.

Composed: 1977–1978.

Publication: Chester Music CH55252 (score), 1978; conductor's score and parts, rental.

Premiere: Academy Hall, Stromness, Orkney, during the St. Magnus Festival, June 18, 1978; Mark Furneaux, mime/juggler; Michael Rippon, baritone; Fires of London conducted by the composer; Stromness Academy Wind Band conducted by Jean Leonard.

Manuscript: British Library nos. 71272–71273, vol. 21–23.

SEE: B5, B12, B41, B52, B79, B124, B134, B178, B223, B260, B287, B312, B313, B373, B386, B397, B414, B423, B430, B474, B639, B651, B661, B669, B690, B709, B722, B730, B787, B904, B907, B944, B945.

W116. Judica Me. (J251)

Voluntary for chamber organ. For Chris Thompson. Arranged at the composer's advice for small school wind ensemble by Chris Thompson for flute, clarinet, muted trumpet, horn and trombone, May, 1992.

Composed: 1992.

Publication: Unpublished.

Premiere: Unknown.

Manuscript: Chris Thompson.

W117. Jupiter Landing. (J226)

Music-theatre work for children to play and sing. Text by Peter Maxwell Davies.

Composed: 1989.

Publication: Score, teacher's book, piano reduction, parts: Longman, 1990; Chester Music, 1994.

Premiere: Queen Elizabeth Hall, London, during Max Fest, April 3, 1990; pupils from the Chase Side Primary School, Enfield conducted by Mark Caswell.

Manuscript: British Library nos. 71291–71292, vol. 40–41.

SEE: B187, B200, B484, B617.

W118. The Kestrel Paced Round the Sun. (J133)

For flute solo.

Composed: 1974–1975.

Publication: Boosey & Hawkes B&H 3799 (flute score), 1976. Published along with **Solita** in **Two Pieces for Flute.** Excerpt **(Recitando--Andante--Allegro)** found in **Contemporary Music for Flute,** Boosey & Hawkes, 1976.

Premiere: University of Surrey, Guildford, BBC Invitation Concert, March 9, 1976; Judith Pearce, flute.

Manuscript: British Library no. 71386, vol. 135, item 2; no. 71387, vol. 136, item 2.

SEE: B498.

W119. Kinloche his Fantassie. (J139)

Arrangement of a fantasie by 16th century Scottish composer William Kinloch. For alto flute, bass clarinet, percussion, viola and cello.

Composed: 1975.

Publication: Boosey & Hawkes B&H 20571 (score) published with **My Lady Lothian's Lilt,** 1978, 1983; conductor's score and parts, rental.

Premiere: Dartington Summer School, Devon, August 19, 1976; Fires of London conducted by the composer.

Manuscript: British Library no. 71388, vol. 137, item 3.

RECORDINGS: D57, D58.

SEE: B51, B726, B945.

W120. Kirkwall Shopping Songs. (J161)

For young voices with recorders, percussion and piano. Text by Peter Maxwell Davies.

Composed: 1979.

Publication: Boosey & Hawkes B&H 20478 (3757) (score & 6 parts); (3758) (recorder parts), 1979, 1980.

Premiere: Kirkwall Primary School, Kirkwall, Orkney, June 16, 1979, as part of the St. Magnus Festival; pupils of the Papdale Primary School conducted by Glenys Hughes.

Manuscript: British Library nos. 71429-71430, vols. 178-179.

SEE: B11, B17, B183, B698, B763, B826.

W121. Leopardi Fragments. (J53)

Cantata for soprano, contralto and instrumental ensemble. Italian text from Leopardi.

Composed: 1961-1962.

Publication: Schott & Co. 10819 (6489) (score), 1965; conductor's score and parts, rental.

Premiere: BBC Invitation Concerts during the City of London Festival, July 19, 1962; Dorothy Dorow, Rosemary Phillips and the New Music Ensemble conducted by John Carewe.

Manuscript: British Library 71404, vol. 153.

RECORDINGS: D59.

SEE: B72, B132, B192, B236, B255, B293, B341, B495, B566, B715, B831, B938, B966.

W122. The Lighthouse. (J162)

Chamber opera in a prologue and one act. Libretto by Peter Maxwell Davies, based on Craig Mair's *A Star for Seamen.*

Composed: 1979.

Publication: Chester Music JWC 55426 (miniature score), 1986; JWC 55350 (vocal score) c. 1982; Libretto 1980; conductor's score and parts, rental.

Premiere: Moray House Gymnasium during the Edinburgh International Festival, September 2, 1980; Neil Mackie, Michael Rippon, David Wilson-Johnson and the Fires of London conducted by Richard Dufallo.

Manuscript: British Library nos. 71277–71278, vols. 26–27.

RECORDINGS: D60, D61.

SEE: B57, B60, B87, B96, B114, B119, B143, B144, B149, B188, B189, B198, B214, B219, B224, B226, B236, B248, B289, B290, B320, B354, B357, B358, B399, B402, B408, B409, B415, B416, B422, B446, B448, B466, B470, B471, B472, B476, B483, B486, B504, B511, B512, B524, B526, B554, B574, B575, B626, B632, B640, B672, B681, B689, B699, B710, B734, B735, B737, B748, B758, B782, B796, B832, B895, B908, B909, B911, B927, B929, B949.

W123. A Little Christmas Music. (J237)

For oboe and violin. For Ian Kellam, Christmas, 1990.

Composed: c. 1990.

Publication: Unpublished.

Premiere: Unknown.

Manuscript: Ian Kellam.

W124. Lord, Thy Word Abideth.

For instruments (undesignated).

Composed: c. 1959–1961.

Publication: Unpublished.

Premiere: Unknown.

Manuscript: British Library no. 71437, vol. 186, item 11.

W125. The Lord's Prayer. (J54)
For SATB chorus unaccompanied.
Composed: 1962.
Publication: Schott, S&Co. 6480 (score), 1962.
Premiere: St. Matthew's Church, Cheltenham, during the Cheltenham Festival, July 1, 1962; Choir of the Cirencester Grammar School conducted by the composer.
Manuscript: British Library no. 71419, col. 168, item 5.

W126. Lullabye for Ilian Rainbow. (J112)
For guitar solo.
Entitled *Ara Coeli: Lullabye for Ilian Rainbow* in *New Grove's*.
Composed: 1972.
Publication: Boosey & Hawkes B&H 20482 (3759) (score), 1978, 1980.
Premiere: Queen Elizabeth Hall, London, September 18, 1972; Timothy Walker, guitar.
Manuscript: Timothy Walker; British Library 71384, vol. 122, item 1.
RECORDINGS: D62.
SEE: B700, B701, B918.

W127. Lullabye for Lucy. (J179)
For SATB chorus unaccompanied. Text by George Mackay Brown.
Composed: 1981.
Publication: Boosey & Hawkes B&H 20591 (MF 52108) (3760) (score), 1982.
Premiere: St. Magnus Cathedral, Kirkwall, Orkney, during the St. Magnus Festival, June 19, 1981; St. Magnus Singers, conducted by the composer.
Manuscript: British Library no. 71431, vol. 180, item 1.
RECORDINGS: D63, D64, D65.
SEE: B63, B444, B617, B698, B886.

W128. 'Ma Fin Est Mon Commencement' by Machaut. (J102)
Arranged for instrumental ensemble. Part of the *Four Quartets: Incidental Music*.
Composed: 1971.
Publication: Unpublished.
Premiere: Unknown.

W129. March: The Pole Star. (J191, J192)

For brass quintet (J191); also arranged for brass band (J192).

Composed: 1981.

Publication: Brass quintet: Chester Music JWC 55652 (score), SOSO1285 (5 parts), 1984. brass band: parts, rental only.

Premiere: Brass band: St. Magnus Festival, Orkney, June 17, 1983; Stromness Academy Brass, conducted by John V. Jones. Quintet: Dartington Summer School, Devon, August 18, 1983; Albany Brass Ensemble.

Manuscript: British Library nos. 71399–71400, vols. 148–149.

RECORDINGS: D66.

SEE: B375, B826.

W130. The Martyrdom of St. Magnus. (J143)

Chamber opera in nine scenes. Libretto by Peter Maxwell Davies, based on the novel *Magnus* by George Mackay Brown.

Composed: 1976.

Publication: Boosey & Hawkes B&H 20136 (vocal score), 1977; B&H 20810, HPS 1141 (miniature score), 1987; libretto, 1977; conductor's score and parts, rental.

Premiere: St. Magnus Cathedral, Kirkwall, Orkney, during the St. Magnus Festival, June 18, 1977; Fires of London conducted by the composer.

Manuscript: British Library no. 71269, vol. 18.

RECORDINGS: D67.

SEE: B45, B68, B111, B167, B172, B187, B192, B198, B239, B256, B257, B268, B281, B283, B292, B295, B360, B403, B426, B451, B452, B453, B454, B462, B473, B476, B492, B501, B515, B531, B544, B553, B565, B577, B579, B589, B614, B673, B820, B856, B880, B923, B929, B944, B966.

W131. The Medium. (J172)

Monodrama for mezzo-soprano. Text by Peter Maxwell Davies.

Composed: 1981.

Publication: Boosey & Hawkes B&H 20665 (6447) (score), 1983.

Premiere: Academy Hall, Stromness, Orkney, during the St. Magnus Festival, June 21, 1981; Mary Thomas, mezzo-soprano.

SEE: B137, B194, B371, B401, B418, B444, B736, B740, B741, B788, B800, B886, B966.

W132. Mercurius. (J271)

For unaccompanied chorus SATB. Alchemical text in Greek and Latin.

Composed: 1994.

Publication: Chester Music (in preparation).

Premiere: Queen's Hall, Edinburgh, November 6, 1994; Cathedral Choir of St. Mary's Cathedral, Edinburgh, conducted by Timothy Byram Wigfield.

W133. A Mirror of Whitening Light. (J149)

For ensemble of 14 instrumentalists.

Composed: c. 1976–1977.

Publication: Boosey & Hawkes B&H 20371 (HPS 908) (miniature score), 1978; conductor's score and parts, rental.

Premiere: Queen Elizabeth Hall, London, March 23, 1977; London Sinfonietta conducted by the composer.

Manuscript: British Library nos. 71389–71390, vols. 138–139.

SEE: B118, B138, B188, B268, B560, B589, B633, B923, B944, B945.

W134. Mishkenot. (J217)

For nine instrumentalists. For Sir William Glock's 80th birthday.

Composed: 1988.

Publication: Boosey & Hawkes B&H 20878 (8474) (score), 1990; conductor's score and parts, rental.

Premiere: BBC Radio 3, May 3, 1988; London Sinfonietta, conducted by Elgar Howarth.

Manuscript: British Library no. 71268, vol. 17.

SEE: B22.

W135. Miss Donnithorne's Maggot. (J121)

Music-theatre work for mezzo-soprano and ensemble. Text by Randolph Stow.

Composed: 1974.

Publication: Boosey & Hawkes B&H 3765 (score), 1977; conductor's score and parts, rental.

Premiere: Town Hall, Adelaide, Adelaide Festival, March 9, 1974; Mary Thomas and the Fires of London conducted by the composer.

Manuscript: British Library no.71268, vol. 17.

RECORDINGS: D68, D69.

SEE: B12, B55, B58, B59, B62, B98, B127, B128, B135, B152, B194, B290, B307, B359, B373, B421, B447, B543, B569, B576, B636, B667, B690, B722, B739, B742, B850, B905, B912, B923, B941, B942, B944, B945, B966.

W136. Missa Super L'Homme Armé. (J75)
For speaker, piccolo/flute, clarinet, percussion, harmonium, harpsichord/celesta/piano, violin and cello.
Composed: 1968.
Publication: Boosey & Hawkes B&H 20472 (3764) (score), 1980; conductor's score and parts, rental.
Premiere: Original version, Conway Hall, London, Macnaghten Concert, February 26, 1968; Mary Thomas and the Pierrot Players conducted by the composer; Revised version, Sagra Musicale Umbra, Perugia, September 28, 1971; Murray Melvin and the Fires of London conducted by the composer.
Manuscript: British Library no. 71405, vol. 154, item 1.
RECORDINGS: D70.
SEE: B62, B80, B97, B300, B303, B566, B570, B650, B657, B703, B704, B793, B923, B930, B931, B941, B962, B964.

W137. 'Moderato' in E Flat. (J1)
For piano solo.
Composed: c. 1942.
Publication: Unpublished.
Premiere: Unknown.
Manuscript: British Library no. 71435, vol. 184, item 1.

W138. Mouvement Perpetuel No. I by Poulenc. (J36)
Arranged for school orchestra.
Composed: c. 1960.
Publication: Unpublished.
Premiere: Pupils of Cirencester Grammar School (date unknown).
Manuscript: British Library no. 71437, vol. 186, item 3.

W139. Movement from 'Il Ballo delle Ingrate' by Monteverdi. (J42)
Arranged for school orchestra.
Composed: c. 1960.
Publication: Unpublished.
Premiere: Pupils of Cirencester Grammar School (date unknown).
Manuscript: British Library no. 71438, vol. 187, item 1.

[W140]. Music in Camera SEE W272 Veni Sancte Spiritus on a Plainsong
In Bayliss's catalog, item **J204** is described as the signature tune for a BBC series entitled *Music in our Time*. The series title was in fact *Music in Camera*, and the composer has identified **Veni Sancte Spiritus on a Plainsong** (now renumbered to **J215A**) as the signature tune. Further details are found at that entry.

W141. My Lady Lothian's Lilt. (J136)

For mezzo soprano obbligato (without words), alto flute, bass clarinet, percussion, viola and cello.

Composed: 1975.

Publication: Boosey & Hawkes B&H 20571 (3791) score, 1983. Published with **Kinloche His Fantassie**. Conductor's score and parts, rental.

Premiere: Dartington Summer School, Devon, August 20, 1975; Mary Thomas and the Fires of London conducted by the composer.

Manuscript: British Library no. 71412, vol. 161.

W142. Nach Bergamo–Zur Heimat. (J124)

For flute, clarinet, percussion, piano, viola and cello.

Composed: 1974.

Publication: Unpublished.

Premiere: Royal Albert Hall, London, September 14, 1974 (Schoenberg Centenary Concert); Fires of London, conducted by the composer.

Manuscript: British Library no. 71384, vol. 133, item. 4.

SEE: B694.

W143. National Anthem. (J48)

'God Save the Queen' arranged for school orchestra.

Composed: c. 1961.

Publication: Unpublished.

Premiere: Pupils of Cirencester Grammar School (date unknown).

Manuscript: British Library no. 71437, vol. 186, item 6.

W144. The No. 11 Bus. (J200)

Music-theatre work for mezzo soprano, tenor, baritone, two dancers and mime; flute (piccolo), clarinet (bass clarinet), violin, cello, piano (celesta), percussion, telephone, 2 tape machines and Klaxon horn. Text by Peter Maxwell Davies.

Composed: 1983–1984.

Publication: Chester Music CH 55788 (miniature score), 1990; libretto, 1984; conductor's score, parts, vocal score, rental.

Premiere: Queen Elizabeth Hall, London, March 20, 1984; Mary Thomas, Donald Stephenson, Brian Raynor Cook, Anne Dickie, Tom Yang, Simon McBurney and the Fires of London conducted by Günther Bauer-Schenk.

Manuscript: British Library nos. 71282–71283, vols. 31–32.

SEE: B21, B123, B290, B312, B370, B377, B399, B406, B481, B576, B682, B739, B756, B759, B767, B823, B966.

W145. Nocturnal Dances. (J88)
Ballet for soprano and instrumental ensemble.
Composed: c. 1969–1970.
Publication: Unpublished.
Premiere: The Place, London, May 31, 1970; London Contemporary Dance Theatre (?). Concert version, Queen Elizabeth Hall, Sep. 19, 1970; Pierrot Players, conducted by the composer.
Manuscript: British Library no. 71262, vol. 11.
SEE: B83, B696, B697.

W146. Nocturne. (J160)
For alto flute solo.
Composed: 1979.
Publication: Boosey & Hawkes B&H 20661 (6446) (score), 1983.
Premiere: Wigmore Hall, London, January 28, 1983; Philippa Davies.
Manuscript: Philippa Davies.

Norn Pater Noster. *SEE* **Westerlings.**

W147. Notre Dame des Fleurs. (J69)
For soprano, mezzo-soprano, counter-tenor, flute, clarinet in A, percussion, piano (celesta), violin and cello. Text by Peter Maxwell Davies.
Composed: 1966.
Publication: Chester Music (miniature score), 1978; score, 1978; conductor's score and parts, rental.
Premiere: Queen Elizabeth Hall, London, March 17, 1973; Vanessa Redgrave, Mary Thomas, Grayston Burgess, and the Fires of London conducted by the composer.
Manuscript: British Library no. 71255, vol. 4.
SEE: B300, B352, B650.

Nowell. *SEE* **Four Carols.**

W148. 'O Haupt Voll Blut und Wunden' by J. S. Bach.
Arranged for SATB chorus unaccompanied.
Composed: c. 1959–1961.
Publication: Unpublished.
Premiere: Pupils of Cirencester Grammar School (date unknown).
Manuscript: British Library no. 71437, vol. 186, item 14.

W149. O Magnum Mysterium. (J39, J40)

> For SATB chorus, instrumental ensemble, and organ. Includes four carols for unaccompanied voices("O Magnum Mysterium," "Haylle, Comly and Clene," "Allelulia, pro Virgine Maria," "The Fader of Heven," two instrumental sonatas for flute, oboe, clarinet, bassoon, horn, percussion, viola and cello; fantasia for organ.
>
> *Composed:* 1960.
>
> *Publication:* *Four Carols from O Magnum Mysterium* (includes "O Magnum Mysterium," "Haylle, Comly and Clene," "llelulia, pro Virgine Maria," "The Fader of Heven"), Schott and Co., Edition 11276 (6492), (score), 1961. *Instrumental Sonatas from O Magnum Mysterium*, Schott and Co. Edition Schott 10825 (6493) (score), 1962; parts available for sale. *Organ Fantasia on O Magnum Mysterium* (J40): Schott and Co. Edition Schott 10826, 1962.
>
> *Premiere:* Organ Fantasia: Festival Hall, London, November 30, 1960; Alan Wicks, organ. Complete work: Cirencester Parish Church, Cirencester, Gloucestershire, December 8, 1960; Alan Wicks, organ, Choir of Cirencester Grammar School, players from the Cirencester Grammar School, conducted by the composer.
>
> *Manuscript:* Carols and Sonatas: British Library 71419, vol. 168, item 2.
>
> *RECORDINGS:* D71, D72, D73, D74, D75, D76, D77, D78.
>
> SEE: B32, B49, B97, B154, B155, B263, B268, B565, B578, B617, B645, B659, B829, B830, B938, B958.

W150. Oggi È Nato un Bel Bambino.

> For SATB choir unaccompanied.
>
> *Composed:* c. 1959–1961.
>
> *Publication:* Unpublished.
>
> *Premiere:* Pupils of Cirencester Grammar School (date unknown).
>
> *Manuscript:* British Library no. 71437, vol. 186, item 17.

W151. Ojai Festival Overture. (J240)

> For orchestra.
>
> *Composed:* 1991.
>
> *Publication:* Boosey & Hawkes HPS 1194 (9020) (miniature score), 1992; conductor's score and parts, rental.
>
> *Premiere:* Libbey Park Bowl, Ojai, California, during the Ojai Festival, June 1, 1991; Scottish Chamber Orchestra conducted by the composer.
>
> *Manuscript:* British Library nos. 71367–71368, vols. 116–117.
>
> *RECORDINGS:* D79, D80, D81.

SEE: B22, B468, B469, B775.

W152. Omnibus Voluptatem. (J252)

For unnacompanied choir, SATB. Text by David E. Griffin. Dedicated to Chris Thompson and the Sandbach School, Cheshire.

Composed: 1992.

Publication: Unpublished.

Premiere: Unknown.

Manuscript: Chris Thompson.

W153. One Star at Last. (J202)

Carol for SATB chorus unaccompanied. Text by George Mackay Brown.

Composed: 1984.

Publication: Score in the *Chester Book of Carols*. 1985.

Premiere: King's College Chapel, Cambridge, during the Nine Lessons and Carols, December 24, 1984. Choir of King's College conducted by Stephen Cleobury.

Manuscript: British Library no. 71344, vol. 93, item 3; no. 71432, vol. 181, item 1.

W154. Orkney Strathspey and Reel Society's Silver Jubilee Salute. (J145)

For septet: flute/piccolo, clarinet, violin, cello, piano/celeste, and percussion. Arrangement of a work composed for Queen Elizabeth II by Ronald Aim in 1978.

Composed: 1979.

Publication: Unpublished.

Premiere: Stromness Academy, Orkney, as part of the St. Magnus Festival, June 17, 1979; Fires of London conducted by Ronald Aim.

Manuscript: British Library no. 71388, vol. 137, 1988.

W155. An Orkney Wedding, With Sunrise. (J205)

For orchestra with highland bagpipe solo.

Composed: 1985.

Publication: Score, Boosey & Hawkes no. 20778 (1985); miniature score no. HPS 1119 (1986); conductor's score and parts, rental.

Premiere: Symphony Hall, Boston, U.S.A., May 10, 1985; Boston Pops Orchestra conducted by John Williams.

Manuscript: British Library no. 71347, vol. 96. Sylvia Junge, short score.

RECORDINGS: D82, D83, D84, D85.

SEE: B106, B133, B207, B210, B227, B228, B253, B276, B340, B419, B424, B445, B479, B485, B493, B494, B503, B519, B523, B598, B616, B684, B757, B774, B791, B799, B857, B896, B902, B949.

Our Father Whiche in Heaven Art *SEE* **Four Instrumental Motets, W85**

W156. Pagoda Fugue. (J62)

For instrumental ensemble. Incidental music for a radio play.
Composed: 1965.
Publication: Unpublished.
Premiere: Unknown.
Manuscript: British Library 71254; Bayliss lists another copy in the BBC Music Library, no. 31559.

W157. Parade.

Suite for piano solo.
Composed: 1949.
Publication: unpublished.
Premiere: BBC Children's Hour c. 1949; Peter Maxwell Davies.
Manuscript: Peter Maxwell Davies.

W158. Pavan and Galliard from the Mulliner Book. (J33)

Arranged for school orchestra.
Composed: 1959.
Publication: Unpublished.
Premiere: Cirencester Grammar School, Cirencester, Gloucestershire, February 3, 1960; Cirencester School Orchestra.
Manuscript: British Library no. 71437, vol. 186, item 2.

W159. Pavan by Newman from the Mulliner Book.

Arranged for wind band.
Composed: c. 1960.
Publication: Unpublished.
Premiere: Students of Cirencester Grammar School, c. 1960.
Manuscript: British Library no. 71437, vol. 186, item 3.

W160. The Peat Cutters. (J207)

For brass band, SATB youth choir and SA children's choir.
Composed: 1985.
Publication: Boosey & Hawkes B&H 20812 (7552) (vocal score), 1987; conductor's score and parts, rental.

Premiere: Usher Hall, Edinburgh, during the Edinburgh International Festival, August 18, 1985; Youth Choir of the Scottish National Orchestra and the Scottish National Youth Band conducted by Geoffrey Brand.

Manuscript: British Library no. 71432, vol. 181, item 3.

SEE: B69, B70, B153, B277, B641, B698, B785, B842, B949.

W161. Plainsong Melodies: Ave Verum Corpus; Ave Maria; Plangiamo [sic] Quel Crudel Basciare; Tantum Ergo.

Format unknown.

Composed: c. 1959–1961.

Publication: Unpublished.

Premiere: Pupils of Cirencester Grammar School?

Manuscript: British Library no. 71437, vol. 186, item 16.

Prayer: Norn Pater Noster *SEE* Westerlings.

W162. Prelude. (J6)

For piano solo.

Composed: 1949.

Publication: Unpublished.

Premiere: Unknown.

Manuscript: British Library no. 71435, vol. 184, item 6.

W163. Prelude and Fugue in C♯ Major by J. S. Bach. (J125)

Arranged for sextet.

Composed: 1974.

Publication: Boosey & Hawkes B&H 20436 (3800) (score), 1978, as part of **Two Preludes and Fugues**; conductor's score and parts, rental.

Premiere: Queen Elizabeth Hall, London, November 27, 1974; Fires of London conducted by the composer.

RECORDINGS: D86.

SEE: B303.

W164. Prelude and Fugue in C♯ Minor by J. S. Bach. (J113)

Arranged for sextet.

Composed: 1972.

Publication: Boosey & Hawkes B&H 20436 (3800) (score), 1978, part of **Two Preludes and Fugues**; conductor's score and parts, rental.

Premiere: Queen Elizabeth Hall, London, October 13, 1972; Fires of London conducted by the composer.

Manuscript: British Library no. 71384, vol. 133, item 2.
RECORDINGS: D87.
SEE: B301, B303.

W165. Prelude from 'Jack-in-the-Box' by Eric Satie. (J34)

Arranged for school orchestra.
Composed: c. 1960.
Publication: Unpublished.
Premiere: Pupils of Cirencester Grammar School (date unknown).
Manuscript: British Library 71437, vol. 186, item 3.

W166. Prolation. (J25)

For orchestra.
Composed: 1957–1958.
Publication: Schott & Co. 10709 (S&Co. 6306) (miniature score) 1961;
    conductor's score and parts, rental.
Premiere: Rome, July, 1959; Radio-Televisione Italiana Orchestra
    conducted by Nino Sanzogno.
Manuscript: British Library nos. 71309–71314, vols. 58–63.
SEE: B177, B249, B350, B923, B958, B962.

Psalm 124 *SEE* Four Instrumental Motets, W86

W167. Pussycat. (J100)

For voice and piano.
Composed: c. 1971.
Publication: Unpublished.
Premiere: Unknown.
Manuscript: Gerald McBurney. He says that the work is found on the
    verso of one of the leaves of the manuscript (probably a copy) of *The
    Boyfriend*.

W168. Quartet Movement. (J12)

For string quartet.
Composed: 1952.
Publication: Chester Music JWC 55681 (miniature score), 1985; parts,
    1983, 1984.
Premiere: Barbican Hall, London, May 23, 1983; Arditti Quartet.
Manuscript: British Library no. 71372, vol. 121, item 1.

W169. Quiet Memory of Bob Jennings. (J163)

For string trio.

Composed: 1979.
Publication: Unpublished.
Premiere: Unknown.
Manuscript: British Library no. 71393, vol. 142, item 1.

W170. The Rainbow. (J174)
 A short music-theatre piece for young children to sing and play with recorders, percussion, violin and piano. Text by Peter Maxwell Davies.
 Composed: 1981.
 Publication: Boosey & Hawkes B&H 20583 (score and parts) 1982; B&H 3768 (vocal score); B&H 3770 (parts only).
 Premiere: St. Magnus Festival, Orkney, June 20, 1981; pupils of the Stromness Primary School conducted by Janet Halsall.
 SEE: B444, B691, B826, B889.

W171. Realisation of a Canon by Michael Praetorius. (J58)
 Composed: c. 1964.
 Publication: Unpublished.
 Premiere: Unknown.
 Manuscript: British Library no. 71378, vol. 127, item 5.

W172. Renaissance Scottish Dances. (J116)
 For flute, clarinet, guitar, violin, cello, and percussion. From anonymous Scottish originals.
 Composed: 1973.
 Publication: Boosey & Hawkes B&H 20406 (3772) (score and parts), 1979.
 Premiere: Dartington Summer School, Devon, July 29, 1973; Fires of London conducted by the composer.
 Manuscript: British Library no. 71383, vol. 132.
 RECORDINGS: D88, D89.
 SEE: B131, B294, B565, B661, B701, B858, B935, B945, B966.

W173. Resurrection. (J216)
 Opera in one act with a prologue. Libretto by Peter Maxwell Davies.
 Composed: 1986–1987.
 Publication: Chester Music JWC60730 (miniature score), 1994; libretto, 1994; conductor's score, vocal score, and parts, rental.
 Premiere: Darmstadt State Theatre, Darmstadt, Germany, September 18, 1988; Staatstheater Darmstadt, conducted by Hans Drewanz.
 Manuscript: British Library nos. 71284–71288, vols. 33–37.

RECORDINGS: D90.

SEE: B14, B46, B117, B180, B186, B236, B312, B315, B334, B392, B433, B547, B607, B637, B684, B760, B853, B898, B966.

W174. Revelation and Fall. (J65)

Monodrama for soprano and instrumental ensemble. Text by George Trakl.

Composed: 1965–1966; revised 1980.

Publication: Boosey & Hawkes B&H 20648 (6259) (score), 1980; conductor's score and parts, rental.

Premiere: Macnaghten Concert, Conway Hall, London, February 26, 1968; Mary Thomas and the Pierrot Players conducted by the composer.

Manuscript: Library of Congress, Washington D.C., autograph; facsimile, British Library nos. 71252–71253, vols. 1–2.

RECORDINGS: D91.

SEE: B80, B97, B100, B187, B236, B329, B356, B538, B569, B618, B657, B706, B714, B716, B738, B754, B859, B864, B919, B923, B929, B932, B941, B943, B950, B958, B964, B966.

W175. Ricercar and Doubles on 'To Many A Well'. (J28)

Octet for flute, oboe, clarinet, bassoon, horn, viola, cello and harpsichord.

Composed: 1959.

Publication: Schott & Co., Edition Schott 10803 (S&Co. 6449), (miniature score), 1963; conductor's score and parts, rental.

Premiere: Dartmouth Festival, Dartmouth, New Hampshire, U.S.A. 1959.

Manuscript: British Library no. 71437, vol. 186, item 3.

SEE: B65, B236, B250, B539, B958, B962.

W176. Richard II. (J47)

Incidental music for a production of the Shakespeare play.

Composed: 1961.

Publication: Unpublished.

Premiere: Old Vic Theatre, London, 1962 (date unknown).

Manuscript: British Library no. 71436, vol. 185, item 3.

W177. Ritornello from 'L'Incoronazione di Poppea' of Monteverdi. (J43)

Arranged for school orchestra.

Composed: c. 1960–1961.

Publication: Unpublished.

Premiere: Pupils of Cirencester Grammar School (date unknown).
Manuscript: British Library no. 71436, vol. 185, item 1; no. 71438, vol. 187, item 2; no. 71439, vol. 188, item 2.

W178. The River. (J5)
For piano solo.
Composed: 1948.
Publication: Unpublished.
Premiere: Unknown.
Manuscript: British Library no. 71435, vol. 184, item 5.

W179. The Road to Colonnus. (J242)
Incidental music for a play by George Mackay Brown.
Composed: 1991.
Publication: Unpublished.
Premiere: Orkney Arts Theatre, Kirkwall, as part of the St. Magnus Festival, June 21, 1991; Scottish Chamber Orchestra Ensemble.

W180. Romance from 'Trois Rag-Caprices' by Milhaud. (J35)
Arranged for school orchestra.
Composed: c. 1960.
Publication: Unpublished.
Premiere: Pupils of Cirencester Grammar School (date unknown).
Manuscript: British Library no. 71437, vol. 186, item 3.

W181. Runes from a Holy Island. (J148)
Sextet for alto flute, clarinet, percussion, celeste, viola and cello.
Composed: 1977.
Publication: Chester Music JWC 55167 (score), 1979; conductor's score and parts, rental.
Premiere: Broadcast: BBC Radio 4, November 6, 1977; Public performance: St. Mary's Cathedral, Edinburgh, during the Edinburgh Festival, September 6, 1978; Fires of London conducted by the composer.
Manuscript: British Library no. 71388, vol. 137, item 6.
RECORDINGS: D92, D93, D94.
SEE: B352, B400, B501, B661.

W182. St. Michael Sonata. (J23)
For 17 wind instruments.
Composed: 1957.

Publication: Schott & Co. Edition Schott 10792 (miniature score), 1963; conductor's score and parts, rental.

Premiere: Cheltenham Town Hall, July 13, 1959; members of the London Symphony Orchestra conducted by the composer.

Manuscript: British Library no. 71377, vol. 126.

RECORDINGS: D95.

SEE: B177, B252, B271, B367, B570, B645, B688, B831, B836, B923, B958, B964.

W183. St. Thomas Wake: Foxtrot for Orchestra. (J78)

Based on a Pavan by John Bull.

Composed: c. 1966-1969.

Publication: Boosey & Hawkes B&H 20050 (HPS 872) (miniature score), 1972; conductor's score and parts, rental.

Premiere: Dortmund, Germany, June 2, 1969; Dortmund Philharmonic Orchestra conducted by the composer.

Manuscript: British Library nos. 71318-71319, vols. 67-68; no. 71382, vol. 131, item 6.

RECORDINGS: D96, D97, D98.

SEE: B7, B72, B99, B178, B181, B216, B236, B369, B429, B534, B558, B656, B864, B923, B944, B956, B964, B966.

W184. Salome. (J156)

Ballet in two acts.

Composed: 1978.

Publication: Boosey & Hawkes B&H 20539 (3790, HPS 963) (miniature score), 1982; conductor's score and parts, rental; version for reduced orchestra, conductor's score and parts, rental.

Premiere: Circus Building, Copenhagen, Denmark, November 10, 1978; Flemming Flindt Circus Company and the Danish Radio Orchestra conducted by Janos Fuerst. Choreography by Flemming Flindt.

Manuscript: British Library nos. 71274-71276, vols. 23-25.

RECORDINGS: D99.

SEE: B50, B381, B500, B606, B750, B795, B805, B906, B941, B945, B965, B966.

W184A. Salome: Concert Suite from the Ballet.

A series of selections from **Salome** indicated by the composer in the published score as appropriate for a concert suite.

Premiere: Royal Festival Hall, London, March 16, 1979; London Symphony Orchestra conducted by David Atherton.

SEE: B16, B82, B147, B378, B568, B674, B695.

W185. Schools Music Association Grace.
For voice and instrument.
Composed: 1986.
Publication: Schools Music Association, 1986.
Premiere: Unknown.
Manuscript: Unknown.
SEE: B542.

W186. Sea Eagle. (J183)
For horn solo.
Composed: 1982.
Publication: Chester Music JWC 55575 (score), 1983.
Premiere: Dartington Summer School, Devon, August 16, 1982; Richard Watkins, horn.
Manuscript: British Library no. 71393, vol. 142, item 4.
RECORDINGS: D100.
SEE: B597, B819.

W187. Sea Runes. (J211)
For unaccompanied choir, AATTBB or SATBBB. Words by George Mackay Brown.
Composed: 1986.
Publication: Chester Music CH 55905 (score) 1989.
Premiere: Alice Tully Hall, Lincoln Center, New York, November 16, 1986; The King's Singers.
Manuscript: British Library no. 71434, vol. 183, item 1.
SEE: B78, B407, B572.

W188. Second Fantasia on John Taverner's 'In Nomine'. (J57)
For orchestra.
Composed: 1964.
Publication: Boosey & Hawkes B&H 19370 (3774) (miniature score), 1968; conductor's score and parts, rental.
Premiere: Royal Festival Hall, London, April 30, 1965; London Philharmonic Orchestra conducted by John Pritchard.
Manuscript: British Library no. 71317, vol. 66.
RECORDINGS: D101.
SEE: B64, B103, B150, B236, B263, B487, B628, B655, B656, B657, B830, B864, B923, B938, B941, B944, B958, B964.

W189. A Selkie Tale. (J250)

Music-theatre work for children. Libretto by Peter Maxwell Davies.
Composed: 1992.
Publication: Chester Music (in preparation).
Premiere: St. Magnus Festival, Orkney, June 19, 1992; pupils of Holm
Primary School, Orkney, conducted by Glenys Hughes.
Manuscript: British Library nos. 71306–71308, vols. 55–57.

W190. The Seven Brightnesses. (J134)

For clarinet in B♭.
Composed: 1975.
Publication: Boosey & Hawkes B&H 20424 (3779), score), 1978.
Premiere: College of William and Mary, Williamsburg, Virginia,
October 12, 1975; Alan Hacker, clarinet.
Manuscript: British Library nos. 71387, vol. 136, item 3.
RECORDINGS: D102.

W191. Seven In Nomine. (J63)

For flute (piccolo), oboe, clarinet, bassoon, horn, harp, violins, viola
and cello.
Composed: c. 1962–1967.
Publication: Boosey & Hawkes B&H 19619 (3780) (score), 1968;
conductor's score and parts, rental.
Premiere: Four movements only: Wardour Castle Summer School,
Wilshire, August 20, 1965; Melos Ensemble conducted by Lawrence
Foster and the composer; First complete performance, Commen-
wealth Institute, London, December 3, 1965; Melos Ensemble
conducted by Lawrence Foster.
Manuscript: British Library nos. 71379–71381, vols. 128–130.
RECORDINGS: D103, D104.
SEE: B501, B638, B923, B962.

W192. Seven Songs Home. (J181)

For a capella children's voices, SSA with divisi. Text by Peter Maxwell
Davies.
Composed: 1981.
Publication: Chester Music JWC 55436 (score), 1983.
Premiere: Congress Hall of the Academy of Sciences, Budapest,
December 13, 1982; Children's Choir of Miskolc Music Primary
School No. 6 conducted by Janos Remenyi.
Manuscript: British Library no. 71431, vol. 180, item 2.
RECORDINGS: D105.

SEE: B260, B763, B826, B887.

W193. Seven Summer Songs. (J257)

For unison children's chorus and small children's instrumental ensemble. Text by Peter Maxwell Davies.

Composed: 1993.

Publication: Chester Music (in preparation).

Premiere: Papdale Primary School, Kirkwall, Orkney, during the St. Magnus Festival, June 18, 1993; pupils of Burray School, Holm School and Papdale School conducted by Frances Gray.

W194. Sextet. (J24)

For flute, clarinet, bass clarinet, violin, cello and piano.

Composed: 1958.

Publication: Unpublished.

Premiere: Dartington Summer School, Devon, 1958; New Music Ensemble conducted by John Carewe. Revised version arranged as a septet, performed at the Purcell Room, London, May 17, 1972; Fires of London, conducted by the composer.

Manuscript: British Library no. 71378, vol. 127, item 1.

SEE: B304, B557.

Septet. *SEE* **Sextet.**

W195. Shakespeare Music. (J59)

For alto flute, oboe, clarinet, bassoon, horn, trombone, percussion, guitar, viola, and double bass.

Composed: 1964.

Publication: Boosey & Hawkes B&H 19779 (score), 1970; 3782 (miniature score), 1970; conductor's score and parts, rental.

Premiere: John Lewis Theatre, London, BBC Invitation Concert, December 8, 1964; Portia Ensemble conducted by John Carewe.

Manuscript: British Library no. 71378, vol. 127, item 5.

SEE: B97, B268, B329, B343, B570, B627, B941, B945, B964.

W196. Shall I Die for Mannis Sake? (J66)

Carol for SA and piano. Text from Richard Hill's *Commonplace Book*.

Composed: 1965.

Publication: Boosey & Hawkes B&H 19481 (3783, 5662) (score), 1967, 1968.

Premiere: London College of Music, 1965 (Details unknown).

Manuscript: British Library no. 71424, vol. 173, item 2.

W197. The Shepherds' Calendar.   (J68)

> For solo voices (SATB), chorus (SATB), and orchestra. 13th Century Latin texts from the Goliard poets.
>
> *Composed:* 1965.
>
> *Publication:* Boosey & Hawkes B&H 19429 (3775), vocal score, 1968; B&H 19703 (score), 1969; conductor's score and parts, rental.
>
> *Premiere:*   Sydney, Australia, May 20, 1965; Students of Sydney University and boys of the Sydney Church of England Grammar School conducted by the composer.
>
> *Manuscript:* British Library no. 71424, vol. 173, item 3.
>
> SEE: B42, B604, B948, B964.

W198. Shepherds of Hoy.   (J263)

> Carol for children. Text by George Mackay Brown. Commissioned for Christmas 1993 by *The Times* (London).
>
> *Composed:* 1993.
>
> *Publication:* Chester Music CH 61068 (1994).
>
> *Premiere:*   Sothebys, New Bond Street, London, May 25, 1994; New London Childrens Choir conducted by Donald Corp.

Si Quis Diligit Me *SEE* Four Instrumental Motets, W83.

W199. Sinfonia.   (J55)

> For orchestra.
>
> *Composed:* 1962.
>
> *Publication:*   Schott & Co. Edition Schott 10820 (miniature score), 1968; conductor's score and parts, rental.
>
> *Premiere:* Royal Festival Hall, London, May 9, 1962; English Chamber Orchestra conducted by Sir Colin Davis.
>
> *Manuscript:* British Library 71316, vol. 65.
>
> *RECORDINGS:* D106.
>
> SEE: B106, B195, B251, B254, B262, B495, B522, B635, B685, B715, B831, B834, B966.

W200. Sinfonia Concertante.   (J185)

> For chamber orchestra, including flute, oboe, clarinet, bassoon, horn, timpani and strings.
>
> *Composed:* 1982.
>
> *Publication:*   Chester Music JWC 55596 (miniature score), 1986; conductor's score and parts, rental.

Premiere: Royal Albert Hall, London, BBC Promenade Concert, August 12, 1983; Academy of St. Martin-in-the-Fields conducted by Sir Neville Marriner.

Manuscript: British Library no. 71338, vol. 87.

RECORDINGS: D107.

SEE: B54, B195, B262, B314, B349, B356, B391, B455, B541, B556, B649, B777, B778, B860, B900.

W201. Sinfonietta Accademica. (J195)

For orchestra.

Composed: 1983.

Publication: Chester Music JWC 55687 (miniature score), 1987; conductor's score and parts, rental.

Premiere: Reid Hall, Edinburgh University, October 6, 1983; Scottish Chamber Orchestra conducted by Edward Harper.

Manuscript: British Library no. 71339, vol. 88; nos. 71341–71342, vols. 90–91.

RECORDINGS: D108.

SEE: B27, B95, B145, B225, B229, B314, B317, B376, B436, B520, B527, B581, B772, B803, B810, B861, B878, B880, B890, B901.

W202. Sir Charles his Pavan. (J255)

For orchestra. Composed in memory of Sir Charles Grove.

Composed: 1992.

Publication: Schott and Co. ED 12438 (score), 1994; conductor's score and parts, rental.

Premiere: Royal Northern College of Music, September 22, 1992; BBC Philharmonic conducted by the composer.

Manuscript: Lady Hilary Groves, London.

RECORDINGS: D109, D110.

SEE: B139.

W203. Six Secret Songs. (J262)

For piano solo. Composed for Ivor Hodgson, double-bass player with the BBC Philharmonic, to celebrate the birth of his daughter, Sara.

Composed: 1993.

Publication: Chester Music (in preparation).

Premiere: Unknown.

Manuscript: Ivor Hodgson, Manchester.

W204. Six Songs for St. Andrew's. (J221)

Song cycle for very young children to play and sing. Text by Peter Maxwell Davies.

Composed: 1988.

Publication: Longman, (score and parts), 1991; Chester, 1994.

Premiere: Kirkwall, Orkney, Papdale Primary School, June 18, 1988; Pupils of St. Andrew's Primary School, Orkney, conducted by Glenys Hughes.

Manuscript: British Library no. 71434, vol. 183, item 2.

SEE: B555, B812, B898.

W205. Solita. (J82)

For flute and optional musical box.

Composed: 1969, 1972.

Publication: Boosey & Hawkes   B&H 3799 (flute score), 1976. Published with **The Kestrel Paced Round the Sun** in **Two Pieces for Flute**.

Premiere: York Festival, June 25, 1969; Judith Pearce, flute.

Manuscript: British Library no. 71382, vol. 131, item 6.

SEE: B571.

W206. Solstice of Light. (J159)

For tenor, chorus (SATB) and organ. Text by George Mackay Brown.

Composed: 1978–1979.

Publication: Boosey & Hawkes, B&H 20477 (3784) (score), 1980.

Premiere: St. Magnus Cathedral, Kirkwall, Orkney, during the St. Magnus Festival, June 18, 1979; Neil Mackie, tenor, Richard Hughes, organ and the St. Magnus Singers conducted by Norman Mitchell.

Manuscript: British Library no. 71389, vol. 138; nos. 71427–71428, vols. 176–177.

RECORDINGS: D111.

SEE: B17, B93, B154, B183, B291, B429, B475, B594, B664, B820, B822.

W207. Sonata for Clarinet and Piano. (J21)

Composed: 1956.

Publication: Chester Music CH 55902 (score and part), 1989.

Premiere: Darmstadt Festival, Darmstadt, Germany, July 20, 1957; Georgina Dobree, clarinet and Peter Maxwell Davies, piano.

Manuscript: British Library no. 71375, vol. 124.

SEE: B129.

W208. Sonata for Guitar. (J201)

For solo guitar.

Composed: 1983–1984.

Publication: Chester Music CH 58941 (score), 1990.

Premiere: St. Magnus Festival, Orkney, June 20, 1987; Timothy Walker, guitar.

Manuscript: British Library no. 71401, vol. 150.

RECORDINGS: D112.

SEE: B21, B292, B880, B918.

W209. Sonata for Organ. (J186)

Purchased by the National Library of Scotland at a benefit auction by the Orkney Artists for Amnesty International.

Composed: 1982.

Publication: Chester Music JWC 55477 (score), 1984.

Premiere: St. Magnus Cathedral, Kirkwall, Orkney, as part of the St. Magnus Festival, June 23, 1982; Richard Hughes, organ.

Manuscript: National Library of Scotland; British Library 71398, vol. 147.

SEE: B154.

W210. Sonata for Piano. (J13)

Composed: 1954.

Publication: Unpublished.

Premiere: Unknown.

Manuscript: Ian Kellam.

W211. Sonata for Piano. (J173)

Composed: 1981.

Publication: Chester Music JWC 55430 (score), 1983.

Premiere: Guildhall, Bath during the Bath Festival, May 23, 1981; Stephen Pruslin, piano.

Manuscript: Stephen Pruslin.

RECORDINGS: D113, D114.

SEE: B19, B466, B668.

W212. Sonata for Trumpet and Piano. (J18)

Composed: 1955.

Publication: Schott & Co., Edition Schott 11067 (score and parts), 1969.

Premiere: Manchester University, Arthur Worthington Hall, 1955; Elgar Howarth, trumpet and John Ogdon, piano.

Manuscript: British Library no. 37373, vol. 122; no. 37374, vol. 123, item 1.
RECORDINGS: D115, D116, D117, D118, D119, D120.
SEE: B138, B495, B837.

W213. Sonatina for Trumpet. (J178)
For solo trumpet.
Composed: 1981.
Publication: In *Contemporary Trumpet*, Boosey & Hawkes B&H 20636, 1984.
Premiere: Unknown.
Manuscript: Unknown.

W214. Sonatine for Violin and Cimbalon. (J198)
Composed: 1984.
Publication: Chester Music JWC 55773 (miniature score), 1984; 2 parts available for sale.
Premiere: Wigmore Hall, London, June 3, 1984; Rosemary Furniss, violin and Gregory Knowles, cimbalon.
Manuscript: British Library no. 71343, vol. 92; no. 71344, vol 93, item 1; no. 71403, vol. 152, item 1.
SEE: B21, B130, B490, B525, B615.

W215. Song. (J103)
For voice and guitar. Text possibly by George Mackay Brown.
Composed: c. 1972.
Publication: Unpublished.
Premiere: Unknown.
Manuscript: British Library no. 71406, vol. 155, item 1.

W216. Song for Jenny and Her New Baby. (J126)
SATB chorus unaccompanied.
Composed: 1974.
Publication: Unpublished.
Premiere: Unknown.
Manuscript: British Library no. 71384, vol. 133, item 4.

W217. Songs. (J87)
For voice and instruments. Numbered II, IV, VI, VIII. Text of No. II, 'O meine müde Füße' from *Leonce und Lena* by Büchner.
Composed: c. 1968.
Publication: Unpublished.

Premiere: Unknown.

Manuscript: British Library, nos. 71252, vol. 1, item 3; 71405, vol. 154, item 2.

W218. Songs of Hoy. (J182)

Masque for children's voices, descant recorders, piano, guitars and percussion. Text by Peter Maxwell Davies.

Composed: 1981.

Publication: Chester Music JWC 55498 (score), 1983; 57034 (voice parts); 57042 (instrumental parts), 1983.

Premiere: Stromness Academy, Orkney, during the St. Magnus Festival, June 21, 1982; children of the North Walls School, conducted by Glenys Hughes.

Manuscript: British Library no. 71281, vol. 30.

SEE: B11, B125, B617, B698, B763, B826.

W219. Songs to Words by Dante. (J27)

For baritone and smallish orchestra.

Composed: c. 1967.

Publication: Unpublished.

Premiere: Unknown.

Manuscript: British Library no. 71322, vol. 71.

W220. Souvenir de Strathclyde. (J256)

For Ian Ritchie.

Composed: 1993.

Publication: Unpublished.

Premiere: Unknown.

W221. A Spell for Green Corn: The MacDonald Dances. (J261)

For violin solo and chamber orchestra. Commissioned by Donald MacDonald, Chairman of the Board of the Scottish Chamber Orchestra as a 60th birthday tribute for the composer and to celebrate the 21st anniversary of the SCO.

Composed: 1993.

Publication: Chester Music CH 60978 (score), 1994; conductor's score and parts, rental.

Premiere: City Hall, Glasgow, November 24, 1993; James Clark, violin; Scottish Chamber Orchestra conducted by the composer.

RECORDINGS: D121.

W222. The Spiders' Revenge. (J241)

Music-theatre work for children to play and sing.   Text by Peter Maxwell Davies.

Composed: 1991.

Publication: Chester (in preparation).

Premiere: St, Magnus Festival, Orkney, June 25, 1991; Pupils of Evie Primary School, Orkney, conducted by Moira Summers.

Manuscript: British Library nos. 71300–71301, vols. 49–50.

SEE: B202, B817, B882.

W223. Stedman Caters. (J76)

For six instruments including flute/piccolo, clarinet in B♭, percussion, harpsichord, viola and cello.

Composed: 1958; revised, 1968.

Publication: Boosey & Hawkes B&H 20496 (3785) (score), 1978, 1980; conductor's score and parts, rental.

Premiere: Purcell Room, London, May 30, 1968; Pierrot Players conducted by the composer.

Manuscript: British Library no. 71382, vol. 131, item 3.

W224. Stedman Doubles. (J20)

For clarinet and percussion.

Composed: 1955; revised 1968.

Publication: Boosey & Hawkes B&H 19964 (3786), (score and parts), 1978.

Premiere: Cardiff University, April 23, 1968; Alan Hacker, clarinet and Tristan Fry, percussion.

Manuscript: British Library nos. 71373, vol. 122; no. 71374, vol. 123, item 3.

SEE: B171, B966.

W225. Stehn am Fuß des Gebirgs. (J8)

For unaccompanied chorus. Text from Rilke.

Composed: c. 1950.

Publication: Unpublished.

Premiere: Unknown.

Manuscript: British library no. 71435, vol. 184, item 7.

W226. Stevie's Ferry to Hoy. (J137)

For piano solo. For Anne Bevan.

Composed: 1975.

Publication: Boosey & Hawkes B&H 20396 (3787) (score), 1978.

Premiere: Unknown.

Manuscript: Archie Bevan; British Library no. 71388, vol. 137, item 2.

SEE: B826, B935.

W227. Stone Litany: Runes From a House of the Dead. (J115)

For mezzo-soprano and orchestra. Text from Viking runic inscriptions on the walls of Maeshowe tomb, Orkney, in Orkney Norn, a dialect of old Norse.

Composed: 1973-1975.

Publication: Boosey & Hawkes, score, 1975; B&H 20670 (HPS 1110) (miniature score), 1975, 1983; conductor's score and parts, rental.

Premiere: City Hall, Glasgow, September 22, 1973; Jan deGaetani with the Scottish National Orchestra conducted by Alexander Gibson.

Manuscript: British Library nos. 71324-71326, vols. 73-74; no. 71408, vol. 157.

RECORDINGS: D122.

SEE: B7, B94, B115, B120, B122, B158, B178, B212, B294, B314, B323, B534, B566, B587, B656, B657, B670, B797, B932, B949, B960.

W228. Strathclyde Concerto No. 1 for Oboe and Orchestra. (J215)

Composed: 1986.

Publication: Boosey & Hawkes HPS 1171 (8099) (miniature score), 1989; BH 8253, reduction for oboe and piano (score and part), 1989; conductor's score and parts, rental.

Premiere: City Hall, Glasgow, April 29, 1988; Robin Miller, oboe, and the Scottish Chamber Orchestra conducted by the composer.

Manuscript: British Library nos. 71351-71352, vols. 100-101.

RECORDINGS: D123.

SEE: B121, B197, B280, B338, B420, B427, B478, B549, B611, B684, B757, B768, B771, B780, B789, B815, B824, B851, B869.

W229. Strathclyde Concerto No. 2 for Cello and Orchestra. (J218)

Composed: 1987.

Publication: Chester Music CH 58933 (miniature score), 1990; CH 59022 (reduction for cello and piano, score and part), 1990; conductor's score and parts, rental.

Premiere: City Hall, Glasgow, February 1, 1989; William Conway, cello and the Scottish Chamber Orchestra conducted by the composer.

Manuscript: British Library nos. 71353-17355, vols. 102-104.

RECORDINGS: D124.
SEE: B187, B201, B205, B206, B327, B338, B385, B389, B410, B521, B616, B623, B687, B731, B768, B770, B780, B815, B819, B824, B851, B887.

W230. Strathclyde Concerto No. 3 for Horn, Trumpet and Orchestra. (J227)
Composed: 1989.
Publication: Boosey & Hawkes B&H 1209 (8778) (miniature score), 1992; B&H 9178 (reduction for horn, trumpet and piano) (score and 2 parts), 1992; conductor's score and parts, rental.
Premiere: City Hall, Glasgow, January 19, 1990; Robert Cook, horn, and Peter Franks, trumpet with the Scottish Chamber Orchestra conducted by the composer.
Manuscript: British Library nos. 71360–71361, vols. 109–110.
RECORDINGS: D125.
SEE: B187, B285, B327, B478, B617, B705, B768, B780, B851.

W231. Strathclyde Concerto No. 4 for Clarinet and Orchestra. (J233)
Composed: 1990.
Publication: Chester Music CH 60875 (miniature score), 1993; CH 60876 (reduction for clarinet and piano, score and part), 1993; conductor's score and parts, rental.
Premiere: City Hall, Glasgow, November 21, 1990; Lewis Morrison, clarinet with the Scottish Chamber Orchestra conducted by the composer.
Manuscript: British Library nos. 71363–71364, vols. 112–113.
RECORDINGS: D126, D127.
SEE: B768, B780, B851, B871.

W232. Strathclyde Concerto No. 5 for Violin, Viola and String Orchestra. (J245)
Composed: 1991.
Publication: Boosey & Hawkes HPS 1236 (9273) miniature score, 1994; Boosey & Hawkes 9487 (reduction for violin, viola and piano, score and two parts), 1993; conductor's score and parts, rental.
Premiere: City Hall, Glasgow, March 13, 1992; James Clark, violin, Catherine Marwood, viola and the Scottish Chamber Orchestra conducted by the composer.
Manuscript: British Library nos. 71365–71366, vols. 114–115.
RECORDINGS: D128.
SEE: B23, B442, B612, B768, B780, B851, B862.

W233. Strathclyde Concerto No. 6 for Flute and Orchestra. (J247)
Composed: 1991.
Publication: Chester Music, CH 60222 (miniature score), 1994; CH 61024 (reduction for flute and piano, score and part), 1994; conductor's score and parts, rental.
Premiere: City Hall, Glasgow, March 13, 1992; David Nicholson, flute and the Scottish chamber Orchestra conducted by the composer.
Manuscript: British Library nos. 71369–71370, vols. 118–119.
RECORDINGS: D129.
SEE: B442, B612, B768, B780, B851, B872.

W234. Strathclyde Concerto No. 7 for Double Bass and Orchestra. (J254)
Composed: 1992.
Publication: Boosey & Hawkes HPS 1266 (9534) (miniature score), 1994; 9760 (reduction for piano and double bass, score and part) 1994; conductor's score and parts, rental.
Premiere: City Hall, Glasgow, November 25, 1992; Duncan McTier, bass, and the Scottish Chamber Orchestra conducted by the composer.
Manuscript:
RECORDINGS: D130.
SEE: B81, B278, B457, B621, B768, B780, B851.

W235. Strathclyde Concerto No. 8 for Bassoon and Orchestra. (J258)
Composed: 1993.
Publication: Chester Music CH 60944 (miniature score) 1995; CH 60945 (reduction for piano and bassoon, score and part) 1995; conductor's score and parts, rental.
Premiere: City Hall, Glasgow November 24, 1993; Ursula Leveaux, bassoon and the Scottish Chamber Orchestra conducted by the composer.
Manuscript: Judy Arnold.
RECORDINGS: D131.
SEE: B768, B780, B851.

W236. Strathclyde Concerto No. 9 for Six Woodwind Instruments. (J272)
Composed: 1994.
Publication: Chester Music (in preparation).
Premiere: City Hall, Glasgow, February 9, 1995; Scottish Chamber Orchestra, conducted by the composer.
SEE: B768, B780, B851.

W237. String Quartet. (J44)

Composed: 1960-1961.

Publication: Schott and Co., Edition Schott 10816 (score), 1962; parts.

Premiere: BBC Maida Vale Studio, London, November 9, 1961; Amici String Quartet.

Manuscript: British Library no. 71378, vol. 127, item 4; no. 71404, vol. 153, item 1.

SEE: B2, B217, B634, B686, B831, B923, B924, B941, B945, B966.

Sub Tuam Protectionem. *SEE* **Two Piano Pieces**.

W238. Sunday Morning. (J268)

For orchestra. 'Signature Tune' for Brian Kay's BBC Radio 3 Program *Sunday Morning*.

Composed: 1994.

Publication: Unpublished.

Premiere: September 18, 1994.

RECORDINGS: D132.

W239. Symphony No. 1. (J142)

Composed: 1975-1976.

Publication: Boosey & Hawkes B&H 20390 (HPS 915) (3792) (miniature score), 1978; conductor's score and parts, rental.

Premiere: Royal Festival Hall, London, February 2, 1978; Philharmonia Orchestra conducted by Simon Rattle.

Manuscript: British Library nos. 71327-71330, vols. 76-79.

RECORDINGS: D133, D134.

SEE: B53, B66, B92, B115, B162, B187, B215, B236, B241, B269, B288, B382, B405, B439, B562, B590, B633, B654, B656, B675, B708, B721, B923, B944, B945, B948, B966.

W240. Symphony No. 2. (J170)

Composed: 1980.

Publication: Boosey & Hawkes B&H 20592 (3821) (miniature score), 1982; conductor's score and parts, rental.

Premiere: Symphony Hall, Boston, U.S.A., February 26, 1981; Boston Symphony Orchestra conducted by Seiji Ozawa.

Manuscript: British Library nos. 71334-71337, vols. 83-84.

RECORDINGS: D135.

SEE: B18, B35, B40, B174, B187, B193, B211, B220, B230, B236, B238, B242, B261, B268, B288, B297, B342, B355, B390, B428,

B458, B491, B510, B564. B582, B593, B610, B622, B677, B707, B720, B749, B790, B867, B945, B949, B966.

W241. Symphony No. 3. (J203)
Composed: 1984.
Publication: Boosey & Hawkes B&H 20747 (HPS 1114) (7127) (miniature score), 1985, 1987; conductor's score and parts, rental.
Premiere: Free Trade Hall, Manchester, February 19, 1985; BBC Philharmonic conducted by Sir Edward Downes.
Manuscript: British Library nos. 71343–71346, vols. 92–95.
RECORDINGS: D136, D137.
SEE: B29, B116, B222, B227, B275. B282, B314, B336, B387, B388, B425, B505, B528, B533, B619, B728, B765, B807, B849, B861, B862, B966.

W242. Symphony No. 4. (J224)
Composed: 1988–1989.
Publication: Boosey & Hawkes HPS 1203 (8555) (score), 1992; conductor's score and parts, rental.
Premiere: Royal Albert Hall, London, September 10, 1989 (BBC Promenade Concert); Scottish Chamber Orchestra conducted by the composer.
Manuscript: British Library nos. 71358–71359, vols.107–108.
RECORDINGS: D138.
SEE: B9, B89, B247, B322, B328, B331, B344, B394, B431, B432, B461, B499, B530, B624, B656, B761, B821, B851.

W243. Symphony No. 5. (J266)
Commissioned by the Philharmonia Orchestra to commemorate their 50th anniversary.
Composed: 1994.
Publication: Boosey and Hawkes (in preparation).
Premiere: Royal Albert Hall, London, Promenade Concert, August 9, 1994; Philharmonia Orchestra conducted by the composer.
Manuscript: Boosey & Hawkes (temporarily).
RECORDINGS: D139.
SEE: B181, B345, B535, B613, B644, B745.

W244. 'Take a Pair of Sparkling Eyes' by Arthur Sullivan. (J182A)
Arranged for flute, B♭ clarinet, piano, violin, cello, and percussion.
Composed: 1982.
Publication: Unpublished.

Premiere: For 'The Musical House That Max Built,' a television profile of the composer on London Weekend Television; The Fires of London conducted by the composer.

Manuscript: British Library no. 71383, vol. 132, item 4.

W245. Taverner. (J92)

Opera in two acts. Libretto by Peter Maxwell Davies.

Composed: 1962–1968; 1970.

Publication: Boosey & Hawkes B&H 20035 (HPS 1103) (6527) (score), 1978, 1984; B&H 20034 (3793) (vocal score), 1972; 3794 (libretto), 1972; conductor's score and parts, rental.

Premiere: Royal Opera House, Covent Garden, July 12, 1972; conducted by Edward Downes.

Manuscript: British Library nos. 71259–71261, nos. 8–10.

SEE: B24, B26, B30, B31, B44, B47, B86, B91, B97, B111, B114, B115, B117, B119, B141, B163, B168, B177, B198, B204, B208, B209, B231, B235, B236, B263, B268, B273, B289, B299, B321, B351, B379, B380, B384, B398, B443, B516, B554, B569, B570, B578, B609, B626, B630, B646, B648, B652, B660, B683, B684, B702, B719, B747, B753, B754, B806, B823, B838, B856, B911, B923, B924, B926. B927, B929, B931, B942, B948, B953, B964, B965, B966.

W246. Taverner: Points and Dances From the Opera. (J93)

For instrumental ensemble.

Composed: 1970.

Publication: Boosey & Hawkes B&H 20414 (HPS 912) (3766) (miniature score), 1978; conductor's score and parts, rental.

Premiere: Queen Elizabeth Hall, London, February 20, 1971; Fires of London conducted by the composer.

Manuscript: British Library no. 71383, vol. 132, item 2.

RECORDINGS: D140.

SEE: B585, B837.

W247. Te Lucis Ante Terminum. (J46)

For SATB chorus, flute, oboe, 2 clarinets, 2 trombones, glockenspiel and guitar.

Composed: 1961.

Publication: Schott & Co. Edition Schott 10817b (score), 1967; conductor's score and instrumental parts, rental.

Premiere: Cirencester Grammar School, Gloucestershire, November 30, 1961; Orchestra and Choir of the Cirencester Grammar School conducted by the composer.

Manuscript: British Library no. 71419, vol. 168, item 3.

SEE: B157, B645, B698, B958.

W248. Tenebrae Super Gesualdo. (J109)

For mezzo-soprano, alto flute, bass clarinet, harpsichord/celesta/chamber organ, marimba/glockenspiel, guitar, violin/viola, and cello.

Composed: 1972.

Publication: Chester Music CH55393 (score), 1980; conductor's score and parts, rental.

Premiere: Queen Elizabeth Hall, London, August 25, 1972; Mary Thomas, Timothy Walker, and the Fires of London conducted by the composer.

Manuscript: British Library no. 71406. vol. 155, item 3.

RECORDINGS: D141, D142.

SEE: B306, B965, B966.

W249. Tenebrae Super Gesualdo (choral version). (J110)

For SATB chorus and instruments.

Composed: 1972.

Publication: Chester Music, JWC 55183 (score), 1980; conductor's score and parts, rental.

Premiere: St. James, Piccadilly, June 28, 1984; St. James's Piccadilly Music Ensemble and Music Ensemble Chorus conducted by Keith Williams.

Manuscript: According to Bayliss, (formerly) at the Scottish Music Information Center; not listed in the British Library inventory.

W250. There Is No Rose of Such Virtue.

Arrangement of an English 15th-century carol for female voices.

Composed: c. 1959–1961.

Publication: Unpublished.

Premiere: Pupils of Cirencester Grammar School?

Manuscript: British Library no. 71437, vol. 186, item 13.

W251. Three Dances by William Byrd. (J31)

Arranged for school or amateur orchestra.

Composed: 1959.

Publication: Schott & Co. Edition Schott 10932 (S&Co. 6630) (score), 1989; parts available for sale.

Premiere: Pupils of Cirencester Grammar School, Gloucestershire, 1959 (?).
Manuscript: British Library no. 71437, vol. 186, item 1.
SEE: B935.

W252. Three German Folksongs.
Arrangement for instruments(?).
Composed: 1960.
Publication: Unpublished.
Premiere: Pupils of Cirencester Grammar School (?) (date unknown).
Manuscript: British Library no. 71437, vol. 186, item 4.

W253. Three Organ Voluntaries. (J138)
For organ solo. For Elizabeth Bevan.
Composed: 1976.
Publication: Chester Music CH55170 (score), 1979.
Premiere: Vestvervig Kirke, Denmark, July 31, 1979; Jesper Jergens Jensen, organ.
Manuscript: Archie Bevan.
RECORDINGS: D143.
SEE: B154.

W254. Three Studies for Percussion. (J135)
For 11 percussionists.
Composed: 1975.
Publication: Chester Music CH55173 (score), 1980; parts for sale.
Premiere: Gosforth High School, Northumberland, October 15, 1975; Gosforth School Percussion Ensemble conducted by Peter Swan.
Manuscript: British Library no. 71388, vol. 137, item 1.
SEE: B411, B935.

W255. Threnody on a Plainsong for Michael Vyner. (J229)
For orchestra. Based on the plainsong *Cor Meum et Caro Mea Exultaverunt in Deum Vivum.*
Composed: 1989.
Publication: Chester Music CH 60356 (miniature score), 1989; conductor's score and parts, rental.
Premiere: Glyndebourne, October 25, 1989; London Sinfonietta conducted by the composer.
Manuscript: British Library no. 71362, vol. 111.
RECORDINGS: D144, D145.
SEE: B618.

W256. Tractus Clausum et Reconditum. (J231)
For mezzo-soprano and guitar.
Composed: 1990.
Publication: unpublished.
Premiere: Purcell Room, London, May 20, 1990; Mary Thomas, mezzo-soprano, and Timothy Walker, guitar.

W257. The Turn of the Tide. (J253)
For orchestra, children's chorus and optional five groups of young instrumentalists.   Commissioned by the Association of British Orchestras.
Composed: 1992.
Publication: Chester Music, CH 60614 (choral score); conductor's score and parts, rental.
Premiere: City Hall, Newcastle, February 12, 1993; Northern Sinfonia conducted by Richard McNichol.
RECORDINGS: D146.
SEE: B139, B631.

W258. Turris Campanarum Sonantium – The Bell Tower. (J97)
For percussion.
Composed: 1971.
Publication: Withdrawn.
Premiere: Queen Elizabeth Hall, London, March 12, 1971; Stomu Yamash'ta, percussion.
Manuscript: lost.
RECORDINGS: D147.
SEE: B246, B966.

W259. The Two Fiddlers. (J153)
Opera in two acts for young people to play and sing. Libretto by Peter Maxwell Davies, based on a short story for children by George Mackay Brown.
Composed: 1978.
Publication: Boosey & Hawkes B&H 20395 (3796) (vocal score), 1978; 3796 (choral score); 3798 (libretto), 1978; conductor's score and parts, rental.
Premiere: Kirkwall Arts Theatre, Kirkwall, Orkney, during the St. Magnus Festival, June 16, 1978; Pupils of the Kirkwall Grammar School conducted by Norman Mitchell.
Manuscript: Sketches in the possession of Boosey & Hawkes; otherwise unknown.

SEE: B15, B17, B33, B43, B221, B232, B233, B237, B243, B298, B313, B325, B346, B368, B374, B396, B502, B517, B595, B698, B711, B723, B733, B826, B870, B876, B944.

W260. Dances from 'The Two Fiddlers'. (J154)
Selections from the opera arranged for violin solo and instrumental ensemble including piccolo, bass clarinet, cello, percussion and piano.
Composed: 1978.
Publication: Boosey & Hawkes B&H 20537 (3740) (score), 1978, 1981; parts for sale.
Premiere: Queen Elizabeth Hall, London, October 6, 1978; Fires of London conducted by the composer.
Manuscript: British Library no. 71391, vol. 140, item 2.
RECORDINGS: D148.
SEE: B176, B449, B763, B875.

W261. Dances From 'The Two Fiddlers'. (J220)
Selections from the opera arranged for violin and piano.
Composed: 1988 (this arrangement).
Publication: Boosey and Hawkes B&H 20864 (8231) (score and part), 1988, 1989.
Premiere: Stromness Academy, Orkney during the St. Magnus Festival, June 19, 1988; György Pauk, violin and Peter Frankl, piano.
Manuscript: British Library no. 71403, vol. 152, item 3.

W262. Two Little Quartets. (J169, J177)
For string quartet.
Composed: **Quartet No. 1**, 1980 (J169); **Quartet No. 2**, 1977; revised 1987 (J177).
Publication: Boosey & Hawkes HPS 1175 (8239) miniature score, 1989; 8258 (parts), 1989.
Premiere: **Quartet No. 1**: Dartington Summer School, Devon, July 26, 1982; Medici String Quartet; **Quartet No. 2**: St. Lawrence University, Canton, New York, November 12, 1987; Alexander String Quartet.
Manuscript: **Quartet No. 1**: British Library no. 71393, vol. 142, item 3. **Quartet No. 2**: British Library no. 71392, vol. 141.

W263. Two Motets by Gesualdo. (J189)
Arranged for brass quintet.
Composed: 1982.

Publication: Chester Music CH 55651 (score), 1984; parts for sale.
Premiere: Dartington Summer School, Devon, August 18, 1983; Albany Brass Ensemble.
Manuscript: British Library nos. 71399–71400, nos. 148–149.

W264. Two Piano Pieces. (J86, J94)
For piano solo.
Composed: No 1: **Sub Tuam Protectionem**: 1969 (J86) ; No. 2: **Ut Re Mi:** 1970–1971 (J94).
Publication: Chester Music CH 55314 (score), 1980.
Premiere: **Sub Tuam Protectionem**: Purcell Room, London, January 13, 1970; Stephen Pruslin, piano. **Ut Re Mi**: Purcell Room, London, January 19, 1971; Stephen Pruslin, piano.
Manuscript: **Sub Tuam Protectionem**: Stepehen Pruslin, autograph; British Library no. 71383, vol. 132, item 1, photocopy. **Ut Re Mi**: Stephen Pruslin, autograph; British Library no. 71383, vol. 132, item 3, photocopy.
SEE: Sub Tuam Protectionem: B240; **Ut Re Mi**: B80, B244, B585.

Two Preludes and Fugues. *SEE* **Prelude and Fugue in C ♯ Major by J. S. Bach; Prelude and Fugue in C ♯ Minor by J. S. Bach.**

W265. Unbroken Circle. (J199)
For chamber ensemble: alto flute, bass clarinet, viola, cello and piano.
Composed: 1984.
Publication: Boosey & Hawkes CH 55686 (miniature score), 1985; conductor's score and parts for sale.
Premiere: Private: Bath Festival, June 1, 1984; London Sinfonietta conducted by Diego Masson; Public: La Mason de la Culture, Rennes, November 30, 1984; Fires of London conducted by the composer.
Manuscript: autograph, Sir William Glock; copy, British Library no. 71401, vol. 150, items 1 and 2.

W266. [Unidentified Arrangement].
Composed: c. 1959–1961.
Publication: Unpublished.
Premiere: Unknown.
Manuscript: British Library no. 71437, vol. 186, item 9.

W267. [Unidentified Sketches/Drafts]. (J16)
Composed: 1950's–1960's.

Publication: Unpublished.
Premiere: Unknown.
Manuscript: British Library nos. 71442–71445, vol. 191–194.

W268. [Untitled Piece]. (J144)
For piano solo.
Composed: c. 1976.
Publication: Unpublished.
Premiere: Unknown.
Manuscript: British Library no. 71388, vol. 137, item 4.

W269. [Untitled Work]. (J104)
For alto flute and marimba.
Composed: c. 1972.
Publication: Unpublished.
Premiere: Unknown.
Manuscript: British Library no. 71383, vol. 132, item 5.

Ut Re Mi. *SEE* **Two Piano Pieces.**

W270. 'Vanitas' by Jan Albert Ban (J246)
Arranged for string orchestra.
Composed: c. 1991.
Publication: Boosey & Hawkes, with the score of **Strathclyde Concerto No. 5**. See entry for that work.
Premiere: Unknown.
Manuscript: British Library no. 71371.

W271. Veni Sancte Spiritus. (J56)
For SAB soloists, mixed chorus and small orchestra.   After John Dunstable
Composed: 1963.
Publication: Boosey & Hawkes B&H 19299 (3801) (miniature score), 1965; vocal score, 1964; 3802 (choral score), 1964; conductor's score and parts, rental.
Premiere: Cheltenham Town Hall, during the Cheltenham Festival, July 10, 1964; Princeton High School Choir and the English Chamber Orchestra conducted by Thomas Hilbish.
Manuscript: British Library nos. 71420–71422, nos. 169–171.
SEE: B118, B132, B303, B467, B518, B570, B599, B830, B831, B835, B938.

W272. Veni Sancte Spiritus on a Plainsong. (J215A)

For flute, clarinet, violin, cello, harpsichord and piano, and percussion. Signature tune for the BBC series *Music In Camera*.

Composed: 1986.

Premiere: Broadcast in 1986.

Manuscript: British Library no. 71403, vol. 152, item 5.

W273. Veni Sancte–Veni Creator Spiritus. (J114)

For flute, clarinet, viola, cello, glockenspiel and harpsichord/piano. After John Dunstable.

Composed: 1972.

Publication: Boosey & Hawkes B&H 20495 (3803) (score), 1978; conductor's score and parts, rental.

Premiere: Queen Elizabeth Hall, London, May 6, 1972; Fires of London conducted by the composer.

RECORDINGS: D149.

SEE: B303, B305, B557.

W274. Vesalii Icones. (J85)

Music-theatre work for dancer, solo cello, and instrumental ensemble.

Composed: 1969.

Publication: Boosey & Hawkes B&H 20286 (7944) (score), 1978; conductor's score and parts, rental.

Premiere: Queen Elizabeth Hall, London, December 9, 1969; William Louther, dancer, Jennifer Ward Clarke, solo cello and the Pierrot Players conducted by the composer.

Manuscript: British Library no. 71258, vol. 7.

RECORDINGS: D150, D151.

SEE: B1, B12, B56, B75, B123, B124, B135, B148, B178, B182, B187, B192, B198, B212, B245, B263, B274, B311, B312, B313, B329, B370, B421, B447, B450, B513, B583, B584, B665, B669, B678, B690, B692, B703, B722, B746, B747, B752, B786, B794, B850, B892, B919, B923, B929, B932, B941, B948, B958.

W275. Walton Tribute. (J105)

For orchestra. Composed as a 70th birthday tribute for Sir William Walton.

Composed: 1972.

Publication: Unpublished.

Premiere: March, 1972; London Symphony Orchestra conducted by the composer.

Manuscript: British Library no. 71323, vol. 72.

W276. Watkins Ale. (J37)

Arranged for school orchestra. Based on an anonymous 16th-Century English tune.
Composed: c. 1960.
Publication: Unpublished.
Premiere: Pupils of Cirencester Grammar School (date unknown).
Manuscript: British Library no. 71437, vol. 186, item 4.

W277. We Met in St. Louis: A Birthday Card. (J196)

For solo cello. For Jonathan Williams's birthday.
Composed: November 19, 1985.
Publication: Unpublished.
Premiere: Unknown.
Manuscript: Jonathan Williams.

W278. Wedding Telegram for Gary Kettel. (J128)

For soprano, guitar and celesta.
Composed: c. 1974.
Publication: Unpublished.
Premiere: Unknown.
Manuscript: British Library no. 71411, vol. 160, item 2.

W279. A Welcome to Orkney. (J168)

For 14 instruments including flute, oboe, clarinet, bassoon, horn, 4 violins, 2 violas, 2 cellos and double bass.
Composed: 1980.
Publication: Boosey & Hawkes B&H 20561 (4873) (score), 1982; 4874 (string parts); 4875 (wind parts).
Premiere: St. Magnus Festival, Orkney, June 30, 1980; Pupils of Chetham's School, Manchester.
Manuscript: British Library no 71393, vol. 142, item 2.
SEE: B826, B935.

W280. The Well – Incidental Music. (J168A)

Incidental music for a play by George MacKay Brown. For speakers, voices and instrumental ensemble (9 instruments).
Composed: 1981.
Publication: Unpublished.
Premiere: Kirkwall Arts Theatre, Orkney, as part of the St. Magnus Festival, June 20, 1981; local musicians conducted by the composer.
Manuscript: British Library 71270–71271, vols. 19–20.
SEE: B444.

W281. Westerlings. (J146)

Four songs and a prayer, with seascapes for unaccompanied SATB chorus. Text by George Mackay Brown.

Composed: 1977.

Publication: Boosey & Hawkes B&H 20563 (3807) (score), 1977. An adaptation from the last section, arranged for mixed chorus and organ, was published by Boosey and Hawkes as **Prayer: Norn Pater Noster** (B&H 6035 (3767) in 1980.

Premiere: Incomplete: Uppsala University, Sweden, May 25, 1977; Uppsala Academy Chamber Choir conducted by Kettil Skarby. Complete: BBC Concert Hall, Broadcasting House, London, October 15, 1977; BBC Singers conducted by John Alldis.

Manuscript: British Library nos. 71425–71426, vols. 174–175. **Norn Pater Noster** only: British Library no. 71389, vol. 138.

SEE: B138, B291, B828.

W282. Winterfold. (J214)

For mezzo-soprano, alto flute, bass clarinet, percussion, guitar, piano, viola and cello. For the Fires of London Farewell.

Composed: 1986.

Publication: Chester Music CH 55869 (miniature score), 1989; conductor's score and parts, rental.

Premiere: Queen Elizabeth Hall, London, January 20, 1987; Mary Thomas, mezzo-soprano and the Fires of London conducted by the composer.

Manuscript: Northwestern University Music Library, Evanston, Illinois, U.S.A.

SEE: B112, B140, B266, B272, B286, B353, B508, B551, B764, B847, B881.

W283. Witch. (J243)

Incidental music to a play by George Mackay Brown.

Composed: 1991.

Publication: Unpublished.

Premiere: Orkney Arts Theatre, Kirkwall, as part of the St. Magnus Festival, June 21, 1991; Scottish Chamber Orchestra Ensemble.

Manuscript: British Library nos. 71302–71303, vol. 51–52.

W284. Woodwind Octet. (J14)

For piccolo, flute, oboe, English horn, clarinet, bass clarinet and two bassoons.

Composed: 1954.

Publication: Unpublished.
Premiere: Unknown.
Manuscript: British Library no. 71372, vol. 121, item 2.

W285. Worldes Blis. (J79)
Motet for Orchestra.
Composed: 1966–1969.
Publication: Boosey & Hawkes FSB 445 (score), 1975; B&h 20299,
    HPS 1198 (9098), (miniature score), 1993; conductor's score and
    parts, rental.
Premiere: Royal Albert Hall, London, BBC Promenade Concert,
    August 28, 1969; BBC Symphony Orchestra conducted by the
    composer.
Manuscript: British Library nos. 71320–71321, vols. 69–70.
RECORDINGS: D152.
SEE: B7, B28, B84, B94, B97, B108, B115, B139, B178, B187, B203,
    B212, B236, B301, B335, B404, B429, B440, B460, B464, B488,
    B534, B558, B566, B656, B657, B666, B852, B864, B923, B943,
    B965, B966.

W286. Yellow Cake Revue. (J165)
Comments in words and music on the threat of uranium mining in
    Orkney. For voice and piano.
Composed: 1980.
Publication: Boosey & Hawkes B&H 20690 (6550) vocal score, 1984.
Premiere: St. Magnus Festival, Kirkwall, Orkney, June 21, 1980;
    Eleanor Bron accompanied by the composer.
Manuscript: British Library no. 71415, vol. 164.
RECORDINGS: See listings for **A Farewell to Stromness**, **Yesnaby
    Ground**.
SEE: B326, B513, B591, B855, B865.

Yellow Cake Revue: *SEE ALSO* **Farewell to Stromness**; **Yesnaby Ground**

W287. Yesnaby Ground. (J167)
Piano interlude from **Yellow Cake Revue**.
Composed: 1980.
Publication: Boosey & Hawkes B&H 20521 (3747), 1980, score.
    Published with **Farewell to Stromness**.
Premiere: St. Magnus Festival, Orkney, June 21, 1980; Peter Maxwell
    Davies.
Manuscript: British Library no. 71415, vol. 164, item 1.

RECORDINGS: D158, D159, D160, D161.
SEE: B935.

W288. Yesterday: Lennon and McCartney. (J130)
Arranged for guitar.
Composed: 1974.
Publication: Unpublished.
Premiere: Unknown.
Manuscript: British Library no. 71384, vol. 133, item 5.
RECORDINGS: D162.

Discography

Antechrist

D1.   Mainstream MS 5001 / c. 1968 / LP
Pierrot Players conducted by the composer.
Album title: *New Music From London*
Includes: Harrison Birtwistle: *Ring a Dumb Carillon*; David Bedford:
Come In Here Child; Richard Orton: *Cycle* (for 2 or 4 players).

D2.   Editions L'Oiseau-Lyre DSLO 2 / 1972 / LP
Fires of London conducted by the composer.
Includes: *From Stone to Thorn, Hymnos, Missa Super L'Homme Armé.*

Ave Maria, Hail Blessed Flower

D3.   Argo RG 446 / 1965 / LP
Argo ZRG 5446 / 1965 / LP
Elizabethan Singers conducted by Louis Halsey.
Album title: *Sir Cristemas*
Includes: *I Saw Three Ships*; *The First Christmas*; *Deck the Hall*; *Dormi
Jesu*; *Here We Come A-Wassailing*; *Our Lady's Song*; *Unto Us Is
Born a Son*; *There Is No Rose*; *We Wish You a Merry Christmas*;
Silent Night; *The Boar's Head Carol*; *Balulalow*; *Out of Your Sleep
Arise*; *Ecce Puer*; *What Cheer*; *From Heaven Winging*; *Welcome
Yule*; *The First Nowell*.

D4.   Odeon HQS 1350 / 1966 / LP
       Album title: *Chichester Cathedral, 900 Years*.
       Includes: Charles Villiers Stanford, *Beati Quorum Via*; Charles Wood, *Short Communion in the Phyrgian Mode: Sanctus and Benedictus*; Ralph Vaughan Williams, *O Taste and See*; Edward C. Barstow, *Let All Mortal Flesh Keep Silence*; Martin Shaw, *Anglican Folk Mass-Creed*; Gustav Holst, *Turn Back O Man*; John Ireland, *Greater Love Hath No Man*; Herbert Howells, *Magnificat*; William Walton, *Set Me as a Seal Upon Thine Heart*; Kenneth Leighton, *Give Me the Wings of Faith*.

Ave Maris Stella

D5.   Unicorn-Kanchana KP 8002 / 1981 / LP
       Fires of London.
       Includes: *Tenebrae Super Gesualdo*.

D6.   Unicorn-Kanchana UKCD 2038 / 1990 / CD
       Fires of London.
       Includes: *Image, Reflection, Shadow*; *Runes From a Holy Island*.

Ave Plena Gracia

D7.   Argo RG 499, ZRG 5499 / LP / 1966
       Elizabethan Singers, conducted by Louis Halsey
       Album title: *Carols of Today*
       Includes: William Mathis, *Wassail Carol*; Benjamin Britten, *Jesu, As Thou Art Our Saviour*; John Joubert, *A Little Child There Is Yborn*; Richard Rodney Bennett, *The Sorrows of Mary*; Alun Hoddinott, *What Tidings?*; P. Racine Fricher, *In Excelsis Gloria*; Nicholas Maw, *Balulalow*; Peter Wishart, *Alleluya, A New Work Is Come on Hand*; John McCabe, *Coventry Carol*; Alan Rawsthorne, *The Oxen*; Gordon Crosse, *Laetabundus*; Phyllis Tate, *The Virgin and Child*; John Gardner, *The Shout*.

Ave Rex Angelorum

D8.   Continuum CCD 1043 / 1991 / CD
       Elysian Singers of London conducted by Matther Greinhall.

Album title: *Child of Light*.

Includes: Benjamin Britten, *Ceremony of Carols*; Judith Weir, *Illuminare Jerusalem*; Robert Saxton, *Child of Light*; John Taverner, *Nativity*; William Walton, *All This Time*; John Byrt, *All and Some*; Kenneth Leighton, *Of a Rose*; Lennox Berkeley, *In Wintertime*;   Francis Poulenc, *Motets pour le Temps de Noël*.

Bairns of Brugh

D9.   Unicorn-Kanchana DKP 9033 / 1984 / LP
Unicorn-Kanchana DKP(L) 9033 / 1984 / Cassette
Fires of London conducted by the composer.
Includes: Davies, *Image, Reflection, Shadow; Runes from a Holy Island*.

D10.   Unicorn-Kanchana UKCD 2068 / 1994 / CD
Fires of London conducted by the composer
Album title: *Vesalii Icones*
Includes: *Vesalii Icones; Runes from a Holy Island*

Black Pentecost

D11.   Collins Classics 13662 / 1993 / CD
Della Jones, David Wilson-Johnson and the BBC Philharmonic conduct-
ed by the composer.
Album title: *Black Pentecost/Stone Litany*
Includes: *Stone Litany*

Black Pentecost (excerpt)

D12.   Collins Classics 14442 / 1994 / CD (from Collins Classics CD 13662)
Della Jones, David Wilson-Johnson, and the BBC Philharmonic
conducted by the composer.
Album title: *Maximum Max*
Includes: *Sunday Morning*; *Sir Charles his Pavan*; *Ojai Festival Overture*; *Yellow Cake Revue: 'Farewell to Stromness,' 'Yesnaby Ground'*; *The Lighthouse* (excerpt); *Caroline Mathilde: Concert Suite from Act I of the Ballet* (excerpts); *O Magnum Mysterium:* carols *'The Fader of Heven,' 'O Magnum Mysterium'*; *Suite from 'The Boyfriend': 'Polly's Dream'*; *Lullabye for Lucy*; *Strathclyde Concerto*

No. 4 for Clarinet and Orchestra (excerpt); *An Orkney Wedding, With Sunrise.*

The Boyfriend: Suite from 'The Boyfriend'

D13. Collins Classics 10952 / 1990 / CD
      Aquarius conducted by Nicholas Cleobury.
      Includes: Davies, *Suite from 'The Devils'*; *Seven In Nomine.*

The Boyfriend: Suite from 'The Boyfriend': Polly's Dream

D14. Collins Classics 30032 / 1992 / CD
      Aquarius, conducted by Nicholas Cleobury
      Album title: *MAX: The Music of Peter Maxwell Davies.*
      Includes: *Ojai Festival Overture*; *Yellow Cake Revue: 'Farewell to Stromness,' 'Yesnaby Ground'*; *Caroline Mathilde: Concert Suite from Act I of the Ballet* (excerpt); *Lullabye for Lucy*; *O Magnum Mysterium:* Carols *'The Fader of Heven,' 'O Magnum Mysterium'*; *Seven In Nomine: 'Gloria Tibi Trinitas,' 'In Nomine'*; *Threnody on a Plainsong for Michael Vyner*; *St. Thomas Wake* excerpt); *An Orkney Wedding, With Sunrise.*

D15. Collins Classics 14442 / 1994 / CD (from Collins Classics CD 10952)
      Aquarius, conducted by Nicholas Cleobury
      Album title: *Maximum Max*
      Includes: *[SEE D12 FOR COUPLINGS]*

Caroline Mathilde: Concert Suite from Act I of the Ballet

D16. Collins Classics 20022 / 1991 / CD
      BBC Philharmonic conducted by the composer.

D17. Collins Classics 13082 / 1991 / CD
      BBC Philharmonic conducted by the composer.
      Includes: *Ojai Festival Overture*; *Threnody on a Plainsong for Michael Vyner*; *St. Thomas Wake.*

Caroline Mathilde: Concert Suite from Act I, excerpt: **Scenes III–IV**

D18.   Collins Classics 30032 / 1992 / CD
       BBC Philharmonic conducted by the composer.
       Album title: *MAX: The Music of Peter Maxwell Davies*.
       Includes: *[SEE D14 FOR COUPLINGS]*

Caroline Mathilde: Concert Suite from Act I, excerpt: **Scenes II–III**

D19.   Collins Classics 14442 / 1994 / CD (from Collins Classics CD 13082)
       BBC Philharmonic conducted by the composer.
       Album title: *Maximum Max*
       Includes: *[SEE D12 FOR COUPLINGS]*.

Chat Moss

D20.   Collins Classics 14602 / 1995 / CD
       BBC Philharmonic conducted by the composer.
       Album title:
       Includes: *Cross Lane Fair*, *Five Klee Pictures*, *Symphony No. 5*.

Concerto for Trumpet and Orchestra

D21.   Collins Classics 11812 / 1991 / CD
       John Wallace, trumpet; Scottish National Orchestra conducted by the
          composer.
       Includes: *Symphony No. 4*.

D22.   Philips 432 075-2 / 1991 / CD
       Håkan Hardenberger, trumpet; BBC Philharmonic conducted by Elgar
          Howarth.
       Album title: *Trumpet Concertos*
       Includes: Harrison Birtwistle, *Endless Parade*; Michael Blake Watkins,
          Concerto for Trumpet.

Concerto for Violin and Orchestra

D23.   Sony Classical SMK 58928 / 198? / CD
       Isaac Stern, violin; Royal Philharmonic Orchestra, conducted by André
          Previn.
       Album title: *British Pageant: Maxwell Davies, Britten*

Includes: Benjamin Britten, *Symphony for Cello and Orchestra*.

D24.   CBS Masterworks MK 42449 / 1987 / CD
CBS Masterworks M 42449 / 1987 / LP
CBS Masterworks MT 42449 / 1987 / cassette
Isaac Stern, Violin; Royal Philharmonic Orchestra, conducted by André
    Previn.
Includes: Henri Dutilleux, *L'Arbre des songes*.

Cross Lane Fair

D25.   Collins Classics 14602 / 1995 / CD
Mark Jordan, Northumbrian pipes, and Rob Lea, Bodhran; BBC
    Philharmonic, conducted by the composer.
Album title:
Includes: *Chat Moss*, *Five Klee Pictures*, *Symphony No. 5*.

Dark Angels

D26.   Nonesuch H71342 / 1977 / LP
Jan deGaetani, mezzo-soprano, and Oscar Ghihlia, guitar.
Includes: R. F. Wernick, *Songs of Remembrance*.

The Devils: Suite from 'The Devils'

D27.   Collins Classics 10952 / 1990 / CD
Aquarius conducted by Nicholas Cleobury.
Includes: Davies, *Suite from 'The Boyfriend'*; *Seven In Nomine*.

Door of the Sun

D28.   Composers Recordings ACS 6016-6018 / 1988 / Cassettes (3)
John Graham, viola: Robert Black, Thomas Muraco, piano.
Album title: *Viola Anthology*.
Includes: Milton Babbitt, *Compositions*; Ralph Shapey, *Evocation*;
    Vincent Persichetti, *Parable No. 16*; Robert Pollock, *Violament*;
    Emmanuel Ghent, *Entelechy*; Stephan Wolpe, *Pieces for Viola Alone*;
    Igor Stravinsky, *Elegy*; David Schiff, *Joycesketch II*; David Wool-
    dridge, *Three Diversions*; Martin Subotnick, *An Arsenal of Defense*;
    Ton-That Tiet, *Terre-Feu*; Bernd Alois Zimmerman, *Sonata for Viola*

and Piano; Dmitrii Shostakovich, *Sonata for Violin and Piano*;
William Bergsma, *Fantastic Variations on a Theme from 'Tristan'*;
Benjamin Britten, *Lachrymae: Reflections on a Song of John
Dowland*.

Eight Songs for a Mad King

D29.   Unicorn RHS 308 / 1971 / LP
       Unicorn UNS 261 / 1971 / LP
       Julius Eastman and the Fires of London conducted by the composer.

D30.   Nonesuch H 71285 / 1973 / LP
       Julius Eastman and the Fires of London conducted by the composer.

D31.   Opus 1 No. 26 / 1975 / LP
       John D'Armand and the University of Massachusetts Group for New
          Music conducted by Charles Fussell.

D32.   Unicorn-Kanchana DKP(C) 9052 / 1987 / cassette
       Julius Eastman and the Fires of London conducted by the composer.

D33.   Unicorn-Kanchana DKP (CD) 9052 / 1987 / CD
       Julius Eastman, baritone; Fires of London conducted by the composer.
       Includes: *Miss Donnithorne's Maggot*.

D34.   Musical Heritage Society MHS 912215 / 1988 / LP
       Musical Heritage Society MHS 312215 / 1988 / Cassette
       Michael Gallup, baritone; New Music Settings Ensemble conducted by
          Rhonda Hess.
       Includes: *Miss Donnithorne's Maggot*.

Fantasia and Two Pavans after Henry Purcell

D35.   Unicorn-Kanchana KP 8005 / 1981 / LP
       Unicorn-Kanchana KP 8005 (CD) / 1991 / CD
       Unicorn-Kanchana UKCD 2044 / 1991 / CD
       Fires of London, conducted by the composer.
       Album title: *Renaissance and Baroque Realisations*.
       Includes: *Fantasia upon One Note*; *Prelude and Fugue in C♯ Minor by
          J. S. Bach*; *Prelude and Fugue in C♯ Major by J. S. Bach*; *Tenebrae*

Super Gesualdo; *Veni Sancte–Veni Creator Spiritus*; *Si Quis Diligit Me*; *All Sons of Adam*; *Our Father Whiche in Heaven Art*; *Kinloche his Fantassie*.

Fantasia Upon One Note

D36.   Unicorn-Kanchana 8005 / 1981 / LP
Unicorn-Kanchana 8005 (CD) / 1991 / CD
Unicorn-Kanchana UKCD 2044 / 1991 / CD
Fires of London, conducted by the composer.
Album title: *Renaissance and Baroque Realisations*.
Includes: *Fantasia and Two Pavans after Henry Purcell*; *Prelude and Fugue in C♯ Minor by J. S. Bach*; *Prelude and Fugue in C♯ Major by J. S. Bach*; *Tenebrae Super Gesualdo*; *Veni Sancte–Veni Creator Spiritus*; *Si Quis Diligit Me*; *All Sons of Adam*; *Our Father Whiche in Heaven Art*; *Kinloche his Fantassie*.

Five Carols

D37.   Argo 436 119-2 / 1992 / CD
Choir of King's College, Cambridge conducted by Stephen Cleobury.
Includes: *Solstice of Light*; *Hymn to the Word of God*.

Five Klee Pictures

D38.   Collins Classics 14602 / 1995 / CD
BBC Philharmonic, conducted by the composer.
Album title:
Includes: *Chat Moss*, *Cross Lane Fair*, *Symphony No. 5*.

Five Pieces for Piano

D39.   His Master's Voice HMV 2029 / 1965 / LP
His Master's Voice APL 2098 / 1965 / LP
Odeon PASD 645 / 1965 / LP
John Ogdon, piano.
Album Title: *Piano Music by Twentieth Century British Composers*.
Includes: Alun Hoddinot. *Sonata No. 2, op. 27*: Alexander Goehr, *Sonata in One Movement, op. 2.*; Harrison Birtwistle, *Precis*; Richard Hall, *Suite*.

Four Carols

Four Carols: 'Jesus Autem Hodie'

D40.   AFKA SK-516 / 1990 / CD
Choir of the Church of the Advent, Mark Dwyer, organist and assistant conductor, conducted by Edith Ho.
Album title: *Duo Seraphim: Angel Songs for Christmas*
Includes: Jacob Handl: *Duo Seraphim*; Juan Esquivel: *Duo Seraphim*; Sebastian Aguilera de Heredia: *Magnificat Octavi Toni*; Judith Weir: *Illuminare, Jerusalem*; Ralph Vaughan Williams: *Down in Yon Forest*; Elizabeth Poston: *The Apple Tree Carol*; Charles Wood, arr.: *King Jesus Hath a Garden*; William Cutter: *Little Lamb*; Ralph Vaughan Williams: *Wither's Rocking Hymn*; Herbert Howells: *Long, Long Ago*; Healey Willan: *What is This Lovely Fragrance?*; Rodney Lister: *Christmas Hymn*; Peter Mathews: *Dans les Ombres de la Nuit*; David Willcocks, arr.: *Angelus ad Virginem*; Peter Warlock: *Bethlehem Down*; Pedro de Cristo: *Quaeramus cum Pastoribus*; Richard Dering: *Duo Seraphim*; Samuel Scheidt: *Duo Seraphim*.

Four Carols: 'Nowell'

D41.   Deutsche Grammophon 413-590-1 / 1984 / LP
Deutsche Grammophon 413-590-4 / 1984 / Cassette
Deutsche Grammophon 413-590-2 / 1984 / CD
Choir of Westminister Abbey; Christopher Herrick, organ, conducted by Simon Preston.
Album title: *Christmas Carols*
Includes: Jacob Praetorius, *Wachet Auf!*; Arthur Oldham, *Remember, O Thou Man*; G. H. Palmer, arr., *There Stood in Heaven a Linden Tree*; Wishart, Peter, *Alleluya, a New Work*; Marc-Antoine Charpentier, *Salve Puerule*; H. Walford Davies, arr., *The Holly and the Ivy*; Elizabeth Poston, *The Apple Tree Carol*; Michael Praetorius, *Resonet in Laudibus*; Charles Wood, arr., *Ding Dong Merrily on High*; Andreas Hammerschmidt, *Alleluja! Freuet Euch!*; G. R. Woodward, arr., *Up Good Christen Folk and Listen: Ding Dong Ding*; R. L. Pearsall, arr., *In Dulcio Jublio*; Felix Mendelssohn, *Hark! The Harold Angels Sing*; Samuel Scheidt, *Puer Natus*; David Wilcocks, arr., *Rocking*; John Gardner, *Tomorrow Shall Be My Dancing Day*; 15th-century English, *Illuminare Jerusalem*; Benjamin Britten, *A Shepherd's Carol*; 16th-Century Swedish, *Good King Wenceslas*.

D42. Meridian E77109 / 1985 / LP
      Choir of Clare College Chapel, Cambridge, conducted by Timothy
        Brown.
      Album title: *In Nativitate Domini*.
      Includes: Plainsong, *Puer Natus est Nobis*; William Byrd, *In Nativitate
        Domini*; Plainsong, *O Magnum Mysterium*; Thomas Luis de Victoria,
        O Magnum Mysterium; Plainsong, *Hodie Christus Natus Est*; Peter
        Maxwell Davies, *O Magnum Mysterium*: carol '*O Magnum Mysteri-
        um*'.

Four Instrumental Motets: Si Quis Diligit Me

D43. Unicorn-Kanchana KP 8005 / 1981 / LP
      Unicorn-Kanchana KP (CD) 8005 / 1991 / CD
      Unicorn-Kanchana UKCD 2044 / 1991 / CD
      Fires of London, conducted by the composer.
      Album title: *Renaissance and Baroque Realisations*
      Includes: *Fantasia and Two Pavans after Henry Purcell*; *Fantasia upon
        One Note*; *Prelude and Fugue in C♯ Minor by J. S. Bach*; *Prelude
        and Fugue in C♯ Major by J. S. Bach*; *Tenebrae Super Gesualdo*;
        Veni Sancte–Veni Creator Spiritus; *All Sons of Adam*; *Our Father
        Whiche in Heaven Art*; *Kinloche his Fantassie*.

Four Instrumental Motets: All Sons of Adam

D44. Unicorn-Kanchana KP 8005 / 1981 / LP
      Unicorn-Kanchana KP 8005 (CD) / 1991 / CD
      Unicorn-Kanchana UKCD 2044 / 1991 / CD
      Fires of London, conducted by the composer.
      Album title: *Renaissance and Baroque Realisations*
      Includes: *Fantasia and Two Pavans after Henry Purcell*; *Fantasia upon
        One Note*; *Prelude and Fugue in C♯ Minor by J. S. Bach*; *Prelude
        and Fugue in C♯ Major by J. S. Bach*; *Tenebrae Super Gesualdo*;
        Veni Sancte–Veni Creator Spiritus; *Si Quis Diligit Me*; *Our Father
        Whiche in Heaven Art*; *Kinloche his Fantassie*.

Four Instrumental Motets: Our Father Whiche in Heaven Art

D45. Unicorn-Kanchana KP 8005 / 1981 / LP

Unicorn-Kanchana KP (CD) 8005 / 1991 / CD
Unicorn-Kanchana UKCD 2044 / 1991 / CD
Fires of London, conducted by the composer.
Album title: *Renaissance and Baroque Realisations*
Includes: *Fantasia and Two Pavans after Henry Purcell*; *Fantasia upon One Note*; *Prelude and Fugue in C♯ Minor by J. S. Bach*; *Prelude and Fugue in C♯ Major by J. S. Bach*; *Tenebrae Super Gesualdo*; *Veni Sancte–Veni Creator Spiritus*; *Si Quis Diligit Me*; *All Sons of Adam*; *Kinloche his Fantassie*.

Four Instrumental Motets: Psalm 124

D46.   Editions de L'Oiseau-Lyre DSLO 12 / 1976 / LP
Fires of London conducted by the composer.
Includes: *Renaissance Scottish Dances; Hymn to St. Magnus*.

From Stone to Thorn

D47.   Editions L'Oiseau-Lyre DSLO 2 / 1972 / LP
Fires of London conducted by the composer.
Includes: *Antechrist*; *Hymnos*; *Missa Super L'Homme Armé*.

Hill Runes

D48.   Paula (Denmark): [number unknown]
Per Dybro Sorensen
[Other information unavailable]

D49.   RCA Red Seal ARL 1-5034 / 1982 / LP
RCA Red Seal RL 25419 / 1982 / LP
RCA Red Seal RK 25419 / 1982 / cassette
RCA Red Seal ARK 1-5034 / 1982 / cassette
Julian Bream, guitar.
Album title: *Dedication*.
Includes: Richard Rodney Bennett, *Five Impromptus*; William Walton, *Five Bagatelles*; Hans Werner Henze, *Royal Winter Music*.

Hymn to St. Magnus

D50.   Editions de L'Oiseau-Lyre DSLO 12 / 1976 / LP
       Mary Thomas, soprano; Fires of London conducted by the composer.
       Includes: *Renaissance Scottish Dances*; *Four Instrumental Motets: Psalm
           124*.

Hymn to the Word of God

D51.   Argo 436 119-2 / 1992 / CD
       Choir of King's College, Cambridge, conducted by Stephen Cleobury.
       Includes: *Five Carols*; *Solstice of Light*.

Hymnos

D52.   Editions de L'Oiseau-Lyre DSLO 2 / 1972 / LP
       Alan Hacker, clarinet; Stephen Pruslin, piano.
       Includes: *From Stone to Thorn; Missa Super L'Homme Armé; Antechrist*.

Image, Reflection, Shadow

D53.   Unicorn-Kanchana DKP 9033 / 1984 / LP
       Unicorn-Kanchana DKP (C) 9033 / 1984 / cassette
       Fires of London.
       Includes: *Bairns of Brugh*; *Runes from a Holy Island*.

D54.   Unicorn-Kanchana UKCD 2038 / 1990 / CD
       Fires of London.
       Includes: *Ave Maris Stella*; *Runes from a Holy Island*

Into the Labyrinth

D55.   Unicorn-Kanchana DKP 9038 / 1985 / LP
       Unicorn-Kanchana DKP (C) 9038 / 1985 / cassette
       Unicorn-Kanchana UKCD 2022 / 1989 / CD
       Neil Mackie, tenor; Scottish Chamber Orchestra conducted by the
           composer.
       Includes: *Sinfonietta Accademica*.

Jimmack the Postie

D56.   Unicorn-Kanchana DKP (CD) 9070 / 1988 / CD
Scottish Chamber Orchestra, conducted by the composer.
Album title: *A Celebration of Scotland*.
Includes: *An Orkney Wedding, with Sunrise; Kinloche, his Fantassie;
Seven Songs Home; Yesnaby Ground; Dances from 'The Two
Fiddlers'; Farewell to Stromness; Lullabye for Lucy; Renaissance
Scottish Dances*.

Kinloche, his Fantassie

D57.   Unicorn-Kanchana 8005 / 1981 / LP
Unicorn-Kanchana 8005 (CD) / 1991 / CD
Unicorn-Kanchana UKCD 2044 / 1991 / CD
Fires of London, conducted by the composer.
Album title: *Renaissance and Baroque Realisations*
Includes: *Fantasia and Two Pavans after Henry Purcell; Fantasia upon
One Note; Prelude and Fugue in C♯ Minor by J. S. Bach; Prelude
and Fugue in C♯ Major by J. S. Bach; Tenebrae Super Gesualdo;
Veni Sancte–Veni Creator Spiritus; Si Quis Diligit Me; All Sons of
Adam; Our Father Whiche in Heaven Art*.

D58.   Unicorn-Kanchana DKP (CD) 9070 / 1988 / CD
Scottish Chamber Orchestra, conducted by the composer.
Album title: *A Celebration of Scotland*.
Includes: *An Orkney Wedding, with Sunrise; Kinloche, his Fantassie;
Seven Songs Home; Yesnaby Ground; Dances from 'The Two
Fiddlers'; Jimmack the Postie; Farewell to Stromness; Lullabye for
Lucy; Renaissance Scottish Dances*.

Leopardi Fragments

D59.   Argo ZRG 758 / 1974 / LP
Odeon ASD 640 / 1965 / LP
Angel 36387 / 1967 / LP
Mary Thomas, soprano; Rosemary Philips, contralto; John Alldis Choir;
Melos Ensemble conducted by John Carewe.
Album title: *Four British Composers*.

Includes: Alexander Goehr, *Two Choruses, op. 14*; Malcolm Williamson, *Symphony for Voice*; Richard Rodney Bennett, *Calendar*.

The Lighthouse

D60. Collins Classics 14152 / 1994 / CD
    Neil Mackie, Christopher Keyte, Ian Comboy, the BBC Philharmonic conducted by the composer.
    Album title: *The Lighthouse*

The Lighthouse (excerpts)

D61. Collins Classics 14442 / 1994 / CD (from Collins Classics CD 14152)
    Neil Mackie, Christopher Keyte, Ian Comboy and the BBC Philharmonic conducted by the composer.
    Album title: *Maximum Max*
    Includes: *[SEE D12 FOR COUPLINGS]*

Lullabye for Ilian Rainbow

D62. Editions de L'Oiseau-Lyre DSLO 3 / 1974 / LP
    Timothy Walker, guitar.
    Includes: Benjamin Britten, *Nocturnal after John Dowland*; Lennon & McCartney, *Yesterday*; Timothy Walker, *Lorelei: Etude*; De Bedford, *You Asked for It*; G. Swayne, *Canto I—Mr Timothy's Troubles*.

Lullabye for Lucy

D63. Unicorn-Kanchana DKP (CD) 9070 / 1988 / CD
    Choir of St. Mary's Music School, Edinburgh, conducted by the composer.
    Album title: *A Celebration of Scotland.*
    Includes: *An Orkney Wedding, with Sunrise; Kinloche, his Fantassie; Seven Songs Home; Yesnaby Ground; Dances from 'The Two Fiddlers'; Jimmack the Postie; Farewell to Stromness; Renaissance Scottish Dances.*

D64. Collins Classics 30032 / 1992 / CD
    The Sixteen conducted by Harry Christophers.
    Album title: *MAX: The Music of Peter Maxwell Davies.*

Includes: *[SEE D14 FOR COUPLINGS]*

D65. Collins Classics 14442 / 1994 / CD
      The Sixteen conducted by Harry Christophers.
      Album title: *Maximum Max*
      Includes: *[SEE D12 FOR COUPLINGS]*

March: The Pole Star

D66. Merlin Records MRF 86041 / 1982 / LP
      Fine Arts Brass Ensemble
      Includes: Witold Lutoslawski, *Mini Overture*; John Casken, *Clarion Sea*;
      Charles Camilleri, *Brass Quintet*; Jonty Harrison, *Sons Transmuta-
      tions/Sans Transmutant*; John Joubert, *Chamber Music for Brass
      Quintet*.

The Martyrdom of St. Magnus

D67. Unicorn-Kanchana DKP (CD) 9100 / 1990 / CD
      Music Theatre Wales; Scottish Chamber Opera Ensemble, conducted by
      Michael Rafferty.

Miss Donnithorne's Maggot

D68. Unicorn-Kanchana DKP (CD) 9052 / 1987 / CD
      Mary Thomas, mezzo-soprano; Fires of London conducted by the
      composer.
      Includes: *Eight Songs for a Mad King*.

D69. Musical Heritage Society MHS 912215 / 1988 / LP
      Musical Heritage Society MHC 312215 / 1988 / Cassette
      Marni Nixon, soprano; New Music Settings Ensemble conducted by
      Rhonda Hess.
      Includes: *Eight Songs for a Mad King*.

Missa Super L'Homme Armé

D70. Editions L'Oiseau-Lyre DSLO 2 / 1972 / LP

Vanessa Redgrave, speaker; Fires of London conducted by the composer.
Includes: *From Stone to Thorn*; *Hymnos*; *Antechrist*.

O Magnum Mysterium

D71.   Argo RG 327 / 1963 / LP
Argo ZRG 5327 / 1964 / LP
Choir and Orchestra of the Cirencester Grammar School, Simon Preston, organ, conducted by the composer.
Album title: *O Magnum Mysterium*
Includes: *Fantasia for organ on 'O Magnum Mysterium'*.

O Magnum Mysterium: Carol *'The Fader of Heven'*

D72.   Collins Classics 30032 / 1992 / CD
Patricia Forbes, soprano, and Caroline Trevor, alto.
Album title: *MAX: The Music of Peter Maxwell Davies*.
Includes: *[SEE D14 FOR COUPLINGS]*

D73.   Collins Classics 14442 / 1994 / CD (from Collins Classics CD 12702)
Patricia Forbes, soprano, and Caroline Trevor, alto.
Album title: *Maximum Max*
Includes: *[SEE D12 FOR COUPLINGS]*

O Magnum Mysterium: Carol *'O Magnum Mysterium'*

D74.   Meridian E77109 / 1985 / LP
Choir of Clare College Chapel, Cambridge, conducted by Timothy Brown.
Album title: *In Nativitate Domini*
Includes: Plainsong, *Puer Natus est Nobis*; William Byrd, *In Nativitate Domini*; Plainsong, *O Magnum Mysterium*; Thomas Luis de Vitoria, *O Magnum Mysterium*; Plainsong, *Hodie Christus Natus Est*; Peter Maxwell Davies, *O Magnum Mysterium*: Carol *'Nowell'*.

D75.   Chesky Records CD83 Digital DDD / 1992 / CD
Westminster Choir, conducted by Joseph Flummerfelt; Nancianne Perrella, organ.
Album title: *O Magnum Mysterium*.

Includes: Edgar L. Bainton, *And I Saw a New Heaven*; Benjamin Britten, *Festival Te Deum*; Tomas Luis de Victoria, *O Magnum Mysterium*; Francis Poulenc, *O Magnum Mysterium*; Olivier Messaien, *O Sacrum Convivium*; W. A. Mozart, *Ave Verum Corpus*; Maurice Duruflé, *Kyrie* (from *Requiem*); William Byrd, *Ave Verum Corpus*; Lukas Foss, *Behold! I Build an House*; Giuseppe Verdi, *Ave Maria*; Anton Bruckner, *Ave Maria*; Igor Stravinsky, *Ave Maria*; Johannes Brahms, *Lass dich nur nichts nicht dauren*; C. Hubert H. Perry, *I Was Glad When They Said unto Me*; Peter C. Lutkin, *The Lord Bless You and Keep You*.

D76.   Collins Classics 30032 / 1992 / CD
The Sixteen conducted by Harry Christophers.
Album title: *MAX: The Music of Peter Maxwell Davies*.
Includes: *[SEE D14 FOR COUPLINGS]*

D77.   Collins Classics 14442 / 1994 / CD (from Collins Classics CD 12702)
The Sixteen conducted by Harry Christophers.
Album title: *Maximum Max*
Includes: *[SEE D12 FOR COUPLINGS]*

O Magnum Mysterium: Fantasia for Organ.

D78.   Argo RG 327 / 1963 / LP
Argo ZRG 5327 / 1964 / LP
Choir and Orchestra of the Cirencester Grammar School, Simon Preston, organ, conducted by the composer.
Album title: *O Magnum Mysterium*.
Includes: *O Magnum Mysterium*.

Ojai Festival Overture

D79.   Collins Classics 13082 / 1991 / CD
BBC Philharmonic conducted by the composer.
Includes: *Caroline Mathilde: Concert Suite I*; *Threnody on a Plainsong for Michael Vyner*; *St. Thomas Wake*.

D80.   Collins Classics 30032 / 1992 / CD
BBC Philharmonic conducted by the composer.
Album title: *MAX: The Music of Peter Maxwell Davies*.
Includes: *[SEE D14 FOR COUPLINGS]*

D81.   Collins Classics 14442 / 1994 / CD (from Collins Classics CD 13082).
       BBC Philharmonic conducted by the composer.
       Album title: *Maximum Max*
       Includes: *[SEE D12 FOR COUPLINGS]*

An Orkney Wedding, With Sunrise

D82.   Unicorn-Kanchana DKP (CD) 9070 / 1988 / CD
       Scottish Chamber Orchestra, conducted by the composer; George
         MacIlwham, highland bagpipes.
       Album title: *A Celebration of Scotland.*
       Includes: *Kinloche, his Fantassie*; *Seven Songs Home*; *Yesnaby Ground*;
         Dances from 'The Two Fiddlers'; *Jimmack the Postie; Farewell to
         Stromness*; *Lullabye for Lucy*; *Renaissance Scottish Dances.*

D83.   Philips 420 946-2 / 1989 / CD
       Boston Pops Orchestra conducted by John Williams; Nanny Tunnicliffe,
         highland bagpipes.
       Album title: *Pops Britannia.*
       Includes: William Walton, *Orb and Sceptre*; Frederick Delius, *Brigg
         Fair*; Percy Grainger, *Irish Tune From County Derry, Danny Boy*;
         Ralph Vaughan Williams, *Fantasia on Greensleeves*; John Williams,
         Jane Eyre, P. Hollenbeck, (arr.), *Scotland the Brave.*

D84.   Collins Classics 30032 / 1992 / CD
       BBC Philharmonic conducted by the composer; George MacIlwham,
         highland bagpipes
       Album title: *MAX: The Music of Peter Maxwell Davies.*
       Includes: *[SEE D14 FOR COUPLINGS]*

D85.   Collins Classics 14442 / 1994 / CD
       Royal Philharmonic Orchestra conducted by the composer; George
         MacIlwham, highland bagpipes.
       Album title: *Maximum Max*
       Includes: *[SEE D12 FOR COUPLINGS]*

Prelude and Fugue in C♯ Major by J. S. Bach

D86.   Unicorn-Kanchana 8005 / 1981 / LP
       Unicorn-Kanchana (CD) 8005 / 1991 / CD

Unicorn-Kanchana UKCD 2044 / 1991 / CD
Fires of London, conducted by the composer.
Album title: *Renaissance and Baroque Relisations*
Includes: *Fantasia and Two Pavans after Henry Purcell*; *Fantasia upon One Note*; *Prelude and Fugue in C♯ Minor by J. S. Bach*; *Tenebrae Super Gesualdo*; *Veni Sancte–Veni Creator Spiritus*; *Si Quis Diligit Me*; *All Sons of Adam*; *Our Father Whiche in Heaven Art*; *Kinloche his Fantassie*.

Prelude and Fugue in C♯ Minor by J. S. Bach

D87. Unicorn-Kanchana KP 8005 / 1981 / LP
Unicorn-Kanchana KO (CD) 8005 / 1991 / CD
Unicorn-Kanchana UKCD 2044 / 1991 / CD
Fires of London, conducted by the composer.
Album title: *Renaissance and Baroque Realisations*
Includes: *Fantasia and Two Pavans after Henry Purcell*; *Fantasia upon One Note*; *Prelude and Fugue in C♯ Major by J. S. Bach*; *Tenebrae Super Gesualdo*; *Veni Sancte–Veni Creator Spiritus*; *Si Quis Diligit Me*; *All Sons of Adam*; *Our Father Whiche in Heaven Art*; *Kinloche his Fantassie*.

Renaissance Scottish Dances

D88. Editions de L'Oiseau-Lyre DSLO 12 / 1976 / LP
Fires of London conducted by the composer.
Includes: *Hymn to St. Magnus*; *Four Instrumental Motets: Psalm 124*.

D89. Unicorn-Kanchana DKP (CD) 9070 / 1988 / CD
Scottish Chamber Orchestra, conducted by the composer.
Album title: *A Celebration of Scotland*.
Includes: *An Orkney Wedding, with Sunrise*; *Kinloche, his Fantassie*; *Seven Songs Home*; *Yesnaby Ground*; *Dances from 'The Two Fiddlers'*; *Jimmack the Postie*; *Farewell to Stromness*; *Lullabye for Lucy*.

Resurrection

D90. Collins Classics 70342 / 1995 / 2 CDs

Della Jones, mezzo-soprano; Christopher Robson, countertenor; Neil Jenkins, Martyn Hill, tenors; Henry Herford, Gerald Finley, baritones; Jonathan Best, bass; Blaze Rock Group with Mary Carewe on vocals; BBC Philharmonic, conducted by the composer.

Revelation and Fall

D91.   Angel S36558 / 1969 / LP
       EMI/HMV ASD 2427 / 1969 /
       Mary Thomas, soprano; Pierrot Players conducted by the composer.
       Includes: Roberto Gerhard, *Collages*.

Runes From a Holy Island

D92.   Unicorn-Kanchana DKP 9033 / 1984 / LP
       Unicorn-Kanchana DKP (C) 9033 / 1984 / cassette
       Fires of London conducted by the composer.
       Includes: Davies, *Image, Reflection, Shadow*; *Bairns of Brugh*.

D93.   Unicorn-Kanchana UKCD 2038 / 1990 / CD
       Fires of London conducted by the composer.
       Includes: Davies, *Ave Maris Stella*; *Image, Reflection, Shadow*.

D94.   Unicorn-Kanchana UKCD 2068 / 1994 / CD
       Fires of London conducted by the composer
       Album title: *Vesalii Icones*
       Includes: *Vesalii Icones; The Bairns of Brugh*.

St. Michael Sonata

D95.   Louisville Orchestra LS 756 / 1975 / LP
       Louisville Orchestra LS 756 / 1977 / LP
       Louisville Orchestra LS 756 / 1987 / LP
       Members of the Louisville Orchestra conducted by Jorge Mester.
       Includes: Ernst Krenek, *Kleine Blasmusik*; *Three Merry Marches*.

St. Thomas Wake: Foxtrot for Orchestra

D96.   Louisville Orchestra LSO 770 / 1980 / LP
       Louisville Orchestra conducted by Richard Dufallo.

Includes: George Antheil, *Symphony No. 5*.

D97. Collins Classics 13082 / 1991 / CD
BBC Philharmonic, conducted by the composer.
Includes: *Ojai Festival Overture*; *Caroline Mathilde: Concert Suite from Act I of the Ballet*; *Threnody on a Plainsong for Michael Vyner*.

St. Thomas Wake: Excerpt

D98. Collins Classics 30032 / 1992 / CD
BBC Philharmonic conducted by the composer.
Album title: *MAX: The Music of Peter Maxwell Davies*.
Includes: *[SEE D14 FOR COUPLINGS]*

Salome

D99. EMI His Master's Voice 157-39270-2 / 1978 / LP
Danmarks Radios Underholdningsorkester conducted by Janos Fürst.

Sea Eagle.

D100. EMI Classics CDC 7 54420 2 / 1992 / CD
Michael Thompson, horn.
Album title: *Virtuosi*
Includes: Paul Dukas: *Villanelle*; Franz Strauss: *Nocturne, op. 7*; Camille Saint-Saens: *Morceau de Concert, op. 94*: Robert Schumann: *Adagio & Allegro in A-Flat, op. 70*; Richard Strauss: *Andante*; Francis Poulenc: *Elgie*; Thomas Dunhill: *Cornucopia*; Alan Abbott: *Alla Caccia*.

Second Fantasia on John Taverner's 'In Nomine'

D101. Argo ZRG 712 / 1973 / LP
New Philharmonia Orchestra conducted by Sir Charles Grove.
Includes: Davies. *'Taverner': Points and Dances from the Opera*.

The Seven Brightnesses

D102. NATO (France) 214
Alan Hacker, clarinet. [other information unavailable]

Seven In Nomine

D103. Collins Classics 10952 / 1990 / CD
Aquarius conducted by Nicholas Cleobury.
Includes: Davies, *Suite from 'The Boyfriend'*; *Suite from 'The Devils'*;

Seven In Nomine: 'Gloria Tibi Trinitas,' 'In Nomine'

D104. Collins Classics 30032 / 1992 / CD
Aquarius, conducted by Nicholas Cleobury.
Album title: *MAX: The Music of Peter Maxwell Davies.*
Includes: *[SEE D14 FOR COUPLINGS]*

Seven Songs Home

D105. Unicorn-Kanchana DKP (CD) 9070 / 1988 / CD
Choir of St. Mary's Music School, Edinburgh, conducted by the
composer.
Album title: *A Celebration of Scotland.*
Includes: *An Orkney Wedding, with Sunrise; Kinloche, his Fantassie;*
Yesnaby Ground; Dances from 'The Two Fiddlers'; Jimmack the
Postie; Farewell to Stromness; Lullabye for Lucy; Renaissance
Scottish Dances.

Sinfonia

D106. Unicorn-Kanchana DKP 9058 / 1986 / LP
Unicorn-Kanchana DKP (C) 9058 / 1986 / Cassette
Unicorn-Kanchana UKCD 2026 / 1989 / CD
Scottish Chamber Orchestra conducted by the composer.
Includes: *Sinfonia Concertante.*

Sinfonia Concertante

D107. Unicorn-Kanchana DKP 9058 / 1986 / LP
Unicorn-Kanchana DKP (C) 9058 / 1986 / Cassette
Unicorn-Kanchana UKCD 2026 / 1989 / CD
Scottish Chamber Orchestra conducted by the composer.
Includes: *Sinfonia.*

Sinfonietta Acccademica

D108. Unicorn-Kanchana DKP 9038 / 1985 / LP
Unicorn-Kanchana DKP (C) 9038 / 1985 / Cassette
Unicorn-Kanchana UKCD 2022 / 1989 / CD
Scottish Chamber Orchestra conducted by the composer.
Includes: *Into the Labyrinth*.

Sir Charles his Pavan

D109. Collins Classics 13902 / 1993 / CD
BBC Philharmonic Orchestra conducted by the composer.
Includes: *Worldes Blis*; *The Turn of the Tide*.

D110. Collins Classics 14442 / 1994 / CD
BBC Philharmonic conducted by the composer.
Album title: *Maximum Max*
Includes: *[SEE D12 FOR COUPLINGS]*

Solstice of Light

D111. Argo 436 119-2 / 1992 / CD
Neil Mackie, tenor; Christopher Hughes, organ; Choir of King's
College, Cambridge conducted by Stephen Cleobury.
Album title: *Solstice of Light*
Includes: *Five Carols*; *Hymn to the Word of God*.

Sonata for Guitar

D112. New Albion Records NA 032 CD AD / 1990 / CD
David Tanenbaum, guitar.
Album title: *Acoustic Counterpoint*.
Includes: Sir Michael Tippett, *The Blue Guitar*; Steve Reich, *Electric
Counterpoint*; Roberto Sierra, *Triptico*; Toru Takemitsu, *All in
Twilight*.

Sonata for Piano (J173)

D113. Auracle AUC 1005 / 1983 / LP

Stephen Pruslin, piano.
Includes: Alexander Goehr, *Capriccio*; *Nonomica*.

D114. Centaur Records CRC 2102 / 1993 / CD
David Holzman, piano.
Includes: Stefan Wolpe, *Music for a Dancer*; Raoul Pleskow, *Sonata No. 1*; *Farewell to Stromness*; *Yesnaby Ground*.

Sonata for Trumpet and Piano

D115. Nonesuch H71275 / 1972 / LP
Gerard Schwarz, trumpet; Ursula Oppene, piano.
Album title: *The New Trumpet*
Includes: L. Dlugoszerski,   *Space is a Diamond*; W. Jellerman, *Passages 13*; *The Fire*.

D116. BIS records (Sweden) LP-287 / 1985 / LP
BIS CD-287 / 1985 / CD
Håkan Hardenberger, trumpet; Roland Portinen, piano.
Album title: *The Virtuoso Trumpet*
Includes: Jean Baptiste Arban:, *Variations on a theme from 'Norma'*; Jean Francaix, *Sonatine for Trumpet and Piano*; Antonie Tisne, *Heraldiques for Trumpet and Piano*; Aurthur Honegger, *Intrada for Trumpet and Piano*; Folke Rabe, *Shazam*; John Hartmean, *Fantasia Brilliante on the Air 'Rule Britannia'*.

D117. Crystal Records S 665 / 1986 / LP
Thomas Stevens, trumpet; Zeta Carno, piano.
Includes: Georges Antheil, *Sonata for Trumpet and Piano*; Thomas Stevens, *A New Carnival of Venice*; Leonard Bernstein, *Rondo for Lifey*; Thomas Stevens, *Variations of Clifford Intervals*.

D118. Crystal Records CD 665 / 1988 / CD
Thomas Stevens, trumpet.
Includes: Georges Antheil, *Sonata for Trumpet and Piano*; Thoms Stevens, *Triangles*; Hans Werner Henze, *Sonatina for Trumpet*; Meyer Kupferman, *Ideas*; Charles Dodge, *Extensions*; Thomas Stevens, *Variations on Clifford Intervals*; *New Carnival of Venice*; Leonard Bernstein, *Rondo for Lifey*; Henri Tomasi, *Triptyque*; Jacques Ibert, *Impromptu*.

D119. International Trumpet Guild ITG 001 / 1991 / CD
Terry Everson, trumpet; Susan Nowicku, piano.
Album title: *International Trumpet Guild Presents Terry Everson.*
Includes: Robert Suderburg, *Chamber Music No. 7: Ceremonies for Trumpet and Piano*; Robert Henderson, *Variation Movements*; Jacques Casterede, *Brèves Rencontres*; Fisher Tull, *Sonata for Trumpet and Piano*; Aaron Copland, *At the River* (arr.).

D120. Virgin Classics VC 5 451003 2 / 1993 / CD
Graham Ashton, trumpet, and John Lenehan, piano.
Album title: *The Contemporary Trumpet*
Includes: André Jolivet, *Heptade*; Michael Nyman, *Flugel and Piano*; Hans Werner Henze, *Sonatina for Solo Trumpet*; Luciano Berio, *Sequenza X*; George Fenton, *Five Parts of the Dance.*

A Spell for Green Corn: The MacDonald Dances

D121. Collins Classics 13962 / 1994 / CD
James Clark, violin and the Scottish Chamber Orchestra conducted by the composer.
Album title: *Strathclyde Concertos*
Includes: Peter Maxwell Davies: *Strathclyde Concerto No. 7 for Double Bass and Orchestra*; *Strathclyde Concerto No. 8 for Bassoon and Orchestra.*

Stone Litany

D122. Collins Classics 13662 / 1993 / CD
Della Jones, David Wilson-Johnson and The BBC Philharmonic conducted by the composer.
Album title: *Black Pentecost/Stone Litany*
Includes: *Black Pentecost*

Strathclyde Concerto No. 1 for Oboe and Orchestra

D123. Unicorn-Kanchana DKP (CD) 9085 / 1989 / CD
Robin Miller, Oboe; Scottish Chamber Orchestra conducted by the composer.
Includes: *Strathclyde Concerto No. 2 for Cello and Orchestra.*

Strathclyde Concerto No. 2 for Cello and Orchestra

D124. Unicorn-Kanchana DKP (CD) 9085 / 1989 / CD
William Conway, cello; Scottish Chamber Orchestra conducted by the composer.
Includes: *Strathclyde Concerto No. 1 for Oboe and Orchestra.*

Strathclyde Concerto No. 3 for Horn, Trumpet and Orchestra

D125. Collins Classics 12392 / 1992 / CD
Robert Cook, horn; Peter Franks, trumpet; Scottish Chamber Orchestra conducted by the composer.
Includes: *Strathclyde Concerto No. 4 for Clarinet and Orchestra.*

Strathclyde Concerto No. 4 for Clarinet and Orchestra

D126. Collins Classics 12392 / 1992 / CD
Lewis Morrison, clarinet; Scottish Chamber Orchestra conducted by the composer.
Includes: *Strathclyde Concerto No. 3 for Horn, Trumpet and Orchestra.*

Strathclyde Concerto No. 4 for Clarinet and Orchestra (excerpt)

D127. Collins Classics 14442 / 1994 / CD (from Collins Classics CD 13292)
Lewis Morrison, clarinet and the Scottish Chamber Orchestra conducted by the composer.
Album title: *Maximum Max*
Includes: *[SEE D12 FOR COUPLINGS]*

Strathclyde Concerto No. 5 for Violin, Viola and String Orchestra.

D128. Collins Classics 13032 / 1994 / CD
James Clark, violin, Catherine Marwood, viola and the Scottish Chamber Orchestra conducted by the composer.
Includes: *Strathclyde Concerto No. 6 For Flute and Orchestra.*

Strathclyde Concerto No. 6 for Flute and Orchestra

D129. Collins Classics 13032 / 1994 / CD
David Nicholson, flute, and the Scottish Chamber Orchestra conducted
by the composer.
Includes: *Strathclyde Concerto No. 5 for Violin, Viola, and String
Orchestra.*

Strathclyde Concerto No. 7 for Double Bass and Orchestra

D130. Collins Classics 13962 / 1994 / CD
Duncan McTier, Double Bass, and the Scottish Chamber Orchestra
conducted by the composer.
Includes: *Strathclyde Concerto No. 8 for Bassoon and Orchestra*; *A Spell
for Green Corn: The MacDonald Dances.*

Strathclyde Concerto No. 8 for Bassoon and Orchestra.

D131. Collins Classics 13962 / 1994 / CD
Ursula Leveaux, Bassoon, and the Scottish Chamber Orchestra conduct-
ed by the composer.
Includes: *Strathclyde Concerto No. 7 for Double Bass and Orchestra*; *A
Spell for Green Corn: The MacDonald Dances.*

Sunday Morning

D132. Collins Classics 14442 / 1994 / CD
BBC Philharmonic conducted by the composer.
Album title: *Maximum Max*
Includes: *[SEE D12 FOR COUPLINGS]*

Symphony No. 1

D133. Decca Head 21 / 1979 / LP
Philharmonia Orchestra conducted by Simon Rattle.

D134. Collins Classics 14352 / 1995 / CD
BBC Philharmonic conducted by the composer.

Symphony No. 2

D135. Collins Classics 14032 / 1994 / CD
BBC Philharmonic conducted by the composer.

Symphony No. 3

D136. BBC REGL 560 / 1985 / LP
BBC Records CD 560 / 1985 / CD
BBC Philharmonic conducted by Edward Downes.

D137. Collins Classics 14162 / 1994 / CD
BBC Philharmonic conducted by the composer.

Symphony No. 4

D138. Collins Classics 11812 / 1991 / CD
Scottish Chamber Orchestra conducted by the composer.
Includes: *Concerto for Trumpet and Orchestra*.

Symphony No. 5

D139. Collins Classics 14602 / 1995 / CD
BBC Philharmonic conducted by the composer.
Includes: *Chat Moss*, *Cross Lane Fair*, *Five Klee Pictures*.

Taverner: Points and Dances from the Opera.

D140. ARGO ZRG 712 / 1973 / LP
Fires of London conducted by the composer.
Includes: *Second Fantasia on John Taverner's 'In Nomine'*

Tenebrae Super Gesualdo

D141. Unicorn-Kanchana PR 8002 / 1981 / LP

Fires of London and Peter Maxwell Davies.
Includes: *Ave Maris Stella*.

D142. Unicorn-Kanchana KP 8005 / 1981 / LP
Unicorn-Kanchana KO (CD) 8005 / 1991 / CD
Unicorn-Kanchana UKCD 2044 / 1991 / CD
Fires of London, conducted by the composer.
Album title: *Renaissance and Baroque Realisations*
Includes: *Fantasia and Two Pavans after Henry Purcell*; *Fantasia upon One Note*; *Prelude and Fugue in C♯ Minor by J. S. Bach*; *Prelude and Fugue in C♯ Major by J. S. Bach*; *Veni Sancte–Veni Creator Spiritus*; *Si Quis Diligit Me*; *All Sons of Adam*; *Our Father Whiche in Heaven Art*; *Kinloche his Fantassie*.

Three Organ Voluntaries: Psalm 124, O God Abufe

D143. ECM New Series ECM 1431 / 1992 / CD
ECM (Germany) CD 849655-2 / CD
Christopher Bowers-Broadbent, organ.
Album title: *Trivium*
Includes: Arvo Part, *Trivium*; *Mein Weg Hat Gipfel und Willentaler*; *Annum per Annum*; *Pari Intervallo*; Philip Glass, *Satyagraha (Act. III, conclusion)*; *Dance No. 4*.

Threnody on a Plainsong for Michael Vyner

D144. Collins Classics 13082 / 1991 / CD
BBC Philharmonic conducted by the composer.
Includes: *Ojai Festival Overture*; *Caroline Mathilde: Concert Suite from Act I of the Ballet*; *St. Thomas Wake*.

D145. Collins Classics 30032 / 1992 / CD
BBC Philharmonic conducted by the composer.
Album title: *MAX: The Music of Peter Maxwell Davies*.
Includes: *[SEE D14 FOR COUPLINGS]*

The Turn of the Tide

D146. Collins Classics 13902 / 1993 / CD

Royal Philharmonic Orchestra, Manchester Cathedral Choir, conducted by the composer.
Includes: *Worldes Blis*; *Sir Charles his Pavan*.

Turris Campanarum Sonantium

D147. London 430 0052 / 1990 / CD
Recorded 1971.
Stomu Yamash'ta, percussion.
Includes: Hans Werner Henze, *Prison Song*; Toru Takemitsu, *Seasons*.

The Two Fiddlers: Dances from 'The Two Fiddlers' (J154)

D148. Unicorn-Kanchana DKP (CD) 9070 / 1988 / CD
Scottish Chamber Orchestra, conducted by the composer.
Album title: *A Celebration of Scotland*.
Includes: *An Orkney Wedding, with Sunrise; Kinloche, his Fantassie; Seven Songs Home; Yesnaby Ground; Jimmack the Postie; Farewell to Stromness; Lullabye for Lucy; Renaissance Scottish Dances*.

Veni Sancte-Veni Creator Spiritus

D149. Unicorn-Kanchana KP 8005 / 1981 / LP
Unicorn-Kanchana KP (CD) 8005 / CD / 1991
Unicorn-Kanchana UKCD 2044 / 1991 / CD
Fires of London, conducted by the composer.
Album title: *Renaissance and Baroque Realisations*
Includes: *Fantasia and Two Pavans after Henry Purcell; Fantasia upon One Note; Prelude and Fugue in C♯ Minor by J. S. Bach; Prelude and Fugue in C♯ Major by J. S. Bach; Tenebrae Super Gesualdo; Si Quis Diligit Me; All Sons of Adam; Our Father Whiche in Heaven Art; Kinloche his Fantassie*.

Vesalii Icones

D150. Unicorn RHS 307 / 1970 /LP
Nonesuch H 71295 / 1974 / LP
Unicorn-Kanchana KPM 7016 / 1984 / LP
Fires of London conducted by the composer.

D151. Unicorn-Kanchana UKCD 2068 / 1994 / CD
Fires of London conducted by the composer
Album title: *Vesalii Icones*
Includes: *The Bairns of Brugh; Runes from a Holy Island*

Worldes Blis

D152. Collins Classics 13902 / 1993 / CD
Royal Philharmonic Orchestra conducted by the composer.
Includes: *The Turn of the Tide*; *Sir Charles his Pavan*.

Yellow Cake Revue

Yellow Cake Revue: Farewell to Stronmess

D153. Unicorn-Kanchana DKP (CD) 9070 / 1988 / CD
Peter Maxwell Davies, piano.
Album title: *A Celebration of Scotland*.
Includes: *An Orkney Wedding, with Sunrise; Kinloche, his Fantassie; Seven Songs Home; Yesnaby Ground; Dances from 'The Two Fiddlers'; Jimmack the Postie; Lullabye for Lucy; Renaissance Scottish Dances.*

D154. Collins Classics 30032 / 1992 / CD
Seta Tanyel, piano.
Album title: *MAX: The Music of Peter Maxwell Davies*.
Includes: Davies, *[SEE D14 FOR COUPLINGS]*

D155. Centaur Records CRC 2102 / 1993 / CD
David Holzman, piano.
Includes: Stefan Wolpe, *Music for a Dancer*; Raoul Pleskow, *Sonata No. 1*; Peter Maxwell Davies, *Yesnaby Ground*; *Sonata for Piano*.

D156. Collins Classics 14442 / 1994 / CD
Peter Maxwell Davies, piano.
Album title: *Maximum Max*
Includes: *[SEE D12 FOR COUPLINGS]*

Yellow Cake Revue: Farewell to Stromness (arr. for solo guitar by Timothy Walker.)

D157. Hyperion CDH 88027 / 1989 / CD
Timothy Walker, guitar.
Album title: *Classical Folk Guitar*
Includes: Narciso Yepes, arr., *Romance: Jeux Interdits*; Jose de Azpiazu, arr., *El Vito*; Manuel de Falla, arr. by Timothy Walker, *Farruca*; Timothy Walker, *Folkish Fancy*; Francis Bebey, *Legende*; Mwenda Jean Bosco, *Masanga*; Timothy Walker, *African Hymn and Dance*; Mauro Giuliani, *Three Irish Airs With Variations: The Last Rose of summer; Gary Owen; My Lodging in on the Cold Ground*; Francis Cutting, *Greensleeves*; Yukijiro Yoko, *Variations on an Old Japanese Folk Tune 'Sakura'*; Matteo Carcassi, arr. by Timothy Walker, *Variations on a Russian Folk Tune*; Hector Ayala, *South American Suite*.

Yellow Cake Revue: Yesnaby Ground

D158. Unicorn-Kanchana DKP (CD) 9070 / 1988 / CD
Peter Maxwell Davies, piano.
Album title: *A Celebration of Scotland*.
Includes: *An Orkney Wedding, with Sunrise; Kinloche, his Fantassie; Seven Songs Home; Dances from 'The Two Fiddlers'; Jimmack the Postie; Farewell to Stromness; Lullabye for Lucy; Renaissance Scottish Dances*.

D159. Collins Classics 30032 / 1992 / CD
Seta Tanyel, piano.
Album title: *MAX: The Music of Peter Maxwell Davies*.
Includes: *[SEE D14 FOR COUPLINGS]*

D160. Centaur Records CRC 2102 / 1993 / CD
David Holzman, piano.
Includes: Stefan Wolpe, *Music for a Dancer*; Raoul Pleskow, *Sonata No. 1*; *Farewell to Stromness*; *Yesnaby Ground*; *Sonata for Piano*.

D161. Collins Classics 14442 / 1994 / CD
Peter Maxwell Davies, piano.
Album title: *Maximum Max*
Includes: *[SEE D12 FOR COUPLINGS]*

Yesterday: Lennon & McCartney

D162. Editions de L'Oiseau-Lyre DSLO 3 / 1974 / LP
   Timothy Walker, guitar.
   Includes: Benjamin Britten, *Nocturnal after John Dowland*; Timothy
      Walker, *Lorelei*: *Etude*; Peter Maxwell Davies, *Lullabye for Ilian
      Rainbow*; De Bedford, *You Asked for It*; G. Swayne, *Canto I—Mr
      Timothy's Troubles*.

A Note on Materials in the British National Sound Archive

The National Sound Archive of the British Library holds a large number of
sound recordings of Peter Maxwell Davies's music, including tapes of
broadcasts and discs produced by the BBC Transcription Service as well as
recordings available commercially.   Recordings exist at this source of many
works, especially early ones, which have not yet been recorded commercially,
although it is necessary to visit the Archive itself in order to listen to them.
Their collection also includes many broadcasts of interviews and other programs
concerning the composer and his music.   At this writing, the Archive is in the
process of computerizing its catalogs to facilitate access.   For further information contact the Curator of Western Art Music at:
      The National Sound Archive, 29 Exhibition Road, London SW7 2AS

Bibliography

Articles and Reviews

B1.   "Anatomy of Outstanding Beauty." *Daily Express* (Nov. 20, 1975).
Review of a concert by the London Contemporary Dance Theater at
Sadler's Wells, Nov. 19, 1975, which included a performance of
Vesalii Icones with dancer William Louther and cellist Jennifer Ward
Clarke, with the Fires of London conducted by the composer: "a
theatrical experience of power and beauty."

B2.   "Concert Notes: Thursday Invitation Concerts." *Strad* v. 72 (Dec.
1961) p. 293.
Includes a review of the premiere of *String Quartet* by the Amici
String Quartet during a BBC Thursday Invitation Concert at the
Maida Vale Studio, Nov. 9, 1961. Comments: "It is not a long
piece, four sections in one movement, and the first excited impression is one of great enthusiasm."

B3.   "Creations." *Brass Bulletin* 64 News Supplement (1988) p. 2.
Announcement of the premiere of *Concerto for Trumpet and
Orchestra* on Sept. 9, 1988: John Wallace, trumpet, with the Royal
Philharmonic Orchestra conducted by Giuseppe Sinopoli in Hiroshi-
ma, Japan.

B4.   "*Eight Songs for a Mad King*." *New York Philharmonic Program Notes*
(Oct. 6, 1972).
Program notes for a concert by the New York Philharmonic
Orchestra conducted by Pierre Boulez at the Loeb Student Center,

New York University, Oct. 6, 1972. Included on the program was a performance of *Eight Songs for a Mad King* with soloist Julius Eastman. Gives information essential to understanding the work.

B5.   "The Fires of London." *Chronicle* (Chester) (Aug. 7, 1981).
Review of a concert by the Fires of London conducted by John Carewe at the Gateway Theatre, Chester, July 31, 1981. The program included *Eight Songs for a Mad King* featuring baritone Michael Rippon, and *Le Jongleur de Notre Dame* with Jonny James, juggler and baritone Michael Rippon.

B6.   "Here & There." *Musical America* 107 no. 2 (1987) p. 7
Brief notice of the composer receiving a knighthood in 1987 and his upcoming U.S. tour in November–December, 1988 with the Scottish Chamber Orchestra.

B7.   "Huddersfield Town Hall: BBC Symphony Orchestra." *Yorkshire Post* (Nov. 12, 1984).
Review of a concert by the BBC Symphony Orchestra conducted by Elgar Howarth, during the Huddersfield Festival at the Huddersfield Town Hall, Nov. 10, 1984. The program featured *St. Thomas Wake*, *Stone Litany*, and *Worldes Blis*.

B8.   "In the News." *Opera* 38 (Feb., 1987) p. 131.
Brief announcement of the composer receiving a knighthood in 1987.

B9.   "A Lyricist Takes Wing." *Times* (Sept. 17, 1989), "Features."
Includes a review of the premiere of *Symphony No. 4* by the Scottish Chamber Orchestra, conducted by the composer, at the Royal Albert Hall, Sept. 10, 1989. Notes that the Symphony was inspired partly by the composer's own fascination with the flight of birds, particularly one occasion in which he watched a golden eagle take flight, and comments: "A soaring, gliding quality is certainly a feature of the woodwind writing, particularly in the Adagio, which contains some of the most singing, lyrical music Maxwell Davies has ever penned, against a constantly shifting background of shimmering, glittering strings." He also notes the work's inspiration from the medieval plainchant *Adorna Thalamum Tuum, Sion*.

B10.   "Max Appeal." *Evening Standard* (Mar. 23, 1990).
Article focusing on the upcoming 'Maxfest' at the Southbank that was to begin on the following Tuesday, Mar. 27, 1990.

B11.   "Max's Maxims." *Times Educational Supplement* (July 8, 1994) p. 29.
Article on the birthday tribute to the composer by Orkney school
children in a concert during the St. Magnus Festival June 23, 1994
at the Phoenix Cinema, Kirkwall, including *Kirkwall Shopping Songs*
and *Songs of Hoy*. A lengthy section deals with the composer's ideas
about children and music and composing original music for children.
With a photograph.

B12.   "Names, Dates, Places." *Opera News* 47 (April 9, 1983) p. 4.
Includes a notice that the composer and the Fires of London would
give five concerts as part of "Britain Salutes New York" activities,
22–24 April, 1983, at Manhattan's Symphony Space, including *Le
Jongleur de Notre Dame*, *Eight Songs for a Mad King*, *Miss
Donnithorne's Maggot*, and *Vesalii Icones*.

B13.   "Nationwide Audience for Island Concert." *Press and Journal* (June 23,
1986).
Review of the premiere of *Concerto for Violin and Orchestra* by
violinist Isaac Stern with the Royal Philharmonic Orchestra conducted by André Previn. Notes the piece was "pronounced a success by
delighted Orcadians."

B14.   "New Operas and Premieres." *Central Opera Services Bulletin* 28 no.
1–2 (1987–1988) p. 18.
Announces the premiere of *Resurrection* in Darmstadt, 17 Sept.
1987.

B15.   "New Operas and Premieres: Foreign Premieres." *Central Opera
Services Bulletin* v. 20 no. 4 (1978) p. 5.
Brief notice of the premiere of *The Two Fiddlers* by pupils from the
Kirkwall Grammar School on June 16, 1978 at the 1978 St. Magnus
Festival.

B16.   "News Section: Composers." *Tempo* no. 128 (Mar. 1979) p. 44.
Notice of the premiere of *Salome: Concert Suite from the Ballet* by
the London Symphony Orchestra conducted by David Atherton at the
Royal Festival Hall, 16 Mar. 1979.

B17.   "News Section: Composers." *Tempo* no. 129 (June, 1979) p. 54.
Notes the premieres of *Solstice of Light*, 18 June 1979 at the St.
Magnus Festival, by the St. Magnus Singers; *Kirkwall Shopping
Songs*, 16 June 1979, at the St. Magnus Festival; and the U.S.

premiere of *The Two Fiddlers*, at the Manhattan School of Music, New York, 21 April 1979.

B18.   "News Section." *Tempo* no. 136 (Mar. 1981) p. 53.
Announcement of the premiere of *Symphony No. 2* by the Boston Symphony Orchestra conducted by Seiji Ozawa at Boston's Symphony Hall, Feb. 16, 1981.

B19.   "News Section." *Tempo* no. 137 (June 1981) p. 56.
Announces premieres of *Hill Runes* for solo guitar at Dartington Summer School by Julian Bream, July 25, 1981, and *Sonata for Piano* by pianist Stephen Pruslin at the Bath Festival, May 23, 1981.

B20.   "News Section." *Tempo* no. 138 (Sept. 1981) p. 69.
Announcement of the premiere of *Suite From 'The Boyfriend'* by the London Sinfonietta conducted by Simon Rattle at the Queen Elizabeth Hall, Aug. 20, 1981.

B21.   "News Section: Composers." *Tempo* no. 149 (June 1984) p. 54.
Announcements of the premieres of *The No. 11 Bus*, Mar. 20, 1984, at Queen Elizabeth Hall, Mar. 20, 1984; *Sonatine for Violin and Cimbalon* featuring violinist Rosemary Furniss and Gregory Knowles, cimbalon, at Wigmore Hall, June 3, 1984; and *Sonata for Guitar* during the St. Magnus Festival, June 17, 1984.

B22.   "News Section: Composers." *Tempo* no. 177 (June 1991) p. 71.
Very brief note of the premieres of *Ojai Festival Overture*, *Mishkenot*, and *Caroline Mathilde: Concert Suite I*.

B23.   "News Section: Composers." *Tempo* no. 178 (Sept., 1991) p. 68.
Announcement of the premiere of *Strathclyde Concerto No. 5 for Violin, Viola and String Orchestra* by James Clark, violin, and Catherine Marwood, viola, with the Scottish Chamber Orchestra conducted by the composer, Glasgow, Dec. 11, 1991.

B24.   "Opera." *Music and Artists* v. 5 n. 4 (Sept.–Oct. 1972) pp. 12–13.
Includes a review of the premiere of *Taverner*, at Covent Garden, July 12, 1972.

B25.   "Peter Maxwell Davies' *Carol*." *Musical Times* 102 (Dec., 1961) p. 777.

Includes a series of excerpts from 18 different reviews of *Ave Maria, Hail Blessed Flower*.

B26.   "Peter Maxwell Davies' *Taverner*: Ein Oper Für Today." *Opernwelt* (Sept. 1983).

Review of a performance of *Taverner* directed by Edward Downes at Covent Garden, July 11, 1983.

B27.   "The Power and Charm of Mozart." *Dundee Courier and Advertiser* (Oct. 27, 1984).

Review of a concert by the Scottish Chamber Orchestra conducted by the composer at the Younger Hall, St. Andrews, Oct. 26, 1984. Program included a performance of *Sinfonietta Accademica*, described as: "An evocative work full of contrasting tempos, rhythms, timbres and techniques."

B28.   "Promenade Concerts." *The Strad* v. 80 (Oct. 1969) p. 282.

Review of the premiere of *Worldes Blis* at a BBC Promenade Concert at the Royal Albert Hall, Aug. 28, 1969, by the BBC Symphony Orchestra conducted by the composer.

B29.   "Proms Profile." *Radio Times* (August 1985).

Brief article announcing the London premiere of *Symphony No. 3* by the BBC Philharmonic Orchestra conducted by Edward Downes in August, 1985. Includes a photograph of the composer.

B30.   "*Taverner* Scrapbook." *About the House* v. 4 no. 1 (1972) pp. 62–63.

Presents a series of photographs taken during rehearsals for the premiere of *Taverner*, July, 1972.

B31.   "*Taverner*—The World." *About the House* v. 4 no. 1 (1972) pp. 20–23.

Photographs of scenes from *Taverner* when it was premiered by the Royal Opera, Covent Garden, July 12, 1972. Also includes excerpts from seven reviews of the performance.

B32.   "Trial by Jury." *Making Music* no. 53 (Autumn, 1963) pp. 7–9.

Includes seven reviews of *O Magnum Mysterium*. One by Gordon Treacher remarks that the music "provides instrumentalists with limited technique an insight into the thoughts of a remarkable English composer."

B33.   *"The Two Fiddlers."* *About the House* v. 5 no. 8 (1979) pp. 52–53.
Series of photographs taken at the English premiere of *The Two Fiddlers* at the Jeannetta Cochrane Theatre, Covent Garden, Dec. 28, 1978, performed by children from the Pimlico School and various areas of London.

B34.   "A Work Dedicated to Isaac Stern." *Jewish Chronicle* (June 20, 1986) p. 16.
Brief article about the *Concerto for Violin and Orchestra* dedicated to Isaac Stern, noting that it was to receive its premiere at the St. Magnus Festival in Kirkwall by Stern with Royal Philharmonic on June 21, 1986.

B35.   "World Premiere." *Symphony Magazine* v. 32 no. 3 (1981) p. 153.
Announcement of the premiere of *Symphony No. 2* by the Boston Symphony Orchestra conducted by Seiji Ozawa at Symphony Hall, Boston, Feb. 26, 1981.

B36.   A. C. *"Jimmack* Brings a Touch of Musical Magic." *Press and Journal.* (June 31, 1987).
Review of a concert by the Scottish Chamber Orchestra conducted by the composer at the Music Hall, Aberdeen, Jan. 30, 1987. Included on the program was a performance of *Jimmack the Postie*. About the music the reviewer remarks, "the clarity of the scoring...was as impressive as the striking conclusion."

B37.   A. C. "Music With Isles of Flavour." *Aberdeen Journal* (April 12, 1986).
Review of a concert by the Scottish Chamber Orchestra conducted by the composer at Mitchell Hall, University of Aberdeen, April 11, 1986. Included on the program was a performance of *Into the Labyrinth* with tenor soloist Neil Mackie. The reviewer notes among other things that the music "expresses concern at the disrupting influences of modern technology...on the Orcadian lifestyle."

B38.   Aitken, Tom. "A Major Work of Chamber Music." *Brass Bulletin* no. 45 (1984) pp. 62–65.
Article about a recording session of the Albany Brass in London to record *Brass Quintet*. The music is described as "richly expressive in its virtuosity." Includes a descriptive analysis of the work as well

as a dialogue between the composer, who was present at the recording session, and the performers.

B39.   Albrecht, Kay, comp.   "High Notes." *Musical Opinion* 114 (Mar., 1991) pp. 79–80.
Includes a brief announcement by Chester Music that the composer had received the first award by the Association of British Orchestras.

B40.   Allenby, David.   "Concerts." *Musical Opinion* 111 (Sept., 1988) p. 317.
Review of a concert by the London Symphony Orchestra conducted by Kent Nagano at the Barbican, May 20, 1988.   Program included a performance of *Symphony No. 2*, about which the reviewer remarks: "The notespinning in the *Symphony* is awesome, and the work is demanding for both performers and audience."

B41.   Amadio, Nadine.   "Sydney." *Music and Musicians* v. 28 (June 1980) p. 66.
Brief review of the final concert of the Australian Music Festival at the Concert Hall, Sydney Opera House, spring, 1980.   Included were performances of *Eight Songs for a Mad King* and *Le Jongleur de Notre Dame*, both by the Fires of London.

B42.   Andrewes, John.   "Peter Maxwell Davies's *The Shepherd's Calendar*." *Tempo* 87 (1968-9) pp. 6–9.

B43.   "Aristides."   "Pied Piper Seizes a Platform." *Times Educational Supplement* (June 10, 1983).
Article on the composer's works for children, primarily the operas and music theater pieces.   Written on the occasion of his becoming President of the Schools Music Association.   Mention is made of *Two Fiddlers* and *Cinderella*, as well as the composer's views on the importance of quality music education in the schools.

B44.   Arnold, Stephen.   "The Music of *Taverner*." *Tempo* no. 101 (1972) pp. 20–39.
Very detailed article about *Taverner*.   Includes a very thorough background of the work and an extensive analysis of the music; many musical examples to illustrate the analysis.

B45.   Baggs, Robin. "Bristol." *Musical Times* 119 (April, 1978) p. 347.
Includes a review of a performance of *The Martyrdom of St. Magnus*
as part of the Arnolfini music program, at Bristol Cathedral, Jan. 31,
1978. Cast included Mary Thomas and Neil Mackie and the Fires
of London. No remarks about the work itself.

B46.   Baker, Richard. "The Magnus Opus." *Now!* (June 20, 1980), p. 81.
Advance article about the coming 1980 St. Magnus Festival,
especially the premiere planned for *Cinderella* (which took place the
following day, June 21). The article discusses rehearsals and closes
with mention of "a new opera for Covent Garden—*Resurrection*—in
the making."

B47.   Barker, Frank Granville. "London." *Opera News* 37 (Sept., 1972) pp.
32–36.
Includes a review of the premiere of *Taverner* at Covent Garden,
July 12, 1972. This reviewer found the work "dull as well as
pretentious," though admitting the score is "undoubtedly skillfully
wrought." Also says the work, rather than being an opera, is "an
oratorio in the tradition of Vaughan Williams' *Pilgrim's Progress*."

B48.   Barnes, Clive. "Bath Festival." *Music and Musicians* 10 (July, 1962)
pp. 28–29.

B49.   Barnes, Clive. "Bath Festival." *Music and Musicians* v. 10 (August
1962) pp. 28–29.
Includes a brief review of a performance of *O Magnum Mysterium*
performed by children form the Cirencester Grammar School at the
Guildhall, during the Bath Festival in mid–June, 1962. The reviewer
notes the piece is one of "overwhelming impact."

B50.   Barnes, Clive. "A Danish Salome That Is More Than Skin–Deep."
New York Post (Jan. 2, 1979) pp. 23ef.
Review of a performance of the premiere production of *Salome* by
the Flemming Flindt Circus Co. at the Cirkus Theater in Copenhagen, late Dec., 1978. The reviewer describes the composer's music
as "one of the most engrossing new ballet scores for years...it may
well be the final statement needed to win for Maxwell Davies the
more general audience he deserves and to confirm his place as
England's finest composer since Britten."

B51. Barry, Malcolm. "Modern Chamber." *Music and Musicians* v. 24 (May 1976) p. 52.

Includes a review of a concert by the Fires of London at the Elizabeth Hall, Jan. 9, 1976. On the program was a performance of *Ave, Maris Stella*, about which the reviewer remarks: "It is chamber music of both a relaxed and vigorous nature...there is great complexity of rhythm and coordination." Also on the were *Dark Angels* (Mary Thomas, soprano, and Tim Walker, guitar) and *Kinloche his Fantassie*.

B52. Barry, Malcolm. "Modern." *Music and Musicians* 28 (April, 1980) pp. 70–71.

Review of a concert by the Fires of London which included a performance of *Le Jongleur de Notre Dame*, Feb. 16, 1972 at the Elizabeth Hall. The reviewer notes there is some "meaty music in the work...and some mickey–mousing."

B53. Barry, Malcolm. "Records: Maxwell Davies' *Symphony*." *Music and Musicians* 28 (Mar., 1980) p. 30.

Review of a recording of *Symphony No. 1* by the Philharmonia Orchestra conducted by Simon Rattle (Head 21). When describing the music the reviewer notes: "There are a couple of moments of choice intonation...however, one is left wondering what all the fuss is about."

B54. Barstow, Chris. "Concert Notes: Orchestral." *Strad* v. 94 (Oct. 1983) p. 367.

Includes a review of a concert by the Academy of St. Martin-in-the-Fields, conducted by Neville Marriner, at the Royal Albert Hall, Aug. 12, 1983. Included on the program was the premiere of *Sinfonia Concertante*, concerning which the reviewer observes, "The Sinfonia is substantial...but elegantly so, without the sombre weightiness of Davies' large orchestral works."

B55. Bauer, Christian. "Zwischen Sexualstau und Tarot." *Oesterreichische Musikzeitschrift* v. 45 (Jan. 1990) pp. 33–34.

Review of *Miss Donnithorne's Maggot* by the Vienna Chamber Opera, conducted by Klaus Zauner, Oct. 11, 1989.

B56. Bawden, Rex. "Inspired by Fires." *Liverpool Daily Post* (Mar. 11, 1982) p. 9.
Review of a concert by the Fires of London conducted by John Carewe at Christ's and Notre Dame College, Woolton, Mar. 10, 1982. On the program were performances of *Vesalii Icones* (with cellist Alexander Baillie and dancer Tom Yang) and *Eight Songs for a Mad King* (with soloist Michael Rippon).

B57. Beaujean, Alfred. "Menschen in extremen Situationen: Blacher's *Die Flut* und *Der Leuchtturm* von P. M. Davies in Aachen." *Opernwelt* v. 28 no. 6 (1987) pp. 62–63.
Review of a performance of *The Lighthouse* by the Aachen Opera, April 2, 1987, conducted by Klaus Rohra.

B58. Berg, Karl Georg. "Karlsruhe: Einakter von Davies und Chaynes." *Opernwelt* v. 31 (June 1990) p. 29.
Review of a performance of *Miss Donnithorne's Maggot* with Clara O'Brien, conducted by Guido Johannes Rumstadt at the Badisches Staatstheater in Karlsruhe, April 14, 1990.

B59. Berkheimer, Martin. "New Group, Nixon Test, New Idea." *Los Angeles Times* (Feb. 27, 1982).
Includes a review of a performance of *Miss Donnithorne's Maggot* featuring soloist Marni Nixon and the New Music Settings Ensemble conducted by Rhonda Kess, at the Little Theatre of Mount St. Mary's College, Los Angeles, late February, 1982. The reviewer remarks: "The protagonist... cackles, gurgles, screeches...a cadenza non-stop...while the tiny ensemble provides witty, parodistic, splotch-and-ripple comments."

B60. Bevan, Clifford. "Thameside Opera at the Wilde Theatre." *Opera* v. 37 (Aug. 1986) pp. 981–982.
Review of a performance of *The Lighthouse* by members of the Thameside Opera conducted by George Badacsonyi at the Wilde Theatre, Brackness, June 20, 1986. Gives a very fine synopsis of the drama but does not address the music so much as the action.

B61. Biermann, David. "German and English Music Educationalists: A Survey of Their Philosophies." *Music Teacher* v. 61 (July 1982) pp. 12–13, 17ff.
Includes a discussion of the composer's contribution to British music education.

B62.   Blanks, Fred R.   "Australia." *Musical Times* 115 (May, 1974) pp.
       413–414.
       Article which includes a review of a concert by the Fires of London
       conducted by the composer, at the Adelaide Festival, Mar. 9, 1974.
       Featured the premiere of *Miss Donnithorne's Maggot* performed by
       Mary Thomas (described as "a vocal and histrionic tour de force").
       Also performed were *Hymn to St. Magnus* (a "rugged piece"),
       Antechrist, and *Missa Super l'Homme Armé*.

B63.   Blezzard, Judith and Orlidge, Robert. "Liverpool." *Musical Times* 124
       (Feb., 1983) p. 116.
       Includes a review of a performance of *Lullabye for Lucy* by the
       Choros Singers in Liverpool at the Philharmonic Hall. Concert was
       conducted by James Wishart, part of a series of concerts during the
       1982 Contemporary Composers Seminar which featured the music of
       Peter Maxwell Davies. Work described as "a tiny but endearing
       fragment."

B64.   Blyth, Alan. "Fantasia II." *Music and Musicians* 13 (July, 1965) pp.
       43–44.
       Review of a concert that included the premiere of the *Second
       Fantasia on John Taverner's 'In Nomine'* by the London Philharmon-
       ic Orchestra, conducted by John Pritchard, Royal Festival Hall, April
       30, 1965. Work described as "a major work of symphonic propor-
       tions."

B65.   Blyth, Alan. "London Sinfonietta." *Musical Times* v. 111 (Feb. 1970)
       p. 182.
       Review of a concert by the London Sinfonietta conducted by David
       Atherton at the Elizabeth Hall, Dec. 29, 1969. Included on the
       program was a performance of *Ricercar and Doubles on "To Many
       a Well'*: "a spare, rather characteristic work in a Webernian mould."

B66.   Blyth, Alan. "Philharmonia/Rattle." *Daily Telegraph* (Feb. 3, 1978).
       Review of the premiere of *Symphony No. 1* by the Philharmonia
       Orchestra conducted by Simon Rattle at the Royal Festival Hall, Feb.
       2, 1978. The reviewer describes the work as: "A bold, uncompro-
       mising and typically rich-hued piece," concluding the composer "has
       enriched the repertory with an uncompromising but very accessible
       work."

B67.   Blyth, Alan. "St. Pancras: Festival Premiere." *Music and Musicians* v. 13 (April, 1965) p. 34.
Review of a concert on Mar. 1, 1965, at the St. Pancras Arts Festival at Friends House. Performance was by the Ambrosian Singers and the English Chamber Orchestra conducted by Norman del Mar. The program included the premiere of *Five Motets*, described as being "remarkable for their antiphonal effects...and for the composer's choral writing."

B68.   Boas, Robert. "Harrogate." *Music and Musicians* v. 28 (Oct. 1979) pp. 54–55.
Review of a performance of *The Martyrdom of St. Magnus* by the Fires of London at Ripon Cathedral, Aug. 10, 1979, during the Harrogate Festival. The reviewer notes the work "seemed somewhat dour and monochromatic although its bleaker tints are suitably evocative of the remote Northern blood feuds."

B69.   Boddice, Nigel. "Celebration of Scottish Youth at Edinburgh International Festival." *British Bandsman* (Aug. 31, 1985) p. 3.
Brief review of the premiere of *The Peat Cutters* by the National Youth Brass Band of Scotland and the Scottish National Orchestra Junior and Youth Choirs, Aug. 18, 1985. Remarks: "Maxwell Davies has created a work to make a social comment on the behaviour of mankind toward nature."

B70.   Boddice, Nigel. "Critic's Corner: National Youth Brass Band of Scotland." *British Bandsman* (Sept. 14, 1985) p. 8.
Review of a concert by the National Youth Brass Band of Scotland conducted by Geoffrey Brand at the Edinburgh Festival, Usher Hall, Aug. 18, 1985. Included on the program was the premiere of *The Peat Cutters* by the Scottish National Orchestra Junior and Youth Choruses conducted by Jean Kidd. Includes a brief analysis of the work. When describing the music the reviewer notes the composer was "inspired...to make a human plea through words and music to stop the many acts of hooliganism on our landscapes."

B71.   Bolley, Richard. "Ancient and Modern. 3." *Early Music* (Oct. 1980) pp. 3, 5.
Features an interview with the composer. The primary focus is the influences of early music on his compositions. In that context mentions such composers as Taverner, Byrd and Dunstable. Also marks the influence of plainsong on his compositions.

B72.   Bonner, Dyl. "Ready-Made Music." *Music and Musicians* v. 23 (Aug., 1975) pp. 28–30.

Focuses on the incorporation of pre-existing music into a newly composed work. In the composer's works, this practice is described as showing "a renaissance-delight in the practical art of parody and cantus firmus..." He says this practice has led the composer to use these techniques of "quotation and pastiche" to provide "an aural backdrop to a symbolic programme." Further: in Davies's case it "has become an actual style elements of composition...[it] can provide the sole material and raison d'être of a work." Cites several works to illustrate this theory, including *Alma Redemptoris Mater*, *Leopardi Fragments*, *St. Thomas Wake*, and *Eight Songs for a Mad King*.

B73.   Bowen, Meirion. "BBCSO/Mata, Festival Hall." *Guardian* (Feb. 23, 1993).

Review of a performance of the *Concerto for Trumpet and Orchestra* featuring Håkan Hardenberger, trumpet with the BBC Symphony Orchestra conducted by Eduardo Mata at the Royal Festival Hall, February, 1993. When describing the piece the reviewer notes it is based on the Gradual for the Mass of St. Francis of Assisi, the solo trumpet being the voice of the Saint. Concludes "Maxwell Davies's skill, craftsmanship and inventiveness have rarely been used together so consistently."

B74.   Bowen, Meirion. "Concerts: Boulez." *Music and Musicians* v. 21 (Oct., 1972) pp. 60–61.

Includes a review of a concert at the Roundhouse, London, May 29, 1972, on which was a performance of *Blind Man's Buff*. Notes: "If the Boulez series produced nothing else, it would have been justified by this piece alone."

B75.   Bowen, Meirion. "Concerts: Contemporary." *Music and Musicians* v. 20 (Mar., 1972) pp. 64–66.

Includes a review of a concert by the Fires of London at the Elizabeth Hall, Sept. 25, 1971. Program included a performance of *From Stone to Thorn*, the music being described by the reviewer as "sounding like a sketch for something more extended." Also performed were *Vesalii Icones* (to which the reviewer compared *From Stone to Thorn*) and *Antechrist* (described as "a parody piece that wears very well").

B76.   Bowen, Meirion. "Contemporary." *Music and Musicians* v. 20 (June 1972) p. 70.
Includes a review of a concert by the Fires of London at the Queen Elizabeth Hall, Feb. 12, 1972. On the program was a performance of *Eight Songs for a Mad King* by baritone William Pearson. The music is described as "a work that learns rather uncomfortably on a semi-verismo dramaturge."

B77.   Bowen, Meirion. "The Fires Brigade." *Guardian* (Jan. 19, 1987) p. 9.
Lengthy article written just before the farewell concert by the Fires of London (Jan. 20, 1987). Focuses on the history of the group.

B78.   Bowen, Meirion. "The King's Singers." *Guardian* (May 19, 1987).
Review of a concert by the King's Singers at Wigmore Hall, mid-May, 1987. Included on the program was a performance of *Sea Runes*, described as "an exercise in technique and little else." Also performed was *House of Winter*, which the reviewer says "gathered together verbal and musical images to create a sense of atmosphere and expectancy."

B79.   Bowen, Meirion. "Kyr Premiere." *Guardian* (Sept. 23, 1983).
Includes a review of a performance of *Le Jongleur de Notre Dame* by the Fires of London conducted by Nicholas Cleobury at the Queen Elizabeth Hall, September, 1983. Soloists were Brian Raynor Cook and juggler Jonny James. The wind and percussion band was from South Hampstead High School for Girls. About the piece the reviewer remarks: "The whole effect of the work was well-timed, witty and charming."

B80.   Bowen, Meirion. "Maxwell Davies." *Music and Musicians* v. 19 (April, 1971) pp. 62-63.
Review of two concerts. One was the first concert by the Fires of London, Dec. 12, 1970 at the Elizabeth Hall, with a program including *Revelation and Fall*, featuring Mary Thomas (which the reviewer said "comes across with inexorable, nerve-shattering power and resilience"); *Missa Super L'Homme Armé*, with Vanessa Redgrave as the Speaker (which the reviewer felt was not cohesive even though it has "a brilliant surface quality"). The second concert was a piano recital by Stephen Pruslin at the Purcell Room, Jan. 19, 1971, including the premiere of *Ut Re Mi*, which the reviewer thought "came over as a series of ambiguous gestures."

B81. Bowen, Meirion. "Maxwell Davies/SCO." *Guardian* (Feb. 18, 1993).
      Review of a concert by the Scottish Chamber Orchestra conducted by
      the composer at the Queen Elizabeth Hall, Feb. 16, 1993. Included
      on the program was the first London performance of the *Strathclyde
      Concerto No. 7 for Double Bass and Orchestra* featuring soloist
      Duncan McTier. The reviewer notes: "All three movements
      emphasised the less exploited lyrical potential of the bass." Also
      included on the program was a performance of *Caroline Mathilde:
      Suite From Act I of the Ballet* about which the reviewer remarks:
      "Fruitful from the start was the interaction of music in past and
      present idioms."

B82. Bowen, Meirion. "Salome Dances Premiere." *Guardian* (Mar. 17,
      1979).
      Includes a review of the premiere of *Salome: Concert Suite from the
      Ballet* by the London Symphony Orchestra conducted by David
      Atherton at the Royal Festival Hall, Mar. 16, 1979. The reviewer
      remarks: "On this hearing, I am inclined to hail it as one of Maxwell
      Davies's finest achievements." Includes a general descriptive
      analysis of the work.

B83. Bowen, Meirion. "South Bank: Pierrot Bows Farewell." *Music and
      Musicians* v. 19 (Nov., 1970) p. 59.
      Review of a concert by the Pierrot Players at the Elizabeth Hall,
      Sept. 19, 1970, which was the final London concert by that group.
      Two works by the composer were included on the program. First
      was the arrangement of Buxtehude's cantata *Also Hat Gott Die Welt
      Geliebt*. When describing the instrumental interlude added by the
      composer to the work, the reviewer notes: "It seemed not just a
      comment on Buxtehude but a reinforcement of the latter's point and
      it added to the anticipation before the final section." Next was the
      new concert version of *Nocturnal Dances*, of which the reviewer
      noted the "cool luminosity and asperity of the scoring" and judged
      it to be one of the composer's finest works.

B84. Bowen, Meirion. "*Worldes Blis*." *Guardian* (July 13, 1978).
      Review of a concert by the London Symphony Orchestra conducted
      by David Atherton at the Royal Festival Hall, July 12, 1978.
      Included on the program was a performance of *Worldes Blis*, which
      the reviewer describes as "a composition of blinding sureness of
      vision and technical accomplishments."

B85.   Bowles, Garrett H. *"Peter Maxwell Davies* by Paul Griffiths." *Opera Quarterly* v. 2 no. 1 (1984) pp 135–136.
Review of Paul Griffith's book, *Peter Maxwell Davies* (New York: Universe Books.   London: Robson Books, 1982.).   Conclusion: "Griffith's book provides an excellent insight into Davies's compositions."

B86.   Brass, Denis. "Opera." *Tablet* (July 16, 1983).
Review of the revival of *Taverner* by the Royal Opera, Covent Garden, June 29, 1983.   Includes a lengthy synopsis of the drama. About the work the reviewer notes: "The music is of a high level of intensity throughout, and never flags."   Further: "there are a number of tantalisingly fertile musical ideas."

B87.   Brennan, Mary. *"The Lighthouse."* *Glasgow Herald* (June 21, 1986).
Review of a performance of *The Lighthouse*.   Soloists were Neil Mackie, Henry Herford and Ian Comboy accompanied by the Fires of London at the Theatre Royal, Glasgow, June 20, 1986.   The work is described as "a superbly constructed piece of music theatre."

B88.   Brown, Antony. "Sir Peter, Orkney's Pied Piper." *Reader's Digest* v. 136 no. 816 (April 1990) pp. 60–64.
Article about the composer's life and selected works.   Very personal, only touching on a selection of his compositions.   Pleasant and informative, especially about his day-to-day routine.

B89.   Bye, Anthony. "Record Reviews." *Tempo* no. 177 (June, 1991) p. 57.
Review of a recording (Collins Classic 11812) of both *Symphony No. 4* and *Concerto for Trumpet and Orchestra* by the Scottish Chamber Orchestra and the Scottish National Orchestra conducted by the composer.   John Wallace was the trumpet soloist in the concerto. About the *Symphony* the reviewer remarks, "Davies has a fine feeling for symphonic proportions"; about the *Concerto*, "Arresting ideas and strong contrasts hold the attention and the three movements proceed with a degree of genuine purposefulness."

B90.   C. F. "Davies' *'Klee Pictures'*." *Music and Musicians* v. 25 (Oct., 1976) pp. 7–8.
Article that presents the background of *Five Klee Pictures* just prior to its premiere Oct. 16, 1976 at St. John's, Smith Square by the Young Musicians' Symphony Orchestra conducted by James Blair. When noting the work is for young orchestra the author remarks:

"Maxwell Davies does not 'talk down'...[the work] contains all sorts of challenges." Further: "it is very much part of Maxwell Davies' development as a composer."

B91. Cairns, David. "The Artist Who Lost His Soul." *Times* (July 3, 1983). Review of a performance of *Taverner* at Covent Garden, June 24, 1983, conducted by Edward Downes. About the work the reviewer remarks: "Davies shows a remarkably sure instinct for dramatic pacing and contrast."

B92. Cairns, David. "The High Ambitions of Maxwell Davies." *Times* (Feb. 5, 1978)
Review of a concert by the Philharmonia orchestra conducted by Simon Rattle at the Royal Festival Hall, Feb. 2, 1978. Included on the program was the premiere of *Symphony No. 1*. The reviewer notes the influence of Sibelius, especially his Symphony No. 5, on the composer's work, finding this "is heard, not only in the work's final chords...but also in certain characteristic textures."

B93. Cairns, David. "Making Music for the Masses." *Times* (Feb. 19, 1984).
Includes a review of a concert given by the Collegium of London conducted by Andrew Parrott at St. Martin-in-the-Fields the weekend of Feb. 11, 1984. Included on the program was a performance of *Solstice of Light*, about which the work the reviewer remarks: "The predominately modal idiom of the choral narrative sounds not stale but freshly apt to the poem's evocation of Orkney's landscape." Includes a descriptive brief analysis.

B94. Cairns, David. "Music From the Wilds." *Times* (Nov. 18, 1984).
Review of a concert by the BBC Symphony Orchestra conducted by Elgar Howarth during the Huddersfield Festival in early November, 1984. Included on the program was a performance of *Stone Litany*, which the reviewer describes as "striking pieces of nature painting." Also on the program was a performance of *Worldes Blis*, which the reviewer asserts is a difficult work to comprehend but then adds, "the slowly accumulating force, the sustained grandeur and momentousness of the conflict it embodies are...awe-inspiring."

B95.   Campbell, Stuart. "Scottish Chamber Orchestra." *Glasgow Herald* (Oct. 30, 1984).

Review of a concert by the Scottish Chamber Orchestra conducted by the composer at City Hall, Glasgow, Oct. 28, 1984. Included on the program was a performance of *Sinfonietta Accademica*. The reviewer notes the Orcadian influence on the piece and remarks, "these inspirations are transformed by mysterious compositional processes to form an immediately likeable piece."

B96.   Cariaga, Daniel. "In Review: San Diego." *Opera News* v. 51 (Oct. 1986) pp. 71–72.

Review of a performance of *The Lighthouse* by the San Diego Opera May 10–18 1986 at the Old Globe, Balboa Park, San Diego. Soloists included Harlan Foss, Michael Ballam, and James Butler; conductor was Karen Keltner. About the music the reviewer writes: "The composer's mastery of instrumental and vocal devices in creating mood and character, tension and relief, sees complete."

B97.   Chanan, Michael. "Dialectics in the Music of Peter Maxwell Davies." *Tempo* no. 90 (Autumn 1969) pp. 12–22.

Lengthy article which focuses upon the composer's use of borrowed and pre-existing material as well as his technique of parody in his compositions. Mentions *Fantasia and Two Pavans after Henry Purcell*, *O Magnum Mysterium*, *Taverner*, *Ecce Manus Tradentis*, *Antechrist*, *Alma Redemptoris Mater*, *Shakespeare Music*, *Missa Super L'Homme Armé*, *Revelation and Fall*, *Eight Songs for a Mad King*, and *Worldes Blis*. Includes musical examples.

B98.   Chanan, Michael. "Modern." *Music and Musicians* v. 22 (July 1974) pp. 51–52.

Includes a review of a concert by the Fires of London conducted by the composer at the Queen Elizabeth Hall, April 23, 1974, including performances of *Eight Songs for a Mad King* (with baritone James Skoog) and *Miss Donnithorne's Maggot*. The reviewer notes the *Eight Songs* "have proved their staying power"; comparing *Miss Donnithorne* with the *Eight Songs*, he says that it is "sufficiently compelling" and that "the instrumental parts are just as brilliantly conceived and the vocal writing...just as taxing."

B99.   Chanan, Michael. "Peter Maxwell Davies." *Listener* (Nov. 8, 1973) pp. 645–646.
Curious article which focuses at one point on *St. Thomas Wake* just prior to a broadcast of that work on BBC Radio 3, Nov. 15, 1973. About the work the author remarks the composer "presents us with musical styles as found cultural objects." Includes a descriptive analysis of the piece.

B100.   Chapman, Ernest. "Boulez at the Roundhouse." *Musical Events* v. 27 (Aug., 1972) pp. 10–11.
Review of a concert which included the premiere of *Blind Man's Buff* by Josephine Narstow and Mary Thomas, with the BBC Symphony Orchestra conducted by Pierre Boulez, May 29, 1972 at the Roundhouse. Compares the music to *Eight Songs for a Mad King,* and remarks, "the music is tightly knit...and...the singing parts are highly effective without going to the vocal extremes of *Revelation and Fall.*"

B101.   Chapman, Ernest. "Maxwell Davies' New Fantasia." *Music Survey* v. 17 (Nov. 1962) pp. 20–21.
Review of the premiere of *First Fantasia on an 'In Nomine' of John Taverner* by the BBC Symphony Orchestra conducted by the composer at the Royal Albert Hall, Sept. 13, 1962. About the work the reviewer notes it is "admirably clear in form, with cleverly varied, transparent orchestration."

B102.   Chapman, Ernest. "Music Survey." *Musical Events* v. 20 (April 1965) pp. 7–11.
Includes a review of the premiere of *Five Motets* by the Ambrosian Singers and the English Chamber Orchestra conducted by Norman Del Mar at Friends House (as part of the St. Pancras Festival) on Mar. 1, 1965. The reviewer notes the work exhibited "poetic beauty and intensity of expression."

B103.   Chapman, Ernest. "Music Survey." *Musical Events* v. 20 (June 1965) p. 29.
Review of a concert by the London Philharmonic Orchestra conducted by Sir John Pritchard at the Royal Festival April 30, 1965. Included on the program was the premiere of *Second Fantasia on John Taverner's 'In Nomine'*: "The range of its melodic, harmonic and orchestral invention is obvious, revealing a powerful mind at work."

B104. Charles, Bruce. *"Hill Runes."* *Classical Guitar* v. 10 (Oct. 1991) pp. 24–25.
Article by guitarist Bruce Charles which includes an analysis of *Hill Runes* for solo guitar. Includes many musical examples. Charles says that the composer "made me think not just about pitch...but also driving rhythm, changing metre and dynamic flux as a means to understand how he feels about *Hill Runes*."

B105. Chatelin, Ray. "Orkney Isolation Feeds Sir Peter's Music." *Province* (Vancouver) (May 17, 1992).
Article about the composer written just prior to a concert of the CBC Symphony Orchestra which the composer was to conduct on May 17, 1992. Largely biographical.

B106. Christiansen, Af Svend. "Peter Maxwell Davies—en Introduktion." *Dansk Musiktidsskrift* v. 65 no. 2 (1990–1991) pp. 39–40, 42–43.
Article about the composer's works prior to the NUT Festival for New Music in Aalborg Oct. 14–19, 1990. On Oct. 16, the composer directed the Aalborg Symphony Orchestra in a program that included performances of his *First Fantasia on an 'In Nomine' of John Taverner, Sinfonia, An Orkney Wedding, With Sunrise*, and *Concerto for Violin and Orchestra*. Focuses on the Violin Concerto, giving a detailed analysis with musical examples.

B107. Clark, David. "Peter Maxwell Davies." *Music and Letters* v. 67 no. 3 (1986) pp. 302–304.
Includes a review of *Maxwell Davies* by Paul Griffiths, (London, Robson Books, 1982). Describes the book as an "introductory study" and notes the author "does point out details of individual works as signposts for listening...even though...the general thrust of his narrative is to elucidate work in terms of each other."

B108. Clark, Timothy Vincent. "Night of Blis." *Riverfront Times* (Oct. 21–27, 1992).
Review of a concert by the St. Louis Symphony Orchestra conducted by Leonard Slatkin at Powell Symphony Hall, St. Louis, Oct. 9, 1992. Included on the program was the first U. S. performance of *Worldes Blis*. The music is described as "eminently listenable." The reviewer notes this is due to, "in equal measure Davies's own musical and dramatic inventiveness..." Includes some background information about the piece.

B109. Clarke, Keith. "Wallace Blows Sir Peter's Trumpet." *Independent*
(Oct. 6, 1988)
Report of an interview with trumpeter John Wallace, for whom the
Concerto for Trumpet and Orchestra was commissioned, as he
prepared for its premiere at the Royal Festival Hall, Oct. 9, 1988.
Wallace describes the Concerto as "a monumental single-movement
work on an epic scale, inhabiting the mystical visionary world of St.
Francis of Assisi...The inexhaustibly fertile imagination of Maxwell
Davies makes the trumpet the voice of St. Francis.   The work
progresses through a multitude of moods and sounds until the ecstatic
vision of St. Francis is finally reached."

B110. Clements, Andrew.   "Composers in Cambridge." *Financial Times*
(Mar. 23, 1993) p. 17.
Includes a review of a concert by the Royal Philharmonic Orchestra
conducted by the composer at the Royal Festival Hall, Mar. 10,
1993.   About the music the reviewer remarks, "the musical argument, so taut and uncompromising (and in the light of his subsequent
development...) remains thrilling."

B111. Clements, Andrew.   "The Festival of St. Magnus." *Music and
Musicians* v. 25 (June 1977) pp. 42–44.
A preview of the first St. Magnus Festival in June 1977.   Mentions
a number of the composer's compositions including *Ave Maris Stella*,
Dark Angels, *Fiddlers at the Wedding* and *Taverner*.   Most of the
article focuses on *The Martyrdom of St. Magnus*, which was to be the
high point of the new festival when it was premiered in June 18,
1977.   Includes a synopsis of the drama and a brief descriptive
analysis.

B112. Clements, Andrew.   "Fires of London Farewell/Elizabeth Hall."
Financial Times (Jan. 22, 1987) p.27.
Review of the farewell concert of and by the Fires of London
conducted by the composer at the Queen Elizabeth Hall, Jan. 20,
1987.   The concert included two premieres: of *Winterfold* by Mary
Thomas, mezzo-soprano (described as "very much chip off the
Orcadian block, without the raw lyricism of its forerunners"), and of
Davies's Dowland realisation, *Farewell–a Fancye* (described as "an
intensely introspective lute piece realised in muted instrumental
colours").   Also included was a performance of *Eight Songs for a
Mad King* featuring David Wilson-Johnson, about which the reviewer

remarks, "it remains an intensely powerful piece...capable of manipulating an audience's emotions as skillfully as ever."

B113. Clements, Andrew. *"First Ferry to Hoy*/Elizabeth Hall." *Financial Times* (Nov. 14, 1985).
Review of a concert by the London Sinfonietta and students from the ILEA Centre for Young Musicians conducted by Elgar Howarth, at the Queen Elizabeth Hall, Nov. 12, 1985. Included on the program was the premiere of *First Ferry to Hoy*, described as "a nicely atmospheric, immaculately paced tone poem."

B114. Clements, Andrew.   "Maxwell Davies Challenges Stockholm." *Financial Times* (Nov. 29, 1984).
Reviews the first Swedish performance of *Taverner* by members of the Swedish Royal Opera at the King's Theatre, Stockholm, Sept. 24, 1984. The reviewer thought the work "lacks the musico-dramatic framework to make it a compelling piece of theatre." (Gives a synopsis of the work). Also reviews a performance of *The Lighthouse* by members of the Swedish Royal Opera at the Swedish Royal Opera House's Rotunda, Sept. 24, 1984 conducted by Kjell Ingebretsen. The reviewer notes: "It is an opera that places a great deal of responsibility upon the three singers to generate and sustain its intensity."

B115. Clements, Andrew.   "Maxwell Davies' New Symphony." *Music and Musicians* v. 26 (Feb., 1978) pp. 24-ff.
Focuses on *Symphony No. 1* prior to its premiere by the BBC Symphony Orchestra in February, 1978. Mentions several earlier works which may have been precursors of the *Symphony*, including *Taverner, Worldes Blis*, and *Stone Litany*. Remarks on the influence of Sibelius, especially as found in that composer's *Symphony No. 5*. Includes a descriptive analysis of the new work and says, "the sureness of the orchestration and the concentration of the thematic procedures are a clear indication of the advance in Davies' music."

B116. Clements, Andrew.   "Maxwell Davies's Third Symphony/Radio 3." *Financial Times* (Feb. 20, 1985) p.
Review of the premiere of *Symphony No. 3* by the BBC Symphony Orchestra conducted by Edward Downes at the Free Trade Hall, Manchester, Feb. 19, 1985. Remarks on the obvious influence of Mahler on the work. Discusses the structure, taking note of the work's 'classical language' and remarking: "The lines seem clean-

er...the music now manages to sustain itself on...fewer contrapuntal lines." Included a descriptive analysis of the work.

B117. Clements Andrew. "*Resurrection* Premiered in Darmstadt." *Financial Times* (Sept. 20, 1988).

Review of the premiere of *Resurrection* in Darmstadt, Sept. 18, 1988. With a brief review history of the work and, throughout, a synopsis of the plot. Notes the parallel with *Taverner*, claiming that that opera must be understood in order to appreciate the new work. At one point the reviewer remarks: "In *Resurrection* the scenes lack any...backbone and float around in a sea of indulgence, for which the music provides no support."

B118. Clements, Andrew. "Sinfonietta Premiere." *Music and Musicians* v. 25 (June, 1977) p. 56.

Review of a series of concerts by the London Sinfonietta. One included the premiere of *A Mirror of Whitening Light* on Mar. 23, 1977, at the Elizabeth Hall, conducted by the composer. Compares the new work to *Ave, Maris Stella* and *Veni, Sancte Spiritus*, when noting the composer's compositional process. Concludes that the work is "as accomplished a work for orchestra as Davies has ever produced."

B119. Clements, Andrew. "Stockholm: Not So Memorable." *Opera* v. 36 (April 1985) pp. 441–442.

Includes first a review of a performance of *Taverner* by the Swedish Royal Opera, Stockholm, Nov. 24, 1984. Says there were many problems, primarily with the staging of the work. Concerning the music itself, the reviewer says: "The real drama in this opera...is going on in the orchestra where Davies's technique of parody and transformation mirror the political and moral metamorphoses that are the opera's raison d'etre." The reviewer thinks the level of the music is too difficult for most listeners to comprehend.

Also includes a review of a performance of *The Lighthouse* by the Swedish Royal Opera, Nov. 24, 1985. Describes the work as "a strongly theatrical piece well plotted," but goes on to add: "The music is perhaps less convincing," even though properly staged as it was, "it can be highly effective."

B120. Clements, Andrew. *"Stone Litany." Music and Musicians* v. 23 (Aug. 1975) pp. 16–18.

Article about *Stone Litany* written just prior to its performance at a Proms concert by the BBC Scottish Symphony Orchestra conducted by Seaman on Aug. 20, 1975, with soloist Jane Manning. The article includes a descriptive analysis of the work. The reviewer notes that the device that sets the piece apart from the composer's earlier orchestral works is "its use of instrumental colour." Further, the piece is described as "the most poetic score Davies has written."

B121. Clements, Andrew. "Wishart's Vox." *Financial Times* (Sept. 15, 1988).

Includes a review of a concert by the Scottish Chamber Orchestra conducted by the composer at the Albert Hall, Sept. 13, 1988. Included on the program was a performance of *Strathclyde Concerto No. 1 for Oboe and Orchestra* featuring oboist Robin Miller. Noting that the work is based on a chant for the liturgy for Pentecost, the reviewer generally feels it lacks excitement and concludes, "Davies' technical processes are now so adroit...the musical surfaces have become almost over-polished."

B122. Coates, Leon. "First Performances: Musica Nova 1973." *Tempo* no. 107 (Dec. 1973) pp. 24–25.

Includes a review of a concert at the City Hall, Glasgow, Sept. 22, 1973. Included on the program was the premiere of *Stone Litany* by Jan deGaetani and the Scottish National Orchestra conducted by Sir Alexander Gibson. The reviewer describes the work as: "Rich in drama, atmosphere and lyricism...one of Davies' most significant creations."

B123. Cockroft, Robert. "The Fires of London." *Yorkshire Post* (Aug. 7, 1984).

Review of a concert by the Fires of London conducted by Nicholas Cleobury at the Harrogate Theatre, Aug. 6, 1984. The program included *The No. 11 Bus*, which the reviewer describes as a very complex work with "a solemn libretto and scarcely memorable score," and *Vesalii Icones* (featuring dancer Tom Yang), about which work the reviewer remarks, "the piece operates on several distinct levels, not all of them immediately comprehensible."

B124. Cockroft, Robert. "Huddersfield Contemporary Music Festival: The Fires of London." *Yorkshire Post* (Nov. 15, 1984).

Review of a concert by the Fires of London under the direction of Günther Bauer-Schenk at St. Paul's Hall, Nov. 13, 1984. on the program were *Vesalii Icones*, featuring dancer Tom Yang (the reviewer describes the piece as a "delicate and neurotic score") and *Le Jongleur de Notre Dame* (which the reviewer says "finds the composer balances its various elements with an absolute assurance of technique").

B125. Cockroft, Robert. "Huddersfield Town Hall: Kirklees School Concert." *Yorkshire Post* (Nov. 7, 1984).

Review of a Kirklees School concert at the Huddersfield Town Hall, Nov. 6, 1984, which included participation of 400 school children from area schools. On the program was a performance of *Songs of Hoy*, about which the reviewer notes: "Textures are clean and uncomplicated, harmonies are simple yet fresh...melodies often folklike and modal in profile."

B126. Cockroft, Robert. "Time to Tear Down the Ivory Tower." *Yorkshire Post* (Nov. 12, 1984).

Article about the composer's life to date and his ideas about composing, especially writing works for young people. It was written while he was composer in residence during the Huddersfield Contemporary Music Festival in 1984.

B127. Cole, Bruce. "*The Blind Fiddler*." *Tempo* no. 117 (June 1976) pp. 32–33.

Gives an analysis of the structure of *The Blind Fiddler*: "the sevenfold structures are apparent...whose ancestry is at once confirmed by its seven songs, seven interludes and the use of a magic square of seven." Mentions *Dark Angels*, *Fiddlers at the Wedding*, *Miss Donnithorne's Maggot* and *Ave Maris Stella*.

B128. Cole, Hugo. "Bath." *Musical Times* v. 116 (July, 1975) p. 645.

Includes a review of a Bath Festival concert at the Theatre Royal, May 27, 1975 by the Fires of London. Included was a performance of *Miss Donnithorne's Maggot* by Mary Thomas. Noted the score "was intricately-textured." Also included a performance of *Ave Maris Stella*, a work the reviewer describes as "austerely beautiful."

B129. Cole, Hugo. "Fires of London." *Guardian* (Feb. 28, 1986).
Review of a concert by the Fires of London conducted by the composer at the Queen Elizabeth Hall, Feb. 26, 1986. Included on the program was the premiere of *Excuse Me*, which is described as "cunningly interlinked and containing some well-planned surprises." The program also included a performance of *Sonata for Clarinet and Piano* by David Campbell, accompanied by Stephen Pruslin.

B130. Cole, Hugo. "Maxwell Davies." *Guardian* (June 5, 1984).
Review of a concert at the Wigmore Hall, London, June 3, 1984. Included on the program was the premiere of the *Sonatine for Violin and Cimbalon* by Rosemary Furniss, violin, and Gregory Knowles, cimbalon. The work is described as: "A lovely piece, that might conceivably lay the foundation for a whole violin-cimbalon repertoire."

B131. Coleman, Tim. "Modern." *Music and Musicians* v. 22 (Dec., 1973) pp. 60–70.
Includes a review of a concert by the Fires of London conducted by the composer at the Elizabeth Hall, Oct. 3, 1973. Program included *From Stone to Thorn*, *Renaissance Scottish Dances*, and *Hymn to St. Magnus*. The latter two works are described as "tough and very impressive." About the *Hymn* the reviewer concludes: "I find it one of the best of the composer's recent works."

B132. Coleman, Timothy. "Modern." *Music and Musicians* v. 21 (Mar., 1973) p. 68.
Article which includes a review of the First London performance of *Veni, Sancte Spiritus* by the Bach Society conducted by Paul Steinitz at the Elizabeth Hall, Nov. 4, 1972. Described as "one of his best scores, on a level with the *Leopardi Fragments*."

B133. Commandy, Robert. "American Symphony—Whirlwind Visit." *San Francisco Chronicle* (Sept. 29, 1986).
Review of a concert by the American Symphony Orchestra conducted by Tamas Vasary at the Masonic Auditorium, San Francisco, Sept. 27, 1986. Included on the program was a performance of *An Orkney Wedding, With Sunrise*: "It is a light, amusing pops work."

B134. Commanday, Robert. "Fires of London Take on Davies' 'King'." *San Francisco Chronicle* (Dec. 9, 1985).

Review of a concert by the Fires of London conducted by the composer at Zellerbach Auditorium, University of California, Berkeley, Dec. 7, 1985. Included on the program was a performance of *Le Jongleur de Notre Dame* featuring mime Jonny James and baritone Andrew Gallacher. Also performed was *Eight Songs For a Mad King*, again with baritone Andrew Gallacher. The review describes the music in the work as "acerbic and not tonal but the dissonance level and texture are light." Includes brief descriptions of each work.

B135. Commanday, Robert. "A N.Y. Sense of Events." *San Francisco Chronicle* (May 4, 1983).

Review of a concert by the Fires of London conducted by John Carewe at New York's Symphony Space, April 24, 1983 as part of the "Britain Salutes New York" Festival. Included on the program was a performance of *Vesalii Icones* featuring dancer Tom Yang and cellist Jonathan Williams. About the score the reviewer remarks: "Otherwise dry and intense, the music variously commented and maintained a semi-separate life." Also performed was *Miss Donnithorne's Maggot* featuring soloist Mary Thomas. The reviewer says: "Davies's fine-line music migrated from instrument to instrument, a sparingly etched underpinning, fragile and telling."

B136. Condi, Gerard. "Les Enfants de Cendrillon." *Le Monde* (Sept. 16, 1987) p. 14.

Review of a performance of *Cinderella* by Jeunesses Musicales de France at the Salle Favart, Paris, mid-September, 1986. The director was Richard Caceres.

B137. Cook, Nicholas. "Orchestral, Choral." *Musical Times* v. 123 (July, 1982) p. 490.

Includes a review of a concert at the Festival Hall, Feb. 11, 1982 by the Philharmonia Orchestra conducted by Simon Rattle, which included the premiere of *Black Pentecost*. The reviewer says that this work is "undoubtedly effective as a whole." However, he thinks that "by Maxwell Davies's standards the music is often thin, even at times banal!"

Also includes a review of a concert at the Elizabeth Hall, May 13, 1982 by the Fires of London which included the first London performance of *The Medium* by Mary Thomas. Described as being in the sale realm as *The Eight Songs for a Mad King*: an "exploration of the borders between imagination and mania."

B138. Cook, Nicholas. "Orchestral." *Musical Times* v. 123 (April, 1982) p. 275ff.

Article includes a review of a concert at the Elizabeth Hall, Feb. 16, 1982 by the London Sinfonietta conducted by Elgar Howarth. Included performances of *A Mirror of Whitening Light*, *Westerlings*, and *Sonata for Trumpet and Piano*. The last is described as "an immensely appealing reworking of the high trumpet sonorities found in Baroque music."

B139. Cook, Paul. "Maxwell Davies: *Worldes Blis*; *Turn of the Tide*; *Plainchant*; *Sir Charles his Pavan*." *American Record Guide* vol. 57 no. 4 (July/August 1994) p. 131.

Review of a recording which includes the following: *Worldes Blis*; *Turn of the Tide*; *Plainchant*; *Sir Charles his Pavan*. About *Worldes Blis* the reviewer notes the work is "robust and clearly developed ...probably a masterpiece of its kind." When describing *Turn of the Tide* the reviewer remarks, "its central weakness...no joy." The other two works are noted to be "pleasant."

B140. Cooper, Colin. "Review Concerts." *Classical Guitar* v. 5 (April, 1987) p. 53.

Review of the farewell concert by the Fires of London at the Queen Elizabeth Hall, Jan. 20, 1987. This included the premiere of *Winterfold* with Mary Thomas, soprano. The reviewer especially focuses on the performance of Timothy Walker, guitar in the piece, noting the function of the guitar in the work, which contributes "to the harmonic pattern to add a tonal dimension to what is already going on." Also on the program was the premiere of *Farewell a Fancye*, which the reviewer thinks "would have sounded better on a solo guitar." Davies's realisation of *Fantasia on a Ground and Two Pavans of Henry Purcell*, performed on the same program, is described as "Very clever and very, very funny."

B141. Cooper, Martin. "Leaving Too Much to the Words." *Opera* v. 23 (Sept., 1972) pp. 795–798.

Review of the premiere of *Taverner* on July 12, 1972 at Covent Garden. Reviewer finds the work problematic. He describes the libretto as being "intellectually over-ambitious." Further, he notes that the composer's "musical language is...a major handicap in setting a many-layered drama of this kind." Review is quite harsh and somewhat pretentious.

B142. Coppler, Peggy. "How I Produced P. M. Davies' *Cinderella.*" *Opera for Youth News* v. 13 no. 3. (1990) p. 8–9.
Short but informative account of a production of *Cinderella* by pupils from the St. Bernard School in Wabash, Indiana, conducted by Peggy Cooper. Not so much a review as an account of the events and activities that led up to the performance.

B143. Corell, Roger. "Opera." *Sydney Morning Herald* (Dec. 3, 1984).
Review of a performance of *The Lighthouse* by members of the Seymour Group Ensemble at the Everest Theatre, Seymour Centre, Sydney, Nov. 30–Dec. 1, 1984. Soloists included Adrian Brand, Garrick Jones and Keith Hampton. The performance was conducted by Myer Friedman. When describing the music the reviewer notes "The instrumental scoring of unfaltering brilliance."

B144. Covello, Richard. "World Report: Chicago Opera Theater." *Opera Canada* v. 31 no. 2 (1990) p. 32.
Brief review of the first Chicago production of *The Lighthouse* at the Chicago Opera Theater, during March and April, 1990. Conducted by Henry Holt, the performance featured Peter Loehle, Nickolas Karousatos and Richard Fracker. Though the reviewer says "the independent Prologue actually promised more than the opera's one act delivered," he adds that "Davies's score admirably builds tension and mystery."

B145. Cox, John. "Music and Words from Orkney." *Southern Evening Echo* (April 2, 1986) p. 27.
Includes a review of a recording of *Sinfonietta Accademica* by the Scottish Chamber Orchestra conducted by the composer, (Unicorn-Kanchana DKP 9038). When describing the work, which was commissioned by Edinburgh University, the reviewer remarks: "This profoundly felt piece is a recollection of Orcadian things past, of men under the earth." Also included on the same recording is *Into the Labyrinth*, featuring tenor Neil Mackie.

B146. Crabtree, Phillip D. "Contemporary British Choral Music." *Choral Journal* v. 17 no. 3 (1976) pp. 15–17.
Includes a review of a DMA dissertation by Marles Preheim (University of Cincinnati, 1972), *The Choral Music of Peter Maxwell*

Davies.   Discusses works composed between 1959–1966.   Also includes the author's abstract of the dissertation.

B147. Crichton, Ronald. "Dances from *Salome.*" *Financial Times* (Mar. 19, 1979).
Review of a concert by the London Symphony Orchestra conducted by David Atherton at Festival Hall, Mar. 16, 1979. Featured on the program was the premiere of *'Salome: Concert Suite from the Ballet.'*.   Includes a discussion of the problem of successfully adapting music for the ballet into the concert hall, while maintaining its dramatic quality and image.   About the composer's score the reviewer remarks: "There is some beautiful, "magic" writing," referring to...intricate textures not unlike those found in certain works of Tippett."

B148. Crisp, Clement. *"Vesalii Icones."* *Financial Times* (Nov. 20, 1975).
Review of a performance of *Vesalii Icones* by dancer William Louther and cellist Jennifer Ward Clarke, with the Fires of London conducted by the composer at Sadlers Wells, Nov. 19, 1975. Gives the background of the work and says: "Davies's score is a superimposition of plainsong, popular music, and his 'own' music inspired by these sources."

B149. Croan, Robert. "Philadelphia Offers Fine *Lighthouse.*" *Pittsburgh Post-Gazette* (Mar. 25, 1989).
Includes a review of a performance of *The Lighthouse* by performers from the Curtis Institute at Center City, Philadelphia, mid-March, 1989, conducted by David Hayes and with soloists Perry Brisbon, Seth Malken, and John Kramer. The work is described as "memorable music theater...a small masterpiece."

B150. Cross, Anthony. "Liverpool." *Musical Times* v. 107 (May, 1966) p.426.
Includes a review of a performance of *Second Fantasia on John Teverner's 'In Nomine'* (1964) by the Royal Liverpool Philharmonic Orchestra conducted by Sir Charles Grove.   The reviewer calls the work "a re-creation of symphonic thought without the artificiality of some latter-day symphonies."

B151. Cruise, Malcolm. "The Fires of London." *Huddersfield Examiner* (Nov. 21, 1983).
Review of a concert by the Fires of London conducted by the composer at St. Paul's Hall, Huddersfield as part of the Huddersfield Contemporary Music Festival, Nov. 20, 1983. Included on the program was a performance of *Image, Reflection, Shadow*, which the reviewer describes as "a big and many-faceted work."

B152. Danler, Karl Robert. "Muenchen: Davies, *Miss Donnithorne's Maggot*" *Opernwelt* v. 32 (May 1991) pp. 54–55.
Review of a performance of *Miss Donnithorne's Maggot* at the Munich Cultural Center, April 1, 1991. The work was conducted by Frank Bayreuther and featured soloist Christina Ascher. Includes a photograph of a scene from the performance.

B153. Davidson, Philippa. "Musical Fireworks." *Times Educational Supplement* (Aug. 30, 1985).
Review of a concert which included the premiere of *The Peat Cutters* by the National Youth Brass Band of Scotland, the Scottish National Orchestra Junior and Youth Choruses, conducted by Geoffrey Brand at Usher Hall, Edinburgh, Aug. 18, 1985. About the work the reviewer notes: "The impact...comes from the composer's masterly integration of poetry, vocal and instrumental forces...create pictorial effect."

B154. Davies, Lyn. "Maxwell Davies' Organ Music." *Musical Times* v. 125 (Sept., 1984) pp. 525–527.
Article about the composer's solo works for organ and also his use of the organ in other of his compositions. Of the *Fantasia on 'O Magnum Mysterium,' Three Organ Voluntaries*, and *Sonata for Organ*, as well as the organ part in *Solstice of Light* the author remarks that these all "reflect both the highly individual and the traditional nature of his musical thought." Includes an analysis of each work with some musical examples.

B155. Davies, Peter Maxwell. "Composing Music for School Use." *Making Music* no. 46 (Summer, 1961) pp. 7–8.
Article by the composer about the necessity for composing original music for school children to perform as opposed to arrangements of previously composed works, simplified to make them accessible to younger performers. Remarks about his experiences while teaching at the Cirencester Grammar School in that regard. Mentions his *Five*

Klee Pictures and *O Magnum Mysterium*, both of which were composed for younger performers.

B156. Davies, Peter Maxwell. "A Letter." *Composer* no. 15 (April 1965) pp. 22–23.
This very articulate piece is a reply to an earlier review of the Princeton University Press's journal *Perspectives of New Music*. He criticizes the author of the review, Alan Walker, describing him as misunderstanding the intent and thrust of the journal as well as noting Walker's lack of understanding of the language of new music. Concludes the journal "is the only 'trade magazine' of musical composition of any seriousness that I know."

B157. Davies, Peter Maxwell. "Music Composition by Children." *Music in Education*: Proceedings of the Fourteenth Symposium of the Colston Research Society held in the University of Bristol, April 2nd–5th, 1962. Willis Grant, ed. (London: Butterworths, 1963) pp. 108–124. Pp. 108–115 are the composer's discussion of some 21 examples of compositions, mostly by his students at Cirencester Grammar School in 1960–61 (though he also includes three short passages from his own works: two of the *Four Canons* and *Te Lucis Ante Terminum*). A number of these examples were reproduced on an LP which accompanied the book. Following the composer's article is a transcript of a discussion of his paper, chaired by Sir Jack Westrup, by the composer and other participants in the Symposium.

B158. Davies, Peter Maxwell. "Pax Orcadiensis." *Tempo* no. 119 (Dec. 1976) pp. 20–22.
Article written by the composer about the background of his move to Orkney. Makes note of his compositions written there, including the film music for Ken Russell's film *The Devils* and *Hymn to St. Magnus*, *Stone Litany*, and *From Stone to Thorn*.

B159. Davies, Peter Maxwell. "Peter Maxwell Davies on Some of His Recent Work." *Listener* vol. 81 (1969) p. 121.

B160. Davies, Peter Maxwell. "Problems of a British Composer." *Listener* (9 Oct. 1959) pp. 563–564.

B161. Davies, Peter Maxwell. "Sets or Series." *Listener* vol. 79 (1968) p. 250.

B162. Davies, Peter Maxwell. "Symphony." *Tempo* no. 124 (Mar., 1978) pp. 2–5.

Article by the composer discussing his *Symphony No. 1* from his first ideas for the work until its completion. Includes a movement-by-movement analysis. He remarks, "I began to feel that I could write the orchestral music...which I had been slowly and intermittently working over the years...the present work could mark the possibility of an orchestral competence."

B163. Davies, Peter Maxwell. "*Taverner*, Synopsis and Documentation." *Tempo* no. 101 (1972) pp. 4–11.

The composer's own account of the development of his plans for *Taverner* and the composition of the opera. He recounts his initial interest, during his student days in 1956 in Manchester, in Taverner's life (in the now-disputed version given by Fellowes) as a possible subject for an opera; his more extensive development of the libretto using the far greater documentary sources available at Princeton University in 1962. He also distinguishes those elements in the opera which he intends as historical from those which are his own inventions, though he begins with the observation: "The 'action' is within Taverner's mind; and so, despite constant references to sixteenth century sources (mostly English), neither time nor place are treated realistically." Following a synopsis of the opera's scenes, the composer gives a reconstruction of the source materials he used for the first conversation between the King and the Cardinal (the composer's sketchbooks were destroyed in a fire after the opera was completed).

B164. Davies, Peter Maxwell. "The Young British Composer." *The Score*, (Mar. 1956) pp. 84–85.

B165. Davies, Peter Maxwell. "The Young Composer in America." *Tempo* no. 72 (Spring 1965) pp. 2–6.

Account of the composer's experiences during his time in the United States when he attended the Graduate school at Princeton University, 1963–1964.

B166. Davis, Peter G. "Bring on the New." *New York* (May 30, 1988) pp. 85–87.

Includes a review of a recording of *Concerto for Violin and Orchestra* featuring Isaac Stern with the New Philharmonia conducted by André Previn (CBS 42449). About the work the reviewer remarks, "it does not take a great deal of imagination to hear how Stern's own generous musical personality has been written into this carefully crafted, very beautiful score."

B167. Dean, Winton. "Aldeburgh." *Musical Times* v. 120 (Aug. 1979) pp. 674–675.
Includes a review of a performance of *The Martyrdom of St. Magnus* featuring Neil Mackie and Brian Raynor Cook. The reviewer thinks that "the piece misses the target through being conceived in intellectual rather than dramatic terms" and, further, "The orchestra enjoys most of the best music."

B168. Dean, Winton. "Music in London." *Musical Times* v. 113 (Sept., 1972) pp. 879–881.
Review of the premiere of *Taverner*, July 12, 1972 at Covent Garden. The reviewer claims the composer has "little or no gift for characterization in music [or] for writing expressive lines for solo voice" and thinks the orchestral writing is most successful, though he concludes that the performance was "most accomplished."

B169. Dehren, Andrew. "Da Capo Chamber Players." *Hi Fi/Musical America* v. 30 (Aug., 1980) p. 24.
Review of a concert by the Da Capo Chamber Players at the Tully Hall, Mar. 25, 1980. Program included a performance of *Ave Maris Stella*, about which the reviewer remarks: "Anyone who likes the self-conscious erudition of Maxwell Davies' scores ought to love this one."

B170. Denisov, Edison. "In Memoriam—Igor Fedorovich Stravinsky: Canons and Epitaphs." *Tempo* no. 97 (1971) pp. 24–25.
Article consisting almost entirely of reproductions of canons written by 10 contemporary composers in memory of the then recently deceased composer, Igor Stravinsky. Maxwell Davies's contribution was entitled *Canon In Memoriam I. S., 1971* (see W32).

B171. Dennis, Brian. "Films, Electronics." *Musical Times* v. 111 (Jan. 1970) p. 66.
Review of an ICA Concert at the Elizabeth Hall, Nov. 17, 1969. Included on the program was a performance of *Stedman Doubles* featuring clarinetist Alan Hacker, which the reviewer says "provided only a pale reflection of the Indian music which had apparently inspired it."

B172. Deutsch, Nicholas. "Maxwell Davies: *The Martyrdom of St. Magnus*." *Fanfare* (July/August, 1991).

Review of a recording of *The Martyrdom of St. Magnus* by Opera Theatre Wales and the Scottish Chamber Opera Ensemble conducted by Michael Rafferty (Unicorn-Kanchana DKP (CD) 9100). Includes a lengthy synopsis of the work. About the music the reviewer notes: "The vocal writing...captures vividly the public or private nature of each character...from the severe...to the hysterical." Very well-written, sensitive review.

B173. Doneldson, Graham. "Postman's Knock for Concert First." *Press and Journal* (June 23, 1986).

Includes the history of what prompted the composer to compose his overture, *Jimmack the Postie* (which had just received its premiere by the Royal Philharmonic Orchestra conducted by Walter Wellet at the Phoenix Cinema, Kirkwall during the St. Magnus Festival, June 22, 1986).

B174. Dove, Jonathan. "Concert Notes." *Strad* v. 92 (Oct. 1981) p. 395.

Includes a review of a concert by the BBC Symphony Orchestra conducted by Gennadi Rozhdestvensky at the Royal Albert Hall, July 23, 1981. The program included the first British performance of *Symphony No. 2*, of which the reviewer says: "he has created a large scale work in which the complexities can be appreciated the more positively because he is working with structures which...are lucid and audible."

B175. Douglas-Home, Colette. "Setting a Score With Destiny." *Scotsman* (July 17, 1989).

Biographical article about the composer, with a photograph of the composer.

B176. Drakeford, Richard. "The Review Section: Poly-Stylism." *Musical Times* v. 132 (Mar., 1991) p. 133.

Review of *Dances from 'The Two Fiddlers'* upon publication of the score by Boosey and Hawkes. Work described as "best regarded as a 'fun piece'...—an exercise in 'poly-stylism' rather in the manner of Schnitke."

B177. Drew, David. "Serielle Komponisten in England." *Melos* v. 29 (May 1962) pp. 143–145.
Includes a brief paragraph about the composer's compositional style, mentioning *Taverner*, *Alma Redemptoris Mater*, *St. Michael Sonata* and *Prolation*.

B178. Dreyer, Martin. "Huddersfield." *Musical Times* v. 126 (Jan. 1985) p. 40.
Brief article about the Huddersfield Contemporary Music Festival which took place Nov. 5–14, 1984. Focuses on *Le Jongleur de Notre Dame*, *Vesalii Icones*, *St. Thomas Wake*, *Stone Litany*, and *Worldes Blis*. The last work is described as having "the longest, slowest crescendo ever written."

B179. Drinkwater, Ros. "How We Met." *Independent* (July 10, 1994) p. 72.
Article which features interviews with the composer and George Mackay Brown. Focuses on the relationship between the two, how they became acquainted as well as why the composer chose to set so many of Mackay Brown's texts to music.

B180. Driver, Paul. "A Boisterous Breath of Old Air." *Times* (Sept. 25, 1988).
Review of the premiere of *Resurrection* in Darmstadt by the Darmstadt Stadtstheater, Sept. 18, 1988. Includes background information about the history of the work, as well as a synopsis of the plot. When describing the opera the reviewer notes: "It is his most parodistic score to date and the musical lampoons are deft...the score has the character of a coolly deliberate re-traversal of the stations of his career."

B181. Driver, Paul. "The Famous Fifth." *Times* (Aug. 14, 1994).
Review of the premiere of *Symphony No. 5* by the Philharmonia Orchestra during a Promenade concert at the Royal Albert Hall, Aug. 9, 1994. After extensive discussion of the composer's earlier symphonies and other major orchestral works, the reviewer says of the new Symphony that "its craggedly thoughtful, intricately patterned form recalls Davies's brilliant orchestral movement, *St. Thomas Wake*...and *Ave Maris Stella*."

B182. Driver, Paul. "The Fires of New York." *Times* (May 1, 1983).
Review of two programs by the Fires of London during late April, 1983 at Symphony Space, New York City, part of the British "Salute

to New York." Included a performance of *Image, Reflection, Shadow*, "an essay in rarefied, beautiful, stringently disciplined textures." The other work of the composer reviewed was a performance of *Vesalii Icones*, featuring dancer Tom Yang and solo cellist Jonathan Williams, conducted by John Carewe.

B183. Driver, Paul. "First Performances: 1979 St. Magnus Festival." *Tempo* No. 130 (Sept., 1979) pp. 35–36, 38.

Focuses on concerts and other arts events at the 1979 St. Magnus Festival. Includes a review of a concert that featured the premiere of *Solstice of Light* for tenor, SATB chorus and organ, on 18 June, at the Kirkwall Cathedral, with Neil Mackie, tenor, Richard Hughes, organist, and the St. Magnus Singers directed by Norman Mitchell. This is described as "a major piece, perhaps one of its composer's most ambitious, even most approachable." Gives a brief, descriptive analysis. Also reviews the premiere of *Kirkwall Shopping Songs* performed by children from the Kirkwall Primary School conducted by Glenys Hughes, June 16, 1976. Music described as "a sequence of light-hearted rhymes...set simply and tunefully to an accompaniment" and further, "an enjoyable and exuberant piece."

B184. Driver, Paul. "First Performances: *Triple Duo* and *Image, Reflection, Shadow*." *Tempo* no. 146 (Sept. 1983) pp. 53–55.

Review of a concert by the Fires of London at Symphony Space, New York City, April, 1985. Included on the program was the American premiere of *Image, Reflection, Shadow*, which the reviewer describes as "an essay in rarefied, beautiful, stringently disciplined textures."

B185. Driver, Paul. "Flattered to Death." *Times Literary Supplement* (July 8, 1994) p. 17.

Review of Mike Seabrook's biography *Max: The Life and Music of Peter Maxwell Davies* (London: Gollancz, 1994). The reviewer says: "it is a thoroughly servile book, and Seabrook's unctuousness gets him nowhere near the character of the composer, whose one obvious trait...is complexity."

B186. Driver, Paul. "Germany: The New Maxwell Davies." *Opera* vol. 39 no. 11 (Nov. 1988) pp. 1345–1347.

Lengthy review of the premiere of *Resurrection* by the Stadtstheater, Darmstadt during the Darmstadt Festival, Sept. 18, 1988. The work was conducted by Hans Drewanz. About the music the reviewer remarks: "It is certainly his most parodistic score to date."

B187. Driver, Paul. "The Grand Old Angry Young Man of Hoy." *Times* (April 8, 1990).

Article about the 13 concerts that took place as part of "Maxfest" in London in late March-early April, 1990. Says of the composer: "At 56 he stands as the country's second-most famous living classical composer." Highlights performances of *Worldes Blis*, *Strathclyde Concerto No. 2*, *Strathclyde Concerto No. 3*, *Vesalii Icones*, *Symphony No. 1*, *Symphony No. 2*, *The Martyrdom of St. Magnus*, *Revelation and Fall*, *Eight Songs for a Mad King*, and *Into the Labyrinth*. Also discusses the premiere of *Jupiter Landing* on April 3, 1990: "a charming music theatre piece for seven to 11-year-olds."

B188. Driver, Paul. "*The Lighthouse*." *Tempo* no. 135 (Dec. 1980) pp. 46–47.

Review of the premiere of *The Lighthouse* during the Edinburgh Festival at Moray House Gymnasium, Sept. 2, 1980. Soloists included Neil Mackie, Michael Rippon and David Wilson-Johnson with the Fires of London conducted by Richard Dufallo. About the work the reviewer remarks: "The musical invention is effective and incisive...Its style resembles that of *A Mirror of Whitening Light* crossed upon Davies's older parodic manners."

B189. Driver, Paul. "*The Lighthouse*: Chilling Fantasy." *Boston Globe* (Nov. 3, 1983) section Arts/Films.

Review of the American premiere of *The Lighthouse*, Nov. 2, 1983. Production was by Peter Sellers for the Boston Shakespeare Company. Conducted by David Hoose, the work featured Michael Brown, Sanford Sylvan and Kenneth Bell. The reviewer says: "The musical text is...free from any hint of poeticism...underpinning the drama with maximal effectiveness." Includes a well-done descriptive analysis of the plot.

B190. Driver, Paul. "London Schools Symphony." *Financial Times* (Sept. 16, 1980).

Review of a concert by the London Schools Symphony Orchestra conducted by John Carewe at the Royal Festival Hall, Sept. 15, 1980. Included on the program was a performance of *Five Klee Pictures*, described as "the most artistically-substantial purpose-written contribution there has been."

B191. Driver, Paul. "Max's Farewell to the St. Magnus Festival." *Times* (June 29, 1986).

Article about the 1986 St. Magnus Festival. Includes a review of the premiere of *Concerto for Violin and Orchestra* by Isaac Stern and the Royal Philharmonic Orchestra conducted by André Previn at St. Magnus Cathedral, Kirkwall, June 21, 1986. The reviewer saw this as a work of "severe, reticent and extreme beauty, lyrical in the best violinistic traditions...neoclassically formal."

Also reviews a concert by the Royal Philharmonic Orchestra conducted by the composer at the Phoenix Cinema, Kirkwall, June 22, 1986, which included the premiere of *Jimmack the Postie*: "a substantial, intricately worked movement in Davies's...fully serious style." Finally, reviews a concert by the King's Singers at the East Church, Kirkwall, June 23, 1986, including the premiere of *House of Winter*. The reviewer says that this piece's "timelessly fresh modality goes back to the composer's early carols but...is akin to the new Violin Concerto."

B192. Driver, Paul. "Maxwell Davies Festival." *Financial Times* (April 10 1990).

Includes a review of a concert by the Fires of London at the Purcell Room, London, April 8, 1990, conducted by Paul Daniel. The program included a performance of *Antechrist* which is described as "brief and scintillating transmogrification of a 13th-century motet." Also on the program was *Vesalii Icones*, featuring Tom Yang, dancer and cellist Jonathan Williams, which the reviewer says "again proved its enduring musical and theatrical power." Rounding out the program were *Leopardi Fragments*, *Ave Maris Stella* and *Image, Reflection, Shadow* (the last described as having "amazing scherzo middle movements").

Also includes a review of a performance of *The Martyrdom of St. Magnus* by the Music Theatre Wales and members of the Scottish Chamber Orchestra at the Queen Elizabeth Hall, April 6, 1990. The reviewer says, "there is violent expressionism in the score...a subtle recreation of the Island sound of Orkney" and that "It is a constructed and quite-moving piece of work." Includes a well-written description and synopsis of the work.

B193. Driver, Paul. "Maxwell Davies's *Second Symphony*." *Tempo* no. 137 (June 1981) pp. 32–33.

Review of the premiere of *Symphony No. 2* performed by the Boston Symphony Orchestra conducted by Seiji Ozawa at Symphony Hall,

Feb. 26, 1981.   Includes a brief description of the music. The reviewer notes: "as a 're-run' of the First, the Second certainly seems to be conventionalizing, rounding and clarifying, putting more flesh on the big structural bones."

B194.   Driver, Paul. "*Miss Donnithorne's Maggot* and *Food For Love*: Theatre de Complicité at the Almeida Theatre." *Opera* v. 40 (Jan., 1989) pp. 114–116.
Includes a review of a performance of *Miss Donnithorne's Maggot* by the Theatre de Complicité at the Almeida Theatre, Nov. 8, 1988. Director was Annabel Arden, conductor Jeremy Arden.   Miss Donnithorne was sung by Lore Lixenberg.   The reviewer mentions *Eight Songs for a Mad King* and *The Medium* when describing the place of the work in the composer's output and claims that by comparison with the latter two compositions, "it cannot boast anything like the same intricacy of design and offers itself as a neatly crafted song-cycle with an added dimension of histrionics."

B195.   Driver, Paul.   "Orchestral 2." *Times* (Sunday, Feb. 8, 1987), p. 105d.
Review of a recording of *Sinfonia Concertante* and *Sinfonia* by the Scottish Chamber Orchestra, conducted by the composer (Unicorn-Kanchana DKP 9058).   Finds the *Sinfonia Concertante* to "go on too long, and in a rather dry and uningratiating idiom"; prefers the *Sinfonia*, of which he writes, "the effect is thoroughly absorbing...the sound has a strenuous beauty."

B196.   Driver, Paul.   "Recordings: Maxwell Davies: Symphony." *Tempo* no. 132 (Mar., 1980) pp. 27–29.
Review of a recording of *Symphony No. 1* (Decca Head 21), by the Philharmonia Orchestra conducted by Simon Rattle.   Notes, "the Philharmonia have responded with a remarkably accurate realization of the Symphony's tricky rhythms, novel phrasing and abstruse polyphony."   Includes an extensive descriptive analysis of the work.

B197.   Driver, Paul.   "Setting the Trend." *Financial Times* (April 30, 1988).
Includes a review of a concert by the Scottish Chamber Orchestra conducted by the composer, at the City Hall, Glasgow, April 29, 1988.   The program featured the premiere of *Strathclyde Concerto No. 1 for Oboe and Orchestra*, with Robin Miller, oboe.   Includes information about the history of the Strathclyde Concerti.   Remarks that the new Concerto, which the reviewer says is "manifestly a

virtuosic work," stems from a chant, part of the liturgy for Pentecost.

B198. Driver, Paul. *"Taverner*. Royal Opera, Covent Garden.*" Opera* v. 34 (Sept., 1983) pp. 1032–1036.
Review of a performance of the revival of *Taverner* by the Royal Opera, Covent Garden, June 29, 1983. Comments scene by scene about the performance, alluding to various "theatrical shortcomings" in each, and concludes this "is an opera of ideas not psychology...the expressive plentitude of the score...irradiates the stage-action and absolves its irregularities." Mentions *The Martyrdom of St. Magnus*, *The Lighthouse*, *Vesalii Icones*, and *Eight Songs for a Mad King*.

B199. Duchen, Jessica. *"The Magic Flute*; *Le Nozze di Figaro.*" *Musical Times* v. 130 (Dec., 1989) p. 755.
Includes a review of a performance by the Glyndebourne Touring Opera of Mozart's *Le Nozze di Figaro*, Oct. 10, 1989, at the Coliseum, conducted by the composer. According to the reviewer, his interpretation of the opera was "ebullient and articulated, but above all warm and sensitive to the tenderness of human frailty."

B200. Dunnett, Roderic. "Max at Large." *Music Teacher* v. 69 (Nov. 1990) pp. 10ff.
Article about the events taking place during "Maxfest" at the South Bank Centre, late March-early April, 1990. Focuses on Davies's works for your people; in a review of the premiere of *Jupiter Landing* by pupils of the Chase Side Primary School, Enfield at the Queen Elizabeth Hall, April 3, 1990. the reviewer says this was perhaps "the best production of the whole South Bank 'Max' day." Also discusses the three Longman's publications, *The Great Bank Robbery*, *Jupiter Landing* and *Dinosaur at Large*.

B201. Dunnett, Roderic. "Maxwell Davies: Cello Concerto." *Strad* v. 102 (July 1991) p. 630.
Review of *Strathclyde Concerto No. 2 for Cello and Orchestra* when the score was published by Chester Music. The reviewer remarks: "One is immensely aware of the overall shape and contours. The piece has just enough excitement and virtuoso writing, balanced against extremely lyrical passages." Includes a well-done analysis of the work. No musical examples.

B202. Dunnett, Roderic. "Space Invaders." *Times Educational Supplement* (July 1991).
Review of the premiere of *The Spiders' Revenge* during the 1991 St. Magnus Festival by students from the Evie Primary School at the Kirkwall Arts Theatre, June 25, 1991. The work is described as "a pot-pourri of song and dance...the work caters well for even the youngest performer." Includes a short synopsis of the plot.

B203. Dyer, Richard. "An Astonishing Piece, a Gripping Performance." *Boston Globe* (Nov. 16, 1992) section Arts/Film p. 32.
Review of a concert by the St. Louis Symphony conducted by Leonard Slatkin at Symphony Hall, Boston, Nov. 15, 1992. Included in the program was a performance of *Worldes Blis*, which the reviewer says is "an astonishing span of music...the piece is of a precision and proportion of design no less remarkable than its penetration of emotions." However, he felt Slatkin's introduction of the work "patronized" the composer and caused confusion for the audience.

B204. Dyer, Richard. "Boston." *Opera* v. 37 (Nov., 1986) pp. 1260–1262.
Includes a review of the American premiere of *Taverner* by the Opera Company of Boston, Mar. 12, 1986, directed by Sarah Caldwell. Includes a description of the music as well as the production, concluding: "Despite the evident intellectual precision, there is something wild...and untameable in the music...that is central to its value."

B205. Dyer, Richard. "The Many Moods of Maxwell Davies." *Boston Globe* (Jan. 4, 1991) section Arts/Film p. 43.
A review of a concert by the Boston Symphony conducted by the composer at Symphony Hall, Jan. 3, 1991, which included a performance of *Strathclyde Concerto No. 2 for Cello and Orchestra* with soloist Ralph Kirshbaum. Notes about the work, which the reviewer describes as a picture in sound reflecting the sights of the composer in Orkney, that "The cello part is almost entirely lyrical...never going where you expect" while the orchestra "provides the stable point of view...the piece is full of the most marvelous and surprising sounds—Maxwell Davies is a complete master of orchestration." Gives a brief descriptive analysis of the work.

B206. Dyer, Richard. "The Puckish Maxwell Davies." *Boston Globe* (Jan. 4, 1991) p. 43.
Includes a review of a concert by the Boston Symphony Orchestra conducted by the composer in Boston, Jan. 3, 1991. On the program was a performance of *Strathclyde Concerto No. 2 for Cello and Orchestra* featuring cellist Ralph Kirshbaum. The article also includes many quotations from the composer regarding his compositions and the influence of the Orkney environment upon them.

B207. Dyer, Richard. "Tanglewood Parade Ends with Mega-Events." *Boston Globe* (Aug. 29, 1985) section Arts/Film p. 76.
Review of concert, part of Tanglewood on Parade, at the Tanglewood Music Center, Aug. 27, 1985. Included on the program was a performance of *An Orkney Wedding, With Sunrise*, by the Boston Pops conducted by John Williams, described as "a wild and wonderful work."

B208. Dyer, Richard. "*Taverner* Challenges at the Opera House." *Boston Globe* (Mar. 13, 1986) section Arts/Film p. 76.
Review of the American premiere of *Taverner* by the Opera Company of Boston, Sarah Caldwell, director, at the Opera House, Boston, Mar. 12, 1986. When describing the score the reviewer notes: "Nearly everything in the opera derives from the music of John Taverner...some derivations are distant...there is work here that will delight the eye of the trained musicians."

B209. Dyer, Richard. "*Taverner* to Premiere in Boston." *Boston Globe* (Mar. 2, 1986) section Arts/Film p. A1.
Article about *Taverner* written just prior to the American premiere by the Opera Company of Boston under the direction of Sarah Caldwell. Includes extensive background information about the work and a synopsis of the drama.

B210. Dyer, Richard. "A Wee Bit of Scotland at the Pops." *Boston Globe* (May 13, 1985) section Arts/Film p. 13.
Review of a concert by the Boston Pops conducted by John Williams at Symphony Hall, May 10, 1985. Included on the program was the premiere of *An Orkney Wedding, With Sunrise*. About the work the reviewer remarks: "The basic dance tunes...are grand ones...harmonies and orchestra misadventures depict the consequences of whiskey..." Notes one really did not need to read the program notes about the work as the story is revealed so clearly in the music.

B211. Dyer, Richard. "A World Premiere." *Boston Globe* (Feb. 22, 1981) section Arts/Film.

Written just prior to the premiere of *Symphony No. 2* by the Boston Symphony Orchestra conducted by Seiji Ozawa. After recalling the composer's career, the reviewer says about the upcoming premiere: "The new symphony is nearly as large as its predecessor...its four movements are also an evocation of the sea." Includes quotes from the composer's own program notes for the work.

B212. East, Leslie. "Maxwell Davies." *Music and Musicians* v. 23 (May, 1975) pp. 47–48.

Includes reviews of: a performance of *Vesalii Icones* with Jennifer Ward Clark, cello and the Fires of London conducted by the composer at the Elizabeth Hall, Feb. 26, 1975 ("throughout the interplay, with which technique Davies' multi-level composition is inevitably concerned, is readily perceptible"); a concert by the Scottish National Orchestra conducted by Alexander Gibson, at the Festival Hall, Mar. 7, 1975, including a performance of *Stone Litany* with soloist Jan deGaetani ("a contemporary tone-poem, an orchestral evocation of the bleak and wild Orkney landscape" and presents "a lasting impression...almost intravenously as well as cerebrally") and a concert by the BBC Symphony Orchestra conducted by Colin Davis at the Festival Hall, Mar. 5, 1975. Program included a performance of *Worldes Blis* ("the score teems with invention which never seems to flag").

B213. Eaton, Quaintance. "Aspen." *Opera News* v. 25 (Sept. 19, 1970) p. 27.

Review of a concert during the Contemporary Music Conference at the Aspen Music Festival, July 30, 1970. Included was a performance of *Eight Songs for a Mad King*, with soloist Julius Eastman. The reviewer says that as this described episodes from the life of George III's "travail," the music "almost excruciatingly depicts his madness."

B214. Eaves, Will. "Peter Maxwell Davies: *The Lighthouse*." *Times Literary Supplement* (July 8, 1994) p. 17.

Review of a performance of *The Lighthouse* by Music Theatre Wales produced by Michael McCarthy at the Playhouse, Oxford. Performers were Philip Creasy, Henry Herford, and Kelvin Thomas. The reviewer notes: "Maxwell Davies is a wonderful mimic...eerie, funny, deranged in turn...There isn't an easy phrase in the whole opera."

B215. Emmerson, Simon. "Carter and Davies." *Music and Musicians* v. 26 (Aug., 1978) pp. 32–33.
Includes a review of a concert at the Royal Festival Hall, Feb. 2, 1978 by the Philharmonia Orchestra conducted by Simon Rattle, which featured the premiere of *Symphony No. 1*. Reviewer subsequently heard a second performance of the work broadcast over BBC 3; the review is based on both hearings. He finds problems with "the unrealistic level of the tuned percussion section" but says that "the memory of the powerful brass and string writing were reinforced, also the feeling of the energetic momentum of the work will assure it many hearings."

B216. Emmerson, Simon. "Modern Prom." *Music and Musicians* v. 26 (Dec., 1977) p. 42.
Includes a review of a performance of *St. Thomas Wake* at a Promenade Concert, Aug. 9, 1977. Includes mention of the *Pavan* by John Bull on which the work is based and says it "is strangely reminiscent of Ives in places."

B217. Evan, Peter A. "Chamber Music: String Quartet." *Music and Letters* v. 44 no. 2 (1963) pp. 191–192.
Review of *String Quartet* upon publication of the score by Schott in 1962. Includes a brief, descriptive analysis of the work, section by section, and characterizes it as another example of the composer's "preoccupation with 'cantus firmus' techniques."

B218. Everett-Green, Robert. "Davies, Scottish Orchestra Serve Up Unusual Cantata, Likeable Lollipop." *Globe and Mail* (Nov. 9, 1988).

B219. Fairman, Richard. "*The Lighthouse*/Bracknell." *Financial Times* (June 24, 1986).
Review of a performance of *The Lighthouse* directed by George Badacsonyi at the Wilde Theatre, Bracknell, June 21, 1986, with principals Jonathan Robarts, Neill Archer and Jeremy White. Reviewer notes: "The opera's strength comes from the way it fills its chosen ground with fertile ideas." He sees the demands of the score to be pushing both the singers and instrumentalists beyond their normal limits and comments on how effective the music is in illustrating the libretto.

B220. Fairman, Richard. "Maxwell Davies/Festival Hall." *Financial Times* (April 4, 1990).
Review of a concert by the Royal Philharmonic Orchestra conducted by Jan Latham-Koenig at the Royal Festival Hall, April 2, 1990. Included on the program was a performance of *Symphony No. 2*, which the reviewer says "is by no means unapproachable, washed along by a strong, atmospheric undercurrent...in a striking view of waves at play." A brief discussion of the work follows, wherein the reviewer finds similarity between the composer's work and Tippett's *Symphony No. 4*.

B221. Fallows, David. "York, Chester, Buxton." *Musical Times* v. 120 (Sept. 1979) pp. 757-759.
Briefly mentions a performance of *The Two Fiddlers* during the 1979 Buxton Festival by a local group conducted by Brian Hughes.

B222. Fanning, David. "Manchester." *Musical Times* v. 126 (June, 1985) p. 362.
Article about *Symphony No. 3* after its premiere by the BBC Philharmonic Orchestra conducted by Edward Downes at the Free Trade Hall, Manchester, Feb. 19, 1985. Compares and contrasts the work to the two earlier *Symphonies*, remaking that it "apparently contains analogies to Renaissance church architecture." The reviewer thinks such a concept is "fragile" and wonders if the composer "has not overestimated the musical potentialities of his magic-square technique."

B223. Feder, Susan. "New York." *Musical Times* v. 124 (July, 1983) p. 444.
Includes a review of performances by the Fires of London in the Spring of 1983 in New York at which *Le Jongleur de Notre Dame* and *Image, Reflections, Shadow* received their American premieres. The latter is described as "mesmerizing; there was a wonderful sense of rightness of proportion among its three movements."

B224. Feggetter, Graeme. "Fringe Performances: *The Lighthouse*." *Opera* v. 35 (April 1984) p. 450.
Review of a performance of *The Lighthouse* by members of the Cambridge University Opera Society at St. Edwards Passage Playroom, Jan. 25, 1984. The review notes: "The composer brilliantly captures the rising anger and fears of the three lighthouse-men both musically and dramatically."

B225. Finch, Hilary. "Concert: Teasing Salute." *Times* (Oct. 8, 1983).
Review of the premiere of *Sinfonietta Accademica* by the Scottish Chamber Orchestra conducted by Edward Harper, at Reid Hall, Edinburgh University, Oct. 6, 1983. About the work the reviewer notes, "the first movement's recapitulation is disguised as development; the second movement develops the first; and the finale is a modified recapitulation."

B226. Finch, Hilary. "Edinburgh Fringe: *The Lighthouse*." *Times* (Sept. 8, 1983).
Review of a performance of *The Lighthouse* by members of the Cambridge University Opera Society in Edinburgh at the Canongate Lodge, early September, 1983. Soloists were Charles Gibbs, John Davies and Simon Berridge. The band was conducted by Christopher Roberts.

B227. Finn, Robert. "New Symphony Grabs Hold of Your Emotions." *Cleveland Plain Dealer* (Nov. 25, 1989)
Review of a concert by the Cleveland Orchestra conducted by the composer at Severance Hall, Nov. 24, 1989, including the American premiere of *Symphony No. 3*, which the reviewer found "wonderfully imaginative" and "thick, the rhythmic layout extremely complex, the harmony often highly dissonant...but also full of arresting and beautiful things." Also performed was *An Orkney Wedding, with Sunrise*. A pre-concert lobby performance of Davies's music for schoolchildren was also presented.

B228. Fisk, Josiah. "Davies' 'Orkney' Suite Debuts." *Boston Herald* (May 11, 1985) p. 17.
Review of the premiere of *An Orkney Wedding, With Sunrise* by the Boston Pops conducted by John Williams, May 10, 1985 at Symphony Hall, Boston. Describes the music as "modal...heavily-ornamented folkdance melodies..." and says, "The orchestra gives the strings and percussion some Hollywood-type moments."

B229. Fleming, Michael. "Conducting His Own Music, Davies Speaks From the Heart." *Saint Paul Pioneer Press* (May 4, 1991) p. 6B.
Review of a concert by the St. Paul Chamber Orchestra conducted by the composer at the Ordway, May 31, 1991, which included the U.S. premiere of *Sinfonietta Accademica*. The reviewer writes: "It is a work both ingeniously made and full of the sound of wind and sea." Also performed was *Fantasia on a Ground and Two Pavanes*

of Henry Purcell, which the reviewer says includes "some bright colors daubed on Purcell and some harmonic smudging" and "went down easily and brought a smile."

B230. Fleming, Shirley. "Boston Beaut." *New York Post* (Mar. 5, 1981).
Review of a performance of *Symphony No. 2* by the Boston Symphony Orchestra conducted by Seiji Ozawa at Carnegie Hall, Mar. 4, 1981. Includes a vivid, colorful description of the work as "a finespun, poetically luminous, sensuously caressing score."

B231. Fleming, Shirley. "Opera Everywhere: Boston." *HiFi/Musical America* v. 35 (July, 1986) pp. 22–23.
Review of the American premiere of *Taverner* by the Opera Company of Boston, Mar. 9, 1986. The reviewer finds the music "spiky, pressured, enormously intense but there is delineation of character in the vocal parts" and concludes that although it is not an opera everyone will appreciate, one is sure to find it unforgettable.

B232. Fletcher, Shane. "Jeannetta Cochrane Theatre: *The Two Fiddlers*." *Music and Musicians* v. 27 (Mar. 1979) pp. 47–48.
Review of the London premiere of *The Two Fiddlers* at the Jeannetta Cochrane Theatre, Dec. 27, 1978–Jan. 6, 1979, by students from the Pimlico School. The reviewer remarks: "The musical style of the piece is wide-ranging—the simple folk melodies contrast with a piano-accompanied recitative style." Includes high praise for the composer's many compositions for children.

B233. Fletcher, Shane. "*The Two Fiddlers*." *Music and Musicians* v. 27 (Dec. 1978) p. 19.
Article about *The Two Fiddlers* written just prior to the work's London premiere on Dec. 27, 1978 at the Jeannetta Cochrane Theatre. Performers were students at the Pimlico School. The reviewer notes, "the greatest promise for *The Two Fiddlers* lies in the fact that words and music are good fun."

B234. Floy, Jerry. "Washington, D. C." *Opera News* v. 47 (July 1982) p. 32.
Includes a brief review of the U. S. premiere of *Cinderella* at the Sheridan School, Washington, D. C., April 1982. Remarks: "the one-and-a-half-hour score...is lyrical and fun for both audience...and cast."

B235. Forbes, Elizabeth. "London: the Royal Opera." *Opera Canada* v. 24 no. 4 (1983) p. 37.

Includes a brief review of the revival of *Taverner* at the Royal Opera, Covent Garden, June 29, 1983. When comparing and contrasting this with the 1972 performance the reviewer notes, "Maxwell Davies's score...yielded even more pleasure; the subject, the conversion of the 16th-century composer from Catholicism to Protestantism has become more relevant."

B236. Ford, Christopher. "Maxwell Davies and the Boston Birthday Symphony." *Times* (Jan. 29, 1980).

Article which focuses on the then recently-commissioned *Symphony No. 2* for the Boston Symphony Orchestra as part of their centenary celebration in 1981. Included biographical material and mentions a number of major works including: *Ricercar and Doubles on 'To Many a Well,' Leopardi Fragments, Revelation and Fall, Second Fantasia on John Taverner's 'In Nomine,' Symphony No. 1, Worldes Blis, St. Thomas Wake, Cinderella, Taverner, The Lighthouse,* and *Resurrection.*

B237. Fowler, John. "Green and Pleasant." *Glasgow Herald* (June 22, 1988) p. 5.

Article about several concerts presented at the 1988 St. Magnus Festival, June, 1988. Included is a review of a performance of *Black Pentecost* on June 20, 1988, of which the reviewer says, "the ominous air of doomsday is pervasive; it is wonderfully captured by the menace of the music." Also reviewed is *The Two Fiddlers* performed by pupils from the Hutcheson's Grammar School, Glasgow; the reviewer found this "a charming piece which does not condescend to young performers."

B238. Fromm, Paul. "World Premieres." *Symphony Magazine* v.32 no. 3 (Oct./Nov., 1981) p. 153.

Mentions the premiere of *Symphony No. 2* by the Boston Symphony Orchestra conducted by Seiji Ozawa on Feb. 26, 1981. Remarks about the success of the work when played on tour by the Boston Symphony, urges Ozawa to integrate the work into the permanent repertoire of the Orchestra.

B239. Furie, Kenneth.   *"The Martyrdom of St. Magnus."*   *Hi-fi/Musical America* v. 28 (Dec. 1978) pp. MA 26–27.
Review of the American premiere of *The Martyrdom of St. Magnus* at the Aspen Music Festival, July 29, 1978. The performance was conducted by Richard Dufallo. The review includes a synopsis of the drama. About the work the reviewer remarks: "Much of Davies's writing for the...instrumental ensemble exhibits his customary flair...the most effective is that linking the opera's nine scenes."

B240. Gill, Dominic. "Barenboim, Pruslin." *Musical Times* v. 111 (Mar. 1970) pp. 294–295.
Review of a recital by pianist Stephen Pruslin at the Purcell Room, on Jan. 3, 1970, which included the premieres of *Sub Tuam Protectionem* ("slight, but neatly formed") and *Cauda Pavonis*.

B241. Gill, Dominic. "Davies's Symphony." *Financial Times* (July 28, 1978).
Review of a Promenade Concert by the Philharmonia Orchestra conducted by Simon Rattle at the Royal Albert Hall, July 26, 1978. Included on the program was a performance of *Symphony No. 1*. When describing the music the reviewer writes, "it is indeed a busy score; full of urgent conversation, the swell and surge of many voices supporting and contrasting even the broadest gesture."

B242. Gill, Dominic. "Davies's 2nd Symphony." *Financial Times* (Feb. 9, 1982).
Review of a performance of *Symphony No. 2* by the BBC Northern Symphony Orchestra conducted by Edward Downes at the Free Trade Hall, Manchester, Feb. 7, 1982. The reviewer says: "The Symphony swells as ardently as any romantic symphony, with a consciousness of natural forces." Includes a brief descriptive analysis of each movement of the work.

B243. Gill, Dominic. "Music in Orkney." *Financial Times* (June 18, 1978)
Article about the 1978 St. Magnus Festival which highlights the premiere of *The Two Fiddlers* on June 17, 1978 by pupils from the Kirkwall Grammar School conducted by Norman Mitchell at the Arts Theatre, Kirkwall. The reviewer notes the work, although simple in design, "neither patronises nor writes down to its performers" and concludes simply, "The piece is fun."

B244. Gill, Dominic. "Stephen Pruslin." *Musical Times* v. 112 (Mar. 1971) pp. 261–262.

Review of a recital by pianist Stephen Pruslin at the Purcell Room, Jan. 19, 1971, which included the premiere of the short work, *Ut Re Mi*. Describes the music as a "tiny, three-part essay with an oddly serial flavour."

B245. Gill, Dominic. "*Vesalii Icones.*" *Musical Times* v. 111 (Feb. 1970) p. 185.

Review of the premiere of *Vesalii Icones* by the Pierrot Players at the Elizabeth Hall Dec. 9, 1969. Soloists were William Louther, dancer and cellist Jennifer Ward Clarke. The music is described as "a fascinating work, richly inventive."

B246. Gill, Dominic. "Yamash'ta." *Musical Times* v. 112 (May 1971) pp. 464–465.

Review of a concert by percussionist Stomu Yamash'ta at the Elizabeth Hall, Mar. 12, 1971. The program included the premiere of *Turris Campanarum Sonantium*, characterized as "a nice little piece" which exhibits "Vesalii-ish visual undertones."

B247. Gillard, David. "A Soaring Symphony." *Radio Times* (Sept. 10, 1989). Article focusing on *Symphony No. 4* written just prior to the work's premiere by the Scottish Symphony Orchestra, Sept. 10, 1989.

B248. Goodman, Peter. "*The Lighthouse*, Operatic Ghost Story." *Newsday* (Dec. 2, 1985).

Review of a performance of *The Lighthouse* with soloists Neil Mackie, Andrew Gallacher, and Christopher Keyte and the Fires of London conducted by the composer at Alice Tully Hall, Nov. 30, 1985. About the score the reviewer remarks: "The musical illustration...is in keeping with the ghost story....full of bangs, thuds, glissandos, wails, chirps, peeps, and ominous treads."

B249. Goodwin, Noel. "Britain's Autumn Bring Many Visitors." *Musical Courier* v. 162 (Dec., 1960) p. 30.

Includes a review of a concert by the Royal Liverpool Philharmonic Orchestra under the direction of John Carewe in London, Autumn, 1960. *Prolation* was performed, which the reviewer says is noted for its "imagination and integrity."

B250. Goodwin, Noel. "The Cheltenham Festival." *Musical Times* v. 101 (Sept., 1960) pp. 572–573.
Article on highlights of the 16th Cheltenham Festival, July 13–15, 1960. One concert included a performance of *Ricercar and Doubles on 'To Many a Well'* by the New Music Ensemble conducted by John Carewe on July 11. The reviewer found this "a strikingly original serial transformation of a medieval English carol...[which] resulted in a pattern of transfixed sounds notable for its grace of form...and skill in instrumental colour."

B251. Goodwin, Noel. "An English Original." *Music and Musicians* v. 10 (Jan. 1962) p. 37.
Review of the premiere of *Sinfonia* by the English Chamber Orchestra conducted by Sir Colin Davis at the Royal Festival Hall, May 9, 1962. The reviewer says this is "a work of real distinction that will certainly be heard with increasing pleasure in the future." Gives a brief analysis of the music.

B252. Goodwin, Noel. "English Summer Festivals." *Musical Courier* v. 160 (Oct., 1959) p. 16.
Includes a description of the 1959 Cheltenham Festival, mentioning the premiere of *St. Michael Sonata* for 17 wind instruments on July 13, 1959. Describes the work as "the musical equivalent of a piece of arresting modern sculpture, imbued with a spirit of medieval beauty."

B253. Goodwin, Noel. "Light and Dark Mixture." *Life and Times* (Oct. 8, 1992) p. 2.
Review of a concert by the Royal Philharmonic Orchestra conducted by the composer, his debut as associate conductor and composer-in-residence for that orchestra. Included on the program was the premiere of *Caroline Mathilde: Concert Suite II* at the Festival Hall, Oct. 5, 1992. Notes the music "came across as a darkly sombre yet graphic tone-poem." The program also included a performance of *An Orkney Wedding, With Sunrise*, a work described as "boisterously inebriate sounding."

B254. Goodwin, Noel. "London." *Music Magazine* v. 164 (July, 1962) p. 32.
Includes a review of a concert on May 9, 1962 by the English Chamber Orchestra conducted by Colin Davis. The premiere of *Sinfonia* was included on that program. About the composition the

reviewer says, "the work achieves contrast of character and a sense of inward calm as well as strength and purpose."

B255. Goodwin, Noel. "London: City Festivals and Cheltenham." *Music Magazine* v. 164 (Sept., 1962) p. 36.
Includes a brief overview of the first City of London Festival in July, 1962, mentioning the premiere of *Leopardi Fragments* with the remark that this piece is impressive because of its "imaginative skill in a modern idiom."

B256. Goodwin, Noel. "Orkney Islands." *Opera News* v. 42 (Sept., 1977) pp. 60, 62.
Review of the premiere of *The Martyrdom of St. Magnus* at the first St. Magnus Festival in the St. Magnus Cathedral, June 18, 1977. Includes a synopsis of the drama. About the music the reviewer remarks: "The vocal lines are exceptionally well written."

B257. Goodwin, Noel. "Orkney: Festival of St. Magnus." *Music and Musicians* v. 25 (Aug. 1977) pp. 48–49.
Article about the first St. Magnus Festival held in mid-June, 1977. Includes a review of the premiere of *The Martyrdom of St. Magnus* by members of the Fires of London conducted by the composer at the St. Magnus Cathedral, June 18, 1977. Very well-written review, including a synopsis of the drama. The reviewer says, "the work's musical character reverts to Davies's less harsh style" and further: "The vocal roles...are exceptionally well written." Also includes a review of a performance of *Dark Angels* by singer Mary Thomas and guitarist Timothy Walker.

B258. Goodwin, Noel. "Pierrot Players." *Musical Times* v. 108 (July, 1967) p. 626.
Review of a concert, the first by the Pierrot Players, on May 30, 1967 at the Elizabeth Hall. The program included the premiere of *Antechrist* conducted by the composer, which the reviewer calls "an attractive suite of instrumental movements in which a medieval dance theme is the subject for free commentary in a modern idiom."

B259. Gray, Yvonne. "Festival." *Musical Opinion* v. 113 (June, 1990) pp. 183, 209–210.
Article about 'Maxfest,' the two-week event on the South Bank during Mar. 27-Apr. 10, 1990 consisting of performances of music by the composer as well as selections chosen by him of other compo-

sers' works. Gray focuses on the three symphonies, which were performed during the festival by the Royal Philharmonic Orchestra. The reviewer acknowledges the composer's use of "conventional musical forms," but says: "However, every conventional, musical structure is transformed by his [Davies'] inimitable use of rhythm and tonality." The author also notes: "Davies is a composer who drinks his surroundings and turns them into music."

B260. Grayson, Barrie. "The Fires of London." *Birmingham Post* (July 8, 1986).
Review of a concert by the Fires of London with the Lichfield Cathedral Choir, Choristers of the Lichfield Cathedral and the Nether Stowe School Wind Ensemble conducted by Günther Bauer-Schenk at Lichfield Cathedral, July 7, 1986. Included on the program was a performance of *Le Jongleur de Notre Dame* featuring Jonny James, juggler and Christopher Keyte, baritone. Also included was *Seven Songs Home*, by the boy choristers of the Cathedral (described as "a miniature masterpiece").

B261. Greenfield, Edward. "BBC/SO." *Guardian* (July 24, 1981).
Review of the London premiere of *Symphony No. 2* by the BBC Symphony Orchestra conducted by Gennadi Rozhdestvensky at the Royal Albert Hall, July 23, 1981. About the music the reviewer remarks: "Davies has used wave-form as a model for various aspects of his musical patterning. One hears direct evocation of the sea."

B262. Greenfield, Edward. "Boldness be My Friend." *Guardian* (Jan. 9, 1987).
Includes a review of a recording of *Sinfonia Concertante* and *Sinfonia* (Unicorn-Kanchana DKP 9058) by the Scottish Chamber Orchestra conducted by the composer.

B263. Greenfield, Edward. "Compositores Britanecos de 'Avant Gard' Peter Maxwell Davies." *Buenos Aires Musical* v. 25 no. 412 (1970) p. 6.
Article on several of the composer's works described as 'avant garde.' Mentions the premiere of *Eight Songs for a Mad King* as well as *O Magnum Mysterium*, *Second Fantasia on John Taverner's 'In Nomine,'* *Vesalii Icones*, and *Taverner*.

B264. Greenfield, Edward. "Just Call Me Max." *Guardian* (Mar. 20, 1990) p. 38.

Biographical article written just a week before the beginning of 'Maxfest,' the South Bank tribute to the composer and his music held in late March and early April, 1990. This article features an interview with the composer focusing on his career to date in light of his then-recent knighthood

B265. Greenfield, Edward. "London Sinfonietta." *Guardian* (Nov. 14, 1985).

Review of a concert by the London Sinfonietta and pupils from the ILEA Centre for Young Musicians conducted by Elgar Howarth, at the Queen Elizabeth Hall, Nov. 12, 1985. Featured on the program was the premiere of *First Ferry to Hoy*, a work the reviewer thought "extraordinary." Includes a descriptive analysis of the work.

B266. Greenfield, Edward. "Max Factor." *Guardian* (Jan. 22, 1987) p. 22.

Review of the farewell concert of the Fires of London conducted by the composer at the Queen Elizabeth Hall, Jan. 20, 1987. Included on the program was the premiere of *Winterfold* featuring soloist Mary Thomas. The work is described as "a haunting new setting of [Davies's] favorite Orkney poet, George Mackay Brown." There was also a performance of *Eight Songs for a Mad King* (which the reviewer says "still stands out...as the most successful examples of music-theatre"), *Fantasia on a Ground and Two Pavans of Henry Purcell*, and *Farewell—a Fancye* ("an ear-tickling rendering").

B267. Greenfield, Edward. "Maxwell Davies." *Guardian* (Sept. 23, 1982).

Includes a review of a concert by the Fires of London at the Queen Elizabeth Hall in September, 1982. Featured on the program was a performance of *Image, Reflection, Shadow* with Gregory Knowles, cimbalon. About the music the reviewer remarks it reveals Davies's talent "to translate evocation into sharp ideas and argument, at times...almost neo-classical."

B268. Greenfield, Edward. "Peter Maxwell Davies." *Hi Fi/Musical America* (Feb., 1981) pp. 1, 4–5.

Article written just prior to the premiere of *Symphony No. 2*. Includes a short, current biography of the composer, focusing on his life in Orkney. Mentions the following works: *The Martyrdom of St. Magnus, Cinderella, Shakespeare Music, A Mirror of Whitening Light, O Magnum Mysterium*, and *Taverner*. Includes a cover portrait.

B269. Greenfield, Edward. "Peter Maxwell Davies: A Major New Work." *HiFi/Music America* 28 (June, 1978) pp. MA 38–39.

Review of a concert which included the premiere of *Symphony No. 1* by the Philharmonia Orchestra conducted by Simon Rattle at the Royal Festival Hall, Feb. 2, 1978. Remarks the work is "a massive four-movement symphony...it has clearly taken the composer into a new stage of his development." Notes the composer "has written with masterful control of orchestral coloring."

B270. Greenfield, Edward. "Sinopoli/Philharmonia." *Guardian* (Oct. 11, 1988).

Review of a concert by the Philharmonia Orchestra conducted by Giuseppe Sinopoli at the Royal Festival Hall, early October, 1988. Included on the program was a performance of *Concerto for Trumpet and Orchestra* featuring John Wallace, trumpet. Giving a brief description of the music, the reviewer says that it is "very much in the line of [Davies's] Orkney inspirations, works which in their rugged elemental references...often hark back to Sibelius." He then compares its structure to that of Sibelius's *Symphony No. 7*.

B271. Greenless, Leslie. "Out of London: Glasgow." *Music and Musicians* v. 10 (July, 1962) p. 49.

Brief article including a review of *St. Michael Sonata* (named in the review *Sonata for 17 Wind Instruments*) performed by members of the Scottish National Orchestra at a Musica Viva concert, conducted by Alexander Gibson, in Glasgow. The reviewer found it "technically clever."

B272. Grier, Christopher. "Fond Fiery Farewell." *Standard* (Jan. 21, 1987) p. 26.

Review of the farewell concert by the Fires of London at the Queen Elizabeth Hall, Jan. 20, 1987. Included on the program was the premiere of *Winterfold* featuring Mary Thomas, mezzo-soprano. The reviewer describes this as "deeply thoughtful" but thought that the performance of *Eight Songs for a Mad King* which followed on the program was "the plum...of the entire concert."

B273. Grier, Christopher. "The Hero's Not For Burning." *Standard* (June 30, 1983).

Review of *Taverner* at Covent Garden, June, 1983. As in the original, this revival was conducted by Edward Downes. The review includes a very short synopsis of the work. The reviewer says that

Taverner belongs to "Maxwell Davies's expressionist, 'shocking' period" and that "the story retains its potency and so does its very demanding score."

B274. Grier, Christopher. "Last Night's Opera." *Standard* (May 20, 1980) p. 17.
Review of a concert by the Fires of London conducted by the composer at the Queen Elizabeth Hall, May 19, 1980. Included on the program was a performance of *Vesalii Icones* featuring William Louther, dancer, and cellist Alexander Baillie. About the work the reviewer notes it "hovers successfully on the border line between the picturesque and the prophetic."

B275. Grier, Christopher. "London Listeners Shore the Music of Sir Max." *Scotsman* (April 12, 1990).
Includes a review of a performance of *Symphony No. 3* by the Royal Philharmonic Orchestra conducted by Edward Downes as part of 'Maxfest' at the Royal Festival Hall, April 10, 1990. The reviewer says this work is "more concerned with transformation, juxtaposition, fluxuations of intensity and pace than with traditional thematic manoeuvres."

B276. Grier, Christopher. "Marvellous Sibelius." *Evening Standard* (Oct. 6, 1992) p. 48.
Review of a concert by the Royal Philharmonic Orchestra conducted by the composer at the Royal Festival Hall, Oct. 5, 1992. Included on the program was the premiere of *Caroline Mathilde: Concert Suite II*, which is described as "riveting stuff in the great tradition of 20th century ballet scores." There was also a performance of *An Orkney Wedding, With Sunrise*, which the reviewer calls "a cleverly scored popular and populist work."

B277. Grier, Christopher. "Resounding Brass." *Scotsman* (Aug. 19, 1985).
Review of a concert at the Edinburgh Festival at Usher Hall, Aug. 18, 1985. Included on the program was the premiere of *The Peat Cutters* by the Scottish National Orchestra Junior Choir and Youth Choruses accompanied by the National Youth Brass Band of Scotland conducted by Geoffrey Brand. About the work the reviewer remarks: "What will strike listeners...is the totally uncompromising nature of the harmonies and fragmented rhythmic notation." Compliments the composer on offering such a challenging but not insurmountable piece to young performers.

B278. Grier, Christopher. "Stirred by the Best of Scottish." *Evening Standard* (Feb. 18, 1993).
Review of a concert by the Scottish Chamber Orchestra conducted by the composer at the Queen Elizabeth Hall, London, Feb. 16, 1993. Included on the program was a performance of the *Strathclyde Concerto No. 7 for Double Bass and Orchestra* featuring soloist Duncan McTier. The music is described as: "A darkling score of acute tonal sensibilities...its three movements fell gracefully and gratefully on the ear." Also performed was *Caroline Mathilde: Concert Suite From Act I of the Ballet*.

B279. Grier, Christopher. "A Trumpet Call From the Orkneys." *Evening Standard* (Oct. 10, 1988).
Review of a concert by the Philharmonia Orchestra at the Royal Festival Hall, Oct. 9, 1988, which included the British premiere of *Concerto for Trumpet and Orchestra* with soloist John Wallace. About the work the reviewer notes it "sounds extremely impressive, bolder in its colours, statements and lineaments than...the composer's recent oboe concerto."

B280. Grier, Christopher. "Visitors in Diversity." *Evening Standard* (Sept. 14, 1988).
Review of a concert by the Scottish Chamber Orchestra conducted by the composer at the Royal Albert Hall, Sept. 13, 1988. Included on the program was the first London performance of *Strathclyde Concerto No. 1 for Oboe and Orchestra*, with oboist Robin Miller. The music is described as: "Mostly quiet, more or less tonal, metrically diverse and faintly enigmatic."

B281. Griffin, Glenn. "Colorado." *Opera News* v. 43 (Nov. 1978) pp. 75–77.
Includes a review of the U.S. premiere of *The Martyrdom of St. Magnus* in the Aspen Amphitheater as part of the 1978 Aspen Music Festival, July 29, 1978. Very brief.

B282. Griffiths, Paul. "BBC Phil/Downes." *Times* (Feb. 20, 1985).
Review of a concert by the BBC Philharmonic Orchestra conducted by Edward Downes at the Free Trade Hall, Manchester, Feb. 19, 1985. Included on the program was the premiere of *Symphony No. 3*, of which the reviewer says, "Davies's music is now more homogenous that he can make the small effects powerfully telling."

B283. Griffiths, Paul. "Body Language." *Times* (May 20, 1987).
Review of a performance of *The Martyrdom of St. Magnus* by Opera
Factory London Sinfonietta at the Donmar Warehouse: "This is often
powerful, often subtle."

B284. Griffiths, Paul. "Characteristically Brisk Beethoven." *Times* (June 24,
1986).
Review of a concert by the Royal Philharmonic Orchestra conducted
by the composer at the Phoenix Cinema, Kirkwall, June 22, 1986
during the St. Magnus Festival. Included on the program was the
premiere of *Jimmack the Postie*. The reviewer remarks about the
piece that it is "quite straight in its rumbustiousness and fierce
changeability of colour."

B285. Griffiths, Paul. "Dangerous Game." *Times* (Jan. 20, 1990).
Review of the premiere of *Strathclyde Concerto No. 3 for Horn,
Trumpet and Orchestra* with soloists Robert Cook, horn and Peter
Franks, trumpet and the Scottish Chamber Orchestra conducted by
the composer, at City Hall, Glasgow, Jan. 19, 1990. The review
notes, "this is music of clear colours and fresh devices...an astonishing orchestral whirlwind."

B286. Griffiths, Paul. "Fires of London." *Times* (Jan. 21, 1987).
Review of the final concert by the Fires of London at the Queen
Elizabeth Hall, Jan. 20, 1987. Included on the program was the
premiere of *Winterfold* with soloist Mary Thomas. The reviewer
describes this as "giving a minor intimation of the somberness of *Into
the Labyrinth*." Also included on the concert were performances of
Fantasia on a Ground and Two Pavans of Henry Purcell and *Eight
Songs for a Mad King*.

B287. Griffiths, Paul. "Fires of London." *Times* (Sept. 22, 1983).
Review of a concert by the Fires of London conducted by Nicholas
Cleobury at the Queen Elizabeth Hall, Sept. 21, 1983. Included on
the program was a performance of *Le Jongleur de Notre Dame*,
which the reviewer finds "by far the most genial of Maxwell
Davies's music theatre pieces."

B288. Griffiths, Paul. "From Out of Tune with Times." *Times* (July 24,
1981).
Review of the British premiere of *Symphony No. 2* by the BBC
Symphony Orchestra conducted by Gennadi Rozhdestvensky at the

Royal Albert Hall, July 23, 1981. Notes when comparing the work to *Symphony No. 1*, "The new work makes a bold step forward in formal definition." Includes high praise for the new symphony.

B289. Griffiths, Paul. "Full Revelation Still Awaited." *Times* (Nov. 27, 1984).

Includes reviews of: *Taverner*, performed by members of the Stockholm Opera at the Royal Opera House, Stockholm, Nov. 24 and 26, 1984, conducted by Gary Berkson; and *The Lighthouse*, performed by members of the Stockholm Opera at the Rotunda, Nov. 24 and 26, 1984, with Lars Magnusson, Magnus Linden and Marti Wallen, conducted by Kjell Ingebretsen.

B290. Griffiths, Paul. "The Heat is On: Peter Maxwell Davies Creates Unique Theatre Pieces for the Fires of London." *Opera News* v. 50 (Nov. 1985) pp. 14, 16–17.

Article about the composer and the Fires of London written prior to their 1985–86 North American tour. Mentions *Eight Songs for a Mad King*, *Miss Donnithorne's Maggot*, *The Lighthouse*, *The No. 11 Bus* and other works.

B291. Griffiths, Paul. "King's Singers." *Times* (June 25, 1986).

Review of a concert by the King's Singers at the 1986 St. Magnus Festival at the East Church, Kirkwall, June 23, 1986. The program included the premiere of *House of Winter*. The reviewer compares it to *Solstice of Light* and *Westerlings*, noting: "The work speaks of the deep community of interest between poet and composer."

B292. Griffiths, Paul. "Lyrical Vein." *Times* (June 23, 1987).

Article about the 1987 St. Magnus Festival. Included is a review of a performance of *The Martyrdom of St. Magnus*. About the work the reviewer remarks: "The best moments in the score are the two big solos for Magnus." There is also a very brief review of the premiere of *Sonata for Guitar* by soloist Timothy Walker ("a pair of dapper, witty two-part Scarlattian allegros around the dark shadow of a lute fantasia").

B293. Griffiths, Paul. "Max: Purcell Room." *Times* (April 11, 1990).

Review of a concert by some members of the then recently disbanded Fires of London in the Purcell Room, early April, 1990. Included on the program were performances of *Ave Maris Stella*, *Image, Reflection, Shadow*, and *Leopardi Fragments*. The reviewer says:

"the performances were so sharply alive and intense that the works seemed absolutely new and not old favorites at all."

B294. Griffiths, Paul. "Maxwell Davies." *Musical Times* v. 114 (Dec. 1973) pp. 1256–1257.
Review of a concert at the Queen Elizabeth Hall, called A Musical Tribute to Northern Britain, Oct. 3, 1973. The performance was by the Fires of London conducted by the composer, and included works either composed or arranged by him: *Si Quis Diliget Me, Renaissance Scottish Dances, From Stone to Thorn, Stone Litany*, and *Hymn to St. Magnus*.

B295. Griffiths, Paul. "Maxwell Davies." *Times* (June 22, 1987).
Includes a review of a performance of *The Martyrdom of St. Magnus* during the 11th St. Magnus Festival by the Fires of London, conducted by Günther Bauer-Schenk. About the music the reviewer notes, "the best moments in the score are the two big solos for Magnus which...look forward to the meditative scena *Into the Labyrinth*."

B296. Griffiths, Paul. "Maxwell Davies Again Delights the Ear." *Times* (Sept. 23, 1982).
Review of a concert by the Fires of London at the Queen Elizabeth Hall, Sept. 21, 1982. Included in the program was the first London performance of *Image, Reflection, Shadow*. About the work the reviewer notes, "this is music of flickering brilliance and elan, taking life from the sound of the cimbalon." Includes a descriptive analysis of the work.

B297. Griffiths, Paul. "Maxwell Davies Concert." *Times* (April 3, 1990).
Review of a concert by the Royal Philharmonic Orchestra conducted by Jan Latham-Koenig at the Royal Festival Hall, April 2, 1990. Included on the program was a performance of *Symphony No. 2*. The reviewer finds this *Symphony* "so much more outward a piece than his First." He notes the exuberance and playfulness of the work and remarks that it is "clearly written for American-style virtuosity." Includes a brief descriptive analysis of the music.

B298. Griffiths, Paul. "A Maxwell Davies School Classic." *Times* (June 19, 1978).
Includes a review of the premiere of *The Two Fiddlers* by pupils from the Kirkwall Grammar School conducted by Norma Mitchell at

the Kirkwall Arts Theatre, June 16, 1987. The reviewer notes the composer has "produced something which can appeal strongly to children's imaginations without being patronizing or embarrassing." Includes a synopsis of the work.

B299. Griffiths, Paul. "Music in London." *Musical Times* v. 113 (Dec. 1972) p. 1204.
Review of a performance of *Taverner* by the Royal Opera, Covent Garden, Oct. 4, 1972. Comparing the performance to the premiere in July of that year Griffiths remarks: "Further exposure to the music uncovers more of its highly organized structure, and suggests how much more will be unravelled as one's acquaintance with the work proceeds." He remarks on the conflict between the difficult "tortuous" music and the smooth, open sets.

B300. Griffiths, Paul. "Music in London." *Musical Times* v. 114 (May 1973) p. 503.
Review of a concert by the Fires of London at the Queen Elizabeth Hall, Mar. 17, 1973. Included a performance of *Blind Man's Buff*. The reviewer notes about the work: "The theme was the characteristic one of parody." The program also included the premiere of *Notre Dame des Fleurs* with Vanessa Redgrave, Mary Thomas and Grayston Burgess, and *Missa Super L'Homme Armé* with Vanessa Redgrave.

B301. Griffiths, Paul. "Music in London: Maxwell Davies." *Musical Times* v. 113 (Dec. 1972) p. 1213.
Review of a concert by the Fires of London at the Elizabeth Hall, Oct. 13, 1972. Three of Davies's works were included on the program. The *Hymn to St. Magnus* had its premiere with soprano Mary Thomas. There is a brief, descriptive analysis of the work, which mentions a similarity of instrumental effects between the new work and Davies's earlier *Blind Man's Buff*. The reviewer also notes the piece calls to mind the composer's *Worldes Blis*. The concert also included the premiere of the composer's arrangement of *Prelude and Fugue in C♯ Minor by J. S. Bach*.

B302. Griffiths, Paul. "Music in London: New Music." *Musical Times* v. 116 (Jan. 1975) p. 63.
Includes a review of a concert by the Fires of London conducted by the composer at the Queen Elizabeth Hall, 27 Nov. 1974, including

the first London performance of *Dark Angels*: "Davies sets the words starkly and simply."

B303.   Griffiths, Paul.   "Music Reviews: Davies Over 12 Years."   *Musical Times* v. 121 (Sept., 1980) p. 568.

Includes a review of *Four Instrumental Motets* when the four were published in a single score by Boosey and Hawkes. The reviewer notes, "all of them are coloured with the percussion sonorities that lighten most of Davies' recent scores." The review also discusses a series of earlier compositions. Of *Fantasia on a Ground and Two Pavans of Henry Purcell*, Griffiths says: "the Pavans are dressed in the exhilarating costume of 250 years later." He characterizes *Missa Super L'Homme Armé* as one of the composer's "most potent" and further remarks, "the work is filled with images of sacred and profane as sides of the same coin." Of the *Prelude and Fugue in C♯ Major by J. S. Bach* and its companion in C♯ minor, he says that the two "could be regarded as preparatory exercises for the chamber work of 1975, [*Ave Maris Stella*]." Finally, reviewing *Veni Sancte Spiritus—Veni Creator Spiritus*, he notes that "the original material and the modern, questioning response are kept separate."

B304.   Griffiths, Paul.   "New Music."   *Musical times* v. 113 (July 1972) p. 683.

Includes a review of a concert by the Fires of London conducted by the composer at the Purcell Room, May 17, 1972. Included on the program was the premiere of *Septet*, a reworked arrangement of the earlier *Sextet* (1958). The piece is described as being divided into two parts, the first "a dense and dark tangle of meandering lines." and the second "produces short, quick figures...brightened by the tone of the glockenspiel." Also reviews a concert by the BBC Symphony Orchestra conducted by Pierre Boulez at the Roundhouse, May 29, 1972 which included the premiere of *Blind Man's Buff* with soloists Josephine Barstow, Mary Thomas and Mark Furneaux. Remarks that the piece "impresses as a much richer work than *Eight Songs for a Mad King*." Further, the work "explores in a sequence of images such questions as: who am I? in what lies my individuality?"

B305.   Griffiths, Paul.   "New Music."   *Musical Times* v. 113 (July 1972) p. 683.

Includes a review of a concert by the Fires of London conducted by the composer at the Elizabeth Hall, May 6, 1972. Featured on the program was the premiere of *Veni Sancte—Veni Creator Spiritus*, which the reviewer found "another beautiful stream of shattered fragments."

B306. Griffiths, Paul. "New Music." *Musical Times* v. 115 (April, 1974) p. 323.
Includes a brief mention of a concert by the Fires of London conducted by the composer at the Elizabeth Hall, 20 Feb., 1974. Included on the program was a performance of *Tenebrae Super Gesualdo* and the premiere of his transcription of the anonymous Scottish motet, *All Sons of Adam*.

B307. Griffiths, Paul. "New Music." *Musical Times* v. 115 (June, 1974) pp. 496–497.
Includes a review of the first London performance of *Miss Donnithorne's Maggot* by Mary Thomas and the Fires of London at the Elizabeth Hall, April 23, 1974. When describing the score the reviewer remarks, "His instrumental music excellently suggests the dry and spidery dustiness of the world inside and outside of Miss Donnithorne's head." Also on the concert was a performance of *Eight Songs for a Mad King* by James Skoog and the Fires.

B308. Griffiths, Paul. "New Music." *Musical Times* v. 116 (May, 1975) p. 467.
Review of a concert by the BBC Symphony Orchestra conducted by Colin Davis, at the Festival Hall, Mar. 5, 1975. Remarks, "Its extended argument, its predominant slowness and its orchestration indicate connections with Mahler."

B309. Griffiths, Paul. "New Music." *Musical Times* v. 117 (Dec., 1976) pp. 1018–1019.
Review of a concert by the Young Musicians Symphony Orchestra conducted by James Blair, 16 Oct., 1976, at St. John's, Smith Square. Program included the premiere of the revised version of *Five Klee Pictures*. Remarks, "as it now stands the work is a short set of studies each a printed interpretation of a work by Klee."

B310. Griffiths, Paul. "New Music." *Musical Times* v. 118 (April, 1977) pp. 319–320.
Includes a review of a concert by the Fires of London at the Elizabeth Hall, Jan. 26, 1977. Mentions performances of three "Orkney" works: *Psalm 124*, *The Blind Fiddler* and *Ave Maris*

Stella. It is the last work which most impressed the reviewer: "unmistakably Orkney music...it is a strong and original composition much less frantic...than much of Davies' work of the late 1960's."

B311. Griffiths, Paul. "New Music." *Musical Times* v. 121 (July, 1980) pp. 453–454.
Includes a review of a performance of *Vesalii Icones* by the Fires of London, at the Elizabeth Hall, May 19, 1980, with Alexander Baillie, cello, and William Louther, dancer. When comparing the performance to an earlier one, reviewer notes that "one's attention is fixed much more on the virtually omnipresent solo cello line...the work has become more inwardly and intimately disturbing."

B312. Griffiths, Paul. "A Night at the Opera." *Opera News* v. 53 (Dec. 10, 1988) pp. 46–47.
Review of the premiere of *Resurrection* by the Darmstadt Staatsoper at the Stadtstheater, Darmstadt, Sept. 18, 1988. The article includes a synopsis of the work and a somewhat psychological analysis as well: "What worries this music is not the crushing effect of social regulations but the absence of strong order, the terrifying fact that anything can be thought or felt." Compares and contrasts the opera to other works of Davies, including *Eight Songs for Mad King*, *Vesalii Icones*, *Le Jongleur de Notre Dame*, and *The No. 11 Bus*.

B313. Griffiths, Paul. "Orkney." *Musical Times* v. 119 (Aug., 1978) p. 707.
Article on the premieres of *The Two Fiddlers* and *Le Jongleur de Notre Dame* in mid-June, 1978 at the St. Magnus Festival, Orkney. Of the *Two Fiddlers*, performed by pupils from the Kirkwall Grammar School on June 16, the reviewer remarks: "There is plenty of simple and charming music in the work...appealing to children's imaginations without being at all patronizing or embarrassing..." Of *Le Jongleur de Notre Dame*, premiered June 18, featuring Mark Furneaux, mime, with the Stromness Academy of Music Ensemble, the reviewer notes the work is a "successor to *Eight Songs for a Mad King* and *Vesalii Icones*." Describes the music as "robust as it is moving...a light-hearted show, with no more than a thread of strenuous cello music to hint at darker currents."

B314. Griffiths, Paul. "Out of the Labyrinth." *Times* (Sept. 5, 1984).
An interview with the composer on Sept. 5, 1984, when he was to conduct a Proms concert including a performance of *Into the Labyrinth*. In the article the reviewer mentions *Black Pentecost*,

Eight Songs for a Mad King, *Sinfonietta Accademica*, *Symphony No. 3*, *Sinfonia Concertante* and *Stone Litany*. Includes a photograph of the composer.

B315. Griffiths, Paul. "Overdue, Overblown, Over There." *Times* (Sept. 21, 1988).
Review of the premiere of *Resurrection* at the Darmstadt Festival by members of Stadtstheater Darmstadt, Sept. 18, 1988. About the piece the reviewer remarks, "its shrill anxiety is laughter in the dark, evincing a craving for the lost authority more than an anti-establishment revolt." Includes a synopsis of the work.

B316. Griffiths, Paul. "Precariously Cogent and Moving." *Times* (June 23, 1986).
Review of the premiere of *Concerto for Violin and Orchestra* featuring violinist Isaac Stern with the Royal Philharmonic Orchestra conducted by André Previn at St. Magnus Cathedral, Kirkwall, during the St. Magnus Festival, June 21, 1986. Includes a descriptive analysis of the work.

B317. Griffiths, Paul. "Promenade Concert." *Times* (June 23, 1984).
Review of a concert by the BBC Scottish Symphony Orchestra conducted by Jerzy Maksymiuk at the Royal Albert Hall, Aug. 22, 1984. Included on the program was a performance of *Sinfonietta Accademica*. The work is described as "indeed an academic exercise and a brilliant one." Includes a descriptive analysis of the work.

B318. Griffiths, Paul. "Recitals: Maxwell Davies." *Musical Times* v. 113 (Feb., 1972) p. 171.
Review of a concert by the Fires of London conducted by the composer at the Elizabeth Hall, Dec. 11, 1971. Program included the premiere of the concert suites of the film scores for *The Devils* and *The Boyfriend*. About *The Devils* music the reviewer remarks that it is "a very good film score" and, when describing the music for *The Boyfriend*, notes it to be "extremely amusing and also disturbing in the vision of a manic ritual dance."

B319. Griffiths, Paul. "Shakespeare Birthday." *Musical Times* v. 113 (June, 1972) p. 577.
Review of a concert by the London Sinfonietta at Southwark Cathedral, April 23, 1972, celebrating Shakespeare's birthday. The program opened with the premiere of *Fool's Fanfare*, conducted by

the composer, with Ron Moody as speaker. Music described as "quiet, sustained...during the speeches" and, in contrast, "erupting into bright and spiky interludes between them."

B320. Griffiths, Paul. "St. Magnus Festival: *The Lighthouse.*" *Times* (June 25, 1986).
Review of a performance of *The Lighthouse* by the Fires of London conducted by Günther Bauer-Schenk at the Phoenix Cinema, Kirkwall during the 1986 St. Magnus Festival. Soloists were Neil Mackie, Henry Herford and Ian Comboy. The reviewer notes the work "is bizarre and grotesque right from the start."

B321. Griffiths, Paul. "*Taverner.*" *Times* (June 30, 1983).
Review of a performance of *Taverner* by the Royal Opera, Covent Garden, June 29, 1983, conducted by Edward Downes. The reviewer describes the opera as "one of the most thrilling, provoking and indeed beautiful operas of recent times...a work of immense richness and vigour."

B322. Griffiths, Paul. "Tumult of Ideas." *Times* (Sept. 11, 1989).
Review of a concert by the Scottish Chamber Orchestra conducted by the composer at the Royal Albert Hall, Sept. 10, 1989. Featured on the program was the premiere of *Symphony No. 4*, of which the reviewer says: "like its predecessors...is...an anti-symphony, an achievement of order regained against the grain." Remarks about the form of the new work and includes a brief, descriptive analysis.

B323. Griffiths, Paul and Evidon, Richard. "Proms." *Musical Times* v. 116 (Oct., 1975) pp. 894–895.
Includes a review of a concert at the Albert Hall, Aug. 20, 1975, by the Scottish Symphony Orchestra directed by Christopher Seaman. Included a performance of *Stone Litany* with soloist Jane Manning. Remarks: "If the work is indeed on evocation of Orkney, the outlook is hard, fractured and menacing."

B324. Gruber, H. K., et al. "Benjamin Britten: Tributes and Memoirs." *Tempo* no. 120 (Mar. 1977) p. 4.
Short memorial for Benjamin Britten written by Davies as part of an article of various tributes and memorials. Davies recalls his final meeting with Britten, during the 1974 Aldeburgh Festival where Davies conducted his *Hymn to St. Magnus* with the Fires of London. It is a very touching remembrance.

B325. Gualerzi, Giorgio. "Turin." *Opera* v. 29 (Dec., 1978) p. 1204.
Brief review of a performance of *The Two Fiddlers* by pupils from the Kirkwall Grammar School, Orkney, at the Turin Conservatory, Sept. 27, 1978: "reveals the inevitable influence exercised by Britten...not without echoes of Gershwin, Scott Joplin."

B326. Halasz, Gabor. "Kaiserslautern: Argyrides, Manoli." *Opernwelt* v. 31 (July 1990) p. 53.
Review of a performance of *Yellow Cake Revue* at the Kaiserslautern Musiktheater on May 31, 1990.

B327. Hall, Alan. "Concerts in London: Max." *Musical Times* v. 151 (June 1990) pp. 321–322.
Includes reviews of performances of *Strathclyde Concerto No. 2 for Cello and Orchestra* and *Strathclyde Concerto No. 3 for Horn, Trumpet and Orchestra*. The reviewer describes these as "Finely crafted and attractive...each conveys a subliminal classicism of form and pitch...and masterly orchestration."

B328. Hall, Alan. "London: Proms." *Musical Times* v. 130 (Nov., 1989) p. 677.
Includes a review of the premiere of *Symphony No. 4* by the Scottish Chamber Orchestra conducted by the composer, Sept. 10, 1989, as part of a Proms concert. The reviewer found it "leaner and more beautiful than its predecessors, retaining a characteristic 'difficultness' and intensity."

B329. Hamilton, D. "Three Composers of Today." *Musical Newsletter* no. 1 (Jan., 1971) p. 18.
Brief article which focuses on the composer's compositional techniques, especially his use of medieval and renaissance sources and musical devices, such as canon, isorhythm, cantus firmus and others. Mentions *Shakespeare Music*, *Eight Songs for a Mad King*, *Revelation and Fall*, and *Vesalii Icones*.

B330. Harrison, Max. "Concerti: Intimate Brilliance." *Times* (Dec. 20, 1982).
Review of a concert by the Albany Brass Ensemble at St. John's, Smith Square, London, Dec. 17, 1982. The reviewer notes the work was "demanding in terms of individual and ensemble techniques."

B331. Harrison, Max. "Fired by a Golden Eagle." *Times* (Sept. 8, 1989).
Notice of the then up-coming premiere of *Symphony No. 4* by the
Scottish Chamber Orchestra conducted by the composer at the Royal
Albert Hall, Sept. 10, 1989. Included remarks about the plainsong
basis of the work. With a photograph of the composer.

B332. Harvey, David. *"Hill Runes."* *Tempo* no. 149 (June 1984) pp. 14–18.
Presents a detailed analysis of *Hill Runes*, giving numerous musical
examples. The author concludes the work "is an entirely characteristic statement on the part of its composer, recreating the harmonic
richness of his recent work in terms of the guitar."

B333. Harvey, Jonathan. "Maxwell Davies's *Eight Songs for a Mad King.*"
Tempo 89 (1969) pp. 2–6.

B334. Hayes, Malcolm. "A Brilliant Composer Who Can't Or Won't Grow
Up." *Sunday Telegraph* (Sept., 1988) p. 26.
Includes a review of the premiere of *Resurrection* by the Darmstadt
Opera conducted by Hans Drewanz at the Staatstheater, Darmstadt,
Sept. 18, 1988. Includes a synopsis of the complex work, remark-
ing, "his opera is composed with a stunning display of technical
expertise that few of his contemporaries would be able to even
contemplate."

B335. Hayes, Malcolm. "Max: Shocking and Serious." *Daily Telegraph*
(April 16, 1990) p. 17.
Includes a review of a performance of *Worldes Blis* by the BBC
Symphony Orchestra conducted by Ronald Zollman at the Royal
Festival Hall during Maxfest, late March-early April, 1990. The
music is described as "the finest and most dramatic evocative of the
Orkney landscape he [Davies] has achieved." Also reviews a
performance of *Into the Labyrinth* featuring tenor Neil Mackie and
the Scottish Chamber Orchestra conducted by the composer at Queen
Elizabeth Hall ("the urgency of its message is the issue that counts").
Both were part of 'Maxfest' at the South Bank late March-early
April, 1990.

B336. Hayes, Malcolm. "Maxwell Davies: *Symphony No. 3.*" *Daily Telegraph* (April 13, 1990).
Review of a performance of *Symphony No. 3* by the Royal Philharmonic Orchestra conducted by Edward Downes in early April, 1990.

The reviewer says the work is "one of the best of Davies's recent scores, written in a relatively defoliated idiom."

B337. Hayes, Malcolm. "Nights and Fires." *Sunday Telegraph* (Jan. 25, 1987).
Review of the farewell concert by the Fires of London conducted by the composer at the Queen Elizabeth Hall, Jan. 20, 1987. Included on the program was a performance of *Eight Songs for a Mad King* with David Wilson-Johnson. About the work the reviewer notes that the composer's "virtuoso display of techniques of distortion and parody...perfectly mirrors the King's situation."

B338. Hayes, Malcolm. "Record Review: Maxwell Davies: *The Strathclyde Concertos*, vol. 1." *Tempo* no. 172 (Mar., 1990) pp. 38–39.
Reviews a recording (Unicorn-Kanchana DKP(CD) 9085) of *Strathclyde Concerto No. 1 for Oboe and Orchestra* (with oboist Robin Miller: "a fine work...") and *Strathclyde Concerto No. 2 for Cello and Orchestra* (with cellist William Conway), both with the Scottish Chamber Orchestra conducted by the composer. Has especially high praise for *Strathclyde No. 2* ("an entirely remarkable one...an ambitious addition to the world repertory" as well as for the performance.

B339. Helm, Everett. "I.S.C.M. Festival in Strasbourg." *Musical Times* v. 99 (Aug., 1958) pp. 446–447.
Focuses on the 1958 ISCM Festival in Strasbourg, 1958. One concert included a performance of *Alma Redemptoris Mater* for wind sextet. About the work the reviewer notes it is "a strange combination of serial technique, Gregorian melody, and ornamentation taken from Dunstable's motet...its composer is clearly thinking in terms of music and sound."

B340. Henahan, Donal. "Humor in a Rustic Vein." *New York Times* (Nov. 11, 1988) p. C3.
Review of a concert by the Scottish Chamber Orchestra conducted by the composer at Carnegie Hall, Nov., 9, 1988. Included on the program was a performance of *Into the Labyrinth* by Neil Mackie, tenor. The reviewer describes the work as "a drably atonal score." Also included on the program was a performance of *An Orkney Wedding, With Sunrise,* which the reviewer found "a howlingly effective musical joke, in the Mozartian sense."

B341. Henderson, Robert. "City of London Festival." *Musical Times* v. 103 (Sept., 1962) pp. 615-617.
Review of the premiere of *Leopardi Fragments* at Stationers Hall, July 19, 1962 as part of the City of London Festival. Notes the influence of Monteverdi on the composer but remarks that "the finished work has all the mystical character of Maxwell Davies and little, if any, of Monteverdi."

B342. Henderson, Robert. "Compelling Sounds From the Sea." *Daily Telegraph* (Mar. 2, 1981).
Review of the premiere of *Symphony No. 2* by the Boston Symphony Orchestra conducted by Seiji Ozawa at Symphony Hall, Boston, Feb. 26, 1981. The reviewer remarks about the obvious influence of the Orkney Islands where the composer lives part of the year, especially the sound of the sea. He notes: "It is a profound and startlingly imaginative achievement, the music breathing and pulsating inexorably in the natural rhythms of man and nature."

B343. Henderson, Robert. "First Performances: Peter Maxwell Davies's *Shakespeare Music*." *Tempo* no. 72 (Spring 1965) pp. 15–18.
Article about *Shakespeare Music*, which was composed on invitation from the BBC for the 400th birthday of William Shakespeare. The article includes some analysis and musical examples. The reviewer concludes that the work "shows the composer working skillfully and confidently with all his favorite technical devices and producing...a fluency and individuality."

B344. Henderson, Robert. "Flamboyant Fourth." *Daily Telegraph* (Sept. 12, 1989).
Review of the premiere of *Symphony No. 4* by the Scottish Chamber Orchestra conducted by the composer during a Proms concert at the Royal Albert Hall, Sept. 10, 1989. The piece is described as "a work of enthralling fascination" and "a work of deep and mysterious undertow, and sharp, coruscating instrumental colours."

B345. Henderson, Robert. "Imperial Pair." *Daily Telegraph* (Aug. 11, 1994).
Review of a concert that included the premiere of *Symphony No. 5* by the Philharmonia Orchestra conducted by the composer during a Promenade Concert at the Royal Albert Hall, Aug. 9, 1994. Remarks on the influence of Sibelius's *Symphony No. 7* apparent in the work. The reviewer says that the new Symphony "has a powerful inner momentum that both shapes and leads it inexorably

on through stark contracts of speed and emphasis to a slow, mysterious ending."

B346. Henderson, Robert. "Maxwell Davies in Rip Van Winkle Vein." *Daily Telegraph* (June 19, 1978).
Review of the premiere of *The Two Fiddlers* by pupils from the Kirkwall Grammar School at the Arts Theatre, Kirkwall, Orkney. It was presented as part of the second St. Magnus Festival on June 16, 1978. About the score the reviewer notes: "While the writing for young singers and players is challenging enough...it never makes unfair demands on their natural talents."

B347. Henderson, Robert. "Peter Maxwell Davies." *Musical Times* v. 102 (1961) pp. 624–626.

B348. Henderson, Robert. "Prom Novelties." *Musical Times* v. 103 (Nov., 1962) p. 780.
Review of a Promenade concert on Sept. 13, 1962, which included a performance of *First Fantasia on an 'In Nomine' of John Taverner* by the BBC Symphony Orchestra conducted by the composer. Notes, "the basic shape of the work is easily followed, rising to a powerful climax...before relaxing to a quiet close, to make its concise, but most effective dramatic point."

B349. Henderson, Robert. "Prom: New Maxwell Davies." *Daily Telegraph* (Aug. 13, 1983).
Review of the premiere of *Sinfonia Concertante* by the Academy of St. Martin-in-the-Fields conducted by Neville Marriner at the Royal Albert Hall, Aug. 12, 1983. The piece is described as "an immediately imposing and substantial work."

B350. Henderson, Robert. "A Question of Time." *Musical Times* v. 102 (June, 1961) pp. 355–357.
Includes a review of *Prolation* upon publication of the score by Schott. Gives a brief, but carefully detailed, descriptive analysis of the piece. Notes, when explaining the meaning of the term 'prolation,' "Maxwell Davies has extended the meaning of the term to govern the relationships between larger and smaller note values...between entire structures from small groups of notes to complete sections." Remarks the basis of the work is a five-note series and explains the significance of the number 5.

B351. Henze, Hans Werner. "Letters to the Editor: *Taverner*." *Tempo* no. 103 (1972) p. 63.

Letter from Hans Werner Henze in response to an article by Joseph Kerman (*Tempo* v. 102) about *Taverner*. Henze takes exception to Kerman's description of the composer's libretto as "misdirected." Remarks he found when hearing the work that he was "deeply moved by the feeling that a major artist was revealing himself with an honesty for which words are hard to find."

B352. Hettergott, Alexandra. "Komponistenporträt Peter Maxwell Davies." *Oesterreichische Musikzeitschrift* v. 45 (Mar.-April 1990) pp. 187–188.

Review of a concert by the ensemble Kontrapunkte directed by Peter Keuschnig at ORF-Sendesaal, Vienna, Nov. 20, 1989. Included on the program were performances of *Runes From a Holy Island*, *Excuse Me*, *Notre Dame des Fleurs*, and *Suite From 'The Devils'*.

B353. Heyworth, Peter. "Farewell to the Fires." *Observer* (Jan. 25, 1987) p. 27.

Includes a review of the farewell concert by the Fires of London at the Queen Elizabeth Hall, Jan. 20, 1987. Included on the program was the premiere of *Winterfold* with soloist Mary Thomas, which the reviewer found "seemed no more than a...mildly attractive setting of a poem by George Mackay Brown." Also premiered on the program was Davies's transcription of Dowland's *Farewell–a Fancye*, which the reviewer thought was "beautifully done, but lasts no more than a few minutes."

B354. Heyworth, Peter. "*The Lighthouse*." *HiFi/Musical America* v. 31 (Jan. 1981) pp. MA36–37.

Review of the premiere of *The Lighthouse* at the Edinburgh Festival, Sept. 2, 1980. Soloists were Neil Mackay, Michael Rippon, and David Wilson-Johnson with the Fires of London conducted by Richard Dufallo, The reviewer says the "music is inspired by a sea- and landscape...The sense of rock, cloud and sea is omnipresent." A rather lengthy, descriptive review that includes several photographs.

B355. Heyworth, Peter. "A Sense of the Sea." *Observer* (Mar. 8, 1981).

Lengthy review of the premiere of *Symphony No. 2* by the Boston Symphony Orchestra conducted by Seiji Ozawa at Symphony Hall, Boston, Feb. 26, 1981. The reviewer notes the work reflects throughout the sea that surrounds the composer on Hoy and says, "this score is no mere seascape...but...a response on an heroic sale to the challenge implicit in symphonic form." Includes a descriptive analysis of the work.

B356. Heyworth, Peter. "Tortoise and Hare." *Observer* (Aug. 14, 1983).
Includes a review of the premiere of *Sinfonia Concertante* by the Academy of St. Martin-In-The Fields, conducted by Neville Marriner at the Royal Albert Hall Aug. 12, 1983. The reviewer remarks that this work "seems to be one of the most sheerly enchanting pieces of music that Davies has given us." Includes a very descriptive analyses of the piece. A very positive review of the work. Also includes a review of *Brass Quintet* performed by the Albany Brass Quintet in a concert in London in early August, 1983. The reviewer describes this as "a piece of complex chamber music" and "a formidable half-hour quintet" and finds it a most demanding work for performers and the listener. Finally, reviews a Proms Concert by the Fires of London conducted by the composer, Aug. 7, 1983, which included performances of *Revelation and Fall* featuring Mary Thomas (the reviewer remarks that "this tour de force is far more than a mere chamber of horrors") and *Suite From 'The Boyfriend'* ("mirrors a passing obsession with foxtrots of the Twenties").

B357. Hiller, Carl H. "Bonn." *Opera* v. 38 (May, 1987) p. 556.
Includes a brief review of a performance of *The Lighthouse* by members of the Bonn Werkstaat, Nov. 9, 1986. Notes the production made "the drama more a crime story than a sophisticated brain twister."

B358. Hiller, Carl H. "Der Kreis nur aüberlich geschlossen: Peter Maxwell Davies' *Leuchtturm* in Bonn." *Opernwelt* v. 28 no. 1 (1987) pp. 48–49.
Review of the first German production of *The Lighthouse* by the Bonn Opera directed by Theo Dorn on Nov. 9, 1986.

B359. Hoffman, Stephan. "Dauer-Braut und Mädchen-Killerin." *Neue Musikzeitung* v. 39 (June–July 1990) p. 32.
Review of a performance of *Miss Donnithorne's Maggot* by Clara O'Brien in Karlsruhe, Spring, 1990.

B360. Holland, Bernard. "Operaworks Presents a New Davies Piece." *New York Times* (Oct. 3, 1984) p. C20.

Review of the New York premiere of *The Martyrdom of St. Magnus* by Operaworks, Sept. 29, 1984 at Larry Richardson's Dance Gallery. The reviewer remarks that the composer's piece "uses a small orchestra with great imagination and a vocal melodic style that...suggests...the plainsong of Mr. Davies's 12th-century setting."

B361. Hollander, Hans. "Cheltenham Festival 1967." *Neue Zeitschrift für Musik* v. 128 (Sept. 1967) p. 361.

Article about the 1967 Cheltenham Festival during July, 1967. Includes a review of the premiere of *Hymnos* by Alan Hacker, clarinet and Stephen Pruslin, piano.

B362. Hoover, Joanne Sheely. "Slapstick! Spice! Kids! Opera!." *Washington Post* (April 17, 1982).

Review of the American premiere of *Cinderella* at the Sheridan School, Washington, D.C., April 16, 1982. The director was Nettie Ruth Brahon. The reviewer notes: "He not only gives the young cast—easily manageable material, but he also makes room for the freshness of their viewpoints within the opera."

B363. Horwood, Wally. "On Screen." *Crescendo International* v. 10 (May, 1972) p. 19.

Review of the Ken Russell film version of *The Boy Friend* for which Davies composed, arranged, and conducted the score. The reviewer remarks that the composer "catches the mood of the period perfectly with some intriguing orchestral touches."

B364. Hughes, Eric, and Timothy Day. "Discographies of British Composers, 2: Peter Maxwell Davies." *Recorded Sound* v. 77 (1980) pp. 81–93.

B365. Hughes-Jones, Llifon. "Fantasia on Taverner." *Music and Musicians* v. 11 (Nov., 1962) pp. 50ff.

Review of a concert by the BBC Symphony Orchestra conducted by the composer on 13 Sept., 1962, Included was the premiere of *First Fantasia on an 'In Nomine' of John Taverner*, which is described as "an exciting and beautiful essay in textures and instrumental colour."

B366. Hurley, Paul. "The Guitar in Song: An Introduction Part V: The Twentieth Century." *Soundboard* v. 17 no. 2 (1990) pp. 50–55.

Includes a section on *Dark Angels*, which it notes was inspired by "the desolate, mystic landscape of the Orkney Islands."

B367. Hussey, Dyneley. "The Cheltenham Festival." *Musical Times* v. 100 (Sept., 1959) pp. 472–473.
Article on the 1959 Cheltenham Festival concerts, including a review of the premiere of *St. Michael Sonata* for 17 wind instruments, by members of the London Symphony Orchestra conducted by the composer, July 13, 1959. The reviewer thought that "it was extremely difficult to make head or tail of this abstrusive music, which gave the impression of having been constructed with the aid of a slide-rule and tabulator."

B368. Ingham, Richard. "*The Two Fiddlers* Played to Crowded Houses." *Orcadian* (June 22, 1978).
Review of the premiere of *The Two Fiddlers* by pupils from the Kirkwall Grammar School, part of the second St. Magnus Festival. The performance took place at the Arts Theatre, Kirkwall, Orkney, June 16, 1978. It includes a detailed synopsis of the work, concerning which the reviewer writes: "The excitement and pace of the score with its fine balance between moods...its messages...are the hallmark of a composer of great standing."

B369. J. D. "Classical Recordings." *Fanfare* v. 4 no. 2 (1980) pp. 134–135.
Review of a recording which included a performance of *St. Thomas Wake* by the Louisville Orchestra conducted ny Richard Dufallo. Work described as an example of "the creation of 'new' music on the attractive remnants of the old."

B370. Jacobs, Arthur. "Harrogate: Maxwell Davies Old and New." *Opera* v. 35 (Nov. 1984) pp. 1204–1205.
Review of a concert by the Fires of London, conducted by Nicholas Cleobury, at the Harrogate Theatre, Aug. 6, 1984. On the program were *The No. 11 Bus* and *Vesalii Icones*. The reviewer compares *No. 11 Bus* unfavorably with *Vesalii Icones*, finding it generally an unsuccessful work.

B371. Jacobs, Arthur. "The Medium." *Opera* v. 33 (June 1982) p. 766.
Review of a performance of *The Medium* by Mary Thomas at Queen Elizabeth Hall, May 20, 1984. The reviewer judges the work "indulgently over-written in both words and music."

B372. Jacobs, Arthur. *"Le Nozze di Figaro*: Glyndebourne Touring Opera at Glyndebourne." *Opera* v. 40 (Dec., 1989) p. 1488.

Review of a performance of Mozart's *Le Nozze di Figaro* by the Glyndebourne Touring Opera Company at Glyndebourne, Oct. 4, 1989, conducted by the composer, who the reviewer says "seized the score at a brisk pace which nevertheless allowed the vocal line to shine."

B373. Jacobson, Robert. "New York." *Opera News* v. 48 (July, 1983) pp. 34–36.

Includes reviews of performances of several of the composer's works by the Fires of London as part of the "Britain Salutes New York" Festival, April 22–24, 1983, in New York's Symphony Space. Performances included *Le Jongleur de Notre Dame* (about which the reviewer notes: "Davies' writing displayed a superb sense of textures and character"); *Eight Songs for a Mad King*; and *Miss Donnithorne's Maggot* (of which the reviewer says "The score concentrates on percussiveness achieving some atmosphere").

B374. Jenyon, Nicholas. "St. Magnus Festival." *Music and Musicians* v. 27 (Oct. 1978) pp. 48–49.

Article about the 1978 St. Magnus Festival, including a review of the premiere of *The Two Fiddlers* by pupils from the Kirkwall Grammar School conducted by Norman Mitchell, June 16, 1978: "Maxwell Davies has provided music that is in the best tradition of children's writing, simple but not trite, pungently orchestrated." Includes a synopsis of the plot.

B375. Johns, Donald. *"March: The Pole Star*, for Brass Quintet." *Notes* v. 44 no. 3 (1988) pp. 590–591.

Review of *March: The Pole Star* upon the publication of the score by Chester, 1984. Notes the composer's "unique use of scale material" and says this is "an engaging work that should be accessible to a great number of groups."

B376. Johnson, David. "Scotland." *Musical Times* v. 125 (May, 1984) p. 285.

Includes a review of a concert by the Scottish Chamber Orchestra conducted by Edward Harper at the Reid Hall, Edinburgh, Oct. 6, 1983. Included on the program was the premiere of *Sinfonietta Accademica*. The reviewer found this work disappointing and "certainly lacked the academic virtues of precision, clear organization and brevity."

B377. Johnson, Stephen. "Recitals." *Musical Times* v. 125 (May, 1984) p. 282.
Reviews the premiere of *The No. 11 Bus* at the Elizabeth Hall, Mar. 20, 1984. In the reviewer's opinion, "Neither the libretto nor the score...are interesting enough...the composer's message...proves fatally obscure."

B378. Joseph, Jeffrey. "Radio and Television." *Music and Musicians* v. 27 (May, 1979) pp. 36–37.
Review of the premiere of *Salome: Concert Suite from the Ballet*, broadcast on BBC Radio 3, Mar. 16, 1979. Performance was by the London Symphony Orchestra conducted by David Atherton. The reviewer judged this to be "massive, grandiose...explicitly articulate high drama to form an eminently gripping concert piece..."

B379. Josephson, David. "In Search of the Historical Taverner." *Tempo* no. 102 (1972) pp. 40–42.
Detailed articled written just prior to the premiere of *Taverner*, focussing on on the history of John Taverner and his music. With extensive bibliography.

B380. Josipovici, Gabriel. "*Taverner*: Thoughts on the Libretto." *Tempo* no. 101 (1972) pp. 12–19.
Historical background of John Taverner and the relationship to the libretto the composer wrote for *Taverner*. Includes quotes from the libretto. The reviewer says, "it is easy to see the fascination exercised by John Taverner over Peter Maxwell Davies."

B381. Kell. "Dance Reviews: *Salome*." *Variety* v. 293 no. 3 (Nov. 22, 1978) p. 128.
Review of a performance of the premiere production of *Salome* in Copenhagen, Nov. 21, 1978, by the Royal Danish Ballet and the Danish State Radio Orchestra conducted by Janos Fuerst. The reviewer thought the music had "dramatic impact without becoming too dominating...it has a soaring lyricism."

B382. Keller, Hans, "The State of the Symphony: Not Only Maxwell Davies's." *Tempo* no. 125 (June, 1978) pp. 6–11.

Describes itself as not just a review of *Symphony No. 1* but of the state of the symphony as a musical form. Attempts, at great length, to define what a "symphony," as a musical form, really is and to explain why the author does not consider Davies's composition a "true" symphony.

B383. Keller, Hans, et. al. "The Symphony Orchestra—Has it a Future?" *Composer* no. 37 (Autumn, 1970) pp. 1–9.

Extracts from a debate at the 1970 Cheltenham Festival which dealt with the possibility of the "ultimate extinction of the symphony orchestra." Hans Keller and the composer argued for that notion while Gerald McDonald and Professor Ivor Kip were against it. Davies's portion of the presentation focused on the following: "The orchestra is becoming a museum." His premise is based on the complexity and experimental nature of contemporary music and the demands it makes on an orchestra, especially in light of the need for adequate rehearsal time, and the lack thereof most of the time. Consequently it is more attractive for composers to write for small ensembles: at least a composer's work might receive more than one or two performances.

B384. Keller, Hans. "Royal Opera, Covent Garden." *Opera* v. 23 (Nov., 1972) pp. 1023–1025.

Short article, not exactly a review of a performance of *Taverner* by the Royal Opera, Covent Garden, Sept. 26, 1972, but more an essay on opera since Wagner. Notes that one of the greatest problems with contemporary opera is communication and remarks about Davies's handling of that in the following: "Few have tackled the contemporary...communication, more comprehensively and indeed with greater originality."

B385. Kennedy, Michael. "Best and Worst in Music." *Daily Telegraph* (Dec. 19, 1989).

Includes a brief mention of *Strathclyde Concerto No. 2 for Cello and Orchestra* as being the most impressive new work of 1989.

B386. Kennedy, Michael. "Fires of London." *Daily Telegraph* (Aug. 1, 1981).

Includes a review of a performance of *Eight Songs for a Mad King* with soloist Michael Rippon and the Fires of London at the Gateway Theatre, Chester, July 31, 1981. About the work the reviewer remarks "remains one of this composer's finest and most moving achievements." Also reviews *Le Jongleur de Notre Dame*, on the same program. The reviewer thinks this work "represents the mellowed side of Max, his version of a Britten church parable."

B387. Kennedy, Michael. "'Max' Sticks His Neck Out." *Daily Telegraph* (Feb. 18, 1985).
Article written just prior to the premiere of *Symphony No. 3* by the BBC Philharmonic Orchestra conducted by Edward Downes Feb. 19, 1985. Focuses on the new work and includes biographical information about the composer.

B388. Kennedy, Michael. "Maxwell Davies' 3rd Symphony." *Daily Telegraph* (Feb. 20, 1985).
Review of the premiere of *Symphony No. 3* by the BBC Philharmonic Orchestra conducted by Edward Downes at the Free Trade Hall, Manchester, Feb. 19, 1985. About the work the reviewer notes it is "a deeply impressive symphony easily related to the classical tradition, both in its basis in tonality and in the severe logicality of its main argument." Includes a photograph of the composer.

B389. Kennedy, Michael. "Maxwell Davies as Soulful Melodist." *Daily Telegraph* (Feb. 3, 1989).
Review of a concert by the Scottish Chamber Orchestra conducted by the composer at City Hall, Glasgow, Feb. 1, 1989. Included on the program was the premiere of *Strathclyde Concerto No. 2 for Cello and Orchestra* featuring soloist William Conway. The reviewer remarks: "The writing for soloist is in long, lyrical lines..." and further "The economical orchestral scoring is etched in brief splashes of colour."

B390. Kennedy, Michael. "Maxwell Davies." *Daily Telegraph* (Feb. 8, 1982).
Review of a performance of *Symphony No. 2* by the BBC Northern Symphony Orchestra conducted by Edward Downes at the Free Trade Hall, Manchester, early Feb., 1982. The reviewer describes the piece as exhibiting "strong, sinewy melodic lines and...marvellously varied harmonic textures."

B391. Kenyon, Nicholas. "ASMF/Marriner." *Times* (Aug. 13, 1983.
Review of a concert by the Academy of St. Martin-in-the-Fields conducted by Neville Marriner. Featured on the program was the premiere of *Sinfonia Concertante*, which the reviewer describes as "a

cool collected essay...complex and restless on the surface." Includes a descriptive analysis of the piece.

B392. Kenyon, Nicholas. "The Exploding Dummy Show." *Observer* (Sept. 2, 1988) p. 38.
Review of the premiere of *Resurrection* by members of the Stadtheater Darmstadt, conducted by Hans Drewanz, Sept. 18, 1988. Includes a vivid, graphic description of the work. The reviewer says, "there are only tiny passages which seem to speak with anything like the eloquence of Davies's current voice...what is disappointing is the lack of musical conviction."

B393. Kenyon, Nicholas. "First Heard on TV." *Observer* (June 29, 1986).
Includes a review of the premiere of *Concerto for Violin and Orchestra* with Isaac Stern and the BBC Symphony Orchestra conducted by André Previn at St. Magnus Cathedral during the St. Magnus Festival, June 21, 1986. The reviewer found this "a cool work, bare in places." Includes a description of each movement but focuses on the second, which is described as "beautifully crafted." He finds that the solo part shows evidence of the influence of Bruch.

B394. Kenyon, Nicholas. "Music." *Observer* (Sept. 17, 1989).
Review of the premiere of *Symphony No. 4* by the Scottish Chamber Orchestra conducted by the composer at the Royal Albert Hall, Sept. 10, 1989. The reviewer notes the work is based upon a, "processional plainsong" and says further "the writing for orchestra is predominately grey and intricately woven."

B395. Kenyon, Nicholas. "Musical Events: Close to Home." *New Yorker* v. 57 (Feb. 1, 1982) p. 127.
Very brief review of a concert by Capricorn at St. Peter's Church, Citicorp Center, New York City, Jan. 19, 1982. Included on the program was the New York premiere of *Anakreontika*, described as "a terse and pungent group of settings of Greek verse."

B396. Kenyon, Nicholas. "Orcadian Root and Branch." *Times* (June 25, 1978).
Review of the premiere of *The Two Fiddlers* by pupils from the Kirkwall Grammar School conducted by Norman Mitchell at the Kirkwall Arts Theatre, June 16, 1987, part of the 1978 St. Magnus Festival. The reviewer says that Davies "provides music which

combines the best qualities of imagination and simplicity." Includes a synopsis of the work.

B397. Kenyon, Nicholas. "St. Magnus Festival." *Music and Musicians* v. 27 (Oct. 1978) pp. 48–49.
Article about the 1978 St. Magnus Festival, including a very brief review of the premiere there of *Le Jongleur de Notre Dame* with mime Mark Furneaux, and Michael Rippon, baritone, and the fires of London conducted by the composer and the Stromness Academy Wind Ensemble conducted by Jean Leonard, June 18, 1978. The reviewer notes: "Maxwell Davies sets this tale as a drama of instrumental solos."

B398. Kerman, Joseph. "Popish Ditties." *Tempo* no. 102 (1972) pp. 20–24.
Lengthy, complex article about *Taverner*, giving a detailed analysis of the work but without musical examples. Includes photographs of scenes from the work at its premiere at Covent Garden. The reviewer thinks "it is a rather marvelous score but rather less marvelous as a theatre piece."

B399. Kerner, Leighton. "Descants: Hell on Wheels." *Village Voice* (Jan. 14, 1986) p. 73.
Review of the U.S. premiere of *The No. 11 Bus* by the Fires of London at the Palace Theater, Stamford, Connecticut, early December, 1985. Includes a lengthy synopsis of the drama. The reviewer says that "The music, however diverting...doesn't divert you from the fable or its possible...meanings" and compares the work to *The Lighthouse*.

B400. Kerner, Leighton. "Hell on Wheels." *Village Voice* (Jan. 14, 1986) p. 73.
Review of a recording by the Fires of London conducted by the composer which included performances of *Image, Reflection, Shadow*, *The Bairns of Brugh*, *Runes from a Holy Island*, (Unicorn-Kanchana DKP 9033). Concentrates upon *Image, Reflection, Shadow*, describing the music a, "big work" but it exhibits "delicacy, lyrical grace and shimmering transparency..." *Bairns* is described as "a delicate threnody." *Runes* is described as "a sometimes awesome tone poem..."

B401. Kerner, Leighton. "Music: A Rare *Medium*." *Village Voice* (Aug. 16, 1983) p. 72.

Article about the 1983 Aldeburgh Festival containing a review of a performance there of *The Medium*. Includes quotes from the composer's own comments about the piece from the festival program and describes the work as "an unaccompanied monologue for a mezzo-soprano which holds the stage for 45 minutes of ranting, raving, cajoling, and hysteria."

B402. Kerner, Leighton. "Music: Intimations of God." *Village Voice* (June 17, 1981) pp. 68ff.

Includes a review of a performance of *The Lighthouse* at the Theatre Royal, during the Bath Festival, May 24, 1981. Gives a detailed synopsis of the work which captures its sinister, mysterious nature, describing the music as "wind-blasted verismo" and "jerky, jabbing."

B403. Kerner, Leighton. "Music: Magnificent *Magnus*." *Village Voice* (Oct. 16, 1984) p. 103.

Review of the New York premiere of *The Martyrdom of St. Magnus* by members of Operaworks at Larry Richardson's Dance Gallery, Sept. 29, 1984. The reviewer says the music is "typically Maxwell Davies in its resonances...from ancient music...in this case Gregorian Chant...into scattered areas of...contemporary pop." The performance was conducted by David C. Leighton.

B404. Kerner, Leighton. "Roast Beef and Fudge." *Village Voice* (Dec. 22, 1992) p. 85.

Includes a review of a concert by the St. Louis Symphony Orchestra conducted by Leonard Slatkin in Carnegie Hall, Nov. 20, 1992. Included on the program was a performance of *Worldes Blis*. About the music the reviewer remarks, "the formidable complexity of Sir Peter's system of pitch-cells pulls the Orchestra and listener through thickets of sound and fury, signifying much."

B405. Kerner, Leighton. "Symphonic Transformations." *Village Voice* (Oct. 30, 1978) pp. 95–96.

Review of the American premiere of *Symphony No. 1* by the New York Philharmonic Orchestra conducted by Zubin Mehta in Avery Fisher Hall, Oct. 12–17, 1978. Includes an analysis of the piece and comments on the influence of Sibelius's *Symphony No. 5* on its second movement. The reviewer also says, "Mahler...is more significantly invoked as regards not the new Symphony's length and

weight but its intensely personal statements, its unorthodox structures, and its variety and impact as sheer sound."

B406. Kimball, Robert. "Fiery Journey on a London Bus." *New York Post*
(Dec. 12, 1985).
Review of the U. S. premiere of *The No. 11 Bus* by the Fires of
London at the Palace Theater, Stamford, Connecticut, December,
1985. The reviewer describes the work as "remarkable, protean,
provocative, humorous, densely packed and dramatically charged."

B407. Kimball, Robert. "Singers Amuse and Dazzle." *New York Post* (Nov.
20, 1986).
Review of a concert by the King's Singers at Alice Tully Hall, Nov.
16, 1986. Included on the program was the premiere of *Sea Runes*,
described as "a 3-minute, haunting setting of six linked poems."
Also performed was *House of Winter*, described by the reviewer as
a piece "that chillingly evokes storm, sea and stillness of an Orkney
December."

B408. Kimball, Robert. "What Happened When the Light Went Out." *New
York Post* (Dec. 2, 1985).
Includes a review of a performance of *The Lighthouse* by the Fires
of London conducted by the composer at Alice Tully Hall, late
November, 1985. The reviewer describes the music as "a dramatic
score, which has many humorous pages as well." Includes a brief
synopsis of the plot.

B409. Kimberly, Nick. *"The Lighthouse." Opera* v. 45 (Sept. 1994) pp.
1117–1118.
Review of a performance of *The Lighthouse* by Music Theatre Wales
at the Queen Elizabeth Hall, London, June 7, 1994. About the music
the reviewer notes: "The score, full of echoes, repeats, borrowings,
adds complexity and contradiction and enigma."

B410. Kiraly, Philippa. "Orchestra, Cello Soloist on a Par." *Akron Beacon
Journal* (Oct. 13, 1989) p. D11.
Review of a concert by the Cleveland Orchestra conducted by
Christoph von Dohnanyi at Severance Hall, Oct. 12, 1989. Included
on the program was a performance of *Strathclyde Concerto No. 2 for
Cello and Orchestra* featuring cellist Ralph Kirshbaum. About the
work the reviewer remarks: "Though the music is dissonant...the
work has a peacefulness and lyricism that is most appealing."

B411. Kleszynski, Kenneth. "Focus on Education: Sir Peter Maxwell Davies' *Three Studies for Percussion*." *Percussive Notes* v. 28 no. 2 (1990) pp. 25–27.

Article about *Three Studies for Percussion*, giving the history of the work and quoting Peter Swann, who commissioned it, on his ideas about what the work should be. Includes a detailed analysis and concludes that the piece "represents one of Davies' most complex formal structures used among his instrumental works for young performers."

B412. Knüppel, Claudio. "Schallplatten: Henri Dutilleux: *L'Arbre des Songes*, Concerto pour violon et orchestre; Peter Maxwell Davies: *Concerto for Violin and Orchestra*." *Neue Zeitschrift für Musik*. v. 150 (June 1989) p. 40.

Review of a recording that includes a performance of *Concerto for Violin and Orchestra* (CBS MK 42 449 Cd/LP).

B413. Knussen, Oliver. "Maxwell Davies' *Five Klee Pictures*." *Tempo* no. 124 (Mar., 1978) pp. 17–21.

Article on *Five Klee Pictures* for junior orchestra. Originally composed in 1959, the score was lost for 15 years. The parts were eventually found, and the composer reconstructed and revised the work. It was premiered by the Young Musicians Symphony Orchestra conducted by John Blair, at St. John's, Smith Square, London, Oct. 16, 1976. The piece is described as "one of the most important and stimulating additions to the youth orchestra repertoire in years...an important minor work by a major artist." Includes an analysis of the piece with musical examples.

B414. Kobrak, Christine. "Radio and Television." *Music and Musicians* v. 27 (Aug., 1979) p. 34.

Includes a review of a BBC Radio 3 previously recorded broadcast of the premiere of *Le Jongleur de Notre Dame* at the St. Magnus Festival, June 18, 1978. The reviewer says that this "was hardly a suitable piece for radio broadcast...a TV slot was necessary to do the work justice."

B415. Kögler, Horst. "Stuttgart." *Opera* v. 40 (June, 1989) p. 720.

Includes a brief review of a performance of *The Lighthouse* in Stuttgart at the Chamber Theatre, Mar. 1, 1989, conducted by Alexander Winterson and featuring soloists Mark Muntikkrick, Gut Renard, and Tero Hannula: "a sort of muted event."

B416. Kögler, Horst. "Stuttgart: P. M. Davies, *Der Leuchtturm.*" *Opernwelt* v. 30 (June 1989) p. 48.
Review of a performance of *The Lighthouse* in Stuttgart directed by Gordon McKechnie, at the Chamber Theater, Mar. 1989. Soloists were Guy Renard, Tero Hannula and Mark Munkittrik. Manages to incorporate a reference to the Bermuda Triangle.

B417. Kopp, Jim. "Guitar Soloist Shines in Demanding Program." *Atlanta Journal* (Mar. 3, 1987).
Review of a concert by guitarist David Tanenbaum at the Academy of Medicine, Atlanta, late Feb., 1987. Included on the program was a performance of *Hill Runes*, which the reviewer saw as "a masterpiece of tone painting."

B418. Kosman, Joshua. "Mezzo Sends a Message in *The Medium.*" *San Francisco Chronicle* (Feb. 3, 1988) p. E3.
Review of a concert by the Composers Chamber Players at the Waterfront Theater, San Francisco. Feb. 1, 1988. Included on the program was a performance of *The Medium* by soloist Lynn Morrow. The reviewer writes: "What impresses is the rawness of the psychic barrage, and the skill with which Maxwell Davies has put the concoction together."

B419. Kosman, Joshua. "Ojai Focus on Maxwell Davies." *San Francisco Chronicle* (June 6, 1988) p. F2.
Article about the 1988 Ojai Festival when Davies was composer-in-residence, with a review of the American premiere of *Into the Labyrinth* featuring Neil Mackie, tenor and the Ojai Festival Orchestra conducted by the composer. Notes that Davies takes a text and "uses it to fashion a musical work of great beauty and emotional power" and comments on the composer's "hard-nosed, resourceful use of the orchestra." Also includes reviews of *Cinderella*, performed by children from Ojai, Ventura County and Los Angeles, observing that it "includes some quasi-operatic writing of minimal difficulty," and a performance of *An Orkney Wedding, with Sunrise* in a new version for chamber orchestra by the Ojai Festival Chamber Orchestra conducted by the composer on June 4, 1988 (which is described as a "small but wonderfully witty bit of musical narrative").

B420. Kosman, Joshua. "Ojai Music Festival Ends on An up Note." *San Francisco Chronicle* (June 7, 1988) p. E6.

Article about the 1988 Ojai Festival during which Davies was composer-in-residence. Includes a review of a concert which featured a performance of *Strathclyde Concerto No. 1 for Oboe and Orchestra*, with soloist Stephen Colburn and the Ojai Festival Orchestra conducted by the composer. The reviewer notes: "Both its dimensions and its character are Mozartian...the soloist ingratiates himself at every turn into the orchestral fabric."

B421. Kraglund, John. "Exuberant Exploration of Madness, Religion." *Globe and Mail* (Toronto) (Nov. 18, 1985).

Review of a concert by the Fires of London conducted by the composer at the Jane Mallett Theatre, Nov. 16, 1985. Included in the program was a performance of *Miss Donnithorne's Maggot* featuring Mary Thomas. The reviewer found the work "dealt with madness in a compassionate fashion." Also on the program was a performance of *Vesalii Icones* by dancer Mark Wraith and cellist Jonathan Williams. The reviewer saw this as "eclectic Davies, music-something at the contemporary combined with plainsong and quotations from other music."

B422. Kraglund, John. "*The Lighthouse* Builds to Stunning Climax." *Globe and Mail* (Toronto) (May 3, 1986).

Review of a performance of *The Lighthouse* at the Guelph Spring Festival, May 2, 1986. Soloists were Ben Heppner, Christopher Cameron and Cornelius Opthof; they were accompanied by the Canadian Chamber ensemble conducted by Stuart Bedford. Of the score, the reviewer says: "The music...was a strange mixture of Davies's version of modern music and almost familiar tunes of the Victorian era."

B423. Kraglund, John. "Music Theatre that Fires the Senses." *Globe and Mail* (Toronto) (Nov. 16, 1985) p. D7.

Review of a concert by the Fires of London, Nov. 15, 1985 at the Jane Mallett Theatre, Toronto. Included on the program was a performance of *Eight Songs for a Mad King* featuring baritone Andrew Gallacher. About the work the reviewer remarks: "The texts...accompanied in a mixture of musical styles from Baroque to twentieth-century Jazz...revealed the range and character of the King's madness." Also performed was *Le Jongleur de Notre Dame*, which the reviewer found "engrossing and sometimes quite touching entertainment."

B424. Kretschmer, Joan Thomson. "Davies Shows Wide Musical Range." *New York Post* (Nov. 11, 1988).
Review of a concert by the Scottish Chamber Orchestra conducted by the composer at Carnegie Hall, Nov. 9, 1988. Included on the program was a performance of *Into the Labyrinth* featuring tenor Neil Mackie. About the music the reviewer notes: "The piece is well-crafted, using dissonance for expressive purpose."   Also performed was *An Orkney Wedding, With Sunrise* ("humorous, programmatic piece").

B425. L. W. "Manchester Free Trade Hall: BBC Philharmonic Orchestra.' *Yorkshire Post* (Feb. 20, 1985) p. 35.
Review of a concert conducted by Edward Downes in the Free Trade Hall, Manchester, Feb. 19, 1985. Included on the program was the premiere of *Symphony No. 3*. The reviewer thought "it simply sounds well ordered and immaculately scored." Includes a descriptive analysis of the work.

B426. Labhart, Walter. "Neue Musik aus Erster Hand." *Züricher-Zeitung* no. 143 (June 22, 1983).
Review of a performance of *The Martyrdom of St. Magnus* by the Fires of London at the Tonhalle-Saal, Zürich, June 17, 1983.

B427. Larner, Gerald. "At the Court of Sir Max." *Guardian* (May 2, 1988).
Review of the premiere of *Strathclyde Concerto No. 1 for Oboe and Orchestra* by oboist Robin Miller and the Scottish Chamber Orchestra conducted by the composer, at City Hall, Glasgow, April 29, 1988. The reviewer notes the piece "is based...on a plainsong which...gives the concerto its own character."

B428. Larner, Gerald. "BBC/NSO." *Guardian* (Feb. 8, 1982).
Review of a performance of *Symphony No. 2* by the BBC Northern Symphony Orchestra conducted by Edward Downes at the Free Trade Hall, Manchester, Feb. 7, 1982. Includes a brief but very well done descriptive analysis of the work. About the music the reviewer notes: "It does...create some interesting melodic shapes and formal patterns...which makes a bruising listening experience."

B429. Larner, Gerald. "BBCSO/Howarth." *Guardian* (Nov. 12, 1984).
Review of an all-Davies concert during the Huddersfield Contemporary Music Festival by the BBC Symphony Orchestra conducted by Elgar Howarth at the Huddersfield Town Hall, Nov., 1984. On the program were *St. Thomas Wake*, *Worldes Blis* (about which the reviewer remarks, "its deliberate progress through its vast arch-form construction are...intense"), and *Solstice of Light*.

B430. Larner, Gerald. "Fires of London." *Guardian* (Aug. 1, 1981).
Review of a performance by the Fires of London conducted by John Carewe at the Gateway Theatre, Chester, during the Chester Festival, late July, 1981. Included on the program was a performance of *Eight Songs for a Mad King*, featuring soloist Michael Rippon, concerning which the reviewer remarks, "apart from the extra-vagrant effects and sensations there are several inspired moments of 18th century decorum, violent distortion, or affectionate parody." Also on the program was *Le Jongleur de Notre Dame* featuring juggler Jonny James.

B431. Larner, Gerald. "Max and Sir Peter." *Listener* (Sept. 7, 1989) pp. 37–38.
Article about *Symphony No. 4* written just prior to its premiere in Sept., 1989. Rather chatty, focuses on earlier works and the composer's career to date rather than on the new symphony. Notes that in the Fourth Symphony "there is orchestration...to clarify the structure by defining areas with distinctive colours...to present his [Davies's] material in dramatically high profile."

B432. Larner, Gerald. "Maxwell Davies Premiere." *Guardian* (Sept. 12, 1989).
Review of a concert by the Scottish Chamber Orchestra conducted by the composer at the Albert Hall, Sept. 10, 1989, including ther premiere of *Symphony No. 4*. The reviewer complains that the Hall was too large in comparison to the size of the orchestra and consequently did not allow the listener to hear the work in all of its glory. Of the *Symphony* itself, he says that "we have some lovely melodic writing for woodwind instruments...some forceful scoring for trumpets and horns, and a general sense of exposed loneliness."

B433. Larner, Gerald. "The Resurrection That Came Too Late." *Guardian* (Sept. 23, 1988).
Review of the premiere of *Resurrection* by the Stadtstheater Darmstadt, Sept. 18, 1988. The reviewer briefly summarizes the work and remarks, "the composer's lifelong preoccupations are exposed and cheapened just as echoes of his earlier music are embarrassed by contrast."

B434. Larner, Gerald. "Ritual of the Reel." *Guardian* (June 24, 1986).
Article principally on the premiere of *Concerto for Violin and Orchestra* by violinist Isaac Stern and the Royal Philharmonic Orchestra conducted by André Previn at St. Magnus Cathedral, during the 10th St. Magnus Festival, June 21, 1986. The music is described as "a formidable piece of violin writing." Includes a description of the piece but not a formal musical analysis. There is also a review of the premiere of *Jimmack the Postie* by the Royal Philharmonic Orchestra conducted by the composer at the Phoenix Cinema, Kirkwall, Orkney during the 10th St. Magnus Festival, June 22, 1986. The reviewer opines that "Davies seems to take some advice from Charles Ives here."

B435. Larner, Gerald. "SCO/Conlon." *Guardian* (Dec. 2, 1983)
Review of a performance of *Into The Labyrinth* on Nov. 30, 1983, featuring Neil Mackie, tenor and the Scottish Chamber Orchestra conducted by James Conlon. The reviewer observes: "It is a beautiful score...which approaches conventional symbolism in a quite new way."

B436. Larner, Gerald. "SCO/Uchida." *Guardian* (Oct. 29, 1984).
Review of a concert by the Scottish Chamber Orchestra conducted by the composer at Younger Hall, St. Andrews, late October, 1984. Included on the program was a performance of *Sinfonietta Accademica*, of which the reviewer remarks, "Davies has never been more successful in communicating the wintry aspect of the Orkney landscape."

B437. [Lavender, E. W.] "Editorial Notes." *Strad* v. 73 (Oct. 1962) p. 197.
Includes a review of a concert by the BBC Symphony Orchestra at the Royal Albert Hall, Sept. 13, 1962, which included the premiere of *First Fantasia on an 'In Nomine' of John Taverner*, conducted by the composer. Remarks: "It sounded like orchestral chamber music,

although there is always a keen sense of individual orchestral timbres."

B438. [Lavender, E. W.] "Editorial Notes." *Strad* v. 87 (Sept. 1976) p. 341.
Includes a review of a concert by the Fires of London conducted by the composer at the Roundhouse in late July 1976. Works performed included *Eight Songs for a Mad King* (reviewer comments: "This hysterical exercise induces fear rather than compassion") and *Dark Angels* (by Mary Thomas and Timothy Walker: reviewer says, "Caught the rawness of the Scotch verse and engaged the attention throughout").

B439. [Lavender, E. W.] "Editorial Notes." *Strad* v. 88 (Mar. 1978) pp. 987ff.
Features a review of the premiere of *Symphony No. 1* by the Philharmonia Orchestra conducted by Simon Rattle at the Royal Festival Hall, Feb. 2, 1978. This very positive review comments: "Each section is exploited to provide line and harmony is achieved often through the promptings provided by the composer's lasting interest in mediaeval music."

B440. Lawson, Peter. "Maxwell Davies's *Worldes Blis*." *Tempo* no. 90 (Autumn 1969) pp. 23–27.
Article on *Worldes Blis* written at its premiere by the BBC Symphony Orchestra conducted by the composer at the Royal Albert Hall, Aug. 28, 1969. Includes a detailed analysis of the piece with musical examples.

B441. Lee-Potter, Linda. "Friday's People." *Daily Mail* (Jan. 29, 1993) pp. 34–35.
Article based on an interview with the composer, largely biographical. Focuses for the most part on his childhood and his works for and with children. Includes a photograph.

B442. Lehman, Mark L. "Maxwell Davies: Strathclyde Concertos 5 & 6." *American Record Guide* vol. 57 no. 5 (Sept./Oct., 1994) p. 160.
Review of a recording of *Strathclyde Concerto No. 5 for Violin, Viola and String Orchestra* and *Strathclyde Concerto No. 6 for Flute and Orchestra*, by the Scottish Chamber orchestra and various soloists conducted by the composer. The reviewer describes the music in both as, "ornate, lyrical, inventive, wordy...that occasionally goes on too long...offer many felicities to the willing ear."

B443. Liebscher, Julia. "Peter Maxwell Davies: *Taverner*." pp. 686–688 in Carl Dalhaus, ed., *Pipers Enzyklopädie des Musiktheaters*, vol. 1. Munich: R. Piper GmbH & Co, 1986.

Article about the opera *Taverner*. Includes a synopsis and information about the premiere and a brief bibliography.

B444. Lindsay, Stuart. "Baby With Her Own Lullaby." *Glasgow Herald* (June 22, 1981).

Brief article about the 1981 St. Magnus Festival focusing on some of the musical events that had taken place. Remarks on the premiere of *Lullabye for Lucy* and the background of the work. Includes a photograph of Lucy Rendall and her parents with the composer. Also mentions the premieres, during the Festival, of *The Rainbow*, *The Medium*, and the incidental music to George MacKay Brown's play *The Well*.

B445. Littler, William. "Scottish Orchestra's Picture Postcard a Delight." *Toronto Star* (Nov. 8, 1988).

Review of a concert by the Scottish Chamber Orchestra conducted by the composer at Roy Thomson Hall, Toronto, Nov. 7, 1988. Included on the program was a performance of *Into the Labyrinth* with Neil Mackie, tenor, which the reviewer says "revealed this score as the almost mystical evocation it is of the changing lifestyle of the Orkneys." Also performed was *An Orkney Wedding, With Sunrise*, of which the reviewer says: "the score is one of the most engaging of its kind in the concert literature...proof of a serious composer's ability to crack a very broad smile."

B446. Littler, William. "*The Lighthouse* a Revelation." *Toronto Star* (May 7, 1986) p. B3.

Review of a performance of *The Lighthouse* at the Guelph Spring Festival in early May, 1986. Focuses on the performance rather than the music itself.

B447. Littler, William. "The Unbalanced Mind Expressed in Music." *Toronto Star* (Nov. 18, 1985).

Includes a review of a performance of *Miss Donnithorne's Maggot* featuring soprano Mary Thomas with the Fires of London at the Jane Mallett Theatre, Toronto, Nov. 16, 1985. About the work the reviewer remarks that Davies "seems to have a special musical insight into the working of the unbalanced mind." Also includes a review of a performance of *Vesalii Icones* on the same concert (with dancer Mark Wraith and cellist Jonathan Williams), concerning which the reviewer says, "bizarre is certainly the word for *Vesalii Icones.*"

B448. Litton, Glenn. "Boston Shakespeare Co.: Davies *The Lighthouse.*" *HiFi/Musical America* v. 30 (April 1984) pp. MA 19-20.
Review of the U.S. premiere of *The Lighthouse* by the Boston Shakespeare Company featuring soloists Michael Brown, Sanford Sylvan and Kenneth Bell, in Boston, Oct. 31, 1983. The reviewer says: "Davies found eloquent musical expression for his creepy tale. His highly theatrical, coloristic score recalled the eerie evocations of Varèse, Schoenberg, Britten and Boulez."

B449. Loppert, Max. "Fires of London/Elizabeth Hall." *Financial Times* (Nov. 7, 1985).
Review of a concert by the Fires of London conducted by the composer at the Queen Elizabeth Hall, Nov. 5, 1985. Included on the program were *Fiddlers at the Wedding* (performed by Elizabeth Söderström) and *Dances from 'The Two Fiddlers'* (described as "piquant").

B450. Loppert, Max. "Fires of London." *Financial Times* (May 20, 1980).
Review of a concert by the Fires of London conducted by the composer at the Queen Elizabeth Hall, May 19, 1980. Included on the program was a performance of *Vesalii Icones* featuring William Luther, dancer and Alexander Baillie, cello. The reviewer writes the work is "the most powerful of all such Maxwell Davies pieces," adding that "the music alone less than half the story." Includes a descriptive analysis of the work.

B451. Loppert, Max. "First Performances: *"The Martyrdom of St. Magnus.*" *Tempo* no. 122 (Sept. 1977) pp. 29-31.
Review of the premiere of *The Martyrdom of St. Magnus* featuring soloists Mary Thomas, Neil Mackie, Michael Rippon, Brian Raynor Cook and the Fires of London conducted by the composer in St. Magnus Cathedral, June 18, 1977. It was performed as part of the St. Magnus Festival. The review contains a lengthy description of the work. The reviewer notes: "Maturity is the mark of the opera, the maturity of many strains...in the decisive manner of a culminating creation."

B452. Loppert, Max. *"The Martyrdom of St. Magnus*/Donmar Warehouse."
Financial Times (May 20, 1987).
Review of a performance of *The Martyrdom of St. Magnus* by Opera
Factory London Sinfonietta at the Donmar Warehouse, May 18,
1987. Soloist included Nigel Robson, Tim Yealland, Adrian Clarke,
Tom McDonnell and Mary King.

B453. Loppert, Max. *"The Martyrdom of St. Magnus."* *Financial Times* (June
22, 1977).
Lengthy review of a performance of *The Martyrdom of St. Magnus*
by members of the Fires of London conducted by the composer,
presented as part of the St. Magnus Festival at St. Magnus Cathedral,
June 18, 1977. Of the work, the reviewer observes, "history, music,
and a powerfully vivid theatrical imagination seemed all to combine
in a dramatic work." Contains a lengthy synopsis of the opera and
a thoughtful review of the performance.

B454. Loppert, Max. *"The Martyrdom of St. Magnus."* *Tempo* no. 122
(Sept. 1977) pp. 29–31.
Review of the premiere of *The Martyrdom of St. Magnus* at the first
St. Magnus Festival, at St. Magnus Cathedral, Kirkwall, June 18,
1977. The reviewer writes that "music and a powerfully vivid
theatrical imagination seemed to combine in a dramatic work of
overwhelming beauty, immediacy and force." Includes a descriptive
analysis of the work. No musical examples.

B455. Loppert, Max. "Maxwell Davies/Albert Hall." *Financial Times* (Aug.
15, 1983).
Review of the premiere of *Sinfonia Concertante* by the Academy of
St. Martin-in-the-Fields at the Royal Albert Hall, Aug. 12, 1983.
The reviewer describes the piece as "a compelling work" and further
notes: "Few new works as complex as this yield quite so much
immediate pleasure." Includes a descriptive analysis of the work.

B456. Loppert, Max. "Maxwell Davies Concerto/Festival Hall." *Financial
Times* (June 26, 1986).
Review of a concert by the Royal Philharmonic Orchestra conducted
by André Previn at the Festival Hall, June 25, 1986. Featured on
the program was the London premiere of *Concerto for Violin and
Orchestra* by Isaac Stern. Includes some background material,
mentioning the world premiere of the piece at the St. Magnus
Festival earlier that month, and a descriptive analysis of the piece.

Concludes: "It is not exciting, as Maxwell Davies' early works were, but it has vitality, intensity, an inner life."

B457. Loppert, Max. "Maxwell Davies's Double Bass Concerto." *Financial Times* (Feb. 18, 1993).
Review of a concert by the Scottish Chamber Orchestra conducted by the composer at the Queen Elizabeth Hall, Feb. 16, 1993. Included on the concert was the first London performance of *Strathclyde Concerto No. 7 for Double Bass and Orchestra* featuring soloist Duncan McTier. The reviewer remarks, "I...admired the self-effacingly expert way the work is moved forward via gradually unfolding melodic devices." The program included a performance of *Caroline Mathilde: Suite from Act I of the Ballet*.

B458. Loppert, Max. "Maxwell Davies Second Symphony." *Financial Times* (July 25, 1981).
Review of a concert by the BBC Symphony Orchestra conducted by Rozhdestvensky, July 23, 1981 at a Promenade Concert. Featured on the program was the British premiere of *Symphony No. 2*. The reviewer notes: "The work itself is thrilling...and the same time a symphonic structure of real power and native energy."

B459. Loppert, Max. "Maxwell Davies Trumpet Concerto." *Financial Times* (Oct. 11, 1988).
Review of a concert by the Philharmonia Orchestra conducted by Giuseppe Sinopoli, at Festival Hall, Oct. 9, 1988. Program included the first British performance of *Concerto for Trumpet and Orchestra*, featuring John Wallace, trumpet. The reviewer remarks: "The lyrical style of trumpet-writing...is certainly chosen to focus...compulsive interest in the solo instrument."

B460. Loppert, Max. "Maxwell Davies: *Worldes Blis*." *Financial Times* (April 2, 1990).
Review of a concert by the BBC Symphony Orchestra conducted by Ronald Zollman at the Royal Festival Hall, Mar. 30, 1990. Included on the program was a performance of *Worldes Blis*, about which the reviewer says: "The piece is not just long but unbroken...moving at a pace of extreme slowness...disrupted by brief, fast-moving contrasts of ferocious violence." This is a 'rave' review.

B461. Loppert, Max. "Maxwell Davies's Fourth." *Financial Times* (Sept. 12, 1989) p. 19.
Review of the premiere of *Symphony No. 4* by the Scottish Chamber Orchestra conducted by the composer at the Royal Albert Hall, Sept. 10, 1989. The reviewer found that "the masterly control of colour makes each sound-image stand out with new distinctiveness."

B462. Loppert, Max. "Orkney, St. Magnus Festival—*The Martyrdom of St. Magnus*." *Opera* v. 28 (Autumn 1977) pp. 46–48.
Review of the premier of *The Martyrdom of St. Magnus* at the first St. Magnus Festival, in St. Magnus Cathedral, June 18, 1977.

B463. Loppert, Max. "Transatlantic Connections/Wigmore Hall." *Financial Times* (Oct. 26, 1983)
Review of a concert by the Albany Brass Ensemble at Wigmore Hall, Oct. 24, 1983. Included on the program was a performance of *Brass Quintet*, which is described as a "formidable and...stirring achievement...three taughtly held movements."

B464. Loppert, Max. "*Worldes Blis*." *Financial Times* (April 2, 1990).
Review of a concert by the BBC Symphony Orchestra conducted by Ronald Zollman at the Royal Festival Hall, Mar. 30, 1990. Featured on the program was a performance of *Worldes Blis*, about which the reviewer remarks: "The experience it attempts to capture, an end of spiritual 'coming into being'...allowed Maxwell Davies no alternatives."

B465. Loskell, Jörg. "Zwischen Wahn und Wirklichkeit: Einakter von Peter Maxwell Davies in Gelsenkirchen." *Opernwelt* v. 29 (April 1988) p. 41.
Review of a performance of *Eight Songs for a Mad King* featuring Richard Suat, conducted by Johannes Kalitzke at the Kleine Haus of the Gelsenkirchen Music Theater, 1988.

B466. Loveland, Kenneth. "Bath." *Musical Times* v. 122 (Aug., 1981) pp. 548-549.
Article about the 1981 Bath Festival concerts. Includes a review of the first English production of *The Lighthouse* during the 1981 Bath Festival by members of the Fires of London with soloists Neil Mackie, Christopher Keyte, and David Wilson-Johnson, conducted by John Carewe. Observes: "The composer's acknowledged gift for creating an atmosphere...is here at its most evocative, as is his

awareness of dramatic structure." Also reviews the premiere of *Sonata for Piano* by Stephen Pruslin, May 23, 1981, remarking that "the new sonata's most striking qualities lie in the juxtaposition of quickly contrasting harmonic ideas."

B467. Loveland, Kenneth. "Cheltenham for the People." *Music and Musicians* v. 13 (Sept., 1964) p. 19.
Review of a concert during the 20th Cheltenham Festival, July 10, 1964, which included the premiere of *Veni, Sancte Spiritus* performed by the Princeton High School Choir and the English Chamber Orchestra conducted by Thomas Hilbish. Review notes: "The music consists of striking choral statements...there is a humanity and serenity that really communicates."

B468. Loveland, Kenneth. "Cheltenham Seasoning." *Musical Times* v. 132 (Sept. 1991) pp. 459–460.
Brief article about the 1991 Cheltenham Festival, July 6–21, 1991. Included is a review of the First British performance of *Caroline Mathilde: Suite from Act I of the Ballet* performed by the BBC Philharmonic Orchestra on July 12 conducted by the composer. The reviewer observes that the composer "shows much craftsmanship in adapting to the requirements of the dance in creating a courtly lyricism." Also includes a review of the first British performance of *Ojai Festival Overture* by the City of London Sinfonia conducted by Paul Daniel, observing that the work "suggest that the spirit of Walton rides again, and makes a bouncy curtain raiser." Davies was composer-in-residence at the Festival that year.

B469. Loveland, Kenneth. "Cheltenham." *Musical Opinion* v. 114 (Nov. 1991) p. 422.
Includes a review of the first British performance of *Caroline Mathilde: Concert Suite from Act I of the Ballet* by the BBC Philharmonic Orchestra conducted by the composer on July 12, 1991, during the Cheltenham Festival. About the work the reviewer notes: "The *Suite*...shows the music to be written with a keen appreciation of the demands of the dance and also strong on atmosphere, courtly and elegant." Also reviews the first British performance of *Ojai Festival Overture* by the City of London Sinfonia conducted by Paul Daniel, which the reviewer describes as: "Seven minutes of infectious vitality."

B470. Loveland, Kenneth. "An Enthralling *Lighthouse*." *South Wales Argus* (May 29, 1981).

Review of a performance of *The Lighthouse* by the Fires of London conducted by John Carewe, late May,1981, during the Bath Festival. About the work the reviewer writes: "The composer uses the instrumental ensemble to accentuate the switches of atmosphere and the mental disturbances of the men in a most sensitive way."

B471. Loveland, Kenneth. "*The Lighthouse*." *Musical Times* v. 121 (Nov. 1980) pp. 718–720.

Includes a review of the premiere of *The Lighthouse* during the Edinburgh International Festival at the Moray House Gymnasium, Sept. 2, 1980. Giving a brief but well-written review of the plot, the reviewer remarks: "Davies's style is of course admirably suited to convey the wild background of sea and storm, the keeper's guilt and despair...the obsessive claustrophobic nature of the whole experience."

B472. Loveland, Kenneth. "*The Lighthouse*: Cardiff New opera Group at Sherman Arena Theatre." *Opera* v. 33 (Sept. 1982) pp. 972–973.

Review of a performance of *The Lighthouse* by members of the Cardiff New Opera Group at Sherman Arena Theatre, June 22, 1980. About the work the reviewer notes: "The force of Peter Maxwell Davies's theatrical thinking, the power of his score...rivet the attention and propel the action..."

B473. Loveland, Kenneth. "Opera: Music Theatre Wales and Maxwell Davies' St. Magnus." *Musical Opinion* v. 112 (July, 1989) p. 250.

Review of a performance of *The Martyrdom of St. Magnus* by members of the Music Theatre Wales at St. Donat's Art Center in Old Tythe Barn, Aug. 11, 1988. The reviewer says that in the piece, "music and drama become vividly interwoven. The only point at which the tension began to sag was the composer's odd decision to move one scene...to the present day."

B474. Loveland, Kenneth. "Style and Stature." *South Wales Argus* (Oct. 14, 1983).

Review of a concert by the Fires of London conducted by John Carewe, part of the Swansea Festival at St. Mary's Church, Swansea, Oct. 13, 1983. The program included a performance of *Image, Reflection, Shadow* about which the reviewer writes, "the composer's intuition in choosing the Hungarian cimbalon for his tuned percussion instrument was revealed in all its genius." There were also performances of *Le Jongleur de Notre Dame* with juggler Jonny James and baritone Andrew Gallagher and the children's band from West Glamorgan ("a little masterpiece"), and the premiere of the complete version of *Birthday Music for John* (composed for conductor John Carewe).

B475. Loveland, Kenneth. "Three Choirs." *Musical Times* v. 121 (Nov. 1980) p. 720.
Includes a review of the English premiere of *Solstice of Light* by the cathedral choirs, part of the 1980 Three Choirs Festival. Describes the music as presenting a "design of deeply-shaded and fluently moving choral textures."

B476. Loveland, Kenneth. "Vale of Glamorgan: *Magnus* Takes Shelter." *Opera* v. 39 (Autumn, 1988) pp. 40–41.
Review of a performance of *The Martyrdom of Saint Magnus* by the Music Theatre Wales during the Vale of Glamorgan Festival in the Old Tythe Barn, Aug. 13, 1988. The chamber orchestra was conducted by Michael Rafferty and the cast included Mary King, Mark Curtis, Richard Morris, Peter Thompson, and Kelvin Thomas. The reviewer judges the work to be "a near masterpiece of its genre...though often appropriately harsh as suites the story, [it] has more fragmentary inner subtleties than that of *The Lighthouse*."

B477. Lucas, John. "Player in a Field of His Own." *Times* (Aug. 28, 1986).
Preview article about the then-new *Concerto for Trumpet and Orchestra* which was premiered at the Yuben-Choken Kaikan Hall, Hiroshima by John Wallace and the Philharmonia Orchestra conducted by Giuseppe Sinopoli. The article focuses on Wallace as he was preparing for the premiere. The writer remarks the work has its basis in the Legend of St. Francis of Assisi but is still a very northern piece, the sounds influenced by the Orkneys.

B478. Mackay, Neil. "First Performances: *Strathclyde Concerto No. 3*." *Tempo* no. 172 (Mar., 1990) p. 28.
Review of the premiere of *Strathclyde Concerto No. 3 for Horn, Trumpet and Orchestra* on Jan. 19, 1990 at Glasgow City Hall by the Scottish Chamber Orchestra conducted by the composer. Soloists were Peter Franks and Robert Cooks. Includes a brief discussion, comparing the new concerto with the two earlier *Strathclyde Concerti*. Describing it as "full of challenge, confrontation and

struggle," the reviewer concludes, "this cudgelling, ironic piece is surely the most substantial *Strathclyde* thus far.

B479. Mackie, Neil. "SCO/Davies." *Guardian* (Mar. 19, 1988).
Review of a concert by the Scottish Chamber Orchestra conducted by the composer at the Queen's Hall, Edinburgh, Mar. 17, 1988. Included in the program was a performance of *Concerto for Violin and Orchestra* featuring soloist Ernst Kovacic ("a masterwork"). Also performed was *An Orkney Wedding, With Sunrise*.

B480. MacMillan, James. "Orcadian Delights." *Guardian* (June 23, 1988).
Article about the performances that took place during the 1988 St. Magnus Festival. Includes a review of a performance of *Black Pentecost* with baritone Alan Oke and soprano LaVerne Williams and the BBC Philharmonic Orchestra conducted by Edward Downes. About the piece the reviewer remarks: "The text is clothed in a forbidding, stark, almost consistently dark-hued orchestrational robe."

B481. Maddocks, Fiona. "Musical Fantasy of a City in Kaleidoscopic Motion." *Times* (Mar. 15, 1984).
Article written just prior to the premiere of *The No. 11 Bus* on Mar. 20, 1984. The reviewer notes: "For Davies the piece enters unfamiliar territory in subject, music and technique. It is the first time he has based his work on the city."

B482. Maddocks, Fiona. "Taking to the Max." *Independent* (Mar. 15, 1990).
Article which presents an interview with the composer just prior to the South Bank event, 'Maxfest,' during Mar.27-Apr. 10, 1990. Mostly biographical; with a photograph of the composer.

B483. Mail, Jens. "Stadtstheater Aachen." *Oper und Konzert* v. 26 no. 5 (1987) pp. 2-3.
Includes a review of *The Lighthouse* at the Stadtstheater Aachen, April 2, 1987.

B484. Main, Carol. "Getting the MAX Habit." *Music Teacher* (Feb., 1990) p. 13.
Article on the then upcoming 'Maxfest' held in late March-early April, 1990, with emphasis on the two music theatre works for children, *Jupiter Landing* (which would be premiered at the Festival) and *The Great Bank Robbery* (which would be given its first London

performance during the same event). Both were scheduled for performance on Children's Day, April 3. The article includes an interview with the composer on the subject of composing really original and interesting music for young people.

B485. Main, Carol. "Scottish Chamber Orchestra," *Glasgow Herald* (July 21, 1986).
Review of a concert by the Scottish Chamber Orchestra conducted by the composer at Music Village, Edinburgh, July 20, 1986. Included on the program was a performance of *An Orkney Wedding, With Sunrise* ("Good fun foot-tapping stuff").

B486. Mann, William. "Aldeburgh Festival: Captivating Mystery." *Times* (June 26, 1981).
Review of a performance of *The Lighthouse* by members of the Fires of London conducted by John Carewe, during the Aldeburgh Festival, June 25, 1981. Soloists were Neil Mackie, Rodney Macann, and Michael Rippon. About the work the reviewer notes: "It is a captivating piece, one of Davies's strongest chamber scores of recent years."

B487. Mann, William. "BBC SO/Pritchard." *Times* (Jan. 22, 1980).
Review of a concert by the BBC Symphony Orchestra conducted by John Pritchard at the Royal Festival Hall, Jan. 21, 1980. Included on the program was a performance of *Second Fantasia on John Taverner's 'In Nomine,'* which the reviewer says "remains a thralling, sober experience...a dramatic experience too."

B488. Mann, William. "LSO/Atherton, Festival Hall." *Times* (July 13, 1978).
Review of a concert by the London Symphony Orchestra conducted by David Atherton at Royal Festival Hall, July 12, 1978. Included on the program was a performance of *Worldes Blis*, which is called "a symphonic examination of the 'form-building potentialities' of an anonymous 13th century song."

B489. Mann, William. "Maxwell Davies Pays His Artistic Debts." *Times* (June 22, 1980).
Includes a review of *Cinderella* when it was given its premiere during the St. Magnus Festival, at the Kirkwall Arts Theatre, June 21, 1980. The performers included pupils from the Papdale Primary school and Kirkwall Grammar School conducted by Glenys Hughes.

The reviewer notes the composer's score is "decently tuneful, strong in its rhythms and spirit and orchestra interest."

B490. Marks, Anthony J. "Recitals." *Musical Times* v. 125 (Aug., 1984) pp. 451–452.
Article that features a review of the premiere of *Sonatine for Violin and Cimbalon* by Rosemary Furniss, violin, and Gregory Knowles, cimbalon, at the Wigmore Hall, June 3, 1984. Work described as "a spacious and enchanting piece full of interesting resonances and effects."

B491. Marks, Anthony. "LSO/Nagano." *Musical Times* v. 129 (Aug., 1988) p. 417.
Review of a concert by the London Symphony Orchestra conducted by Kent Nagano at the Barbican, May 26, 1988. Included was a performance of *Symphony No. 2*, which is described as "enticing and satisfying." The reviewer further notes that the music is "so rich in detail that one loses sights of the whole."

B492. Marks, Anthony. "*The Martyrdom of St. Magnus.*" *Musical Times* v. 128 (Aug., 1987) pp. 448–449.
Review of a performance of *The Martyrdom of St. Magnus* by the Opera Factory and the London Sinfonietta conducted by Stephen Langridge at the Donmar Warehouse, May 23, 1987, with soloists Timothy Yealland, Adrian Clarke, Mary King, Nigel Robson and Tom McDonnell. Reviewer found the work "a surprise and delight," with music having "idiosyncratic complexities" but also "a particularly luminous texture."

B493. Marsh, Robert C. "Maxwell Davies Finds Inspiration on Scottish Isle." *Chicago Sun-Times* (Oct. 30, 1980) p. E11.
Written just prior to a concert by the Scottish Chamber Orchestra conducted by the composer scheduled for Oct. 31, 1980 in Orchestra Hall, Chicago. *An Orkney Wedding, With Sunrise* and *Into the Labyrinth* were on the program; the article is largely an interview with the composer commenting on the influence the Orkney setting and its people have had on those compositions.

B494. Marsh, Robert C. "Scottish Chamber Group Deserves an Encore Here." *Chicago Sun-Times* (Nov. 1, 1988) p. 44.
Review of concert by the Scottish Chamber Orchestra conducted by the composer at Orchestra Hall, Chicago, Oct. 31, 1988. Included

on the program was a performance of *Into The Labyrinth* with Neil Mackie, tenor.   Also performed was *An Orkney Wedding, With Sunrise*, which the reviewer described as "delightful."

B495.   Mason, Colin.   "Benjamin Britten's Monumental *War Requiem*."   *Canon* v. 16 (Feb., 1963) pp. 8–9
Includes a review of the premiere of *Four Carols* by the London New Music Singers at St. Pancras Town Hall, Nov. 26, 1962. Mentions other new works of the composer that had recently been performed, including *Sinfonia, [First] Fantasia on an 'In Nomine' of John Taverner* and *Leopardi Fragments*.   Also includes a review of a 'revival' performance of *Sonata for Trumpet and Piano*.

B496.   Mason, Colin.   "*Five Pieces for Piano*."   *Music and Letters* v. 39 no. 4 (Oct., 1958) pp. 416–417.
Review of *Five Pieces for Piano* upon the publication of the score by Schott.   Remarks that the pieces "show some influence of Webern, but in musical character and quality sound they are nearer to Schoenberg."

B497.   Mathez, Jean-Pierre.   "Sir Peter Maxwell Davies: L'écriture de feu." *Brass Bulletin* no. 76 (1991) pp. 58–61, 63, 65.
Article which focuses on the composer's compositions for brass. Includes an interview with the composer as well as a list of the major works for brass instruments and a discography.

B498.   Maycock, Robert.   "Fires of London."   *Music and Musicians* v. 25 (Dec., 1976) p. 60.
Includes a review of a concert which featured the premiere of *Anakreontika* Mary Thomas and the Fires of London conducted by the composer at the Elizabeth Hall, Sept. 17, 1976.   Remarks the composer "reveals a new lightness and relaxed sensuality."   The program also included performances of *Door of the Sun* by violinist Duncan Druce (described as "evocative and interesting in its ideas"); *The Kestrel Paced Round the Sun* by flautist Judith Pearce; and Davies's interpolation to Buxtehude's cantata, *Also Hat Gott die Welt Geliebet* (which the reviewer thought was "musically, if not psychologically irrelevant").

B499. Maycock, Robert. "Stormy Voyage." *Independent* (Sept. 12, 1989) Arts section p. 14.

Review of a concert by the Scottish Chamber Orchestra conducted by the composer at a Proms concert, Royal Albert Hall, Sept. 10, 1989. Included on the program was the premiere of *Symphony No. 4.* Notes: "The four movements' edges are blurred...so that essentially there is a forty-minute argument" which follows the opening statement of the orchestra.

B500. Mazur, Carole. "Steamy *Salome* Lacks Consistency." *Albuquerque Journal* (Aug. 1, 1982).

Review of a performance of *Salome* choreographed by Flemming Flindt presented by the Dallas Ballet at Sweeny Center, Santa Fe, July 29, 1982. The reviewer notes a problem with the "stylistic consistency" throughout the entire work and remarks: "Even Peter Maxwell Davies's commissioned score goes from romantic to movie dramatic to modern symphonic." Nevertheless, he did find the work enjoyable.

B501. McBurney, Gerard. "Record Reviews." *Tempo* no. 176 (Mar., 1991) pp. 32–33.

Reviews several CDs of the composer's music. First is a recording of *The Martyrdom of St. Magnus* by the Music Theatre Wales and the Scottish Chamber Opera Ensemble conducted by Michael Rafferty (Unicorn-Kanchana DKP CD 9100). Reviewing performances by the various singers, he objects strongly only to the scene in which the singers become newspaper and television reporters and "rush around uttering cliches like characters on our Gulf screens...I just can't imagine...singers voices making these deliberately bland and awkward speeches convincing." Instead, he suggests that the composer might wish to replace the singers with actors at that point in the work.

Also reviews of a recording of three works by Davies, *Ave Maris Stella, Image, Reflection, Shadow*, and *Runes From a Holy Island*, by the Fires of London, conducted by the composer (Unicorn-Kanchana UKDC0238). Remarks, "it is good to have these Fires' performances of two of Davies' finest chamber works, (plus the little *Runes*)...sounding spruce and dandy."

Finally, reviews a recording of *Suite from 'The Devils,' Suite from 'The Boyfriend,'* and *Seven In Nomine* by Acquarius conducted by Nicholas Cleobury (Collins Classics 10952). *The Boyfriend* music is described as the composer's "deliciously affectionate send-ups...a concert lollipop to gladden the heart." However, the reviewer encounters problems with *The Devils* score, "slightly more awkward as a concert piece...individual numbers have the oddly weightless open-endedness characteristic of film music."

B502. McBurney, Gerard. *"The Two Fiddlers."* *Tempo* no. 126 (Sept. 1978) pp. 33–35.

Article about *The Two Fiddlers*. Includes a description of the plot and also an analysis of the score. The reviewer concludes: "What is striking is the musical sanity with which one thing follows another, the attentiveness...with which the notes connect...the composer actually cares how one is going to hear what happens."

B503. McClellan, Joseph. "Davies' Scottish Mischief." *Washington Post* (Nov. 12, 1988) sect. Style p. C02.

Review of a concert by the Scottish Chamber Orchestra conducted by the composer, Nov. 11, 1988 at Kennedy Center Concert Hall, including performances of *Into the Labyrinth* (described as a story of "the advance of a human spirit from a static, almost timeless mode of existence into the dynamic, fascinating...world of tomorrow") and *An Orkney Wedding, With Sunrise* ("a folksy and hilarious tone poem").

B504. McCleod, John. "Regional Reports: Scotland." *Composer* no. 71 (Winter 1980–1981) pp. 32–33.

Includes a mention of a performance of *The Lighthouse* at the 1980 Edinburgh Festival. Notes "the opera turned out to be one of the big successes of the Festival."

B505. McGinnis, S., and De Souza, C. "First Performance and Commissions." *Composer* no. 85 (Summer 1985) p. 31.

Notice of the premiere of *Symphony No. 3* by Edward Downes at the Free Trade Hall, Manchester, Feb. 19, 1985."

B506. McGinnis, S., and De Souza, C. "First Performances and Commissions." *Composer* no. 89 (Winter 1986) p. 30.

Notice of the premieres of *Concerto for Violin and Orchestra* at the St. Magnus Festival, June 21, 1986 with soloist Isaac Stern and the Royal Philharmonic Orchestra conducted by André Previn; *Jimmack the Postie* at the St. Magnus Festival by the Royal Philharmonic Orchestra conducted by the composer, June 22, 1986; and *House of*

Winter by the King's Singers in Kirkwall during the St. Magnus Festival, June 22, 1986.

B507. McGinnis, S., and De Souza, C. "First Performances and Commissions." *Composer* no. 87 (Spring 1986) p. 35.
Notice of the premiere of *First Ferry to Hoy* by the London Sinfonietta and members of the ILEA Centre for Young Musicians conducted by Elgar Howarth at the Queen Elizabeth Hall, Nov. 12, 1985.

B508. McGinnis, S., and De Souza, C. "First Performances, Commissions." Composer no. 91 (Summer 1987) p. 28.
Notice of the premieres of *Farewell—A Fancye* and *Winterfold* by the Fires to London at the Queen Elizabeth Hall, Jan. 20, 1987.

B509. McGrath, Sandra. "Max the Master of Music." *Australian* (Mar. 13, 1980) p. 10.
Interview with the composer during the 1980 Adelaide Festival. Mostly biographical, focusing on the composer's philosophy of music education for young people.

B510. Mendl-Schrama, Heleen. "Engelse Componisten Vertellen Over Eigen Werk." *Mens en Melodie* v. 38 (Nov. 1983) pp. 471–472.
Article about various composers who participated in the 1983 Dartington Summer School of Music. Mentions *Brass Quintet*, premiered by the Empire Brass Quintet, as well as *Symphony No. 2*.

B511. Mercer, Ruby. "Boston Opera." *Opera Canada* v. 25 no. 5 (1984) p. 32.
Brief review of the U.S. premiere of *The Lighthouse* by the Boston Opera in November, 1983. The work is described as "musically dynamic, dramatically compelling." The production was by Peter Sellars.

B512. Millington, Barry. "Aldeburgh." *Musical Times* v. 122 (Aug. 1981) p. 548.
Includes a review of a performance of *The Lighthouse* when it was given at the 1980 Aldeburgh Festival. Soloists were Neil Mackie, Michael Rippon and Rodney Macann with the Fires of London conducted by John Carewe. Notes the music "ranges from ominous, atmospheric textures to quasi-revivalist choruses."

B513. Millington, Barry. "Orchestral, Choral." *Musical Times* v. 125 (July, 1984) pp. 400–401.

Includes a review of a concert by the Fires of London at the Elizabeth Hall, May 17, 1984. Included on the program were *The Yellow Cake Revue*, with Mary Thomas, soprano, in its first London performance of the piece (the reviewer says that the singer "could not disguise the vacuity of the verbal and musical content") and *Vesalii Icones* by Tom Yang, dancer, and Jonathan Williams, cello, all conducted by Günther Bauer-Schenk ("Hectic, mocking music, drama of shocking impact, a message communicated with uncompromising force").

B514. Millington, Berry and Williams, Martyn. "Proms." *Musical Times* v. 125 (Nov., 1984) pp. 656–657.

Includes a review of a concert by the Scottish Chamber Orchestra, conducted by the composer, Sept. 5, 1984, at the Albert Hall. Included on the program was the London premiere of *Into the Labyrinth*, with soloist tenor Neil Mackie. About the work the reviewer remarks: "The instrumentation is economical, masterly and often very beautiful...and the composer...can now communicate to no less powerful effect...with minimal gestures."

B515. Milnes, Rodney. *"The Martyrdom of St. Magnus." Opera* v. 38 (June, 1987) pp. 944–945.

Review of a performance of *The Martyrdom of St. Magnus* by members of Opera Factory London Sinfonietta at the Donmar Warehouse, May 23, 1987. The reviewer was not impressed by the performance. Consequently he chose to address the music about which he remarks: "Sir Peter writes as excitingly for the voice as he does for instruments." The cast included Mary King, Nigel Robson, Adrian Clark, Tom Mcdonnell and Timothy Yealland. The performance was conducted by Paul Webster.

B516. Milnes, Rodney. *"Taverner* in the Town." *Spectator* (July 23, 1972) p. 142.

Review of the premiere of *Taverner* at Covent Garden, July 12, 1972. Acknowledges the composer's skill as a librettist as well as a composer. Remarks that the work is "deeply thoughtful" and "earns its place among the most satisfying operas introduced to London since the war."

B517. Milnes, Rodney. "*The Two Fiddlers*: ILEA/Pimlico School at the Jeannetta Cochrane Theatre." *Opera* v. 30 (Mar. 1979) pp. 286–287.

Review of the first English performance of *The Two Fiddlers* by students from the Pimlico School at the Jeannetta Cochrane Theatre, Dec. 27, 1978. After describing the production the reviewer concludes: "I cannot think of a more successful work for young people since (musically, at least) *The Little Sweep*."

B518. Mitchell, Donald. "Cheltenham Festival." *Musical Times* v. 105 (Sept., 1964) pp. 672–673.

Includes a review of the premiere of *Veni Sancte Spiritus* by the Princeton High School Choir and the English Chamber Orchestra conducted by Thomas Hilbish, July 10, 1964 during the Cheltenham Festival. Reviewer enthusiastically remarks, when speaking of Davies as a composer: "The kind of clarity and accessibility that mark the new piece I prefer to consider the result of artistic maturity...Davies is a leading talent among composers." After listing notable portions of the piece, the reviewer concluded: "The work should be heard again at the earliest possible moment."

B519. Monelle, Raymond. "Building in a Sunshine Conductor." *Independent* (Nov. 15, 1986).

Includes a review of a concert by the Scottish Chamber Orchestra conducted by the composer at Queen's Hall, Edinburgh, Nov. 13, 1986. Included on the program was the first performance of *An Orkney Wedding, With Sunrise* in an arrangement for chamber orchestra, with piper James MacDonald Reid. The reviewer notes, "the new small-scale arrangement seemed incisive and well-judged...it brought the house down."

B520. Monelle, Raymond. "A Jot Too Nostalgic." *Independent* (Aug. 13, 1987).

Review of a concert by the Scottish Chamber Orchestra conducted by the composer at Usher Hall, Edinburgh, Aug. 11, 1987. Included on the program was a performance of *Sinfonietta Accademica*, which the reviewer says reveals "the usual quality of Davies's imagination, his varied colour and sharp observation." Includes a descriptive analysis of the piece.

B521. Monelle, Raymond. "Lonely Sea and the Sky." *Independent* (Feb. 4, 1989) Weekend Arts p. 31.

Review of the premiere of *Strathclyde Concerto No. 2 for Cello and Orchestra* by William Conway, cello and the Scottish Chamber Orchestra conducted by the composer. The reviewer remarks the work is "completely dominated by the soloist" and that the orchestra "throws a pall of atonal smoke over the struggling passage work of the soloist." However, the composer avoids the jagged sounds of so much modern scoring for the orchestra by "relying solidly on the string band."

B522. Monelle, Raymond. "Queen's Hall: Scottish Chamber Orchestra." *Scotsman* (Feb. 28, 1987).

Review of a concert by the Scottish Chamber Orchestra conducted by the composer at Queen's Hall, Edinburgh, Feb. 27, 1987. Included on the program was a performance of *Sinfonia*. Very complimentary of the composer's conducting about which the reviewer remarked that it was "the modern piece that made the evening."

B523. Monelle, Raymond. "Sir Peter Maxwell Davies and SCO." *Scotsman* (Mar. 19, 1988).

Review of a concert by the Scottish Chamber Orchestra conducted by the composer at the Queen's Hall, Edinburgh, Mar. 17, 1988. Included on the program was a performance of *Concerto for Violin and Orchestra* with Ernst Kovacic, violin. Also performed was *An Orkney Wedding, with Sunrise*.

B524. Monelle, Raymond. "An Unsentimental Saint." *Independent* (June 4, 1990) p. 15.

Review of a performance of *The Lighthouse* by the Music Theatre Wales and the Scottish Chamber Orchestra conducted by Michael Rafferty at the Tramway, Glasgow in early June, 1990. When describing the music the reviewer notes "this amazingly rich score adds a refinement of instrumental texture, an interest in the grotesque, an explicit concern for the modern world."

B525. Money, David. "New Maxwell Davies Sonata." *Daily Telegraph* (June 5, 1984).

Brief review of a concert at the Wigmore Hall, London, June 3, 1984. Included on the program was the premiere of the *Sonatine for Violin and Cimbalon* be Rosemary Furniss, violin, and Gregory

Knowles, cimbalon. The work is described as one, "with fascinating patterns of sound and colour."

B526. Moore-Morgan, Derek. "Perth: From Lehar to Davies." *Opera* v. 36 (April, 1985) pp. 422–423.
Review of a performance of *The Lighthouse* during the Festival of Perth at the University of Wellington, Australia's Octagon Theatre by members of the Western Australia Opera Company, Aug. 14, 1984. Performers included Adrian Brand, Garrick Jones and Keith Hampton and the Western Australia Arts Orchestra Ensemble conducted by Myer Friedman. The reviewer says that the composer "has shown himself...to be a considerable master of chamber opera" and, in the case of *The Lighthouse*, "he is as adept as ever at making big effects with small forces."

B527. Morrison, Richard. "Music Rings Out At Last." *Times* (Aug. 13, 1987).
Includes a review of a concert by the Scottish Chamber Orchestra conducted by the composer at Usher Hall, Edinburgh, Aug., 1987. On the program was a performance of *Sinfonietta Accademica*, of which the reviewer says: "One thinks particularly of the jagged brass outbursts, wildly imaginative in detail, or the mellow desolation of the slow movement."

B528. Morrison, Richard. "Promenade Concerts." *Times* (Sept. 2, 1985).
Review of a concert by the BBC Philharmonic Orchestra conducted by Edward Downes Aug. 31, 1985. Included on the program was a performance of *Symphony No. 3*. About the music the reviewer notes, "Davies's famously angular melodic contours have been softened...the harshness of his chromaticism has been tempered."

B529. Morrison, Richard. "Sturdy Champion of Living Music." *Times* (June 19, 1986).
A long interview with violinist Isaac Stern a few days before he premiered *Concerto for Violin and Orchestra* at the St. Magnus Festival June 21, 1986.

B530. Mundy, Simon. "First Cousins." *Classical Music* (Sept. 9, 1989) p. 31.
A preview of *Symphony No. 4* just prior to its premiere by the Scottish Chamber Orchestra, Sept. 10, 1989.

B531. Mundy, Simon. "Scots in Wales." *Independent* (Aug. 13, 1988).
Review of a performance of *The Martyrdom of St. Magnus* by Music
Theatre Wales in the Old Tythe Barn, St. Donat's Arts Center,
August, 1988. Comments: "the moments of magic owe more to the
instinctive meeting of music and dramatic craft than to any mid-
1970s gimmickry." The reviewer objects to the seventh Scene,
where the setting moves to the present day, as disrupting the
atmosphere of the piece.

B532. Murray, David. "A Bright Baton." *Financial Times* (Feb. 22, 1993).
Review of a concert by the BBC Symphony Orchestra conducted by
Eduardo Mata at Festival Hall, Feb. 19, 1993. Included on the
program was a performance of *Concerto for Trumpet and Orchestra*
featuring Håkan Hardenberger, trumpet. The work is described as
a "sort of mini-opera with the trumpet in the role of St. Francis."

B533. Murray, David. "Davies' Third Symphony/Radio 3." *Financial Times*
(Sept. 2, 1985).
Review of a concert by the BBC Philharmonic Orchestra conducted
by Edward Downes, at the Albert Hall, Aug. 31, 1985, including a
performance of *Symphony No. 3*. Remarks: "Intricate though the
design of the Third is, Davies has this time made everything audible:
the power of the music doesn't have to be taken on trust." Gives a
descriptive analysis of the work.

B534. Murray, David. "Huddersfield Festival—I." *Financial Times* (Nov. 14,
1984) p.
Article about the 1984 Huddersfield Festival held in early November,
1984. Among the works performed were *St. Thomas Wake* (which
the reviewer says "sinks 1930's fox-trots in a truly Titanic disaster");
Stone Litany (described as a "masterly conjuring-up of ancient air
and mystery") and *Worldes Blis*, performed by the BBC Symphony
conducted by Elgar Howarth (described as "unheard-of sketches
of...anguished polyphony"). Also reviews a performance of *Brass
Quintet* by the Albany Quintet, observing that "the polyphony is
tough but necessarily transparent" and that this compels the listener
to understand it better.

B535. Murray, David. "Maxwell Davies' New Fifth." *Financial Times* (Aug.
11, 1994).
Review of the premier of *Symphony No. 5* by the Philharmonia
Orchestra conducted by the composer during a Promenade Orchestra

at the Royal Albert Hall, Aug. 9, 1994. Compares the new work to the composer's earlier Symphonies, noting the influence of Sibelius, and remarks, "it is superbly compact and exercises a relentless symphonic grip."

B536. Murray, David. "Nash Ensemble." *Financial Times* (Dec. 2, 1980) p. Review of a concert by the Nash Ensemble at the Roundhouse, late November, 1980. Included on the program was a performance of *Ave Maris Stella*. Work described as "an integrated masterpiece."

B537. Murray, David. "*Pollicino* (Henze) and *Cinderella* (Peter Maxwell Davies)." *Opera* v. 32 (Mar. 1981) pp. 295–296.
Review of a performance of *Cinderella* at the Jeanetta Cochrane Theatre, Dec. 16, 1980, concerning which the reviewer remarks: "Davies's music functions like a modest score for a light musical comedy."

B538. Murray, David. "Superlative Performance and Deft Ending." *Financial Times* (Aug. 10, 1983) p.
Review of a concert by the Fires of London at the Albert Hall, Aug. 7, 1983. Included on the program was a performance of *Revelation and Fall* conducted by John Carewe with soloist Mary Thomas (which the reviewer says remains "the best and richest of all the partly theatrical works of Davies' expressionist period"). Also on the program was a performance of *Suite from 'The Boyfriend'* conducted by the composer (an "affectionately jokey suite").

B539. Myers, Rollo. "British Music." *Canon* v. 14 (Jan.-Feb. 1961) p. 110.
Includes a review of the first London performance of *Ricercar and Doubles on 'To Many a Well'* by the New Music Ensemble conducted by John Carewe. About the music the reviewer remarks: "Mr. Davies has considerable technical ability" but complains that "The music...suffers from a too purely intellectual approach leaving the ear unsatisfied."

B540. Myers, Rollo. "London Music." *Canon* v. 16 (Nov. 1962) pp. 77–78.
Review of the premiere of *First Fantasia on an 'In Nomine' of John Taverner* by the BBC Symphony Orchestra conducted by the composer at the Royal Albert Hall, Sept. 13, 1962. About the music the reviewer remarks: "The idiom is unmistakably modern, but the composer us less uncompromising than usual...paying more attention...to such things as colour and rhythmic variety."

B541. Nagley, Judith. "Proms." *Musical Times* v. 124 (Oct., 1983) pp. 629–630.

Includes a review of a concert which featured the premiere of *Sinfonia Concertante*, by the Academy of St. Martin-in-the-Fields conducted by Neville Marriner, Aug. 12, 1983. Reviewer remarks about the music: "Although much of the writing is densely contrapuntal there are some marvelous 'mood moments'" and concludes the work "will yield up more treasures with better acquaintance."

B542. Nash, Ian. "Pied Piper Heralds Age of Barbarism." *Teacher* v. 41 no. 18 (Jan. 18, 1985) p. 1.

Article which features excerpts from a lecture the composer delivered, as President of the Schools Music Association at a North of England Education Conference. The thrust of the talks was directed at the cuts made from support of music in the British Schools Music program by the government.

B543. Naslund, Erik. "Stockholm." *Opera Canada* v. 22 no. 2 (1981) pp. 41–42.

Brief article which includes a review of a performance of *Miss Donnithorne's Maggot* at the Stockholm Opera in the Rotunda, Feb., 1981. Soloist was Kerstin Meyer.

B544. Neubauer, Simon. "Der heilige Pazifist." *Opernwelt* (Nov. 1983).

Review of a performance of *The Martyrdom of St. Magnus* by members of the Bremer Theater conducted by Günther Bauer-Schenk at Bremen, der Kirche Unser Lieben Frauen, Sept. 23, 1983.

B545. Noble, Jeremy. "Music in London." *Musical Times* v. 106 (April, 1965) p. 279.

Includes a review of a concert by the Ambrosian Singers and the English Chamber Orchestra conducted by Norman del Mar, at Friends House, Mar. 1, 1965, which featured the premiere of *Five Motets*. Remarks about the music: "These were impressive in a seized-up sort of way; individual chordal structure revealed an individual harmonic sense...the antiphonal effects were beguiling."

B546. Norris, David Owen. "The Bearable Lightness of Being." *BBC Music Magazine* (Sept. 1994) pp. 44–47.

Article about the composer written of his 60th birthday (Sept. 8, 1994). It features an interview with the composer about aspects of his life and works and future plans. Includes many photographs and a brief discography.

B547. Norris, Geoffrey. "Davies's Brave New World." *Daily Telegraph* (Sept. 20, 1988).
Review of the premiere of *Resurrection* by the Darmstadt Opera conducted by Hans Drewanz at the Stadtstheater, Darmstadt, Sept. 18, 1988. Of the opera, the reviewer says, "Musically, Davies is eclectic...pop, gospel hymns, chant and 1930's songs parodied or absorbed into his own idiom."

B548. Norris, Geoffrey. "Davies's Violin Concerto." *Daily Telegraph* (June 23, 1986) p. 8.
Review of the premiere of *Concerto for Violin and Orchestra* by Isaac Stern with the Royal Philharmonic Orchestra conducted by André Previn at St. Magnus Cathedral during the St. Magnus Festival, June 21, 1986. Describing the music the reviewer writes, "Davies has created a work of taut thematic organisation...dramatic in its violin writing, pointed in its application of orchestral colours."

B549. Norris, Geoffrey. "A Doubtful Modern Haydn." *Daily Telegraph* (Sept. 15, 1988).
Review of a concert by the Scottish Chamber Orchestra conducted by the composer at the Royal Albert Hall, Sept. 13, 1988. Included on the program was a performance of *Strathclyde Concerto No. 1 for Oboe and Orchestra* featuring Robin Miller, oboe. The reviewer says that the work is "not Davies at his most inspirational, though it is firmly constructed and structurally balanced."

B550. Norris, Geoffrey. "Festival Spirit Here to Stay." *Daily Telegraph* (June 14, 1986).
A description of concerts and other events which were scheduled to take place at the 1986 St. Magnus Festival, June, 1986.

B551. Norris, Geoffrey. "The Fires' Farewell." *Daily Telegraph* (Jan. 22, 1987) p. 10.
Review of the farewell concert by the Fires of London conducted by the composer at the Queen Elizabeth Hall, Jan. 20, 1987. Included on the program was the premiere of *Winterfold* by Mary Thomas, which the reviewer found "a characteristically haunting, still and chilly setting of the Orcadian poet, George Mackay Brown."

B552. Norris, Geoffrey. "Island Life Under Threat." *Daily Telegraph* (June 22, 1988).
Article which includes a review of a performance of *Black Pentecost* by soloists LaVerne William and Alan Oke with the BBC Philharmonic Orchestra conducted by Edward Downes at the Phoenix Cinema, Kirkwall, Orkney, June 19, 1988.

B553. Norris, Geoffrey. "A Modern Saga of a Saint." *Daily Telegraph* (May 21, 1987).
Review of a performance of *Martyrdom of St. Magnus* by Opera Factory London Sinfonietta at the Donmar Warehouse in mid-May 1987, produced by Stephen Langridge.

B554. Norris, Geoffrey. "A Swedish *Taverner*." *Daily Telegraph* (Nov. 26, 1984).
Features reviews of productions of *The Lighthouse* and *Taverner* by the Swedish Royal Opera in the Royal Theatre, Stockholm, Nov. 24, 1984.

B555. Norris, Geoffrey. "A Toast to St. Magnus." *Daily Telegraph* (June 20, 1988).
Article about performances at the 1988 St. Magnus Festival. Included is a review of the premiere of *Six Songs for St. Andrew's* by pupils of St. Andrew's Primary School conducted by Glenys Hughes at the Papdale Primary School, Kirkwall, June 18, 1988. The reviewer describes the work as "challenging, marvellously inventive and colourful miniatures of music theatre."

B556. Northcott, Bayan. "Always Somebody New." *Sunday Telegraph* (Aug. 14, 1983).
Includes a review of the premiere of *Sinfonia Concertante* by the Academy of St. Martin-in-the-Fields conducted by Neville Marriner at the Royal Albert Hall, Aug. 12, 1983. The reviewer says that "in scoring the lay-out is often closer to baroque than classical...like some latter day Brandenburg concerto."

B557. Northcott, Bayan. "Chamber Groups." *Music and Musicians* v. 21 (Sept., 1972) pp. 88ff.
Includes a review of a concert by the Fires of London at the Elizabeth Hall, May 6, 1972. Included in the concert was the premiere of *Veni Sancte-Veni Creator Spiritus*, which the reviewer judged to be "a bright little medieval transcription." Also performed

were *Hymnos* ("one of the richest, most varied and ambivalently musical of all Davies's pieces") and *Septet*, a revised version of the 1958 *Sextet* ("displayed a glittering diaphany of sound rare in Davies's subsequent music").

B558. Northcott, Bayan. "Composers of the Sixties." *Music and Musicians* v. 18 (Jan. 1970) p. 34.
Article about important composers in the 1960's. The section on Davies mentions *St. Thomas Wake*, *Worldes Blis* and *Eight Songs for a Mad King* and concludes: "The intriguing question for the 70's is whether Davies will achieve some intermediate and humanistic mode of expression."

B559. Northcott, Bayan. "Damping Down the Flames." *Independent* (Jan. 20, 1987) p. 12.
Written just prior to the Fires of London's Farewell Concert in London at the Queen Elizabeth Hall, Jan. 20, 1987. Gives a brief history of the group and mentions works by Davies and other composers written for it.

B560. Northcott, Bayan. "First Performances: Maxwell Davies's *A Mirror of Whitening Light*." *Tempo* no. 121 (June 1977) pp. 33–34.
Review of the premiere of *A Mirror of Whitening Light* by the London Sinfonietta conducted by the composer at the Queen Elizabeth Hall, May 23, 1977. The reviewer says the work had a positive reception and thinks it "may well prove the last, most finished product of a particular phase."

B561. Northcott, Bayan. "First Performances: Maxwell Davies's *Anakreontika*." *Tempo* no. 119 (Dec. 1976) pp. 49–50.
Short review of the premiere of *Anakreontika* by Mary Thomas and the Fires of London conducted by the composer at the Queen Elizabeth Hall Sept. 17, 1976. Describing briefly several of the songs, the reviewer comments: "In several ways *Anakreontika* conveys an intermezzo-like character."

B562. Northcott, Bayan. "Gale From the North." *Sunday Telegraph* (Feb. 5, 1978).
Review of the premiere of *Symphony No. 1* by the Philharmonia Orchestra conducted by Simon Rattle at the Royal Festival Hall, Feb. 2, 1978. The reviewer writes that the work is "a masterpiece...no

doubt that it is his boldest and bravest offering yet." Includes a lengthy description.

B563. Northcott, Bayan. "Just as You'd Expect." *Sunday Telegraph* (June 29, 1986).
Includes a review of a concert which featured the premiere of *Agnus Dei* by members of the Almeida Festival Players conducted by Oliver Knussen at the Union Chapel, Islington, June 23, 1986, as part of the Almeida Festival. The reviewer saw this as "a memento of Davies's idiosyncratic early Medievalry." Also includes a review of the first London performance of *Concerto for Violin and Orchestra* by Isaac Stern with the Royal Philharmonic Orchestra conducted by André Previn at the Royal Festival Hall, June 25, 1986. The reviewer says that the work "flows, sounds, feels like conventional late-romantic concerto—except for its notes."

B564. Northcott, Bayan. "Marches Past." *Sunday Telegraph* (July 26, 1981).
Includes a review of a performance of *Symphony No. 2* by the BBC Symphony Orchestra conducted by Gennadi Rozhdestvensky at the Royal Albert Hall, July 23, 1981. After a description of the work the reviewer concludes, "while the large-scale gestures of the music suggest Davies' frankest endorsement of the rhetoric of late romanticism...this only seems to emphasize the paucity of plain statement and the flux of 'transformations'."

B565. Northcott, Bayan. "One Foot in Eden," *Tempo* no. 124 (Mar., 1978) p. 32.
Short review of a film about the composer, *Orkney and Music of Peter Maxwell Davies* (produced by Platypus Films for the Arts Council of Great Britain), shown on Jan. 19, 1978. Notes some of the works that were excerpted in the film, including *Renaissance Scottish Dances*, *Ave Maris Stella*, *O Magnum Mysterium*, and *The Martyrdom of St. Magnus* (remarking about the last that it "should win Maxwell Davies many new listeners").

B566. Northcott, Bayan. "Opening Up: British Concert Music Since the War." *Musical Newsletter* v. 5 no. 3 (1975) p. 9.
Article on major British composers since the War. The author describes Davies's compositional style as "a combination of avant-garde number-working and Medieval cantus firmus techniques." He writes that *Leopardi Fragments* (1961) are "introverted...in their darkly melismatic counterpoint"; *Missa Super L'Homme Armé* (1967)

threatens to "denigrate altogether into phantasmagoria of parody foxtrots and sentimental Victorian hymns"; and *Worldes Blis* (1969) and *Stone Litany* (1973) "reveal a calm and atmospheric lyricism after the storm."

B567. Northcott, Bayan. "Peter Maxwell Davies." *Music and Musicians* vol. 17 (1969) pp. 36-40, 80-81.

B568. Northcott, Bayan. "Pioneer Core." *Sunday Telegraph* (Mar. 18, 1979). Includes a review of the premier of *Salome: Concert Suite from the Ballet* by the London Symphony Orchestra conducted by David Atherton at the Royal Festival Hall, Mar. 16, 1979. The reviewer comments: "It is certainly as a sequence of specifically orchestral, sonorous images that the Suite proves most immediately memorable." Gives a brief background about the ballet.

B569. Northcott, Bayan. "Since Grimes: A Concise Survey of the British Musical Stage." *Musical Newsletter* v. 4 n. 2 (1974) p. 21. Survey which includes a short section on several of Davies's "theatrical and dramatic works" including *Revelation and Fall, Eight Songs for a Mad King, Blind Man's Buff, Miss Donnithorne's Maggot* and *Taverner*. About *Taverner* the writer remarks that "it remains an open question whether the dark beauty and power of the music...really articulates the drama or merely parallels and decorates it."

B570. Northcott, Bayan. "*Taverner*." *Music and Musicians* v. 21 (Sept., 1972) pp. 62–64. Lengthy review of *Taverner*, after the reviewer had "experienced the work four times." Article mentions other compositions by the composer: *St. Michael Sonata, Veni Sancte Spiritus, Ecce Manus Tradentis, Shakespeare Music, Antechrist*, and *Missa Super L'Homme Armé*. He writes, "the opera had become almost continuously absorbing...I have found my mind much occupied by the question as to just what it adds up to."

B571. Northcott, Bayan. "Thin Programme." *Music and Musicians* v. 18 (Dec., 1969) p. 56. Review of a concert by the Pierrot Players conducted by the composer on Oct. 1, 1969 at the Elizabeth Hall. Included on the program was the first London performance of *Solita*, by flautist Judith Pearce.

B572. Northcott, Bayan. "The Winces Consort." *Independent* (May 18, 1987).
Review of a concert by the King's Singers at Wigmore Hall, May 15, 1987. Included on the program was a performance of *House of Winter* described as "remote and haunting for the most part in Sir Peter's best Orkney manner." Also performed was *Sea Runes*.

B573. Northcott, Bayan. "With God in Tow." *Independent* (Aug. 5, 1987).
Includes a review of a performance of *Eight Songs For a Mad King* by Opera Factory London Sinfonietta at the Queen Elizabeth Hall, early August, 1987, with soloist Richard Suat. The work is described as "a sequence of musical forms and quotations from the time of George III." The reviewer comments that David Freeman's production employed what he describes as "the usual Freeman tactics."

B574. Norton-Welsh, Christopher. "Salzburg." *Opera* v. 34 (Aug., 1983) pp. 867–868.
Review of a performance of *The Lighthouse* on Mar. 27, 1983 in Austrian Radio's Salzburg studio. Notes the set "caught the claustrophobic character of the work."

B575. Norton-Welsh, Christopher. "Vienna." *Opera* v. 35 (June 1984) pp. 630–631.
Review of a performance of *The Lighthouse* by Studio K, Vienna, Feb. 24, 1984.

B576. Norton-Welsh, Christopher. "Vienna." *Opera* v. 40 (Dec., 1989) pp. 1444–1445.
Review of a double-billed production which included both *Miss Donnithorne's Maggot* and *The No. 11 Bus* in Vienna at the Studio K, (n.d.). Program was performed four times during Oct. 11–18, 1989. No real review of the music but only of the performances. For Guri Egge's *Miss Donnithorne's Maggot*, there is high praise. The reviewer felt the translation to German probably removed some of the jokes from *The No. 11 Bus*, but remarks, "I have nothing but praise for the realization."

B577. Norton-Welsh, Christopher. "Vienna." *Opera* v. 36 (Autumn 1985) pp. 55–56.
Includes a review of a performance of *The Martyrdom of St, Magnus* by members of the Vienna Chamber Opera at Studio K, May 22, 1985. The work is described as "a proven artistic success."

B578. Nyman, Michael. "The Manchester School." *Musical Events* v. 24 (Dec., 1969) pp. 12–14.

Article about an upcoming concert by the London Sinfonietta, on 29 Dec., 1969, featuring the music of the 'Manchester School' represented by composers Alexander Goehr, Harrison Birtwistle, and Davies. Includes a brief description of Davies's career as a composer and also remarks on his work as a music educator, describing the latter aspect as "remarkable...witness *O Magnum Mysterium.*" Also speculates (in 1969) that the composer's "fantastic opera [*Taverner*] is likely to remain unperformed as long as there are still forms of religious censorship in force."

B579. Oakes, Meredith. "Death of a Pacifist Viking." *Independent* (May 21, 1987).

Reviews *The Martyrdom of St. Magnus* performed by Opera Factory during London's International Opera Festival at the Donmar Warehouse in May, 1987. The score is described as "restrained by comparison with some earlier Maxwell Davies's pieces...thematic in scoring and plot...to intrigue, teach and entertain."

B580. Oakes, Meredith. "Television (Fires of London)." *Music and Musicians* v. 25 (Oct. 1976) pp. 38–40.

Article on television productions of major musical works. Includes a review of an earlier live production (July 27, 1976) of a Promenade concert at the Roundhouse which featured a performance of *Eight Songs For a Mad King.* It was filmed and televised on BBC-1 Aug. 15, 1976. The reviewer saw this work as "good music theatre" and writes: "A successful performance of this piece is a rite crystallising an important idea: the unnatural degree to which Nature allows us to suffer."

B581. Oliver, Michael. "Maxwell Davies." *Gramophone* v. 63 no. 751 (Dec. 1985) p. 793.

Review of a recording (Unicorn-Kanchana DKP9038; DKPC9038) of *Into the Labyrinth* (with tenor Neil Mackie) and *Sinfonietta Accademica* by the Scottish Chamber Orchestra conducted by the composer. The reviewer writes that in the first piece "Davies's music matches the text...with subtlety and moving directness," while the second is a "landscape" work, evocative of the Orkney Islands where Davies lived and composed. He notes the composer's "use of cunningly-wrought musical processes as analogues for meditation upon time and transience."

B582. Oliver, Michael. "Maxwell Davies: *Symphony No. 2.*" *Gramophone* (Sept. 1994) p. 54.

Review of a recording of *Symphony No. 2* by the BBC Philharmonic Orchestra conducted by the composer (Collins Classics 1403-2 CD): "richly full but immaculately detailed." Includes a description of the work.

B583. Orga, Ates. "South Bank." *Music and Musicians* v. 18 (Feb., 1970) pp. 50ff.

Review of a concert which included the premiere of *Vesalii Icones* at the Elizabeth Hall, Dec. 9, 1969, choreographed and danced by William Louther with Jennifer Ward playing the obbligato cello part. The reviewer comments: "repetitive elements have entered [Davies's] music, and I sense a certain obscurity and eccentricity of direction."

B584. Orr, Buxton. "Commissions and First Performances." *Composer* no. 34 (Winter 1969–1970) p. 41.

Announcement of the premiere of *Vesalii Icones* at the Queen Elizabeth Hall, Dec. 9, 1969.

B585. Orr, Buxton. "First Performances and Commissions." *Composer* no. 39 (Spring, 1971) p. 34.

Notices of the premiere of *Ut Re Mi* by Stephen Pruslin at the Purcell Room, London, Jan. 19, 1971, and of *Taverner: Points and Dances from the Opera* [by the Fires of London], at the Elizabeth Hall, Feb. [20], 1971.

B586. Orr, Buxton. "First Performances and Commissions." *Composer* no. 40 (Summer, 1971) p. 32.

Announcement of the premiere of *From Stone to Thorn* for mezzo-soprano and instrumental ensemble, in Oxford, June, 1971. Work was commissioned by Jesus College.

B587. Orr, Buxton. "First Performances and Commissions." *Composer* no. 49 (Autumn, 1973) p. 27

Announcement of the premiere of *Stone Litany* Sept. 22, 1973 in Glasgow, by the Scottish National Orchestra.

B588. Orr, Buxton. "First Performances and Commissions." *Composer* no. 55 (Summer, 1975) p. 2.

Announcements of the premiere of *Ave Maris Stella* May 27, 1975 at the Bath Festival.

B589. Orr, Buxton. "First Performances and Commissions." *Composer* no. 60 (Spring, 1977) p. 3.

Announcement of the premiere of two works: *A Mirror of Whitening Light*, Mar. 23, 1977 by the London Sinfonietta at the Queen Elizabeth Hall, and *The Martyrdom of St. Magnus*, June 18, 1977 at the St. Magnus Festival, Kirkwall.

B590. Orr, Buxton. "First Performances and Commissions." *Composer* no. 62 (Winter, 1977–78) p. 2.

Announcement of the premiere of *Symphony No. 1*, Feb. 2, 1978 by the Philharmonia Orchestra at the Royal Festival Hall.

B591. Osborne, Robert. *"The Yellow Cake Revue*: Comments in Words and Music on the Threat of Uranium Mining in Orkney." *Notes* v. 42 no. 3 (1986) pp. 657–658.

Review of *Yellow Cake Revue* upon the publication of the score by Boosey and Hawkes in 1984, Includes a clear and concise descriptive analysis of the work, which is described as "a politically challenging work that questions the very future of our planet." Notes the songs are "spiced with intriguing rhythmic subtleties."

B592. Owen, Albert Alan. "First Performances, Commissions." *Composer* no. 71 (Winter 1980–1981) p. 37.

Announcement of the premiere of *Cinderella*, June 21, 1980 at the St. Magnus Festival, Kirkwall, Orkney, by students from the Papdale Primary School and Kirkwall Grammar School Choir conducted by Glenys Hughes.

B593. Owen, Albert Alan. "First Performances, Commissions." *Composer* no. 73 (Summer, 1981) p. 30.

Announcement of the premiere of *Symphony No. 2* in Boston, 26 Feb., 1981, by the Boston Symphony Orchestra.

B594. Owens, Peter. *"House of Winter*; *Jimmack the Postie."* *Music and Letters* 69 no. 4 (1988) pp. 567–568.

Review of *House of Winter* and *Jimmack the Postie* when the scores of both works were published by Chester, 1987. After a brief description of *House of Winter*, the reviewer notes: "The gentle rise and fall of melodic construction...is most strongly reminiscent of *Solstice of Light*...and...*First Ferry to Hoy*." He judges the work to be "a most attractive and effective piece." Of *Jimmack*, he writes: "Though manipulation of pitch class sequences and the organizations of durations in the piece relate clearly to the technique explored in Davies' larger orchestral works, its textures are predominately lighter."

B595. P. G. *"The Two Fiddlers." Music in Education* v. 142 (1978) no. 396 p. 327.
Review of the premiere of *The Two Fiddlers* at the second St. Magnus Festival, Kirkwall, Orkney, June 16, 1978. Performers included students from the Kirkwall Grammar School; conductor was Norman Mitchell. Article includes a synopsis of the libretto. Of the music the reviewer remarks "this is a school opera which is neither patronizing nor embarrassing."

B596. Page, Frederick. "New Zealand." *Musical Times* v. 107 (Feb., 1966) pp. 139-140.
Includes mention of a series of lectures the composer delivered at 4 major New Zealand universities: "His topics were the training of a musician as he saw it...and his own teaching at Cirencester."

B597. Page, Tim. "Concert: Davies Piece for Solo Horn." *New York Times* (June 10, 1984) p. 12.
Review of a concert by the Chamber Players of the League of Composers—International Society for Contemporary Music at Symphony Space, New York City, early June, 1984. Included on the program was a performance of *Sea Eagle* performed by William Purvis. The reviewer says that the music "possesses a near Sibelian bleakness...a lyrical utterance with few gratuitous effects."

B598. Paterson, Wilma. "SCO." *Glasgow Herald* (Nov. 15, 1986).
Review of a concert by the Scottish Chamber Orchestra conducted by the composer at City Hall, Glasgow, Nov. 14, 1986. Included on the program was a performance of *An Orkney Wedding, With Sunrise*, which the reviewer thought "a most evocative and enthralling 'picture postcard record' of an Orkney Wedding."

B599. Payne, Anthony. "First Performances." *Tempo* no. 70 (Autumn 1964) pp. 15-16.
Includes a review of a performance of *Veni Sancte Spiritus* at the Cheltenham Festival, July 10, 1964. More than a mere review: also includes a detailed analysis of the piece with musical examples.

B600. Payne, Anthony. "Full Gamut." *Music and Musicians* v. 11 (Jan., 1963) p. 44.
Review of a concert at the St. Pancras Town Hall, Nov. 26, 1962, which included the premiere of *Four Carols* by the New Music Singers conducted by Graham Treacher. Remarks that the composer has "recaptured the beautiful austerity of Christmas as it was before the big department stores gave it an overdose of sugar."

B601. Payne, Anthony. "Peter Maxwell Davies' *Five Motets*." *Tempo* no. 72 (Spring 1965) pp. 7–11.
Article on *Five Motets* (composed in 1959 and revised in 1962), including an analysis and many musical examples. The author remarks: "Stylistically, the work moves away from the strict techniques characteristic of the composer's preceding works...towards a greater freedom of melodic and harmonic expression."

B602. Payne, Anthony. "Philharmonia/Simon Rattle." *Daily Telegraph* (July 27, 1978).
Review of a Promenade Concert by the Philharmonia Orchestra conducted by Simon Rattle at the Royal Albert Hall, London, July 26, 1978. The reviewer notes, "the work makes a magnificent impression, sustaining its argument through four wide spanned movements."

B603. Payne, Anthony. "The Problems of Pierrot." *Music and Musicians* v. 15 (Aug., 1967) p. 4.
Review of the first concert given by the Pierrot Players at the Elizabeth Hall, May 30, 1967. Included in the program was the premiere of *Antechrist*, a work here described as "a sequence of anonymous mediaeval dances arranged by the composer and interspersed with original interludes."

B604. Peart, Donald. "Peter Maxwell Davies: The Shepherds' Calendar." *Miscellanea Musicologica* v. 1 (Mar., 1966) pp. 249–255.
Both historical and analytical, focusing on *Shepherds' Calendar* prior to its performance at the 1966 Adelaide Festival of Arts. The reviewer writes that the work is "delightful and imaginative" and says that "The melodic writing...owes something to Bartok's methods of developing folksong scales." The analysis includes musical examples.

B605. Percival, John. *"Caroline Mathilde." Dance Magazine* (April/May, 1991) p. 33.
Review of the premiere of *Caroline Mathilde: A Ballet in Two Acts* by the Royal Danish Ballet at the Royal Theatre, Copenhagen, Mar. 14, 1991. Compares the music to that of *Eight Songs for a Mad King*, noting the new score uses many of the same techniques but that "they are transformed into a longer development drawing on his later symphonic experience." The reviewer also comments: "One interesting feature is the use of unusual instruments."

B606. Percival, John. *"Salome." Times* (Nov. 28, 1978).
Review of the ballet *Salome* at its premiere by the Royal Danish Ballet at the Circus Building, Copenhagen, Nov. 10, 1978. Music was provided by a recording made by the Danish radio Orchestra conducted by Janos Furst. About the piece the reviewer notes: "In its theatrical context it supports and enhances the production at all points, glossing occasional weaknesses in the choreography."

B607. Persche, Gerhard. "Interview." *Opernwelt* v. 29 (Nov. 1988) pp. 64–66.
Interview of the composer by Gerhard Persche. Focuses on *Resurrection*, after the premiere of that work in Sept., 1988 at Darmstadt. Includes the composer's views on the purpose and meaning of his operas.

B608. Peschl, B. "Mürztaler Werkstatt '87: Peter Maxwell Davies: *Cinderella." Oesterreichischer Bundesverlag* v. 41 (Feb. 1988) p. 133.
Review of a performance of *Cinderella* at the 1987 Mürztaler Workshop in Krieglach, Austria, conducted by Hans Held.

B609. Petrie, Jonathan. "Magnificently Captured Agony." *Catholic Herald* (July 8, 1983).
Review of the revival of *Taverner* by the Royal Opera, Covent Garden, June 29, 1983. The reviewer notes: "The musical argument contained in an often difficult score, succinctly underlines the dilemma in which Taverner...finds himself." Includes a synopsis of the plot.

B610. Pettitt, Stephen. "Aromas Enjoyed." *Times* (May 27, 1988).
Review of a concert by the London Symphony Orchestra conducted by Kent Nagano at the Barbican Hall, May 26, 1988. Included on the program was a performance of *Symphony No. 2*, which the

reviewer judged to be "a work of deep and lasting substance which crowned the evening."

B611. Pettitt, Stephen. "Clearer Structures in New Classic." *Times* (Sept. 14, 1988.
Review of a concert by the Scottish Chamber Orchestra conducted by the composer at the Royal Albert Hall, Sept. 13, 1988. Included on the program was a performance of *Strathclyde Concerto No. 1 for Oboe and Orchestra* with oboist Robin Miller. Of this piece the reviewer notes its classic form and says that "one of Davies's main achievements has been to forge a new classicism, a music of reason which manages to be at once entirely original."

B612. Pettitt, Stephen. "Dark and Secretive." *Times* (Mar. 16, 1992).
Review of a concert by the Scottish Chamber Orchestra conducted by the composer at City Hall, Glasgow, Mar. 13, 1992. Included on the program was the premiere performance of *Strathclyde Concerto No. 6 for Flute and Orchestra* with soloist David Nicholson. The reviewer remarks the composer "toys with motifs and colours." Also on the program was the premiere of *Strathclyde Concerto No. 5 for Violin, Viola and String Orchestra* with soloists Jane Clark and Catherine Marwood. The reviewer notes the musical sources for the work "suggested dark themes of emptiness and loneliness."

B613. Pettitt, Stephen. "Davies Finds Room to Breathe Life." *Times* (Aug. 11, 1994).
Review of the premiere of *Symphony No. 5* by the Philharmonia Orchestra conducted by the composer at the Royal Albert Hall, Aug. 9, 1994. About the work the reviewer notes: "This is a tough, uncompromising piece...It challenges the orchestra severely, although it presents the listener with plenty of clear hooks." Includes a colorful description of the work.

B614. Pettitt, Stephen. "Effectively Simple." *Times* (April 9, 1990).
Review of a performance of *The Martyrdom of St. Magnus* as part of 'Maxfest,' April, 1990 at the Queen Elizabeth Hall, by members of Music Theatre Wales accompanied by the Scottish Chamber Orchestra conducted by Michael Rafferty. The reviewer notes the work "stands at a crucial moment of his composing career, straddling what might be very broadly categorized as the shocking and the lyrical phases of his style."

B615. Pettitt, Stephen. "Furniss/Knowles." *Times* (June 4, 1984).
Review of a concert at the Wigmore Hall, London, June 3, 1984. Included on the program was the premiere of the *Sonatine for Violin and Cimbalon* by Rosemary Furniss, violin and Gregory Knowles, cimbalon. About the work the reviewer remarks: "Neither partner is allowed to dominate the other. Instead, both are given their fair share of melodic prominence."

B616. Pettitt, Stephen. "Guided Tour by the Composer." Times (April 3, 1990).
Includes a review of a concert by the Scottish Chamber Orchestra conducted by the composer at the Queen Elizabeth Hall, during 'Maxfest,' Mar. 31, 1990. On the program was the first London performance of *Strathclyde Concerto No. 2 for Cello and Orchestra* featuring cellist William Conway. About the music the reviewer says: "To say that the piece exudes feelings of space, wonder, and poignant solitude give the impression of something utterly romantic. So it is." Also performed were *Into the Labyrinth*, with tenor Neil Mackie (the reviewer remarks, "Mackay Brown's atmospheric words are inextricably bound up with the flavour of the place and the people") and *An Orkney Wedding, With Sunrise* ("effervescent, cannily contrived").

B617. Pettitt, Stephen. "Having Fun, Naturally." *Times* (April 5, 1990).
Includes a review of the premiere of *Jupiter Landing* during the South Bank Maxfest on Children's Day at the Queen Elizabeth Hall, April 3, 1990, by pupils from the Close Side Primary school conducted by Mark Caswell. The reviewer describes the music as "simple but not too simple. Davies know how far he can stretch young musicians." Also includes a brief review of the English premiere of *Strathclyde Concerto No. 3 for Horn, Trumpet and Orchestra* with soloist Robert Cook, horn, and Peter Franks, trumpet and the Scottish Chamber Orchestra conducted by the composer at the Queen Elizabeth Hall, April 8 ("a work which tests the technique of its soloists....to the full...which is a compelling, beautifully coloured struggle for supremacy and reconciliation") and brief mention of performances of a number of other works as part of Children's Day: *Cinderella, Songs of Hoy, The Great Bank Robbery, Lullabye for Lucy, O Magnum Mysterium* and *Farewell to Stromness*.

B618. Pettitt, Stephen. "In Memoriam, Michael Vyner." *Times* (Oct. 23, 1989).

Review of a concert by the Birmingham Contemporary Music Group conducted by Oliver Knussen at Adrian Boult Hall, Birmingham in October, 1989. Included on the program was a performance of *Revelation and Fall* featuring Linda Hurst, soprano. The reviewer remarks the work is "surely representing the last work in the paradoxes of expressionism, at once austere and extravagant."

B619. Pettitt, Stephen. "RPO/Downes." *Times* (April 13, 1990).

Review of a concert by the Royal Philharmonic Orchestra conducted by Edward Downes at the Royal Festival Hall, April, 1990. Included on the program was a performance of *Symphony No. 3*. The reviewer notes: "It may not be an easy work to assimilate" and concludes, "possibly a masterpiece."

B620. Pettitt, Stephen. "SCO/Maxwell Davies/Boettcher." *Times* (Sept. 6, 1984).

Review of a concert by the Scottish Chamber Orchestra conducted by the composer at the Royal Albert Hall, Sept. 5, 1984. On the program was the English premiere of *Into the Labyrinth*, with tenor Neil Mackie. The reviewer says: "It is not so much a hymn to raw nature as a confrontation through George Mackay Brown's magical, evocative text, between the natural state and the real world...of technology." Includes a brief analysis of the work.

B621. Pettitt, Stephen. "Touching Bass." *Times* (Feb. 18, 1993).

Review of a concert by the Scottish Chamber Orchestra conducted by the composer at the Queen Elizabeth Hall, London, Feb. 16, 1993. Included on the program was a performance of the *Strathclyde Concerto No. 7 for Double Bass and Orchestra* featuring soloist Duncan McTier. When describing the work the reviewer notes, "the first impression is of a pregnant rhapsody, richly harmonized and orchestrated." Also included on the program was *Caroline Mathilde: Suite From Act I of the Ballet*.

B622. Pfeifer, Ellen. "Boston Symphony: Davies' *Symphony No. 2*." *Hi Fi/Musical America* v. 31 (July, 1981) pp. MA 37–38.

Review of the premiere of *Symphony No. 2* in Boston, by the Boston Symphony Orchestra conducted by Seiji Ozawa, Feb. 26, 1981. Describes the music as exemplifying the composer's "uniquely reinterpreted tonality" and says that it "takes both pictorial and architectural inspiration from the sea."

B623. Pfeiffer, Ellen. "Conductor Peter Davies Hits Right Note With BSO." *Boston Herald* (Jan. 4, 1991).
Review of a concert by the Boston Symphony Orchestra conducted by the composer at Symphony Hall, Boston, Jan. 3, 1991. Included on the program was the U.S. premiere of *Strathclyde Concerto No. 2 for Cello and Orchestra* featuring cellist Ralph Kirshbaum. About the piece the reviewer remarks, "it is a half-hour piece of haunting and poignant mood...almost unrelievedly somber and passionate."

B624. Phillips, Roddy. "Sir Peter Maxwell Davies: *Symphony No. 4*." *Aberdeen Evening News* (Mar. 24, 1990).
Review of a performance of *Symphony No. 4* by the Scottish Chamber Orchestra conducted by the composer in the Music Hall, Aberdeen, May 10, 1990. The reviewer notes: "The work was provocative, exciting, haunting, ironic, refreshing."

B625. Pincus, Andrew L. "St. Magnus Festival." *Musical America* v. 107 no. 1 (1987) pp. 55–56.
Includes a series of descriptions and reviews of performances during the 1986 10th St. Magnus Festival. One concert reviewed was the premiere of *Concerto for Violin and Orchestra* on June 21, 1986 by violinist Isaac Stern with the Royal Philharmonic Orchestra conducted by André Previn. The reviewer writes, "The violin part is virtuosic, lyrical and attractive," set against "a dark, orchestral accompaniment." Also reviews premiere of *Jimmack the Postie* by the Royal Philharmonic Orchestra conducted by the composer at the Phoenix Cinema, Kirkwall, June 22, 1986, noting the "folksy" character of the music but commenting, "with its disjointed, desiccated gestures, Jimmy seemed pretty thin malt whisky."

B626. Pincus, Andrew L. "*Taverner*—at Last." *Berkshire Eagle* (Mar. 29, 1986).
Primarily a lengthy review of the U.S. premiere of *Taverner* by the Opera Company of Boston, staged and conducted by Sarah Caldwell. About the piece the reviewer remarks: "As an early work *Taverner* lacks the tautness of the music that was to come, such as *The Lighthouse*." Includes a synopsis of the plot.

B627. Pirie, Peter J. "Broadcasting." *Musical Times* v. 106 (Feb., 1965) p. 123.

Includes a review of the premiere of *Shakespeare Music* performed by the Portia Ensemble, Dec. 8, 1964. After brief remarks about several sections of the work the reviewer notes, "the trouble seems...to be a combination of sounds so exacerbated that great ingenuity must have gone to their devising."

B628. Pirie, Peter J. "Broadcasting." *Musical Times* v. 106 (June, 1965) p. 451.

Reviews the premiere of *Second Fantasia on John Taverner's 'In Nomine'* by the Royal Philharmonic Orchestra conducted by Sir John Pritchard at the Royal Festival Hall, Apr. 30, 1965 (this was also broadcast). Of the music the review says: "This is [Davies's] best work so far, a piece that adds up clearly and convincingly, has something to say, and is full of pouncing invention."

B629. Pitt, Charles. "France: More Philidor." *Opera* v. 30 (June 1979) pp. 592–595.

Includes a review of a performance of *Eight Songs for a Mad King* by baritone David Wilson-Johnson and the Ensemble Intercontemporain in Paris at the Salle Favart, Mar. 14, 1979. Reviewer observes: "one likes or dislikes the extraordinary range of screams, whispers, groans and, occasionally, sung notes that represent George III's tragic madness, but there is no denying the intensity and boldness of the composer's imagination nor its theatrical impact."

B630. Porter, Andrew. "England." *Opera Canada* v. 13 no. 3 (1972) pp. 76–77.

Includes a review of *Taverner* when it was premiered at by the Royal Opera, Covent Garden, July 12, 1972. After hearing the work several times the reviewer says, "I was gripped by its theatricality and passion and no longer deterred by the multi-layered complications." He concludes it is "a most exciting piece of music drama."

B631. Porter, Andrew. "Everyone Burst Out Singing." *Observer* (Mar. 7, 1993).

Review of the premiere performance on Feb. 12 of a work for children mostly composed by the composer, *The Turn of the Tide*, at the Barbican by the London Symphony Orchestra and ensembles from five Islington junior schools, all conducted by Richard McNicol. The reviewer notes: "I was bowled over as much by the event as by the work—hundreds of children involved in making contemporary music."

B632. Porter, Andrew. "Guelph Festival." *Financial Times* (June 20, 1986). Review of a performance of *The Lighthouse* conducted by Stuart Bedford with the Canadian Chamber Ensemble at the Guelph Festival, June, 1986. Cast included Cornelius Opthof, Ben Heppner and Christopher Cameron. Notes the work is "complicated...guilt is not unearned and retribution not unmerited." Includes a detailed description of the production.

B633. Porter, Andrew. "Island Symphony." *New Yorker* (Oct. 30, 1978) pp. 145-148.
Includes a review of the American premiere of *Symphony No. 1* by the New York Philharmonic conducted by Zubin Mehta in October, 1978. About the music the reviewer notes: "It is...an essay in harmonizing the bright spore, luminous sonorities projected in his chamber works of recent years and the sonic surge and tempest that can be summoned by a full symphony orchestra." Also reviews a performance of *A Mirror of Whitening Light* by members of Music Project conducted by Gerard Schwarz at Town Hall, April 1978.

B634. Porter, Andrew. "Maxwell Davies's *Quartet*." *Musical Times* v. 103 (Jan., 1962) p. 40.
Review of a BBC Invitation Concert, 9 Nov., 1961 by the Amici Quartet, which featured the premiere of *String Quartet*. The reviewer says this "seems to me a small and perfect piece." Following a brief description of the piece, he concludes it "seemed like something one could hold and examine in changing lights."

B635. Porter, Andrew. "Maxwell Davies' *Sinfonia*." *Musical Times* v. 103 (July, 1962) pp. 477-478.
Review of a concert by the English Chamber Orchestra conducted by Sir Colin Davis at the Royal Festival Hall, May 9, 1962. Included on the program was the premiere of *Sinfonia*, a work the reviewer says "has basic simplicity of form, simplicity of basic ideas." This reviewer loves Davies's music "because it is free from artifice."

B636. Porter, Andrew. "*Miss Donnithorne's Maggot*." *New Yorker* (Dec. 12, 1988) p. 111.
Review of a performance of *Miss Donnithorne's Maggot* by Lynne Vardaman accompanied by members of the American Chamber

Opera Company at the Manhattan Marymount Theatre, New York. About the work the reviewer notes: "The dramatic force of the score had never been in doubt. I had not realized before how beautiful it is."

B637. Porter, Andrew. "Music in Action." *New Yorker* (Oct. 24, 1988) p. 103.
Review of the second performance of *Resurrection* performed at the Darmstadt Staatstheater, late September, 1988, conducted by Hans Drewanz. Reviewer remarks: "The music is...eclectic, ranging from jingles and commercial pop to Davies's most refined." He was not impressed by the singing. With brief synopsis of the libretto.

B638. Porter, Andrew. "Musical Events: Airs of Earth and Heaven." *New Yorker* (Mar. 18, 1985) pp. 103-104, 106.
Includes a review of a concert in Feb., 1985 by the ensemble Musical Elements in the Great Hall at Cooper Union. Included on the program was a performance of *Seven In Nomine*. The reviewer remarks: "The sequence as a whole brings the past into the present...proclaims the steps and leaps of plainchant as basic metaphors relating music for life."

B639. Porter, Andrew. "Musical Events: Alternatives." *New Yorker* (Dec. 8, 1986) pp. 136-140.
Review of a concert by the New York New Music Ensemble at St. Paul's Chapel, Columbia University, November, 1986. Included on the program was a performance of *Le Jongleur de Notre Dame* directed by David Ostwald. Reviewer describes the instrumental solos as "quirky" but concludes that the work is "excellently composed music."

B640. Porter, Andrew. "Musical Events: Musical Elements." *New Yorker* (May 26, 1986) p. 88.
Includes a review of a performance of *The Lighthouse* at the Guelph Spring Festival, by Cornelius Opthof, Christopher Cameron, and Ben Heppner with the Canadian Chamber Ensemble conducted by Stuart Bedford. Notes: "Davies has conjured a marvelous range of sounds, and his music reveals new subtleties at each hearing." Gives a synopsis of the work.

B641. Porter, Andrew. "New Music/Edinburgh Festival." *Financial Times* (Aug. 22, 1985).
Review of the premiere of *The Peat Cutters* by the National Youth Brass Band of Scotland and the Scottish National Orchestra junior chorus and youth chorus conducted by Geoffrey Brand at Usher Hall, Edinburgh during the Edinburgh Festival, Aug. 18, 1985. Notes: "The music is rhythmically difficult. The harmonies are bold and strong." Includes notes on the text and its implications.

B642. Porter, Andrew. "Nightingales and Eagles." *New Yorker* (Dec. 16, 1985) pp. 134–136.
Article about the Fires of London and Peter Maxwell Davies written when the group was in New York touring in late November, 1985.

B643. Porter, Andrew. "Peter Maxwell Davies: A Personal View." *Keynote Magazine* (1980) pp. 15–19.
Lengthy, informative article, primarily biographical, on Davies and his compositions to date. Very well presented chronological account. The author notes: "Maxwell Davies became a master of Medieval and Renaissance techniques of prolation, isorhythm, hocket and 'parody' in its special musical sense." Includes photographs.

B644. Porter, Andrew. "Peter Maxwell Davies's Fifth Symphony." *Observer* (Aug. 14. 1994).
Review of the premiere of *Symphony No. 5* by the Philharmonia Orchestra conducted by the composer during a Promenade concert at the Royal Albert Hall, Aug. 9, 1994. Includes a lengthy account of the composer's life and works leading up to the premiere.

B645. Porter, Andrew. "Some New British Composers." *Musical Quarterly* v. 51 no. 1 (1965) pp. 12–21.
Includes a short account of Davies, primarily focusing on his style of composing. Says that he began with "an exuberant avant-garde start" and then "turned to contemplation of medieval music"; concludes "His latest compositions have a curiously timeless quality." Mentions *St. Michael Sonata*, *O Magnum Mysterium*, and *Te Lucis Ante Terminum*.

B646. Porter, Andrew. "*Taverner*." *Financial Times* (July, 1972).
Lengthy review of a performance of *Taverner* at its premiere at the Royal Opera, Covent Garden, July 12, 1972. With synopsis of the libretto. The music is described as: "A powerful and brilliant piece

of music theatre, product of a fiery imagination wedded to a prodigious craft."

B647. Potter, Keith. *"Blind Man's Buff." Music and Musicians* v. 21 (Mar., 1973) pp. 66ff.
Review of a concert which included a performance of *Blind Man's Buff* by the Fires of London at The Place, Nov. 24, 1972. The performance featured Mary Thomas, soprano and Mark Furneaux, mime. The reviewer remarks on the similarity of subject matter to *Eight Songs for a Mad King* and says, "certain new elements are appearing in Davies' musical style which may herald a move away from music theatre and a return to purely instrumental...music."

B648. Potter, Keith. "Britain's Best Since Budd Returns to the Stage." *Classical Music* (June 25, 1983) p. 7.
Article about *Taverner* written just prior to its revival ar the Royal Opera, Covent Garden, June 29, 1983. Includes an interview with Edward Downes, who conducted the 1972 premiere and was scheduled to conduct all of the performances in 1983.

B649. Potter, Keith. "Contemporaries at the Proms." *Classical Music* (Sept. 17, 1983).
Article which includes a review of the premiere of *Sinfonia Concertante* by the Academy of St. Martins-In-the-Fields conducted by Neville Marriner at a Promenade Concert at the Royal Albert Hall, London, Aug. 12, 1983. The review notes: "The *Sinfonia Concertante* is a substantial and sustained half-hour in three movements modelled fairly clearly along very classical lines." Includes a descriptive analysis of the piece.

B650. Potter, Keith. "Davies and Gerhard." *Music and Musicians* v. 21 (June, 1973) pp. 78ff.
Includes a review of a concert on Mar. 17, 1973 by the Fires of London at the Elizabeth Hall. Program included the premiere of *Notre Dame des Fleurs* by Vanessa Redgrave, Mary Thomas and Grayston Burgess (the reviewer dismisses this as "a piece of rather unsubstantial nonsense"). Also performed were *Antechrist* and *Missa Super L'Homme Armé*.

B651. Price, Cyril. "Fires of London." *Cheshire Observer* (Aug. 7, 1981).
Review of a concert by the Fires of London conducted by John Carewe at the Gateway Theatre, Chester, July 31, 1981. Included on

the program were *Eight Songs for a Mad King* (featuring baritone Michael Rippon) and *Le Jongleur de Notre Dame*. The latter work is described as "the aural and the visual blend of music and mime in an intensified treatment of subject matter."

B652. Pruslin, Stephen. "An Anatomy of Betrayal." *Music and Musicians* v. 20 (July, 1977) pp. 28–30.
Article about *Taverner* written just prior to its premiere in July, 1972. It includes an act and scene by scene synopsis of the drama. The author describes the work as "concerned with the idea that what seems a betrayal on one level may be a constructive act on another." He observes that "Davies has arranged things so that the actual music of John Taverner could be used."

B653. Pruslin, Stephen. "*Max: The Life and Music of Peter Maxwell Davies*." *BBC Music Magazine* vol. 3. no. 5 (Jan. 1995) p. 47.
Review of Mike Seabrook's biography of the composer. Though noting that "Mr. Seabrook's enthusiasm sometimes stops just short of the sycophantic," Pruslin describes the book overall as "a readable portrait of a human being who happens to be a great composer, achieved with an essential largeness of spirit."

B654. Pruslin, Stephen. "Maxwell Davies' *Symphony*—an Introduction." *Tempo* no. 124 (Mar., 1978) pp. 6–9.
Written just prior to the premiere of *Symphony No. 1* on 2 Feb., 1978, by the Philharmonia Orchestra conducted by Simon Rattle at the Royal Festival Hall, this article discusses the history of the symphony as a form from the classical through the 19th and 20th century. Pruslin focuses on Sibelius as really establishing the return of the true symphony as a generic form and says: "The relationship between Davies, Sibelius and Beethoven resonates inside the new Symphony and gives it dimension."

B655. Pruslin, Stephen. "Maxwell Davies's Second Taverner Fantasia." *Tempo* no. 73 (Summer 1965) pp. 2–11.
Lengthy article the focus of which is *Second Fantasia on John Taverner's 'In Nomine'*. Includes some background information, sources material, etc. Primarily, it is a well-presented analysis of the piece with musical examples.

B656. Pruslin, Stephen. "Peter Maxwell Davies' *Symphony No. 4.*" *Musical Times* v. 130 (Sept., 1989) pp. 520–523.

Based on an interview with the composer just prior to the premier of his *Symphony No. 4* scheduled for Sept. 10, 1989. Opens with a brief background sketch which focuses on the sources of material in the new work, including *Second Fantasia on John Taverner's 'In Nomine,' Worldes Blis, St. Thomas Wake, Stone Litany*, and *Symphony No. 1*. Pruslin writes: "the new *Symphony No. 4*, a large-scale work in four movements played without a break [which] caps all of his chamber orchestra music thus far."

B657. Pruslin, Stephen. "Returns and Departures: Recent Maxwell Davies." *Tempo* no. 113 (June 1975) pp. 22–28.

Focuses primarily on *Worldes Blis*, giving an analysis of the piece with musical examples. The reviewer remarks the work "represents a homecoming to the spiritual territory that had been left behind with the *Second Taverner Fantasia* and replaced by a head-on confrontation with Expressionism." As examples of the latter, the reviewer cites *Hymnos, Missa Super L'Homme Armé* and *Revelation and Fall*. Also includes an analysis of *Stone Litany*, remarking on the influence of Debussy and Sibelius on the piece and adding that the work "is somehow one of those pieces one wants to cherish rather than analyse." With musical examples.

B658. Pruslin, Stephen. "The Triangular Space: Peter Maxwell Davies's *Ave Maris Stella.*" *Tempo* no. 120 (Mar. 1977) pp. 16–22.

Primarily an analysis of *Ave Maris Stella* with musical examples. The author concludes: "*Ave Maris Stella* is a great and glowing work."

B659. Ramey, Basil. "Contemporary Organ Music." *Musical Times* v. 102 (Jan., 1961) p. 36.

Review of a concert by organist Allan Wicks, 30 Nov., 1960 at the Festival Hall. Program included the premiere of the *Organ Fantasia* from '*O Magnum Mysterium*,' of which the unsympathetic review remarks, "we reach a form of higher mathematics that requires a lengthy, explanatory note from the composer" and concludes: "Whatever Mr. Maxwell Davies is doing certainly requires all the verbal explanation he can muster."

B660. Ratcliffe, Michael. "One-Man Musical Reformation." *Times* (June 16, 1983).

An interview with the composer during the 1983 St. Magnus Festival, June, 1983, just prior to the revival of *Taverner* at Covent Garden on June 29.

B661. Rayment, Malcolm. "Brilliance of the Fires Draws the Crowds." *Glasgow Herald* (Sept. 7, 1978).

Review of a concert by the Fires of London conducted by the composer at St. Mary's Cathedral, Edinburgh, during the Edinburgh Festival, September, 1978. Included on the program was the first public performance of *Runes From a Holy Island*, *Renaissance Scottish Dances*, and *Le Jongleur de Notre Dame*, this being described as "a brilliant piece of music theatre."

B662. Rayment, Malcolm. "Captivating 'Cinders'." *Glasgow Herald* (June, 1980).

Review of the premiere of *Cinderella* by pupils from the Papdale Primary and Kirkwall Grammar Schools conducted by Glenys Hughes at the Orkney Arts Theatre, during the St. Magnus Festival, June 21, 1980. Remarks: "The humour on stage...is matched by a most attractive score."

B663. Rayment, Malcolm. "Neil Mackie and the Scottish Chamber Orchestra." *Glasgow Herald* (Dec. 1, 1983).

Review of a concert by the Scottish Chamber Orchestra conducted by James Conlon at the Queen's Hall, Edinburgh, Nov. 30, 1983. Included on the program was a performance of *Into the Labyrinth* with Neil Mackie, tenor. The reviewer says the work "was hailed as a masterpiece...a claim that now seems in no way exaggerated."

B664. Rayment, Malcolm. "Premiere of Davies Work." *Glasgow Herald* (June 21, 1979).

Article about the 1979 St. Magnus Festival which includes a review of the premiere of *Solstice of Light* performed by Neil Mackie, the St, Magnus Cathedral Choir, and organist Richard Hughes, conducted by Norman Mitchell. Described as a "major new work." Very complimentary review!

B665. Rayment, Malcolm. "Truly Outstanding Music-Theatre Performances."
       Glasgow Herald (June, 1980).
       Reviews a performance of *Vesalii Icones* by dancer William Louther
       and cellist Alexander Baillie with the Fires of London conducted by
       the composer at the Orkney Arts Theatre, Kirkwall, June 23, 1980
       during the St. Magnus Festival. Includes a description of the work.
       Also reviews a performance of *Dark Angels* by Mary Thomas,
       soprano, and Timothy Walker, guitarist, at the St. Magnus Cathedral
       in late June, 1980 (described as "a setting of two grim poems by
       George MacKay Brown separated by a guitar interlude"). The
       concert also included a performance by Timothy Walker of his own
       guitar arrangement of *Farewell to Stromness*.

B666. Raynor, Henry. "The Promenade Concerts 1969." *Music Review* v. 31
       no. 1 (1970) pp. 83–84.
       Includes a review of the premiere of *Worldes Blis* by the BBC
       Symphony Orchestra at the Albert Hall, Aug. 28, 1969. After some
       discussion the writer says: "The events in *Worldes Blis* are simply
       sonorities, each of a different sort to those we have been hearing
       before."

B667. Redvall, Eva. "Stockholm." *Opera News* v. 46 (Sept., 1981) pp.
       40–41.
       Review of a performance of *Miss Donnithorne's Maggot* at the Royal
       Opera, Stockholm, theatre-in-the-round, Feb. 7, 1981. Noted the
       work "is told in a monologue of confusion, full of sexual symbolism
       and poetic imagery, matched by Davies' music expressing anguish,
       twisted by anguish."

B668. Reich, Howard. "Pianists Find Direct Route to New Music." *Chicago
       Tribune* (Feb. 25, 1987) sec: Chicagoland p. 14.
       Review of a concert by pianists Lambert Orkis and Stephen Pruslin
       at the Mandel Hall, University of Chicago, Feb. 24, 1987. Included
       on the program was a performance of *Sonata for Piano* by Pruslin,
       which the reviewer says "nearly bursts with all its motivic ideas and
       transformations."

B669. Rich, Alan. "Playing With Fires." *Newsweek* (Dec. 9, 1985) p. 94.
       Includes highlights from a series of concerts by the Fire of London
       conducted by the composer in late 1985 at the St. Laurence Centre,
       Toronto. Includes reviews of performances of *Eight Songs for a
       Mad King*, featuring baritone Andrew Gallacher ("the music veers

from the Handelian style of George's own time to a gritty contemporary style that mocks the other"); *Vesalii Icones*, with dancer Mark Wraith and cellist Jonathan Williams (the solo cello music "groans, exults and seemingly mirrors the dancing"); and *Le Jongleur de Notre Dame* ("the instrumental lines become the wordless censures of monks scowling their disapproval as the juggler makes his offering to the Virgin").

B670. Richards, Denby. "The Contemporary Scene." *Musical Opinion* v. 98 (May, 1975) p. 400.
    Includes a review of a performance of *Stone Litany* by the Scottish National Orchestra directed by Alexander Gibson at the Festival Hall, Mar. 7, 1975. The work is described as "a musical miracle" and "a dramatic, enthralling study in the origin and growth of language."

B671. Roberts, David. "*Cinderella*." *Musical Times* v. 122 (Feb. 19, 1981) pp. 118–119.
    Review of the London premiere of *Cinderella* at the Jeannetta Cochrane Theatre, Dec. 30, 1980.   The reviewer notes: "At its best...the music was quite affecting."

B672. Roberts, David. "*The Lighthouse* (Sadler's Wells)." *Musical Times* v. 122 (Sept. 1981) pp. 615–616.
    Review of a performance of *The Lighthouse* at Sadler's Wells, July 14, 1981, with soloists Neil Mackie, Michael Rippon, and David Wilson-Jones, conducted by John Carewe. The reviewer remarks on the "spectacular range of colour and texture and surprising power" of the music.

B673. Roberts, David. "Maxwell Davies in Orkney—*The Martyrdom of St. Magnus*." *Musical Times* v. 118 (Aug. 1977) pp. 633–635.
    Lengthy review of *The Martyrdom of St. Magnus* at the first St. Magnus Festival June 18, 1977. Includes a detailed synopsis of the drama as well as a descriptive music analysis but no musical examples. Concludes, "it is...a major work of enduring importance that deserves to be widely heard."

B674. Roberts, David. "New Music." *Musical Times* v. 120 (May, 1979) p. 420.
    Review of the premiere of *Salome: Concert Suite from the Ballet* by the London Symphony Orchestra conducted by David Atherton, at the Festival Hall, Mar. 16, 1979. Remarks about the music, "the

most striking feature was the brilliance of the orchestral sound, with the textures complex yet pellucid."

B675. Roberts, David. "Proms." *Musical Times* v. 119 (Sept., 1978) p. 777.
Includes a review of a concert that featured the second London performance of *Symphony No. 1* by the Philharmonia Orchestra conducted by Simon Rattle, Royal Festival Hall July 26, 1978. Comparing the work to Sibelius's *Symphony No. 5*, which was performed on the same program, the reviewer notes Davies's work is "so radically original, entailing nothing far short of a new musical rhetoric, that it must be listened to according to its own internal logic."

B676. Robinson, Ray. "Book Review." *Choral Journal* v. 27 no. 8 (1987) pp. 33–35.
Article which features reviews of two volumes written about the composer and his music. Of the first, *Peter Maxwell Davies* by Peter Griffiths (London: Robson Books, 1983), the reviewer states: "It is because Peter Maxwell Davies has dared to grapple with the deepest issues of the human dilemma" that he is a composer "who truly "reaches" his audience." The reviewer characterizes the second volume, *Peter Maxwell Davies: Studies From Two Decades*, edited by Stephen Pruslin (London: Boosey & Hawkes, 1979), as an "informative and analytical" collection of twenty articles.

B677. Rockwell, John. "An English Composer Matures." *New York Times* (Mar. 1, 1981) p. D21.
Article written just prior to the New York premiere of *Symphony No. 2* by the Boston Symphony Orchestra at Carnegie Hall, Mar. 4, 1981. Very interesting for its biographical content.

B678. Rockwell, John. "Music: Capricorn Offers Davies's *Anakreontika*." *New York Times* (Jan. 22, 1982) p. 18.
Includes a brief review of a performance of *Vesalii Icones* at its New York premiere by Capricorn, at St. Peter's Church, Jan. 19, 1982. Also on the program was a performance of *Anakreontika*, sung by Lisa Nappi, of which the reviewer writes: "Although the vocal line is modernistically chromatic, the effect is as voluptuous and sensuous as the texts themselves."

B679. Rockwell, John. "Music: Da Capo Players." *New York Times* (Mar. 28, 1980) p. C28.
Review of a concert by the Da Capo Chamber Players at Alice Tully Hall, late Mar., 1980. Included on the program was a performance of *Ave Maris Stella*. The work is described as "a rapt, intense meditation on death...wonderfully evocative, almost a blend of the austerity of Webern."

B680. Rockwell, John. "Which Works of the 70's Were Significant." *New York Times* (July 27, 1980) pp. 19, 22.
Article focusing on the significant musical works of the 1970's. Included in the list of ten is *Ave Maris Stella*, of which the writer says, "it combines Mr. Maxwell Davies' medieval mysticism, his skill at writing for the new virtuosos...and his intense musicality into one supremely successful work."

B681. Rosenthal, Harold. *The Lighthouse." Opera* v. 32 (Sept. 1981) pp. 967–968.
Review of a performance of *The Lighthouse* by the Fires of London at Sadler's Wells Theatre, July 17, 1986. About the score the reviewer remarks: "Davies's music for each of the three men is carefully contrasted and the song each one sings is a brilliantly conceived musical parody." Includes a brief synopsis of the work.

B682. Rosenthal, Harold. "*The No. 11 Bus*, The Fires of London at the Queen Elizabeth Hall, London." *Opera* v. 35 (May, 1984) pp. 563–564.
Very critical review of the premiere of *The No. 11 Bus* at Queen Elizabeth Hall, Mar. 20, 1984. Reviewer found it "an over-blown self-indulgent non-starter, full of in-jokes and out-moded undergraduate humor."

B683. Rosenthal, Harold and Kerensky, Oleg. "*Taverner*—Two Points of View." *Opera* v. 23 (Sept., 1972) pp. 789–794.
Includes two reviews of *Taverner* when it was premiered at the Royal Opera, Covent Garden, July 12, 1972. Rosenthal admires the works as a but contends that, although the writing for the voice is quite well done in Act II, "a little judicious pruning, especially in the second part of Act I could help tighten the dramatic tension." Kerensky's views are harsher and much less sympathetic. He describes the libretto as "obscure and pretentious," and thinks perhaps the entire works is "intended to appeal maybe to the younger generation" and

is a more appropriate a piece for "multi-media theatre or a pop festival."

B684. Rostron, Tim. "The Sense of Adventure." *Daily Telegraph* (Sept. 12, 1988).

An interview with the composer by Tim Rostron just prior to performance of *Strathclyde Concerto No. 1 for Oboe and Orchestra* by the Scottish Chamber Orchestra at the Royal Albert Hall, Sept. 13, 1988. Includes some biographical material. Mentions *An Orkney Wedding, With Sunrise*, *Taverner*, and *Resurrection*.

B685. Sadie, Stanley. "Maxwell Davies' *Sinfonia*." *Musical Events* v. 17 (July 1962) p. 28.

Includes a review of the premiere of *Sinfonia* by the English Chamber Orchestra conducted by Colin Davis, at the Royal Festival Hall, May 9, 1962. A brief article, though the reviewer remarks: "Among the *Sinfonia's* immediately impressive features are the significant group of note patterns...and the profoundly moving music of the last movement."

B686. Sadie, Stanley. "New, New, New." *Music and Musicians* v. 10 (Jan., 1962) p. 25.

Includes a review of an ISCM Festival concert in Nov. 1961 at the BBC Maida Vale Studios, including the premiere of *String Quartet* by the Amici Quartet. Work described as displaying "something new in its...treatment of harmony and line."

B687. Salisbury, Wilma. "Premiere Presents Challenge." *Cleveland Plain Dealer* (Oct. 13, 1989)

Review of a concert by the Cleveland Orchestra conducted by Christoph von Dohnanyi in Severance Hall, Oct. 12, 1989, which included the American premiere of *Strathclyde Concerto No. 2 for Cello and Orchestra* (with cellist Ralph Kirshbaum). The reviewer thought the piece "dark in tone and brooding in mood...with a Nordic accent reminiscent of Sibelius."

B688. Salzman, Eric. "Terrific Modern Music for the Wind Band." *Stereo Review* v. 39 (July 1977) p. 132.

Review of a recording (Louisville First Editions LS756) featuring members of the Louisville Orchestra conducted by Jorge Meister. Includes a performance of *St. Michael Sonata*, which is described as "combining serialism with Renaissance brass music traditions in a skillful post-Webern manner."

B689. Samuelson, Dorothy. "Chicago." *Opera* v. 41 (Dec., 1990) pp. 1438, 1459.

Includes a review of a performance of *The Lighthouse* by members of the Chicago Opera Theater, Mar. 21, 1990. Cast included Richard Fracker, Nickolas Karousatos, and Peter Loehle; conductor was Henry Holt. Remarks about the music: "The dissonant score is for the greater part of the work, unsparingly rigorous." Includes a very brief synopsis of the work.

B690. Sandow, Gregory. "New Music: Fire From Maxwell Davies." *Wall Street Journal* (Nov. 19, 1985) p. 28.

Article written in Toronto when the composer and the Fires of London began a 1985 North American tour. Comments on the works the group was touring with, including *Le Jongleur de Notre Dame* (noting "Davies's music might seem to distract from his story or...to give it extra depth"), *Vesalii Icones*, *Eight Songs for a Mad King*, and *Miss Donnithorne's Maggot*.

B691. Scherzer, E. "War immer schon ein Vollblutmusiker: Uraufführung von György Ligetis Klavierkonzert in sterischen herbst." *Neue Zeitschrift für Musik* no. 1 (Jan. 1987) p. 33.

Includes a brief mention of a performance of *The Rainbow* at the Mürztaler Workshop, Krieglach, Austria, November, 1986.

B692. Schiffer, Brigitte. "Berichte aus dem Ausland: Avantgarde in Oxford." *Melos* v. 37 (June 1970) pp. 249-250.

Includes a brief mention of a performance of *Vesalii Icones* by Jennifer Ward Clarke, cello, and dancer William Louther in Oxford during April 1970.

B693. Schiffer, Brigitte. "London." *Schweizerische Musikzeitung* v. 115 no. 6 (1975) pp. 19–20.

Includes a review of the premiere of *Ave Maris Stella* by the Fires of London, May 27, 1975 during the Bath Festival.

B694. Schiffer, Brigitte. "London: BBC-Aufträge für die Promenadenkonzerte." *Melos* v. 1 no.1 (1975) pp. 47–49.

Includes a brief mention of a Schoenberg Centenary Concert by the Fires of London at the Royal Albert Hall, Sept. 14, 1974. Included on the program was the premiere of *Nach Bergamo–Zur Heimat*, composed to open the concert.

B695. Schiffer, Brigitte. "Londres." *Schweizerische Musikzeitung* v. 119 no. 3 (1979) p. 158.
Review of the London premiere of *Salome: Concert Suite from the Ballet* by the London Symphony Orchestra at the Royal Festival Hall, conducted by David Atherton, Mar. 16, 1979.

B696. Schiffer, Brigitte. "Mixed Media in Londoner Musikleben." *Melos* v. 37 (July-August 1970) p. 308.
Includes a review of the unpublished work *Nocturnal Dances* performed by the Pierrot Players at The Place, London, June (?) 1970.

B697. Schiffer, Brigitte. "Rock und Pop in Londons Konzertsaalen." *Melos* v. 37 (Dec. 1970) p. 519.
Includes a review of the final concert by the Pierrot Players in London at The Place, June (?) 1970. Included on the program was a performance of a concert version of *Nocturnal Dances*.

B698. Schlotel, Brian. "Personalities in World Music Education No. 12: Peter Maxwell Davies." *International Journal of Music Education* no. 17 (1991) pp. 43–47.
Article on Davies's compositions for young performers and his interest in music education. In that context mentions works including *Kirkwall Shopping Songs*, *The Great Bank Robbery*, *Five Klee Pictures*, *Te Lucis Ante Terminum*, *Songs of Hoy*, *The Two Fiddlers*, *Peat Cutters*, *First Ferry to Hoy*, and *Lullabye for Lucy*.

B699. Schmidgall, Gary. "Reports: Philadelphia." *Opera News* v. 50 (July 1985) p. 36.
Includes a review of a performance of *The Lighthouse* at the Academy of Vocal Arts, Philadelphia, May 15, 1985. Soloists were Robert Rowland, David Neal, and Todd Thomas, accompanied by an orchestra made up of the Philadelphia Concert Soloists conducted by Theodore Antoniou. About the work the reviewer notes: "Musically, there was a visceral excitement, Davies being a virtuoso at arresting the ear and giving sound to the demons of the mind."

B700. Schneider, John. "The Contemporary Guitar: Peter Maxwell Davies."
      Soundboard v. 10 no. 1 (1983) pp. 43–45.
      Article on the composer's uses of the guitar in both his ensemble
      music as well as his solo compositions. It emphasizes the solo works
      Lullabye For Ilian Rainbow, *Dark Angels*, and *Hill Runes* and gives
      musical examples from those compositions. Concludes that the
      composer "has proven to be an important and very creative composer
      for the guitar for both solo and ensemble settings."

B701. Schneider, John. "Peter Maxwell Davies." *Guitar Review* no. 65
      (Spring, 1986) pp. 1–7.
      Article which features an interview with the composer originally
      broadcast on KPFK-FM, Los Angeles. In it the composer talks
      about the Fires of London and his works for guitar. Includes a very
      brief works list, brief discography and short bibliography. Includes
      a reproduction of the fourth movement of *Lullabye for Ilian Rainbow*
      and the third of *Renaissance Scottish Dances*.

B702. Schott, Howard. "Boston." *Musical Times* v. 127 (July 1986) pp.
      401–402.
      Includes a review of the American premiere of *Taverner* by the
      Opera Company of Boston, conducted by Sarah Caldwell, between
      Mar. 9–16, 1986. Very brief but very positive: describes the work
      as "a theatrical tour-de-force."

B703. Schwartz, Elliott. "Current Chronicle: The Netherlands." *Musical
      Quarterly* v. 58 no. 4 (1972) pp. 655–658.
      Article about the 1972 summer Holland Festival. During that time
      one program was devoted to the music of Peter Maxwell Davies.
      Included were performances of *Missa Super L'Homme Armé* as well
      as *Vesalii Icones*. The latter work is described as "an exciting
      theatrical experience, particularly because it relates its visual and
      sonic aspects in provocative ways."

B704. Schwartz, Elliott. "Reviews of Records: Peter Maxwell Davies: *From
      Stone to Thorn*." *Musical Quarterly* v. 62 no. 2 (1976) pp. 302–305.
      Review of an all-Davies recording (L'Oiseau-Lyre DSLO 2) which
      includes *From Stone to Thorn*, *Hymnos*, *Antechrist*, and *Missa Super
      L'Homme Armé*, all performed by members of the Fires of London
      conducted by the composer. About *Antechrist* and *Hymnos* the
      reviewer remarks: "Whether brutal or still, the music is always

gripping." He also notes the composer's use of parody, a compositional device that is one of his hallmarks.

B705. Scott, Robert Dawson. "Concerto for Leading Composer and 75 Teenagers." *Times* (Jan. 21, 1990).
Includes a review of a concert by the Scottish chamber Orchestra conducted by the composer at City Hall, Glasgow, Jan. 19, 1990. Featured on the program was the premiere of *Strathclyde Concerto No. 3 for Horn, Trumpet and Orchestra*, with soloists Robert cook, horn and Peter Franke, trumpet.

B706. Shawe-Taylor, Desmond. "At the Proms." *Times* (Aug. 14, 1983).
Review of a concert by the Fires of London at a Proms concert, during the second week in August, 1983. Included on the program was a performance of *Revelation and Fall* featuring soloist Mary Thomas; this is described as a "highly charged expressionist setting." Also performed was *Suite From the Boyfriend*, again with soloist Mary Thomas.

B707. Shawe-Taylor, Desmond. "The Battle For the Proms." *Times* (July 26, 1981).
Includes a review of the London premiere of *Symphony No. 2* by the BBC Symphony Orchestra conducted by Gennadi Rozhdestvensky at the Royal Albert Hall, July 23, 1981. About the music the reviewer notes, "the material itself and the orchestral textures are striking and alluring."

B708. Shawe-Taylor, Desmond. "This Astonishing New Symphony." *Times* (July 30, 1978).
Review of a performance of *Symphony No. 1* by the Philharmonia Orchestra conducted by Simon Rattle at the Royal Albert Hall, London, July 26, 1978. The reviewer remarks: "The work is astonishing, dumbfounding: intricate certainly, and, in a sense, tough."

B709. Shere, Charles. "'Fires of London' Sweeps from Madness to Simply Theatrical." *Oakland Tribune* (Dec. 9, 1985).
Review of a concert by the Fires of London which included performances of *Le Jongleur de Notre Dame* and *Eight Songs for a Mad King*. Notes both works are, "dramatic and theatrical." About *Le Jongleur*, the reviewer says that the music has "rather thin, predict-

able ...qualities." However, he finds the music of the *Eight Songs* "rich, probing and ultimately tragic...exquisitely-composed."

B710. Siedhoff, Thomas. "Peter Maxwell Davies: *The Lighthouse.*" pp. 688–689 in Carl Dalhaus, ed., *Pipers Enzyklopädie des Musiktheaters*, vol. 1. Munchen: R. Piper GmbH & Co., 1986.
Article about the opera *The Lighthouse.* Includes a synopsis of the work and information about the premiere as well as a brief bibliography.

B711. Silsbury, Elizabeth. "Peter Maxwell Davies' *Two Fiddlers* at the Adelaide Festival." *Australian Journal of Music Education* no. 27 (Oct., 1980) p. 65.
Review of the Australian premiere of *The Two Fiddlers*, in March, 1980 at the Adelaide Festival, by children from schools in the area, under the direction of Dean Patterson. Music described as "not easy but rewarding" and as "musically and dramatically very strong, and lots of fun."

B712. Simmons, David. "London Music." *Musical Opinion* v. 95 (Aug., 1972) p. 567.
Includes a review of a concerts, part of the 1972 Westminster Festival, 17 June, 1972 by members of the London Sinfonietta. Included was a performance of a composite work by 17 composers, entitled *Canons and Epitaphs*, dedicated to the memory of Igor Stravinsky. Maxwell Davies's contribution (*Canon in Memoriam Igor Stravinsky*) is described as a "little canon...in the form of one of his tender jeux d'esprit."

B713. Simmons, David. "London Music." *Musical Opinion* v. 95 (Feb. 1972) pp. 231–232.
Reviews a concert by the Fires of London in the Queen Elizabeth Hall, Dec. 11, 1971. Featured on the program were performances of *Suite from 'The Devils* and *Suite from 'The Boyfriend'*. Of the former the reviewer writes, one got the "agonies of torture"; of the latter, "It came as a welcome relief that this composer can relax." Also includes a review of a concert by the New Philharmonia Orchestra conducted by Sir Charles Grove in London, early 1972. Included on the program was a performance of *Second Fantasia on John Taverner's 'In Nomine'*. The music is described as "a terrifyingly complex score." Gives a brief description of the work."

B714. Simmons, David. "London Music." *Musical Opinion* v. 96 (Sept. 1973) pp. 601–603.
Includes a review of a performance of *Revelation and Fall* by Mary Thomas and the Fires of London at the Albert Hall (described as a "decadent piece"). Also includes a brief note of the premiere of *Fantasia upon One Note*, by the Fires of London at the Albert Hall, July 24, 1973, of which the reviewer says, "the flux of fun plus seriousness is never lost."

B715. Simmons, David. "More Maxwell Davies." *Music and Musicians* v. 11 (Sept. 1962) pp. 36–37.
Short review of a concert by the New Music Ensemble conducted by John Carewe at Stationer's Hall, London, July 19, 1962. Included on the program was the premiere of *Leopardi Fragments*. The reviewer notes the scoring "seemed highly appropriate to the new piece which, like the composer's...*Sinfonia*...is acknowledged as homage to Monteverdi."

B716. Smaczny, Jan. "Simplest Course." *Independent* (Oct. 23, 1989) Arts section, p. 13.
Review of a concert by the Birmingham Contemporary Music Group conducted by Oliver Knussen at Adrian Boult Hall, Oct. 21, 1989. Included on the program was a performance of *Revelation and Fall* featuring soprano Linda Hirst (described as a "highly personal distillation of Expressionism").

B717. Smalley, Roger. "Some Recent Works by Peter Maxwell Davies." *Tempo* 84 (1968) pp. 2–5.

B718. Smith, Carolyn J. "Davies, (Sir) Peter Maxwell." *International Dictionary of Opera*, ed. C. Steven Larue. 2 vols., London: St. James Press, 1993.
Brief biographical entry concentrating on the composer's operatic compositions.

B719. Smith, Carolyn J. "*Taverner*." *International Dictionary of Opera*, ed. C. Steven Larue. 2 vols., London: St. James Press, 1993.
Presents the historical background of *Taverner* and gives a synopsis of the work, with some analytical points.

B720. Smith, Patrick J. "Boston." *Musical Times* v. 122 (April, 1981) p. 259.

Review of the premiere of *Symphony No. 2* by the Boston Symphony Orchestra (who commissioned the work) conducted by Seiji Ozawa, Feb. 26, 1981. Remarks that the composer "has used...the ceaseless changes of wind and wave on the sea outside his Orkney home...as a basis for the...continually changing pattern subservient to the outward forms of the movements."

B721. Smith, Patrick J. "New York." *Musical Times* v. 120 (Jan. 3, 1979) pp. 62–63.

Includes brief mention of the American premiere of *Symphony No. 1* by the New York Philharmonic Orchestra conducted by Zubin Mehta in the autumn of 1978 ("a work that attempts more than it accomplishes").

B722. Soria, Dorle J. "Peter Maxwell Davies and The Fires of London." *Hi Fi/ Musical America* v. 33 (Sept., 1983) MA pp. 6, 8ff.

Article on the Fires of London written during the Britain Salutes New York Festival in late April, 1983 includes portions of interviews with the composer's agent Judy Arnold, mostly about the history of the Fires. Also reviews a concert by the Fires of London, April 23, 1983 at New York, Symphony Space. Program included *Le Jongleur de Notre Dame* (described as "a moving score"); *Miss Donnithorne's Maggot*, *Vesalii Icones*, and *Eight Songs For a Mad King* (described as "strange and fascinating").

B723. Spencer, Roderick. "*The Two Fiddlers*." *Music Teacher* v. 58 (June 1979) p. 22.

Review of the first London performance of *The Two Fiddlers*, by students from the Pimlico School and several other London area musicians at the Jeannetta Cochrane Theatre during Dec. 27, 1978–Jan. 6, 1979. The reviewer notes: "The music is, in itself, not difficult, but needs considerable skill in being able to put it all together."

B724. Stadlen, Peter. "Albany Brass Ensemble." *Daily Telegraph* (Dec. 20, 1982).

Review of a concert by the Albany Brass Ensemble at St. John's, Smith Square, London, Dec. 17, 1982. Included on the program was a performance of *Brass Quintet*, described as an "exceptional and important work."

B725. Stadlen, Peter. *"Fiddlers at the Wedding." Daily Telegraph* (Nov. 7, 1985).
Review of a concert by the Fires of London conducted by Günther Bauer-Schenk at the Queen Elizabeth Hall, early November, 1985. Included on the program was a performance of *Fiddlers at the Wedding* with soloist Elisabeth Söderström. About the work the reviewer notes, "the elusiveness of this song cycle from 1973 lies in a new-Webernesque sparseness of textures."

B726. Stadlen, Peter. "Fires of London." *Daily Telegraph* (Sept. 23, 1982).
Review of a concert by the Fires of London at the Queen Elizabeth Hall, September, 1982. Included on the program was a performance of *Image, Reflection, Shadow*. The reviewer notes the piece is based on a poem by Charles Senior and states further, "the thoughts and images conveyed by the words are reflected in the varied moods of the music." Also performed was *Kinloche His Fantassie*.

B727. Stadlen, Peter. *"First Ferry to Hoy." Daily Telegraph* (Nov. 14, 1985).
Review of a concert by the London Sinfonietta and performers from the ILEA Centre for Young Musicians, conducted by Elgar Howarth at the Queen Elizabeth Hall, Nov. 12, 1985. Included on the program was the premiere of *First Ferry to Hoy*. About the work the reviewer remarks: "The comparatively simple score...lacks any trace of condescension."

B728. Stadlen, Peter. "In Search of a New Order." *Daily Telegraph* (Sept. 2, 1985).
Review of the first London performance of *Symphony No. 3* by the BBC Philharmonic Orchestra conducted by Edward Downes at the Royal Albert Hall, August, 1985.

B729. Stadlen, Peter. "Peter Maxwell Davies." *Daily Telegraph* (July 25, 1981).
Review of a concert by the BBC Symphony Orchestra conducted by Gennadi Rozhdestvensky at the Royal Albert Hall, July 23, 1981. Very brief.

B730. Stadlen, Peter. "Premiere of Kyr's *Maelstrom*." *Daily Telegraph* (Sept. 23, 1983).
Includes a review of a concert by the Fires of London conducted by Nicholas Cleobury at the Queen Elizabeth Hall, September, 1983.

Included on the program was a performance of *Le Jongleur de Notre Dame*. The reviewer describes the work as "lighthearted."

B731. Stearns, David Patrick. "'Holy' Falls from Grace." *USA Today* (Oct. 16, 1989) p. 7D.
Includes a brief review of a performance of *Strathclyde Concerto No. 2 for Cello and Orchestra* by the Cleveland Symphony Orchestra. Remarks about the work: "Its directness....and strong musical narrative suggest it could be a significant addition to the modern concert repertoire."

B732. Steptoe, Roger. "Peter Maxwell Davies." *Composer* no. 90 (Spring, 1987) p. 24.
Short, descriptive, largely biographical article, written upon the composer being elected President of the Composers' Guild in 1986. Remarks that the composer "belongs to the eighteenth-century breed of composers;—industrious and entrepreneurial."

B733. Stiller, Andrew. "*2 Fiddlers* Opera for Children." *Philadelphia Inquirer* (Nov. 17, 1988) Section: Features Daily Magazine, p. E4.
Review of a performance of *The Two Fiddlers* by a group from Swarthmore College, the Swarthmore College Singers and Chamber Orchestra on Nov. 16, 1988 at the Lang Concert Hall, Swarthmore. Included a brief synopsis of the work. Concludes: "Composer Davies tones down his savage satirical bent for the kiddies but not his booby-trapped brand of musical postmodernism."

B734. Stöckl, Rudolf. "Ein Solohorn stillt Fragen: *Der Leuchtturm* von P. M. Davies in Coburg." *Orchester* v. 35 (May 1987) p. 528.
Review of a performance of *The Lighthouse* by members of the Coburg State Theatre at the Reithalle, conducted by Marcel Meier, no date included.

B735. Stöckl, Rudolf. "Regensburg: P. M. Davies, *Der Leuchtturm*." *Opernwelt* v. 30 (Mar. 1989) p. 57.
Review of a performance of *The Lighthouse* conducted by Christian Pyhrs at the Regensburger Theater Jan. 23, 1989. Soloists were Berthold Gronwald, Bruno Balmelli, and Jorgen Kristensen.

B736. Stöckl, Rudolf. "Selbstironie mit künstlerischem Ernst." *Opernwelt* v. 29 (Mar. 1988) p. 50.
Includes a review of a performance of *The Medium* by Janet Walker, at the Komödie, Augsburg, Jan. 26, 1988.

B737. Stöckl, Rudolf. "Unbewältigte Vergangenheit: Peter Maxwell Davies' Kammeroper *Der Leuchtturm* in Coburg." *Opernwelt* v. 28 no. 5 (1987) p. 58.
Review of a performance of *The Lighthouse* conducted by Marcel Meier at the Landestheater, Coburg, Mar., 1987.

B738. Stockmeier, Wolfgang. "Neue Noten: Werke con Bialas und Davies." *Musik und Kirche* v. 55 no. 4 (1985) pp. 196–197.
Review of the score of *Revelation and Fall* when it was published by Boosey & Hawkes.

B739. Sträter. Lothar. "Wien: Einakter von P. Maxwell Davies." *Opernwelt* v. 30 (Dec. 1989) pp. 52–53.
Review of a performance of *Miss Donnithorne's Maggot* and *No. 11 Bus* by the Vienna Chamber Opera, Fall, 1989.

B740. Sutcliffe, James Helme. "Aldeburgh." *Opera* v. 34 (Autumn 1983) pp. 73–77.
Review of the 1983 Aldeburgh Festival, including an unsympathetic review of *The Medium*, performed by Mary Thomas on June 24, 1983: "initial fascination is soon replaced by exhaustion and the search for meaning abandoned long before the protagonist's cries of 'Rapist!' submerge in distance and darkness."

B741. Sutcliffe, James Helme. "Aldeburgh." *Opera News* v. 48 (Dec. 10, 1983) pp. 79–80.
Review of a concert on June 24, 1983 at Aldeburgh which included a performance of *The Medium*, by Mary Thomas. About the music the reviewer remarks, "Davies, who wrote his own text, takes the confusion so far that the audience...begins to doubt its own sanity."

B742. Sutcliffe, James Helme. "Berlin." *Opera* v. 39 (Dec. 1988) p. 1469.
A review of a performance of *Miss Donnithorne's Maggot* by members of Norske Opera conducted by Terje Boye in Berlin, Aug. 26–27, 1988. Includes a brief description of the performance.

B743. Sutcliffe, James H. "Kassel: Henze u.a. *Der heiße Ofen.*" *Opernwelt* v. 30 (May, 1989) p. 42.

Review of the premiere of the opera *Der Heiße Ofen* by various artists, the opera chorus and orchestra of the Staatstheaters Kassell, and the Rock'N'Roll-Clubs Kassel, at the Staatstheater Kassell, Mar. 18, 1989. Davies was one of the "project" composers commissioned by Hans Werner Henze to compose music for the work. The critic concludes: Too many cooks spoil the stew.

B744. Sutcliffe, Tom. "Having a Ball." *Guardian* (Dec. 30, 1980).

Article based on an interview with the composer just prior to the London premiere of *Cinderella.*

B745. Sutcliffe, Tom. "Majestic Max." *Guardian* (Aug. 10, 1994).

Review of a Promenade Concert by the Philharmonia Orchestra conducted by the composer at the Royal Albert Hall, Aug. 9, 1994. Featured on the program was the premiere of *Symphony No. 5.* Which the reviewer says "has some of the attributes of a concerto for orchestra, with meaty and strongly characterised solos for various winds and brass." After a descriptive analysis of the music, he concludes the work is "a soulful, arrestingly affirmative achievement."

B746. Sutcliffe, Tom. "The Origins of *Vesalius*: Peter Maxwell Davies Talks to Tom Sutcliffe." *Music and Musicians* v. 18 (Dec. 1969) pp. 24, 74.

Article which features an interview with the composer focusing on the background of his *Vesalii Icones.* Little real musical analysis but does provide some historical background.

B747. Sutcliffe, Tom. "A Question of Identity." *Music and Musicians* v. 20 (June 1972) pp. 26–28.

Article written just prior to the premiere of *Blind Man's Buff* at the Roundhouse, May 29, 1972. Part of the article is an interview with the composer by the author. Davies is quoted as describing his new work as "a light piece." Mentions *Ave Maria-Hail, Blessed Flower*, *Eight Songs for a Mad King*, *Vesalii Icones*, the film scores for *The Devils* and *The Boyfriend*, and *Taverner*.

B748. Sutcliffe, Tom. "Sadler's Wells: *The Lighthouse*." *Guardian* (July 17, 1981).

Review of a performance of *The Lighthouse* at Sadler's Wells, July, 1981, with soloists Neil Mackie, Michael Rippon and David Rippon-Jones accompanied by the Fires of London conducted by John Carewe. About the work the reviewer remarks: "The music...defines the isolation of the place and the mania of the inhabitants."

B749. Swan, Annalyn. "The Musical Hermit of Hoy." *Newsweek* (Mar. 9, 1981) p. 49.

Lengthy article about the composer's life and works to date, written on the event of the premiere of *Symphony No. 2* by the Boston Symphony Orchestra conducted by Seiji Ozawa. About the music the reviewer remarks, "the Symphony is a masterly work, full of color and contrasts, the ghost of tonality and, everywhere, the ebb and flow of the sea." Includes biographical material about the composer and a descriptive analysis of the work.

B750. Swan, Peter. "Recordings: *Salome*." *Tempo* no. 130 (Sept., 1979) pp. 43–44ff.

Review of a recording of *Salome* (Danish EMI 157-39270). Performance by the Danish Radio Concert Orchestra conducted by Janos Furst. Article includes a scene by scene description and explanation of the work. Concludes it is "one of the most exciting new works...this year...a must not only for Maxwell Davies enthusiasts but for anyone interested in exploring modern music."

B751. T. M. C. "St. Paul's Hall, Huddersfield, Huddersfield Contemporary Music Festival—The Fires of London." *Yorkshire Post* (Nov. 21, 1983).

Review of a concert by the Fires of London conducted by the composer at St. Paul's Hall, Huddersfield as part of the Huddersfield Contemporary Music Festival, Nov. 20, 1983. Included on the program was a performance of *Image, Reflection, Shadow*. The reviewer notes: "The work contains much calm, a massive and complicated scherzo and a fantasy-like dance in the final movement."

B752. Taylor, Michael. "First Performances: Maxwell Davies's *Vesalii Icones*." *Tempo* no. 92 (Spring 1970) pp. 22–27.

Primarily a very detailed analysis of *Vesalii Icones*. The author holds that the material of the work exists on three levels—plainsong, popular, and the composer's own music. Includes musical examples.

B753. Taylor, Paul. "Opera and Ballet in London." *Musical Opinion* v. 106 (Sept. 1983) pp. 366–367.

Includes a review of *Taverner* by the Royal Opera, Covent Garden, June 29, 1983, giving a brief synopsis of the complicated work. About the score the reviewer remarks that "in this opera music plays a subordinate role to drama and staging." Thinks more of the drama is related by the words and stage effects rather than the music.

B754. Thomas, Sarah. "*Taverner* at Covent Garden." *Musical Events* v. 27 (Aug. 1972) pp. 4–6.

Review of the premiere of *Taverner* by the Royal Opera, Covent Garden, July 12, 1972. Includes some background material and a very brief synopsis of the work. Describes the score as "impressive" and notes links between it and *Revelation and Fall* and *Blind Man's Buff*. Remarks: "The density of the music or rather its concentration of ideas...revealed an unexpected variety of experience."

B755. Tressider, Megan. "Fires of London." *Horizon* (April, 1983) pp. 48–51.

Article about the Fires of London and the composer prompted by a series of concerts scheduled by the group at Symphony Space, New York, April 22–24, 1983. Focuses on the composer's work with the Fires and remarks he had written over 50 compositions for that group—roughly, at that time, half of his compositions. When describing Davies's music generally, the author remarks it is "suffused with the harmonies and progressions of music from the Middle Ages and Renaissance...always has an underlying coherence...it is extremely varied."

B756. Trilling, Ossia. "Letzen Endes eine Lappalie." *Opernwelt* (May, 1984).

Review of the premiere of *The No. 11 Bus* by Mary Thomas, Donald Stephenson, Brian Raynor Cook, Simon McBurny, mime, and dancers Anne Dickie and Tom Yang and the Fires of London. Performance was at the Queen Elizabeth Hall, Mar. 20, 1984.

B757. Tucker, Marilyn. "A Vigorous Performance by the Scottish Orchestra." *San Francisco Chronicle* (Oct. 24, 1988) p. F3.

Review of a concert by the Scottish Chamber Orchestra conducted by the composer, at Herbst Theatre, San Francisco, Oct. 22, 1988. The program included the American premiere of *Strathclyde Concerto No. 1 for Oboe and Orchestra* with Robin Miller, oboe. Remarks about the music: "The work is structured on an ancient plainsong that pictures tongues of fire...the solo writing is brilliant." The program also included a performance of *An Orkney Wedding, With Sunrise*, of which the reviewer says: "the work was...a hoot, the mind's recreation of a wedding the composer attended on the island where he has lived for many years...a fetching work."

B758. Tumelty, Michael. "1986 St. Magnus Festival." *Glasgow Herald* (June 27, 1985).
Article which focuses on performances to be presented at the 1986 St. Magnus Festival. Includes an announcement that *Concerto for Violin and Orchestra* would be premiered at that time, featuring soloist Isaac Stern, and that *The Lighthouse* would be performed.

B759. Tumelty, Michael. "Apocalypse Wow!" *Glasgow Herald* (Mar. 20, 1984).
Article about *The No. 11 Bus* written just prior to the premiere of the piece. Features an interview with the composer and a description of the work, punctuated throughout by the composer's comments.

B760. Tumelty, Michael. "Black Comedy Covent Garden Wouldn't Touch." *Glasgow Herald* (Sept. 20, 1988).
Review of the premiere of *Resurrection* by members of the Stadtstheater, Darmstadt, conducted by Hans Drewanz. Notes the work "represents a climatic statement of everything Davies has practiced in his theatrical output." Includes a lively description of the work and concludes the opera is "a withering and hilariously assault on all that society has become."

B761. Tumelty, Michael. "City Hall, Glasgow: SCO." *Glasgow Herald* (April 12, 1990).
Review of a performance of *Symphony No. 4* by the Scottish Chamber Orchestra conducted by the composer in City Hall, Glasgow, April 11, 1990. The reviewer notes: "The Symphony is a nature piece...a superb, if long and exhausting study."

B762. Tumelty, Michael. "Damp Kick-Off in Kirkwall." *Glasgow Herald* (June 20, 1994).
Article about the 1994 St. Magnus Festival which took place in late June, 1994. Includes a very brief review of a concert by the BBC Philharmonic Orchestra conducted by the composer at St. Magnus Cathedral, Kirkwall, Orkney, June 18, 1994. About the work the

reviewer notes that it was, "inspired by memories of a childhood day at a Salford fair, this is a cracker of a piece."

B763. Tumelty, Michael. "Endgame in Kirkwall." *Glasgow Herald* (June 24, 1994).
Report of a concert in honor of the composer's then-upcoming 60th birthday by children from Orkney schools during the St.Magnus Festival at the Phoenix Cinema, Kirkwall, June 23, 1994. Included on the program were performances of *Kirkwall Shopping Songs*, *Songs of Hoy*, *Seven Songs Home*, and *Dances from 'The Two Fiddlers'*.

B764. Tumelty, Michael. "Fires of London." *Glasgow Herald* (Jan. 22, 1987).
Review of the Fires of London's farewell concert conducted by the composer at the Queen Elizabeth Hall, Jan. 20, 1987. Included on the program was the premiere of *Winterfold* with soloist Mary Thomas, which the reviewer says "contains a typical evocation of some shivering landscapes with some of the composer's rich, pictorial word-setting."

B765. Tumelty, Michael. "Maxwell Davies's Third Symphony." *Glasgow Herald* (Feb. 21, 1985).
Review of a concert by the BBC Philharmonic Orchestra conducted by Edward Downes at the Free Trade Hall, Manchester, Feb. 19, 1985. Featured on the program was the premiere of *Symphony No. 3*. Remarks: "The new Symphony inhabits different territory from its predecessor...The sweep of the work is unmistakable." Includes a brief description of each movement.

B766. Tumelty, Michael. "New Music for Festival Goers." *Glasgow Herald* (June 17, 1986).
Article about the then upcoming 10th St. Magnus Festival in June, 1986. Includes notice that three of the composer's works would be premiered: *House of Winter*, *Jimmack the Postie*, and *Concerto for Violin and Orchestra*.

B767. Tumelty, Michael. "*The Number 11 Bus*." *Glasgow Herald* (Mar. 22, 1984).
Review of the premiere of *The Number 11 Bus* at the Queen Elizabeth Hall, Mar. 20, 1984. Performers included mime Simon McBurney; singers Donald Stephenson, Brian Raynor and Mary

Thomas; and dancers Anne Dickie and Tom Yang, all accompanied by the Fires of London conducted by Günther Bauer-Schenk. About the work the reviewer remarks that it is in the "brilliantly counterpointed...pungent and parodistic musical composition that the originality and of the piece resides."

B768. Tumelty, Michael. "Region to Sponsor 10 Concerts for SCO." *Glasgow Herald* (Mar. 26, 1987) p. 8.
Article announcing the composer's commission of the 10 Strathclyde Concerti for the Scottish Chamber Orchestra, to be composed over a five-year period.

B769. Tumelty, Michael. "Royal Philharmonic Orchestra." *Glasgow Herald* (June 23, 1986).
Review of a concert by the Royal Philharmonic Orchestra conducted by André Previn during the 10th St. Magnus Festival at the St. Magnus Cathedral, June 21, 1986. Featured on the program was the premiere of *Concerto for Violin and Orchestra* by violinist Isaac Stern. The article includes a sensitive, descriptive analysis of the work, concluding that it is "an important complex, and, immediately fascinating work."

B770. Tumelty, Michael. "SCO." *Glasgow Herald* (Feb. 3, 1989).
Review of a concert that included the premiere of *Strathclyde Concerto No. 2 for Cello and Orchestra* performed by cellist William Conway and the Scottish Chamber Orchestra conducted by the composer. The music is described as "a three movement work of ostensibly classical proportions" and "a work that may well reveal itself to be central to Davies's output." The review includes a brief analysis of the work.

B771. Tumelty, Michael. "SCO." *Glasgow Herald* (April 30, 1980).
Review of a concert by the Scottish Symphony Orchestra conducted by the composer at City Hall, Glasgow, April 29, 1988. Includes a review of the premiere of *Strathclyde Concerto No. 1 for Oboe and Orchestra*. Soloist was Robin Miller. Describing this as a "tough" work, the reviewer remarks: "Much of the work is immediately outstanding—the poignant plainchant, the still atmospheric slow movements."

B772. Tumelty, Michael. "SCO." *Glasgow Herald* (Aug. 12, 1987).
Review of a concert by the Scottish Chamber Orchestra conducted by the composer at Usher Hall, Edinburgh, Aug. 11, 1987. Included on the program was a performance of *Sinfonietta Accademica*: "a work of rare delicacy and exquisite construction."

B773. Tumelty, Michael. "SCO." *Glasgow Herald* (Feb. 2, 1987).
Review of a concert by the Scottish Chamber Orchestra conducted by the composer at City Hall, Glasgow, Feb. 1, 1987. Included on the program was a performance of *Jimmack the Postie*. The work is described as one in which "a portrait of a subject emerged, with clear purpose...and some marvellously witty gestures...some marvellously witty gestures on whooping horns, raucous trumpet flourishes and slurping trombones."

B774. Tumelty, Michael. "SCO." *Glasgow Herald* (Mar. 19, 1988).
Review of a concert by the Scottish Chamber Orchestra conducted by the composer at City Hall, Glasgow, Mar. 18, 1988. Featured on the program was a performance of *Concerto for Violin and Orchestra* with violinist Ernst Kovacic. Also performed was *An Orkney Wedding, With Sunrise*."

B775. Tumelty, Michael. "SCO at the Royal Concert Hall, Glasgow." *Glasgow Herald* (Dec. 21, 1991).
Review of a concert by the Scottish Chamber Orchestra conducted by the composer at the Royal Concert Hall, Glasgow, Dec. 11, 1991. Included on the program was a performance of the *Ojai Festival Overture*. The work is described as a "foot tapping romp in Max's wittier vein." Also performed was *Caroline Mathilde: Concert Suite from Act I of the Ballet* described as, "fine music, at once subtle and direct."

B776. Tumelty, Michael. "SCO, City Hall, Glasgow: Breathtaking." *Glasgow Herald* (Nov. 26, 1992).
Review of a concert by the Scottish Chamber Orchestra conducted by the composer at City Hall, Glasgow, Nov. 25, 1992. Included on the program was the premiere of *Strathclyde Concerto Co. 7 for Double Bass and Orchestra* with soloist Duncan McTier. About the work the reviewer remarks: "From start to end...this piece beguiles with melody...it threatens, in its broad soloistic sweep, to become almost Elgarian."

B777. Tumelty, Michael. "Scottish Chamber Orchestra." *Glasgow Herald* (June 27, 1985).
Article on concerts presented during the 1985 St. Magnus Festival. It includes a review of a performance of *Sinfonia Concertante* by the Scottish Chamber Orchestra conducted be Nicholas Cleobury. The reviewer notes that despite "its rigorously intellectual composition the *Sinfonia Concertante* reveals itself...as on of the essential Orkney-inspired works."

B778. Tumelty, Michael. "Scottish Chamber Orchestra." *Glasgow Herald* (Nov. 5, 1984).
Review of a concert by the Scottish Chamber Orchestra conducted by the composer at City Hall, Glasgow, Nov. 4, 1984. Included on the program was a performance of *Sinfonia Concertante*. About the music the reviewer remarks, "the *Sinfonia Concertante* contains some of Maxwell Davies's most beautifully expressive composition."

B779. Tumelty, Michael. "Signposts to a Masterwork." *Glasgow Herald* (Mar. 15, 1988).
Article about *Concerto for Violin and Orchestra* written just prior to a performance by violinist Ernst Kovacic. Includes a descriptive analysis of the work as well as a "plain person's guide" to the first movement.

B780. Tumelty, Michael. "Sir Peter Maxwell Davies and the Strathclyde Concertos." *Scottish Chamber Orchestra Yearbook* (1988) pp. 33–35.
An account of the history of the Strathclyde Concertos project.

B781. Tumelty, Michael. "St. Magnus Festival." *Glasgow Herald* (June 24, 1986).
Review of a concert by the royal Philharmonic Orchestra conducted by the composer in Kirkwall during the 10th St. Magnus Festival, June 22, 1986. Included on the program was the premiere of *Jimmack the Postie*, which the reviewer calls "a lively character piece, particularly in the rumbustious climax."

B782. Tumelty, Michael. "St. Magnus Festival." *Glasgow Herald* (June 26, 1986).
Review of a performance of *The Lighthouse* at the 1986 St. Magnus Festival in Kirkwall at the Phoenix Cinema. Soloists were Neil Mackie, Henry Herford and Ian Comboy with the Fires of London

conducted by Günther Bauer-Schenk. The reviewer notes: "Davies allows no unequivocal explanation in his music for the disappearance of the lighthouse keepers."

B783. Tumelty, Michael. "St. Magnus." *Musical Times* v. 127 (Aug., 1986) p. 455.
Article about the 10th St. Magnus Festival. Includes a review of the premiere there of *House of Winter*, by the King's Singers at the Phoenix Cinema, Kirkwall, July 23, 1986. Notes: "The strikingly atmospheric [work] evokes the chill, black stillness of a winter landscape." Also reviews the premiere of *Concerto for Violin and Orchestra* by violinist Isaac Stern with the Royal Philharmonic Orchestra conducted by André Previn at St. Magnus Cathedral, June 23, 1986. The reviewer notes, "the music, though lyrical and intense, is characteristically ascetic." Also contains a very brief review of the premiere of *Jimmack the Postie* by the Royal Philharmonic Orchestra conducted by the composer, June 22, 1986 ("a rumbustious character sketch").

B784. Tumelty, Michael. "Wealth of Music Donated to Public." *Glasgow Herald* (Dec. 23, 1986).
Article on the collection of the composer's manuscripts housed at the Scottish Music Information Centre in Glasgow. (This collection is now in the British Library.)

B785. Tumelty, Michael. "Youth Band and Choirs." *Glasgow Herald* (Aug. 19, 1985).
Review of a concert by the Scottish Youth Brass Band and the Scottish National Orchestra Junior and Youth Choruses at Usher Hall, Edinburgh, Aug. 18, 1985. Included on the program was the premiere of *The Peat Cutters*, which is described as "a work of compelling intensity" and "complex and wiry though thoroughly accessible writing."

B786. Turner, J. Rigbie. "The Juilliard School." *Music Journal* v. 31 (April, 1973) pp. 52–53.
Includes a review of the American premiere of *Vesalii Icones* at the Juilliard Theater. Reviewer complains that the work was "ambiguous and disparate, and at times incoherent and simply noisy."

B787. Ulrich, Allan. "Berkeley Welcomes the Fires of London." *San Francisco Examiner* (Dec. 9, 1985), p. E2.
Review of a concert by the Fires of London conducted by the composer at Zellerbach Hall, University of California, Berkeley, Dec. 7, 1985. Included on the program were performances of *Eight Songs For a Mad King* and *Le Jongleur de Notre Dame*, this work with the assistance of the Young People's Symphony Orchestra. Baritone Andrew Gallacher was soloist in both works and juggler Jonny James was featured in the latter.

B788. Ulrich, Allan. "Mezzo's Maximum *Medium*." *San Francisco Examiner* (Feb. 3, 1988).
Review of a concert by the Composers Chamber Players at the Waterfront Theater, San Francisco, Feb. 1, 1988. Included on the program was a performance of *The Medium* with soloist mezzo-soprano Lynn Morrow. The reviewer describes the piece as "a shattering work, buoyed by an awesome theatrical intelligence."

B789. Ulrich, Allan. "Musical Gems in Shangri-La." *San Francisco Examiner* (June 7, 1988) p. B7.
Article about the 1988 Ojai Festival when Davies was composer-in-residence. Includes a review of the American premiere of *Into the Labyrinth* featuring Neil Mackie, tenor and the Ojai Festival Orchestra conducted by the composer. Described as a work that "reflects, pleads and warns, all in eloquent cantilena, while the orchestra shifts its timbral personality." Also reviews *Strathclyde Concerto No. 1 for Oboe and Orchestra* performed by soloist Stephen Colburn on June 5, 1988 (the work "grows organically from strings to oboe...the composer seems more concerned with arresting textures...setting soloist against orchestra") and *Ave Maris Stella* performed by the California E.A.R. Unit, June 4, 1988 ("the work's elegaic mood masks a complex plan in which one attends to the sound...without...comprehending the organizing idea").

B790. Ulrich, Alan. "Ozawa Returns to S.F. With Guns Blazing." *San Francisco Examiner* (Mar. 13, 1981).
Review of concert by the Boston Symphony Orchestra conducted by Seiji Ozawa at Davies Hall, San Francisco, Mar. 12, 1981. Included on the program was a performance of *Symphony No. 2*, of which the reviewer remarks, "the latest, magnificently sustained 50-minute work is a composition of unparalleled scope and wonder."

B791. Ulrich, Allan. "Viva American Symphony." *San Francisco Examiner* (Sept. 29. 1986) p. E4.

Review of a concert by the American Symphony Orchestra conducted by Tamas Vasary, at the Masonic Auditorium, San Francisco, September, 1986. Included on the program was a performance of *An Orkney Wedding, With Sunrise*, characterized as a combination of "repeated fiddle tunes...sudden metrical shifts, the playful exchange of material."

B792. Unwin, Russell. "Caught in the Act." *Melody Maker* v. 46 (Dec. 18, 1971) p. 26

Review of a concert which featured the premieres of *Suite from 'The Devils'* and *Suite from 'The Boyfriend'* on 11 Dec., 1971, by the Fires of London directed by the composer at the Queen Elizabeth Hall. Of the *Devils* music the reviewer notes it "is a manifestation of Maxwell Davies' hard edge serious expressiveness"; by contrast, the *Boyfriend* music is "Light-hearted and extremely camp."

B793. Unwin, Russell. "Contemporary Classics." *Melody Maker* v. 47 (Dec. 2, 1972) p. 67.

Review of a recording of *Missa Super L'Homme Armé, From Stone to Thorn, Hymnos*, and *Antechrist*, performed by Mary Thomas, Vanessa Redgrave, Alan Hacker, Stephen Pruslin, and the Fires of London conducted by the composer. (L'Oiseau-Lyre DSLO 2). The music on the recording is described as "refreshingly different" and proof that "it is still possible to produce exciting, original music."

B794. Varnai, Peter. "Royani Fesztival—1970." *Musika* v. 13 (June 1970) pp. 30–31.

Includes reviews of performances of *Vesalii Icones* and *Eight Songs For a Mad King* at the 1970 Royani Festival.

B795. von Bachau, Stephanie. "Reports: Santa Fe." *Ballet News* v. 4 (Nov., 1982) pp. 36–37.

Review of a performance of *Salome* by the Dallas Ballet, July 29, 1982 in Santa Fe. About the score the reviewer remarks it is "mainly percussive but in a delicate, pointillistic manner...lots of bell-like sound." She found the work as a whole unexciting and lacking in dramatic focus.

B796. von Rhein, John. "Beacon of Darkness." *Chicago Tribune* (Mar. 23, 1990) section Tempo, p. 3.

Review of a performance of *The Lighthouse* by members of the Chicago Opera Theater at the Athenaeum Theatre, Chicago, Mar. 21, 1990. The cast included Richard Fracker, Nikolas Karousatos, and Peter Loehie, conducted by Henry Holt. Describes the work as "a taut psychological thriller, as dark and unsettling as its subject." Further notes: "Davies' strong, mostly atonal score is frightfully hard to perform." With a synopsis of the work.

B797. von Rhein, John. "Composer Peter Maxwell Davies: Looking for an Audience, Not a Cult." *Chicago Tribune* (May 22, 1983) section 6, pp. 16–17.

Article about Davies as a composer focusing on his style and accomplishments to date. Includes a review of a performance of *Stone Litany* with Jan deGaetani and the Chicago Symphony conducted by Raymond Leppard on April, 1983.

B798. von Rhein, John. "Group Rules Wide Kingdom of Song." *Chicago Tribune* (Oct. 13, 1986) section Chicagoland p. 7.

Review of a concert by the King's Singers at Orchestra Hall, Chicago, Oct. 12, 1986. Included on the program was the American premiere of *House of Winter*, said to be "drenched in the eerie stillness of an Orkney winter." Further, "the dramatic contrast between the raptly sustained unison declamation...and the agitated part writing...made a quietly powerful claim on the listener."

B799. von Rhein, John. "Scottish Orchestra, Davies bridge 2 Musical Worlds." *Chicago Tribune* (Nov. 1, 1988) Section: Chicagoland, p. 10.

Review of a concert by the Scottish Chamber Orchestra conducted by the composer at Orchestra Hall, Chicago, Oct. 31, 1988. On the program were *Into the Labyrinth*, with Neil Mackie, tenor (the reviewer remarks: "The music is as stark as the gull cries and raging sea...painted in shades of gray") and *An Orkney Wedding, With Sunrise* ("an exhilarating, amusingly programmatic evocation of a nuptial ceremony on...Hoy").

B800. Wagner, Regina. "Experimentelles Musiktheater in der Augsburger Komödie." *Musica* v. 142 no. 2 (1988) pp. 183–184.

Review of a performance of *The Medium* by soloist Janet Walker, directed by Kornelia Repschläger, no date cited.

B801. Walker, Timothy. "Sir Peter Maxwell Davies, Part II." *Classical Guitar* v. 6 (Jan., 1988) pp. 19–20ff.
Second part of an article which features an interview of the composer by guitarist Timothy Walker, especially focusing on his compositions for solo guitar or including guitar parts.

B802. Walker, Timothy. "Sir Peter Maxwell Davies." *Classical Guitar* v. 6 (Dec., 1987) pp. 11–12ff and cover portrait.
First part of a two-part series in conversation with the composer by Timothy Walker. Features a personal portrait of Davies's early life and focuses on his interest in the guitar and composing for that instrument.

B803. Walsh, Stephen. "Creative Energy." *Observer* (Oct. 9, 1983).
Review of the premiere of *Sinfonietta Accademica* by the Scottish Chamber Orchestra conducted by Edward Downes at Reid Hall, Edinburgh University, Oct. 6, 1983. The reviewer describes the piece as a "difficult and exhilarating three-movement work"; commenting on the Orkney influence, he says that the work presents "the composer's mental picture of the spirit of dead souls" in an old church in the island of Hoy.

B804. Walsh, Stephen. "Impressive Image." *Observer* (Sept. 26, 1982).
Includes a review of a concert by the Fires of London at the Queen Elizabeth Hall, Sept. 21, 1982. On the program was the first complete London performance of *Image, Reflection, Shadow*. Includes a description of the work, focusing on the images it conveys. Terms such as "delicate" and "dearingly simple" are used. The reviewer notes the special role of the cimbalon in the work, here played by Gregory Knowles, and says it "is a beautifully integrated and beautifully satisfying piece."

B805. Walsh, Stephen. "New Dances From Salome." *Observer* (Nov. 1987).
Review of *Salome* at its first performance by the Royal Danish Ballet in Copenhagen, November, 1978. Focuses more on the music than on the choreography. About the score the reviewer notes, "the music always closely follows the course of the action, both in mood and pace." Notes the care taken in each section and the notable balance the composer achieves.

B806. Walsh, Stephen. *"Taverner."* *Musical Times* v. 113 (July, 1972) pp. 653–655.

An interview between the composer and Stephen Walsh, focusing on the background of *Taverner* and with mention of earlier works that the author feels are related to it.

B807. Walsh, Stephen. "With as Much Power as Possible." *Observer* (Feb. 24, 1985).

Review of the premiere of *Symphony No. 3* by the BBC Philharmonic Orchestra conducted by Edward Downes at the Free Trade Hall, Manchester, Feb. 19, 1985. The article includes a vivid description of the work, often stressing the unique compositional elements present in it. The reviewer describes the piece as "a huge four-movement score of massive intricacy" and finds evidence of the influence of Sibelius and Mahler apparent in it.

B808. Walsh, Stephen and David Roberts. "Peter Maxwell Davies." in *The New Grove Dictionary of Music and Musicians*, 1980.

B809. Walton, Kenneth. *"Black Pentecost."* *Glasgow Herald* (June 22. 1988).

Review of a concert at the St. Magnus Festival, June 20, 1988 by the BBC Philharmonic Orchestra conducted by Edward Downes. Included on the program was a performance of *Black Pentecost* by LaVerne Williams, mezzo-soprano, and Alan Oke, baritone. Music described as "a glinting, picturesque, refreshingly abstract impression of an Orkney seascape."

B810. Walton, Kenneth. "Maxwell Davies and SCO." *Daily Telegraph* (Oct. 30, 1984).

Review of a concert by the Scottish Chamber Orchestra conducted by the composer at City Hall, Glasgow, Oct. 28, 1984. Included on the program was a performance of *Sinfonietta Accademica*.

B811. Walton, Kenneth. "Maxwell Davies Cantata." *Daily Telegraph* (Dec. 2, 1983).

Review of a performance of *Into the Labyrinth* featuring tenor Neil Mackie and the Scottish Chamber Orchestra conducted by James Conlon at Queen's Hall, Edinburgh, Nov. 30, 1983. About the music the reviewer remarks: "It is the deft orchestra writing...which heightens this work to meet the claims of masterpiece."

B812. Walton, Kenneth. "School Concerts." *Glasgow Herald* (June 20, 1988).
Review of a concert on June 18, 1988 at the St. Magnus Festival, in Kirkwall, Orkney. Included on the program was the premiere of *Six Songs for St. Andrew's* by pupils from the St. Andrew's Primary School. These are called "classroom songs, with simply but imaginatively constructed melodies...inviting a certain amount of creativity from the kids."

B813. Walton, Kenneth. "SCO/Maxwell Davies." *Daily Telegraph* (Feb. 3, 1987).
Review of a concert by the Scottish Chamber Orchestra conducted by the composer at City Hall, Glasgow, Feb. 1, 1987. Included on the program was a performance of *Jimmack the Postie*, which the reviewer says is "a self-contained musical statement which is both logically constructed and brimming over with sparkling and vivid ideas."

B814. Walton, Kenneth. "St. Magnus: Ideals Upheld." *Classical Music* (Aug. 11, 1984).
Article about the 1984 St. Magnus Festival. Included is a review of the first Scottish performance of *Brass Quintet*, by the Albany Brass Ensemble. About the work the reviewer remarks he "found it to be one of the most exhilarating works of the festival; rich in rhythmic and harmonic interest, cohesive in structure."

B815. Warnaby, John. "CDs." *Musical Opinion* v. 113 (April, 1990) p. 141.
Review of a CD recording of *Strathclyde Concerto No. 1 for Oboe and Orchestra* and *Strathclyde Concerto No. 2 for Cello and Orchestra*, with soloists Robin Miller, Oboe, and William Conway, cello and the Scottish Chamber Orchestra conducted by the composer, (Unicorn-Kanchana, DKP 9085). Notes the music "fulfills the composer's intention of writing contemporary music that...is capable of appealing to a wide audience" and concludes: "Both works exhibit craftsmanship of the highest order."

B816. Warnaby, John. "CDs." *Musical Opinion* v. 114 (Oct., 1991) pp. 380–381.
Review of a CD which includes a performance of *Concerto for Trumpet and Orchestra* with Håkan Hardenberger on trumpet and the BBC Philharmonic Orchestra conducted by Elgar Howarth. When describing the work the reviewer notes: "The idea of thematic

transformation has long been associated with the music of Maxwell Davies, but he has tended to favour more extended melodies, and this is particularly true of the *Trumpet Concerto.*"

B817.   Warnaby, John. "Festival: St. Magnus." *Musical Opinion* v. 114 (Nov. 1991) pp. 420–421.
Reviews performances during the 1991 St. Magnus Festival, including: a recital by Håkan Hardenberger, trumpet accompanied by pianist John Constable at the Stromness Town Hall, June 23; *Image, Reflection, Shadow*, performed by Nouvelles Images, June 26; and a brief account of the premiere of *The Spiders' Revenge* by pupils of the Evie Primary School, June 25.

B818.   Warnaby, John. "Festivals." *Musical Opinion* v. 113 (July, 1990) pp. 248–249.
Article about 'Maxfest' held during Mar. 27–Apr. 10, 1990 at the South Bank. Describes the event as having "exemplified the extent to which Maxwell Davies has fulfilled his ambition of combining creativity with the practical aspects of music-making."

B819.   Warnaby, John. "Festivals." *Musical Opinion* v. 114 (Jan., 1991) pp. 25–27.
Review of concerts and other arts events at the 14th annual St. Magnus Festival, June, 1990. One event was the premiere of *Dangerous Errand* on June 24, performed by children of the Papdale Primary School. The reviewer says: "An element of improvisation is one of the more important ingredients of the work...this was often associated with some surprisingly lively outbursts." Another concert by members of the Music Theatre Wales at Hoy, Kirkwall, included a performance of *Sea Eagle* for solo horn. A third, by the Scottish Chamber Orchestra conducted by the composer, featured a performance of the composer's *Strathclyde Concerto No. 2 for Cello and Orchestra* with soloist William Conway; this work "revealed further subtleties that cannot be dealt with in the space available."

B820.   Warnaby, John. "Festivals: St. Magnus." *Musical Opinion* v. 114 (Nov. 1991) pp. 420–421.
Includes a review of a concert by the Scottish Chamber Singers on June 26, 1991, the final concert of the 1991 St. Magnus Festival. Tenor Neil Mackie performed three arias from *The Martyrdom of St. Magnus* and a revival of *Solstice of Light* (featuring organist Richard Hughes).

B821. Warnaby, John. "First Performance: Maxwell Davies's *Fourth Symphony*." *Tempo* no. 171 (Dec., 1989) pp. 44–45.

Article about *Symphony No. 4* just following the work's premiere by the Scottish Symphony Orchestra conducted by the composer at a Promenade Concert, at the Albert Hall, Sept. 10, 1989. Primarily a descriptive analysis of the piece. The reviewer remarks: "By deliberately blurring the distinction between the Symphony's four movements he [Davies] has constructed a continuous discourse."

B822. Warnaby, John. "First Performances." *Tempo* no. 146 (Sept. 1983) pp 55–57.

Review of the premiere of *Into the Labyrinth* featuring tenor Neil Mackie and the Scottish Chamber Orchestra conducted by James Conlon. It took place on June 22, 1983 in St. Magnus Cathedral as part of the 1983 St, Magnus Festival. The article includes a descriptive analysis of the work and mentions *The Blind Fiddler*, *Black Pentecost*, and *Solstice of Light*.

B823. Warnaby, John. "First Performances." *Tempo* no. 149 (June 1984) pp. 47–49.

Review of the premiere of *The No. 11 Bus* by the Fires of London and others at the Queen Elizabeth Hall, Mar. 20, 1984, conducted by Günther Bauer-Schenk, The reviewer says that: "The supporting music is also constructed from a complex network of references...permeated by fragments of plainsong...allusions to popular song...rock music" and notes the important relationship to *Taverner*.

B824. Warnaby, John. "Maxwell Davies: Strathclyde Concerti Nos. 1 and 2." *Musical Opinion* v. 113 (April 1990) p. 141.

Review of a recording by the Scottish Chamber conducted by the composer (Unicorn-Kanchana DKP 9085) that includes *Strathclyde Concerto No. 1 for Oboe and Orchestra* with Robin Miller, oboe (the reviewer says "the main inspirational source has been Mozart's *Oboe Concerto*") and *Strathclyde Concerto No. 2 for Cello and Orchestra* featuring William Conway, cello ("This work shows that contemporary music can be beautiful").

B825. Warnaby, John. "Maxwell Davies's Violin Concerto in Orkney." *Tempo* no. 158 (Sept., 1986) pp. 46–47.

Review of the premiere of *Concerto for Violin and Orchestra* at the 10th St. Magnus Festival by violinist Isaac Stern (for whom it was composed) and the Royal Philharmonic Orchestra conducted by

André Previn, at the St. Magnus Cathedral, June 21, 1986. About the work the reviewer remarks: "The solo violin is naturally regarded as an extension of the human voice...its dramatic potential is immediately apparent in the interplay between the soloist and the different sections of the orchestra." Includes a descriptive analysis of the work.

B826. Warnaby, John.   "Peter Maxwell Davies' Educational Music—the Orkney Years." *Music Teacher* (April 1985) pp. 10–11.
Article on Davies's then-recent compositions for young persons. Discusses *The Two Fiddlers* (with a brief synopsis of that piece), *Cinderella*, *The Rainbow*, *Kirkwall Shopping Songs*, *Songs of Hoy*, *Seven Songs Home*, *Five Klee Pictures*, *Welcome to Orkney*, *March: The Pole Star*, and *Stevie's Ferry to Hoy*. Includes a photograph of the composer.

B827. Warnaby, John.   "Peter Maxwell Davies' Orchestral Music." *Music and Musicians* v. 33 (Dec., 1984) pp. 6–8.
Lengthy article that focuses on the composer's major orchestral compositions to date. Some biographical material is included as well as a photograph of the composer.

B828. Warnaby, John.   "*Westerlings*: A Study in Symphonic Form." *Tempo* no. 147 (Dec. 1983) pp. 15–22.
An analysis of *Westerlings*, with many musical examples and quotes from the text, all used to illustrate the author's premise that although it is a choral work, "it is...possible to discern a 'symphonic' outlook underlying the work's organization as well as overall form."

B829. Warrack, John.   "Children in Harmony." *Sunday Telegraph* (Feb. 5, 1991).
Includes a lengthy critique of Davies as a composer of brilliant, original music for children. Focuses on his techniques and mentions *O Magnum Mysterium* which was given its premiere by the Cirencester Grammar School Choir at Cirencester Parish Church, Dec. 8, 1960.

B830. Waterhouse, John C. G. "Meeting Point." *Music and Musicians* v. 13 (Oct., 1964) pp. 24–26.
Analytical article, the primary focus being on "the fusions of styles" in *Veni, Sancte Spiritus* (which was premiered at the Cheltenham Festival July 10, 1964). Davies is described as being "perhaps the

most important English composer younger than Britten." The article includes a complete analysis of the work with musical examples. Remarks on the relationship of the *Veni, Sancte Spiritus* to *O Magnum Mysterium* and the two *Taverner Fantasias*.

B831. Waterhouse, John C. G. "Peter Maxwell Davies: Towards an Opera." *Tempo* no. 69 (Summer 1964) pp. 18–25.
Article which begins by announcing that the composer had begun working on an opera. The author then presents an overview of the composer's works to date, including *St. Michael Sonata*, *Alma Redemptoris Mater*, *String Quartet*, *Leopardi Fragments*, *Sinfonia*, *First Fantasia on an 'In Nomine' of John Taverner*, and *Veni Sancte Spiritus*. Includes musical examples.

B832. Webster, Daniel. "*The Lighthouse*, a Mystery Opera." *Philadelphia Inquirer* (Mar. 18, 1989) p. 8-c.
Review of a performance of *The Lighthouse* by performers from the Curtis Institute, Mar. 17, 1989. The conductor was David Hayes; soloists were Perry Brisbon, John Kramar, and Seth Malken. When describing the music the reviewer remarks that the composer "has made his brief ghost play a setting where musical style clash together, juxtaposing unabashed tone painting and taut psychological representation."

B833. Webster, E. M. "Cheltenham: Blight on the Band-Wagon." *Musical Opinion* v. 90 (Sept., 1967) pp. 677–685.
Article about the 1967 Cheltenham Festival. One concert reviewed included the premiere of *Hymnos* played by Alan Hacker, clarinet and Stephen Pruslin, piano. Remarks: "It is a more violent work than his [Davies's] wont, but it still burns with his own peculiar brand of fiery intensity." Another concert, on July 15, featured the premiere of *Homage to Stravinsky*, a set of 12 pieces each by a different young composer, in honor of Igor Stravinsky. The reviewer finds Davies's contribution, *Canon ad Honorem I[gor]. S[travinsky].*, "as spellbinding as he [Davies] always is, even in this small fragment." Finally, reviews a concert by the Pierrot Players conducted by the composer on July 16 which included *Antechrist*, remarking, "with all the fun and games, late medieval technique...the work remains personally characteristic and alive."

B834. Webster, E. M. "Cheltenham: Festival of Temporary Music." *Musical Opinion* v. 85 (Sept., 1962) p. 723.

Article about the 1962 Cheltenham Festival, including a review of a performance of *Sinfonia* (which had received its premiere earlier on May 9 of that year, in London). Giving a brief descriptive analysis of the work, the reviewer says it "is a vivid and compelling piece, based...on the Monteverdi *Vespers*" and is "a work of grave beauty, warm texture and lyric intensity."

B835. Webster, E. M. "Cheltenham: Growing Child of Our Time." *Musical Opinion* v. 87 (Sept., 1964) p. 708.

Article about the 1964 Cheltenham Festival, including a review of a concert on 10 July which included the premiere of *Veni Sancte Spiritus* by the Princeton High School Choir and the English Chamber Orchestra conducted by Thomas Hilbish. Music described as "full of Pentecostal fire...of compelling serenity and maturity of thought" and "a work of exceptional genius."

B836. Webster, E. M. "Cheltenham's Twenty-First Valorous Discretion." *Musical Opinion* v. 88 (Sept., 1965) p. 723.

Article about the various concerts at the 1965 Cheltenham Festival. Includes a brief review of a performance of *St. Michael Sonata* on 7 July, describing it as "awkward, fiendishly difficult to play, wildly original in concept...brilliantly and absurdly inventive and a colossal failure from the listener's point of view."

B837. Webster, E. M. "Communication Coinage." *Musical Opinion* v. 94 (April, 1971) p. 349.

Includes a review of a concert by the Fires of London, 20 Feb., 1971 at the Elizabeth Hall, with performances of the composer's realisation of Machaut's *Hoquetus David* ("lightly percussive and contrapuntally pointed") and the premiere of *Taverner: Points and Dances from the Opera* ("The rhythmic structure remained extremely tight and formal, giving a true medieval flavour"). Also includes a review of a concert on Feb. 26, 1971, with a performance of *Sonata for Trumpet and Piano* by Elgar Howarth, trumpet and John Constable, piano at the Queen Elizabeth Hall. Remarks, "it has the clear authority of a whole new school of thought."

B838. Webster, E. M. "Twentieth Century Opera: The Light and the Dark."
Musical Opinion v. 95 (Aug., 1972) pp. 573–575.
Includes a lengthy review of the premiere of *Taverner* by the Royal
Opera, Covent Garden, July 12, 1972. Gives a descriptive analysis
of the work, characterizing the music as: "Turbulent, violent, ironic,
pitiful, white-hot, cold as death." Further: the entire work "burns
with deadly fire from Taverner's opening innocence...to his final
disintegration as a human soul."

B839. Webster, Elizabeth. "Bath Festival." *Musical Opinion* v. 98 (Aug.,
1975) p. 557.
Includes a review of a concert by the Fires of London at the Theatre
Royal on May 27, 1975 (as part of the Bath Festival) which featured
the premiere of *Ave Maris Stella*. Calling this work "serious and
profound," the reviewer says, "it is difficult to say why one is so
moved...but one is."

B840. Webster, Elizabeth. "Bath." *Music and Musicians* v. 24 (Aug., 1975)
pp. 48–49.
Includes a review of the premiere of *Ave Maris Stella* performed by
the Fires of London at the Bath Festival, May 27, 1975. The work
is described as "deeply concerned with Time." The reviewer notes
that it has "a quiet, contemplative insistence, spiralling towards a
fierce climax."

B841. Weissmann, J. S. "'Your Concert Night' at St. Pancras." *Musical
Events* v. 18 (Feb. 1963) p. 29.
Review of a concert by the New Music Singers conducted by
Graham Treacher at the St. Pancras Town Hall early in 1963.
Included on the program was the premiere of *Four Carols*, which the
reviewer found "Beautiful; very enjoyable."

B842. Wells, William. "*The Peat Cutters*, for Brass Band, Youth Choir
(SATB) and Children's Choir (SA)." *Notes* v. 45 (1989) p. 864.
Review of *The Peat Cutters* upon the publication of the score by
Boosey and Hawkes, 1987; with a synopsis of the text, as well as a
descriptive analysis of the music, movement by movement.
Remarks: "The composer makes no concessions to his young
performers in the richness or complexity of the harmony."

B843. White, Harry. "The Holy Commandments of Tonality." *Journal of Musicology* v. 9 (1991) pp.254–268.

Response to an article by Arnold Whittall ("The Theorist's Sense of History": see B863) which used Davies as one of six examples of twentieth-century composers in arguing that theorists should strive for greater "contemporaneity" by recognizing that "there is no turning back from the emancipation of the dissonance." Whittall argued that tonal elements could only compromise the musical integrity of atonal compositions by conveying a "unifying confidence of outlook" (the latter phrase is from the composer) that violates the aesthetics of late 20th-century composition. White responds, from a music historian's point of view, that strict devotion to atonality leads to a music which is incapable of referring to anything else, even other music, and is thus without historical location.

B844. White, Michael John. "Albany Brass Ensemble." *Daily Telegraph* (Dec. 20, 1982).

Review of a concert by the Albany Brass Ensemble at St. John's, Smith Square, London, Dec. 17, 1982. Included on the program was a performance of *Brass Quintet* by the Albany Brass Ensemble which the reviewer describes as "a memorable event," noting "The three movements...follow Davies's continuing interest in classical structures."

B845. White, Michael. "At 60, the Real Maxwell Davies." *Independent* (Aug. 14, 1994).

Article about the composer (with a photograph of him) written just prior to his 60th birthday on Sept. 8, 1994.

B846. White, Michael John. "*Eight Songs for a Mad King*." *Opera* v. 36 (Dec., 1985) p. 1446.

Review of a performance of *Eight Songs for a Mad King* by members of the Innererklang Players in the public cafeteria of the Innererklang Lyric Theatre, Hammersmith, Aug. 20, 1985. Notes the "musical borrowings...are not an academic exercise in composition. They are more like beacons, aural stimulants for the audience."

B847. White, Michael John. "Glowing Last Embers for the Fires." *Independent* (Jan. 22, 1987).

Review of the farewell concert of the Fires of London conducted by the composer at the Queen Elizabeth Hall, Jan. 20, 1987. Included on the program was the premiere of *Farewell–A Fancye by John*

Dowland, which the reviewer describes as "a charming, fragile piece..." Also on the program was the premiere of *Winterfold*, which is given a performance review only.

B848. White, Michael John. "Maxwell Davies Premiere." *Arts Guardian* (Sept. 6, 1984).
Review of a concert by the Scottish Chamber Orchestra conducted by the composer at the Royal Albert Hall, Sept. 5, 1984, including the English premiere of *Into the Labyrinth* with Neil Mackie, tenor. The reviewer says the piece "pleased with an eloquent and open lyricism that surpasses in its beauty anything Davies has written during the past 10 years."

B849. White, Michael John. "Maxwell Davies Premiere." *Guardian* (Sept. 2, 1985).
Review of a concert by the BBC Philharmonic Orchestra conducted by Edward Downes at the Royal Albert Hall, Aug. 31, 1985. Included on the program was the first London performance of *Symphony No. 3*. The reviewer remarks, "the music reads less like an intellectual game...more like a vehicle of...passion and all the raw material of the romantic artist."

B850. White, Michael. "Maxwell Davies' Shockers Sprout Again in Brussels." *Independent* (April 10, 1994).
Includes a review of performances of *Vesalii Icones*, *Eight Songs for a Mad King*, and *Miss Donnithorne's Maggot* by members of Kameropera Antwerpen Transparant in Brussels during the weekend of April 2–3, 1994.

B851. White, Michael John. "Purer Forms Where Fewer Notes Do Harder Work." *Independent* (Mar. 25, 1990).
Article primarily based on an interview with the composer written just prior to the 1990 Maxwell Davies Festival at the South Bank, London, Mar. 27–April 10, 1990. Some is biographical and certainly promotional. Focuses on the *Strathclyde Concertos* and *Symphony No. 4*. Includes photograph of the composer.

B852. White, Michael. "More Than an Average Wind-Up." *Independent* (Mar. 14, 1993) p. 21.
Includes a review of a performance of *Worldes Blis* by the Royal Philharmonic Orchestra conducted by the composer at the Royal Festival Hall, Mar. 10, 1993. Describing the work as "an orchestral

juggernaut, whose slow, massive progression....made tough demands on the initial 1960's audience," the reviewer admits this performance revealed "more radiant qualities than I remembered."

B853. White, Michael John. "The Second Coming." *Independent* (Sept. 21, 1988) p. 12.
Lengthy review of the premiere of *Resurrection* by Stadtstheater Darmstadt, conducted by Hans Drewanz, Sept. 18, 1988. After stating that Covent Garden had turned down the libretto, the reviewer concedes that the opera appears to be dated in theme, and that "the slapstick...will have Davies' critics ticking off yet another lapse of judgment." However, he responds, first, that the work is not dated but actually reflects an earlier point in the composer's career, since its ideas "were set down in 1963 when Davies was still studying in America; and they are his response to the American consumer culture." As a consequence, *Resurrection* "chronologically...is itself...the originating agenda, once hidden but now revealed, from which the [other music theatre pieces] sprang...it is the key to a whole genre of his work." And he concludes that "a sense of order somehow prevails, musically, over a barrage of ideas with no obvious linear relationship; and despite the wild diversity of input...there is an engaging tightness of expression which manages to contain everything in an 80-minute running time."

B854. Whittall, Arnold. "*Image, Reflection, Shadow*, for Chamber Ensemble." *Music and Letters* v. 68 (1987) pp. 306–308.
Review of the score of *Image, Reflection, Shadow* when it was published by Chester, 1984. Describes the piece as "a formidable demonstration of the composer's "international" style at full symphonic stretch."

B855. Whittall, Arnold. "*Into the Labyrinth*." *Music and Letters* v. 68 (1987) pp. 306–308.
Review of the score of *Into the Labyrinth* when it was published by Chester, 1986. Remarks that the work is a "satisfying demonstration of how intense expressiveness can survive the abandonment of expressionistic rhetoric, and yield a purified...still more intense effect." Mentions links with *Black Pentecost* and *The Yellow Cake Revue*.

B856. Whittall, Arnold. "*The Martyrdom of St. Magnus*." *Music and Letters* v. 69 (1988) pp. 136–137.

Review of *The Martyrdom of St. Magnus* upon publication of the score by Boosey and Hawkes, 1987.   Compares the work to *Taverner*, stressing the differences between the two. Also mentions Britten's church parables as another point of comparison. Concludes the work "is a fascinating, gripping and resourceful composition" but that Davies has yet to achieve "a completely satisfying confrontation between good and evil."

B857. Whittall, Arnold.   *"An Orkney Wedding, With Sunrise." Music and Letters* v. 68 (1987) pp. 306–308.
Review of *An Orkney Wedding, With Sunrise* when the score was published by Boosey and Hawkes, 1985.   Noting that the work makes blatant use of "folk or folk-like materials," the reviewer says that although the composer has made use of such elements before, "never so consistently in an orthodox concert work."

B858. Whittall, Arnold.   "Records: Taverner and Maxwell Davies." *Music and Musicians* v. 25 (June, 1977) p. 49.
Includes a review of a recording of *Renaissance Scottish Dances*, *Hymn to St. Magnus*, and *Psalm 24* (L'Oiseau-Lyre DSLO 12), all performed by the Fires of London conducted by the composer. Focuses on *Hymn to St.Magnus* and notes: "With its substantial dimensions and often macabre textures the *Hymn* disturbs and provokes...the work grips like a vice throughout its 35-minute span."

B859. Whittall, Arnold.   *"Revelation and Fall." Music and Letters* v. 66 (1985) pp. 191–193.
Includes a review of *Revelation and Fall* when the score was published by Boosey & Hawkes, 1984.   The reviewer notes: "*Revelation and Fall* is one of Davies's finest works...its violent emotions are channelled compositionally, rather than simply being allowed to assault the audience in virtually unmediated form."

B860. Whittall, Arnold.   *"Sinfonia Concertante." Music and Letters* v. 69 (1988) pp. 137–138.
Review of *Sinfonia Concertante* for chamber orchestra upon publication of the score by Chester, London, 1986.   After a descriptive analysis of the composition, during which the reviewer frequently remarks on the lack of balance between the two parts, he observes: "The 'concertante' is a full wind quintet, with strings and timpani in support, but Davies appears to experience difficulty at

many points in preventing the work from turning into a horn concerto."

B861. Whittall, Arnold. "*Sinfonietta Accademica* for Chamber Orchestra." *Music and Letters* v. 69 (1988) pp. 313–314.

Review of *Sinfonietta Accademica* for chamber orchestra upon the publication of the score by Chester, London, 1987. Includes a brief descriptive analysis of the work, movement by movement. Although noting that the composer describes the piece as a "game...with sonata form references," the reviewer considers it more rather "a game...between those references and the music's post-Schoenbergian process of developing variation." Concludes that the piece might be considered a preview to *Symphony No. 3*.

B862. Whittall, Arnold. "*Symphony No. 3*." *Music and Letters* v. 69 (1988) pp. 137–138.

Review of *Symphony No. 3* upon the publication of the score by Boosey and Hawkes, London, 1987. Includes a descriptive analysis of the work, remarking that the "symphony is the composer's most successful attempt so far to sustain harmonic as well as rhythmic continuity in large structures in which the degree of tonal focus is...far from uniform."

B863. Whittall, Arnold. "The Theorist's Sense of History." *Journal of the Royal Musical Association* v. 92 (1987) pp. 1–20.

Argues for the importance of tonality as a concept for analyzing the historical place of compositions, and undertakes to study the presence and absence of tonality in compositions of Alban Berg, Anton Webern, Pierre Boulez, Peter Maxwell Davies, Harrison Birtwistle, and Elliott Carter.

B864. Whittall, Arnold. "A Transatlantic Future?" *Music and Letters* v. 51 (1970) pp. 259–264.

Curious article focusing on contemporary composers and the future of their music. Compares Davies with Stockhausen and concludes, at one point: "If Stockhausen seeks to eliminate our conventional sense of time by increasingly static musical events, Davies seeks to dramatize it by increasingly kaleidoscopic events." Considers *Revelation and Fall*, *St. Thomas Wake*, *Eight Songs for a Mad King*, *Worldes Blis*, and *Second Fantasia on John Taverner's 'In Nomine'*.

B865. Whittall, Arnold. "*The Yellow Cake Revue*." *Music and Letters* v. 66 (1985) pp. 191–193.

Review of *Yellow Cake Revue* when the score was published by Boosey & Hawkes, 1984. Includes a description of the piece and a brief analysis of the music.

B866. Wickert, Max. "Librettos and Academies: Some Speculations and an Example." *Opera Journal* v. 7 no. 4 (1974) pp. 6–16.
Article which deals with opera librettos and their authors, with emphasis on contemporary operas. Includes a section about *Eight Songs for a Mad King* (the text of which is by Randolph Stow). Although not concentrating on the score, the author does say the music is a "brilliantly inventive and deeply disturbing score." Article includes sources for the text.

B867. Wilder, Mark. "The High Days and the Hoy Days." *Daily Mail* (Mar. 10, 1981) p. 28.
Article written just prior to the premiere of *Symphony No. 2* by the Boston Symphony Orchestra. Mostly biographical with many good insights into the composer.

B868. Williams, Nicholas. "The View From Within." *Independent* (Oct. 7, 1992) p. 22.
Review of a concert by the Royal Philharmonic Orchestra conducted by the composer at Festival Hall, Oct. 5, 1992. Included on the program was the premiere of *Caroline Mathilde: Concert Suite II*. Remarks about the music, "through much of this seven-movement suite, a parade of distorted courtly dances lurched in and out."

B869. Wilson, Conrad. "Back to Classic Beauty." *Scotsman* (May 2, 1988) p. 9.
Review of the premiere of *Strathclyde Concerto No. 1 for Oboe and Orchestra* by Robin Miller, oboe and the Scottish Chamber Orchestra conducted by the composer at City Hall, Glasgow, April 29, 1988. The reviewer notes the work presents "a distinguished modern composer's response to musical history and to the island surroundings in which he works."

B870. Wilson, Conrad. "Cautionary Tales in Orkney." *Scotsman* (June 22, 1988).
About the 1988 St. Magnus Festival. Reviews a performance of *The Two Fiddlers* by children from the Hutcheson's Grammar School, Glasgow conducted by Norman Mitchell at the Kirkwall Arts Theatre, June 21, 1988. Emphasizes the moral message in the piece,

the reviewer describes it as "a little opera, for a multiplicity of vocal and instrumental resources...a tricky piece." Also reviews a concert by the BBC Philharmonic Orchestra conducted by Edward Downes at the Phoenix Cinema, Kirkwall, on June 21. which featured a performance of *Black Pentecost* with soloists La Verne Williams and Alan Oke.   The reviewer remarks: "It is a powerful, serious, ambitious score...its local relevance remains strong."

B871. Wilson, Conrad.   "Clarinet Theme Hauntingly Beautiful." *Scotsman* (Nov. 23, 1990).
Review of a concert by the Scottish Chamber Orchestra conducted by the composer at Queens Hall, Edinburgh, Nov. 22, 1990. Included on the program was the premiere of *Strathclyde Concerto No. 4 for Clarinet and Orchestra* with soloist Lewis Morrison. The reviewer remarks: "The work is magical in its instrumentation, with the sound of the soloist reflected in the gleam of the crotales in the first movement." Continuing in that vein, the reviewer emphasizes the special effects produced by various instruments.

B872. Wilson, Conrad.   "Common Touch From Davies." *Glasgow Herald* (Mar. 16, 1992).
Review of a concert by the Scottish Chamber Orchestra conducted by the composer at the Queen's Hall,Glasgow, Mar. 13, 1992. Included on the program were the premieres of *Strathclyde Concerto No. 5 for Violin, Viola and String Orchestra* with soloists James Clark and Catherine Marwood (the reviewer notes, "the double concerto was startling in its freshness") and also of *Strathclyde Concerto No. 6 for Flute and Orchestra* (which the reviewer says "seemed content to be a sketch, a vehicle for the SCO's principal flute, David Nicholson").

B873. Wilson, Conrad.   "Cycle of Concertos." *Scotsman* (Nov. 15, 1986).
Notice that the composer had been commissioned to compose the 10 *Strathclyde Concertos* for the Scottish Chamber Orchestra.

B874. Wilson, Conrad.   "Davies Captures Spirit of Orkney." *Scotsman* (June 23, 1986).
Includes a review of a concert by the Royal Philharmonic Orchestra conducted by André Previn during the St. Magnus Festival at the St. Magnus Cathedral, June 21, 1986. The featured work was the premiere of *Concerto for Violin and Orchestra* performed by violinist Isaac Stern. In a vivid description of the new work, the reviewer

says that it is "definitely not only a concerto for a great soloist but a work with Scottish and Orcadian fingerprints."

B875. Wilson, Conrad. "Davies Fascinates with Beethoven." *Scotsman* (June 21, 1988).
Includes a review of a concert by György Pauk, violin and Peter Frankl, piano, during the 1988 St. Magnus Festival at the Stromness Academy, Orkney, June 19, 1988. Included on the program was the premiere of *Dances From 'The Two Fiddlers'* arranged for violin and piano. The music is described as "a witty tribute to Orkney fiddle music."

B876. Wilson, Conrad. . "Davies Scores With New Opera. *Scotsman* (June 19, 1978).
Review of the premiere of *The Two Fiddlers* by pupils from the Kirkwall Grammar School conducted by Norman Mitchell at the Kirkwall Arts Theatre, June 16, 1978. About the work the reviewer remarks, "Davies...is not only able but eager to write music which...is related to the community where he now lives." Gives a synopsis of the piece and the plans for future performances.

B877. Wilson, Conrad. "Davies Writes Rousing Score for Orkney Schoolchildren." *Scotsman* (June 23, 1980).
Review of the premiere of *Cinderella* during the 1980 St. Magnus Festival, by pupils of the Papdale Elementary School and Kirkwall Grammar School conducted by Glenys Hughes at the Kirkwall Arts Theatre on June 21. The reviewer says: "The music...has its local links...incorporating a charming Scottish dance of the kind which Davies has written time to time...for the instrumentalists in the Fires of London." Includes a detailed description of the performance and a vivid synopsis of the plot.

B878. Wilson, Conrad. "Double-Barrelled Triumph." *Scotsman* (Aug. 13, 1987).
Review of a concert by the Scottish Chamber Orchestra conducted by the composer at Usher Hall, Edinburgh, August, 1987. Included on the program was a performance of *Sinfonietta Accademica*, of which the reviewer says: "As a series of Orcadian scenes in symphonic form it beguiled and teased the ear."

B879. Wilson, Conrad. "Edinburgh: SCO." *Scotsman* (Dec. 1, 1983).
Review of a concert by the Scottish Chamber Orchestra conducted by James Conlon at Queen's Hall, Edinburgh, Nov. 30, 1983. Included on the program was a performance of *Into the Labyrinth* with tenor Neil Mackie. Observing that "the music wove its Orcadian spell," the reviewer pronounces the work "a masterpiece."

B880. Wilson, Conrad. "Eroica Performance Will Put Davies to the Test." *Scotsman* (Aug. 10, 1987) p. 4.
includes mention of the commission for the composition of the ten *Strathclyde Concerti* and some discussion of *Sinfonietta Accademica*, *The Martyrdom of St. Magnus*, and *Sonata for Guitar*.

B881. Wilson, Conrad. "The Fires of London Go Out in Style." *Scotsman* (Jan. 22, 1987).
Review of the farewell concert of the Fires of London conducted by the composer at the Queen Elizabeth Hall, Jan. 20, 1987. Included on the program was the premiere of *Winterfold* with soloist Mary Thomas. The reviewer describes this as "a thoroughly Orcadian piece...The sound was as unpolluted as the Orkney air." Also on the program were the premiere of *Farewell-A Fancye* and a performance of *Eight Songs for a Mad King*.

B882. Wilson, Conrad. "International Music, Perfectly at Home." *Scotsman* (June, 1991).
Article about the 1991 St. Magnus Festival. Includes a review of the premiere of *The Spiders' Revenge* by students from the Evie Primary School at the Kirkwall Arts Theatre, June 25, 1991. Observing that the piece is "essentially a simplification of Ravel's *L'Enfant et les Sortilèges*," the review notes: "in tone, accent and rhythm, the music seemed devised for young Orkney voices." Also includes a review of a performance of *Image, Reflection, Shadow* by members of Nouvelles Images at St. Magnus Cathedral, on June 25. Remarks about the piece that it is "one of the purest, most beautiful and intricate of adult works which Davies has written in Orkney in recent years" and comments on its remarkable orchestration.

B883. Wilson, Conrad. "Jimmy the Postie at Orkney." *Scotsman* (June 24, 1986).
Review of a concert by the Royal Philharmonic Orchestra conducted by the composer during the St. Magnus Festival at the Phoenix Cinema, Kirkwall, June 22, 1986. Included on the program was the

premiere of *Jimmack the Postie*. The reviewer remarks that the composer attempted "to express something of Jimmy's many-sided ebullient personality."

B884. Wilson, Conrad. "Magic Union of Storyteller and the Composer." *Weekend Scotsman* (June 21, 1980).
Article on the relationship between Davies and the Orkney author, George Mackay Brown. Addresses the composer's various works that set texts by Brown.

B885. Wilson, Conrad. "Maxwell Davies With the SCO." *Scotsman* (April 11, 1986).
Review of a concert by the Scottish Chamber Orchestra conducted by the composer at Queen's Hall, Edinburgh, April 10, 1986. Included on the program was a performance of *Into the Labyrinth* with Neil Mackie, tenor. The reviewer remarks, "the score as a whole proved as powerful as it was picturesque."

B886. Wilson, Conrad. "Midsummer Magic and Music." *Scotsman* (June 22, 1981).
Article about the 1981 St. Magnus Festival. Includes a review of the premiere of *The Medium* by mezzo-soprano Mary Thomas at Academy Hall, Stromness, on June 21, (described as "Davies's latest mad scene—a piece of unaccompanied music theatre").   Also includes a review of the premiere of *Lullabye for Lucy* by the St. Magnus Singers conducted by the composer at St. Magnus Cathedral on June 19 (described as a "sweetly melodious setting").

B887. Wilson, Conrad.   "Orkney Composer Rises to Sibelian Heights." *Scotsman* (Feb. 3, 1989).
Includes a review of a concert by the Scottish Chamber Orchestra conducted by the composer at City Hall, Glasgow, Feb. 1, 1989. Featured on the program was the premiere of *Strathclyde Concerto No. 2 for Cello and Orchestra*, with soloist William Conway. Noting the influence of Sibelius on the piece, the reviewer writes: "In a score both powerful and economic, the soloist contributes the main element of warmth to unorchestrated texture otherwise of often bare."   Also includes a review of a concert by children from the St. Mary's Music School at the Scottish National Gallery on Feb. 2, 1989. On the program was a performance of *Seven Songs Home*. These pieces are described as "more general studies of Orkney life,

but ones with their own onomatopoetic references to the ever present sea."

B888. Wilson, Conrad. "Orkney Out of Tune With Man of Music." *Scotsman* (June 21, 1986).
Article about the composer and his relationship with Orkney and its inhabitants, especially his connection with the St. Magnus Festival. Very interesting and highly anecdotal.

B889. Wilson, Conrad. "Orkney's Enchanting Rainbow." *Scotsman* (June 24, 1981).
Review of a performance of *The Rainbow* by pupils of the Stromness Elementary School conducted by Janet Halsall in Stromness, June 22, 1981. This performance followed the premiere in Kirkwall. About the piece the reviewer notes: "The tone is amiable, amusing, mildly subversive."

B890. Wilson, Conrad. "Peter Maxwell Davies Premiere." *Scotsman* (Oct. 7, 1983).
Review of a concert by the Scottish Chamber Orchestra conducted by Edward Harper at Reid Hall, Edinburgh University, Oct. 6, 1983. Included on the program was the premiere of *Sinfonietta Accademica*. About the work the reviewer notes, "an impression was conveyed of the overall sweep of the music, of its whirlwind activity, its sudden fierce blasts."

B891. Wilson, Conrad. "*Postie* Witty Touch at SCO Concert." *Scotsman* (Feb. 2, 1987).
Review of a concert by the Scottish Chamber Orchestra conducted by the composer at Queen's Hall, Edinburgh, June 31, 1987. Included on the program was a performance of *Jimmack the Postie*, of which the reviewer remarks, "the gradual invasion of the music by Scotch snap rhythms brings with it a nervy atmosphere of Scottishness."

B892. Wilson, Conrad. "Queen's Hall Concert." *Scotsman* (Nov. 5, 1986).
Review of a concert by members of the Scottish Chamber Orchestra conducted by Alasdair Nicolson at Queen's Hall, Edinburgh, Nov. 4, 1986. Included on the program was a performance of *Vesalii Icones* featuring dancer Tom Yang and cellist William Conway. The reviewer notes the music featured "piercing flute and clarinet, sensitive viola and vivid percussion."

B893. Wilson, Conrad. "St. Magnus Festival Masterpiece." *Scotsman* (June 24, 1983).

Review of a concert during the St. Magnus Festival by the Scottish Chamber Orchestra conducted by James Conlon at St. Magnus Cathedral, June 22, 1983. Included on the program was the premiere of *Into the Labyrinth*, with tenor Neil Mackie. About the work the reviewer remarks, "there is in the new cantata an almost Sibelius-like force and sweep." Includes a descriptive analysis of the piece.

B894. Wilson, Conrad. "St. Magnus Festival: King's Singers." *Scotsman* (June 25, 1986).

Includes a review of a concert by the King's singers during the 1986 St. Magnus Festival at East Kirk, Kirkwall, June 23, 1986. Featured on the program was the premiere of *House of Winter*, in which the reviewer finds the text is "resourcefully worked by Davies's music, which makes vivid use of flow, frozen tones...scale passages." Notes the work was the high point of the concert.

B895. Wilson, Conrad. "St. Magnus Festival: *The Lighthouse*." *Scotsman* (June 26, 1986).

Review of a perfomrnace of *The Lighthouse* during the 1986 St. Magnus Festival at the Phoenix Cinema, Kirkwall, on June 24. The performers included Neil Mackie, Ian Comboy, and Henry Herford and the Fires of London conducted by Günther Bauer-Schenk. The reviewer describes the piece as "a work in which a number of Davies's musical obsessions meet and strike sparks with each other."

B896. Wilson, Conrad. "Scottish Chamber Orchestra." *Scotsman* (Nov. 14, 1986).

Review of a concert by the Scottish Chamber Orchestra conducted by the composer at Queen's Hall, Edinburgh, Nov. 13, 1986. Included on the program was the first performance of *An Orkney Wedding, With Sunrise* in the reduced version for small orchestra. When describing this version the reviewer remarks: "Quite apart from the advantage of hearing it indoors...raw, often witty rhythms and textures seemed conspicuously sharper."

B897. Wilson, Conrad. "Sea Change for Orkney Composer." *Scotsman* (Mar. 26, 1990).

Review of a concert by the Scottish Chamber Orchestra conducted by the composer, Mar. 24, 1990. About the work the reviewer notes:

"In structure the music has points in common with Sibelius's Seventh Symphony." Notes influence on the piece of the Orkney landscape and, especially, of the sea.

B898. Wilson, Conrad. "A Shock Opera Orkney May Never See." *Scotsman* (June 20, 1988).
Includes an announcement of the forthcoming premiere of *Resurrection* at Darmstadt in September, 1988. About the work the reviewer writes: "Approaching his subject in his own bizarre, surrealistic way, Davies appears to have produced a work which is more anti-opera than opera." Also reviews the premiere of *Six Songs for St. Andrew's* by pupils from the St. Andrew's Primary School near Kirkwall during the 1988 St. Magnus Festival, on June 18. The reviewer remarks: "The latest songs...were intended for classroom use but are fun to hear and see." Includes a brief description of the songs.

B899. Wilson, Conrad. "Teachers Smooth Over the Anti-Max Factor." *Scotsman* (Dec. 10, 1983) p. 2.
Article about the composer, the St. Magnus Festival and the residents of Orkney. Describes various problems that have arisen between the composer (and the Festival) and the people of Orkney.

B900. Wilson, Conrad. "Uchida's Mozart Cycle of Quality." *Scotsman* (Nov., 1984).
Review of a concert by the Scottish Chamber Orchestra at Queen's Hall, Edinburgh, Oct. 31, 1984. Included on the program was a performance of *Sinfonia Concertante* conducted by the composer. When describing the work the reviewer remarks that "Davies has tackled for the first time the writing of a concerto and the music shows his exhilarating response to his...quintet for solo instruments."

B901. Wilson, Conrad. "Well-Balanced Concert With Visual Appeal." *Scotsman* (Oct. 29, 1984).
Review of a concert by the Scottish Chamber Orchestra conducted by the composer at Queen's Hall, Edinburgh, Oct. 27, 1984. Included on the program was a performance of *Sinfonietta Accademica*, which the reviewer describes as "a work of considerable rhythmic complexity and tensions...a powerful, bleaker and more abstract picture of Orcadian life."

B902.   Wilson, Kenneth.   "BBC Philharmonic."   *Glasgow Herald* (June 23, 1988).
Review of a concert by the BBC Philharmonic Orchestra conducted by the composer at the St. Magnus Festival, June, 1988.   Included on the program was a performance of *An Orkney Wedding, with Sunrise*.   The music is described as being: "Riotous whoops...from the horns...together with drunken antics...from the trumpets...had all the trappings of a revelrous wedding."

B903.   Wilson, Timothy.   "Fires Leave a Warm Glow."   *South China Morning Post* (Feb. 11, 1984).
Review of a concert by the Fires of London as part of the 1984 Hong Kong Arts Festival, early Feb., 1984.   Included on the program was a performance of *Ave Maris Stella*, of which the reviewer remarks: "Here serialism has clearly reached its maturity both in rhythmic complexity and in aesthetic diffusion."

B904.   Wilson, Timothy.   "Interesting Fiery Fare."   *South China Morning Post* (Feb. 9, 1984).
Review of a concert by the Fires of London conducted by the composer, part of the 1984 Hong Kong Arts Festival, Feb. 7, 1984.   Included on the program were performances of *Le Jongleur de Notre Dame* and *Eight Songs for a Mad King* (with baritone Andrew Gallagher).   The reviewer says of both works: "Disjointed, hectic music that was once labelled 'new' now seems rather bland."

B905.   Wolf, Hans.   "Sweden: Two Novelties."   *Opera* v. 32 (July 1981) p. 741.
Includes a brief review of a performance of *Miss Donnithorne's Maggot* by singer Kerstin Meyer, conducted by Thomas Schuback, at the Rotunda, Royal Opera, Stockholm, Feb. 7, 1981.

B906.   Woodward, Ian.   "The Naked Salome."   *Evening News* (Nov. 24, 1978) p. 29.
Lengthy review of the ballet *Salome* following its premiere at the Circus Building, Copenhagen, Nov. 10, 1978.   It was an amazing success and sold our most every performance.   Though the music is described as "a stunning score by Britain's foremost serious music composer," most emphasis is focused on Vivi Flindt, who dances the role of Salome, especially on her nude dance at its conclusion. Includes a somewhat popular synopsis.

B907. Zakariasen, Bill. "The Fires of London in New York." *New York Daily News* (April 25, 1983).
Includes a review of a performance of *Le Jongleur de Notre Dame* by the Fires of London conducted by the composer at Symphony Space, New York, late April, 1983. About the work the reviewer notes: "Davies's clever, medieval-hued score is spikely attractive and makes all the unusual points the composer attempts."

B908. Zimmermann, Christoph. "Gelsenkirchen." *Opera* v. 35 (Oct. 1984) p. 1145.
Very brief review of a performance of *The Lighthouse* in Bremen by Gelsenkirchen, Feb. 25, 1984.

B909. Zimmermann, Christoph. "Oper der Stadt Bonn." *Oper und Konzert* v. 25 no. 1 (1987) p. 5.
Includes a review of a performance of *The Lighthouse* by the Oper der Stadt Bonn, Nov. 25, 1986. Soloists included Lorenz Minth, Marcel Gasztecki, and Roderic Keating. The performance was directed by Theo Dorn.

Books, Theses, and Dissertations

B910. Adams, Richard. *A Book of British Music Festivals*. London: Robert Royce Limited, 1986.
pp. 175–180.
Brief but informative discussion of the St. Magnus Festival.

B911. Anderson, James. *Bloomsbury Dictionary of Opera and Operetta*. London: Bloomsbury Publishing Limited, 1989.
pp. 331, 367, 562.
Includes a short biography of the composer as well as entries on *The Lighthouse* and *Taverner*.

B912. Anhalt, Istvan. *Alternative Voices: Essays of Contemporary Vocal and Choral Compositions*. Toronto: University of Toronto Press, 1984.

pp. 6, 161, 164, 170, 172–174, 200, 204, 211 215–216, 217, 235, 239.

Features discussions of *Eight Songs for a Mad King*, and *Miss Donnithorne's Maggot*.

B913.   Bawtree, Michael. *The New Singing Theatre: A Charter Movement for the Music Theatre Movement*. New York: Oxford University Press, 1991. pp. 11–12; 173–174.

Includes a discussion of *Eight Songs for a Mad King*.

B914.   Bayliss, Colin. *The Music of Sir Peter Maxwell Davies: An Annotated Catalogue*. Beverly (U. K.): Highgate Publications, 1991.

First published annotated catalogue of works and premieres in a single volume, with details on the compositions through 1990 (up to **J239**) and other information.

B915.   Bazelon, Irwin. *Knowing the Score*. New York: Van Nostrand Reinhold Company, 1975.

pp. 37–38, 197, 202, 208, 288.

Brief discussion of Davies as a composer of film scores.

B916.   Borwick, Douglas Bruce. *Peter Maxwell Davies' "Antechrist": An Analysis*. Doctoral Dissertation: Eastman School of Music, University of Rochester, 1979.

B917.   Brown, George Mackay. *Portrait of Orkney*. London: John Murray (Publishers) Ltd., 1988.

Includes a charming personal account of the composer's move to Hoy and of the St. Magnus Festival. Photograph of the composer with Isaac Stern in St. Magnus Cathedral.

B918.   Cargile, Donald Wayne. *Music by Sir Peter Maxwell Davies for the Guitar: An Analysis by Pitch Reduction of the Solo Works*. Master's Thesis: University of Texas at El Paso, 1989.

Discusses *Dark Angels*, *Lullabye for Ilian Rainbow*, *Hill Runes*, and *Sonata for Guitar*.

B919.   Crawford, John C. and Dorothy L. Crawford. *Expressionism in Twentieth-Century Music*. Bloomington: Indiana University Press, 1993. pp. 276, 278–279.

Discusses *Eight Songs for a Mad King*, *Revelation and Fall*, and *Vesalii Icones*.

B920. Finnissy, Michael, Malcolm Hayes and Roger Wright, eds. *New Music–1988*. Oxford: 1988.
pp. 85–90.
Includes an article by Stephen Pruslin which focuses on the history of The Fires of London.

B921. Flerlage, Alice K, *The Use of Pre-existent Material in the Works of Peter Maxwell Davies and George Rochberg*. M.M. Thesis: Northwestern University, 1978.

B922. Foreman, Lewis., ed. *British Music Now* London: Paul Elek, 1975.
pp. 7, 11, 12, 17, 27, 41, 48, 61, 62, 71–85, 97, 120, 165, 167, 173, 199, 200.
Includes a chapter by Stephen Arnold on the composer's work to 1975 (pp. 71–85), with some musical examples.

B923. Griffiths, Paul. *Modern Music: The Avant Garde Since 1945*. London: J.M. Dent & Sons, Limited, 1981.
pp. 189–195, 201, 252, 259, 260–262, 269.
Mentions *Alma Redemptoris Mater*, *Ave Maris Stella*, *Blind Man's Buff*, *Ecce Manus Tradentis*, *Eight Songs for a Mad King*, *First Fantasia on an 'In Nomine' of John Taverner*, *Martyrdom of St. Magnus*, *A Mirror of Whitening Light*, *Missa Super L'Homme Armé*, *Miss Donnithorne's Maggot*, *Prolation*, *Revelation and Fall*, *St. Michael Sonata*, *St. Thomas Wake*, *Second Fantasia on John Taverner's 'In Nomine,'* *Seven In Nomine*, *String Quartet*, *Symphony No. 1*, *Taverner*, *Vesalii Icones*, and *Worldes Blis*. Includes musical examples from *A Mirror of Whitening Light* and *Taverner*.

B924. Griffiths, Paul. *Peter Maxwell Davies*. London: Robson Books, 1982.
In the series "The Contemporary Composers," this general introduction to the composer and his works surveys his compositional output as of its date, with musical analyses of *String Quartet*, *Antechrist*, and *Ave Maris Stella*. A section "Around Taverner" examines his uses of John Taverner's music and life; another, "*Pax Orcadiensis*," explores the importance of Orkney to his compositions. With a "List of Works and Recordings" and a Bibliography.

B925. Griffiths, Paul. *New Sounds, New Personalities: British Composers of the 1980s in Conversation with Paul Griffiths*. London: Faber Music Ltd., 1985. pp, 19, 31–38, 40, 41, 97, 103.
Chapter 3 (pp. 31–38) is a lengthy interview with the composer, including a photograph of him at home on Hoy.

B926. Hall, Michael. *Harrison Birtwistle*. London: Robson Books, 1984. pp. 6, 7, 8, 9, 12, 27, 50, 155, 159, 160.
Mentions *Alma Redemptoris Mater*, *Antechrist*, and *Taverner*.

B927. Hamilton, Mary. *A–Z of Opera*. New York: Facts on File, 1990. pp. 118, 135, 200.
Includes brief articles on *The Lighthouse*, "Peter Maxwell Davies," and *Taverner*.

B928. Hanke, Ken. *Ken Russell's Films*. Metuchen, New Jersey: Scarecrow Press, 1984.
pp. 122, 149, 152, 153, 172, 173, 413.
Includes discussions of Ken Russell's films *The Devils* and *The Boyfriend*, with comments on how the scores enhanced the films.

B929. Headington, Christopher, et. al. *Opera: A History*. London: Bodley Head, 1987.
pp. 344–346.
Includes a section on *Taverner* and mentions *Revelation and Fall*, *Vesalii Icones*, *The Lighthouse*, and *The Martyrdom of St. Magnus*.

B930. Henze, Hans Werner. *Music and Politics*. Ithaca, New York: Cornell University Press, 1982.
pp. 22, 216, 223, 263, 267.
Includes a discussion of *Psalm 24* and *Missa Super L'Homme Armé*. Also remarks on Davies's involvement in Henze's opera project *Der Heiße Ofen*, which began in 1975 and was premiered in 1989.

B931. Hutcheon, Linda. *A Theory of Parody: The Teaching of Twentieth-Century Art Forms*. New York: Metheun, Incorporated, 1985.
p. 15.
Mentions the composer's use of parody as a compositional technique, citing *Antechrist*, *Taverner*, and *Missa Super L'Homme Armé*.

B932. Jacob, Jeffrey. *Peter Maxwell Davies' Vesalii Icones: Origins and Analysis*. Dissertation: Peabody Conservatory of Music, 1979.
Discusses *Hymn to St. Magnus*, *Stone Litany*, *From Stone to Thorn*, *Hymnos*, *Revelation and Fall*, in the course of a thorough analysis of *Vesalii Icones*.

B933. Jeutner, Renate, ed. *Peter Maxwell Davies: Ein Komponistenporträt*. Bonn: Musikverlag Boosey & Hawkes, 1983.
A small but significant life and works volume. Contains musical examples. Also contains a chronological works list.

B934. Karolyi, Otto, *Modern British Music: The Second British Musical Renaissance—From Elgar to P. Maxwell Davies*. Cranbury, New Jersey: Associated University Presses, 1994.
pp. 104, 107, 109, 112, 116–129.
Includes a chapter devoted to Davies's life and works.

B935. Kleszynski, Kenneth A. *Peter Maxwell Davies' Instrumental Music for Young Performers*. Doctoral Dissertation: Michigan State University, 1984.
Discusses selected works for young performers, with emphasis on *Stevie's Ferry to Hoy*, *Farewell to Stromness*, *Yesnaby Ground*, *Renaissance Scottish Dances*, *Three Studies for Percussion*, *Three Dances by William Byrd*, *Five Voluntaries*, *Five Klee Pictures*, and *A Welcome to Orkney*.

B936. Lippman, Samuel. *Arguing for Music/ Arguing for Culture*. Boston: David R. Godine, 1990.
pp. 79–80.
Briefly focuses on a performance of *Ave Maris Stella* by the New York New Music Ensemble conducted by Robert Black in New York City, as part of 'Horizons '83,' June 2, 1983.

B937. Manville, Roger and John Huntley. *The Technique of Film Music*. Revised and Enlarged edition. New York: Hastings House Publishers, 1975.
pp. 234, 235, 246–253.
Includes a section on the film score for Ken Russell's *The Devils*, with reproduction of several pages of the score,

B938. Mellers, Wilfred. *Caliban Reborn: Revival in Twentieth-Century Music*.
London: Victor Gollancz, Limited, 1968.
pp. 150, 174–177.
Includes mention of *Four Carols from O Magnum Mysterium*,
Leopardi Fragments, *Veni Sancte Spiritus*, and *Second Fantasia on
John Taverner's 'In Nomine'*.

B939. Miller, Maureen. *Vocal Music of Peter Maxwell Davies Based on the
Poetry of George Mackay Brown*.   Dissertation: Florida State
University School of Music, 1984.
Focuses on settings of texts by George Mackay Brown.

B940. Montgomery, Joy L. *Dualism in Eight Songs for a Mad King by Peter
Maxwell Davies*.   Master's Thesis: Southern Illinois University,
1978.

B941. Morgan, Robert P. *Twentieth-Century Music: A History of Musical Style
in Modern Europe and America*.   New York: W. W. Norton &
Company, Inc., 1991.
pp. 277, 415, 419, 446, 450, 482.
Features discussion of *Alma Redemptoris Mater*, *Antechrist*, *Eight
Songs for a Mad King*, *Fantasias on an 'In Nomine' of John
Taverner Nos. 1 and 2*, *Missa Super L'Homme Armé*, *Miss Donni-
thorne's Maggot*, *Revelation and Fall*, *Salome*, *Shakespeare Music*,
String Quartet, and *Vesalii Icones*.

B942. Northouse, Cameron. *Twentieth Century Opera in England and the
United States*.   Boston: G. K. Hall & Company, 1976.
pp. 130, 146, 147, 155, 280.
Mentions *Eight Songs for a Mad King*, *Blind Man's Buff*, *Taverner*,
and *Miss Donnithorne's Maggot*.

B943. Orga, Ates. *The Proms*.   London: David & Charles, 1974. pp. 150,
165, 176, 177, 182.
Discusses *First Fantasia on an 'In Nomine' of John Taverner*,
Worldes Blis, *Blind Man's Buff*, and *Revelation and Fall*.

B944. Porter, Andrew. *Music of Three More Seasons: 1977–1980*.   New
York: Alfred A, Knopf, Incorporated, 1981.

pp. 16, 18, 26, 29, 66, 89, 215, 221, 229–230, 237–244, 281, 302, 334, 387–388, 521, 573.

This volume includes references and some more lengthy discussion of *Alma Redemptoris Mater, Ave Maris Stella, Black Pentecost, Dark Angels, Le Jongleur de Notre Dame, The Martyrdom of St. Magnus, Mirror of Whitening Light, Miss Donnithorne's Maggot, St. Thomas Wake, Second Fantasia on John Taverner's 'In Nomine,' Symphony No. 1*, and *The Two Fiddlers*.

B945. Porter, Andrew. *Musical Events, A Chronicle: 1980–1983*. New York: Summit Books, 1987.

Includes discussion of *Ave Maris Stella, Brass Quintet, Cinderella, Eight Songs for a Mad King, Fantasia and Two Pavans after Henry Purcell, Image, Reflection, Shadow, Le Jongleur de Notre Dame, Kinloche His Fantassie, A Mirror of Whitening Light, Miss Donnithorne's Maggot, Renaissance Scottish Dances, Salome, Shakespeare Music, String Quartet, Symphony No. 1*, and *Symphony No. 2*.

B946. Porter, Andrew. *A Musical Season*. New York: Viking Press, 1974.
pp. 32–33, 35.
Briefly discusses *Eight Songs for a Mad King*.

B947. Preheim, Marles Clair. *The Choral Music of Peter Maxwell Davies*. DMA Thesis: University of Cincinnati, 1972.

B948. Pruslin, Stephen, ed. *Peter Maxwell Davies: Studies from Two Decades*. London: Boosey and Hawkes, 1979.

Highly useful collection of articles from the 1960s and 1970s by the composer and others (including John Andrewes, Stephen Arnold, Michael Chanan, Jonathan Harvey, Robert Henderson, Gabriel Josipovici, Oliver Knussen, Stephen Pruslin, Michael Taylor, J. C. G. Waterhouse); the editor was pianist for the Fires of London. Discussion of *Taverner*, the *Taverner* Fantasias, *Ave Maris Stella, Shepherds' Calendar, Five Motets, Eight Songs for a Mad King, Vesalii Icones, Symphony No. 1, Five Klee Pictures*.

B949. Purser, John. *Scotland's Music*. Edinburgh: Mainstream Publishing Company, Limited, 1992.
pp. 267–268, 272, 274.
Mentions *Concerto for Violin and Orchestra, An Orkney Wedding, With Sunrise, The Lighthouse, The Peat Cutters, Stone Litany*, and *Symphony No. 2*.

B950. Read, Gardiner. *20th-Century Microtonal Notation.* Westport, Connecticut: Greenwood Press, 1990. pp. 54, 72, 155.
Briefly discusses *Eight Songs for a Mad King* and *Revelation and Fall.*

B951. Roeder, Michael Thomas. *A History of the Concerto.* Portland, Oregon: Amadeus Press, 1994.
pp. 344, 451.
Includes a discussion of *Concerto for Violin and Orchestra* ("a concerto of distinction").

B952. Routh, Francis. *Contemporary British Music: The Twenty-Five Years From 1945 to 1970.* London: Macdonald and Company, 1972. pp. 229–244.
Includes a chapter on Davies's life and works.

B953. Sadie, Stanley. *History of Opera.* London: Macmillan Press Limited, 1989.
pp. 11, 265, 306, 309–310.
Includes a description of *Taverner.*

B954. Schafer, Murray. *British Composers in Interview.* London: Faber and Faber, 1963.
Pp. 173–182.
Interview with the composer early in his career.

B955. Schlotel, Brian Kenneth. *A Study of Music Written for Use in Education by Some Modern British Composers.* Doctoral Thesis: University of Reading, 1974.
Includes a section featuring an interview with the composer on his philosophy of music education (pp. 142–152).

B956. Schwartz, Elliott and Daniel Godfrey. *Music Since 1945: Issues, Materials and Literature.* New York: Schirmer Books, 1993.
pp. 230–232, 244, 252, 442.
Includes sections on Davies's *Eight Songs for a Mad King*, including musical examples, *St. Thomas Wake*, and *Antechrist.*

B957. Seabrook, Mike. *Max: The Life and Music of Peter Maxwell Davies.* London: Gollancz, 1994.
First full-length biography of the composer to appear. Intended more as a popular introduction than a scholarly treatment, but contains

much information, with discussions of the compositions and material from interviews with the composer and others.

B958. Searle, Humphrey and Robert Layton. *Britain, Scandinavia and The Netherlands*. (*Twentieth Century Composers III*.) New York: Holt, Rinehart and Winston, 1973.
pp. 118, 119–121, 122, 185.
The section on Davies mentions *Prolation, St. Michael Sonata, O Magnum Mysterium, Te Lucis Ante Terminum, Alma Redemptoris Mater, Ricercar and Doubles on 'To Many a Well,' First Fantasia on an 'In Nomine' of John Taverner, Second Fantasia on John Taverner's 'In Nomine,' Eight Songs for a Mad King, Revelation and Fall*, and *Vesalii Icones*.

B959. Silsbee, Ann Loomis. *Seven Rituals for Orchestra*. Part I of a Doctoral Thesis: Cornell University, 1979.

B960. Silsbee, Ann Loomis. *Peter Maxwell Davies' Stone Litany: Integration and Dynamic Process*. Part II of a Doctoral Thesis: Cornell University, 1979.
Intense study and analysis of *Stone Litany*.

B961. Skoog, James A. *Pitch Material in Peter Maxwell Davies's Eight Songs For a Mad King*. Masters Thesis: Eastman School of Music, University of Rochester, 1976.

B962. Smith-Brindle, Reginald. *The New Music: The Avant-Garde Since 1945*. Oxford: Oxford University Press, 1987. pp. 140–142, 149.
Includes a brief discussion of Davies's works including *Alma Redemptoris Mater, Antechrist, Eight Songs for a Mad King, Missa Super L'Homme Armé, Hymn to St. Magnus, Prolation, Ricercar and Doubles on 'To Many a Well,'* and *Seven In Nomine*.

B963. Taylor, Dorothy. *Music Now*. Milton Keynes: The Open University Press, 1979.
Pp. 17, 45.
Focuses on the compositions for school orchestras. Mentions the composer's term at Cirencester (1959–1962).

B964. Tongier, Cheryl A. *Pre-Existent Music in the Works of Peter Maxwell Davies*. Dissertation: University of Kansas, 1983.

Discusses *Alma Redemptoris Mater, St. Michael Sonata, First Fantasia on an 'In Nomine' of John Taverner, Shakespeare Music, The Shepherds' Calendar, Revelation and Fall, Missa Super L'Homme Armé, St. Thomas Wake, Second Fantasia on John Taverner's 'In Nomine,' Antechrist*, and *Eight Songs for a Mad King*, but by far the greatest amount of attention is given to *Taverner*.

B965. Watkins, Glenn. *Pyramids at the Louvre: Music, Culture, and Collage from Stravinsky to the Postmodernists*. Cambridge, Massachusetts: Belnap Press of Harvard University Press, 1994.

pp. 307, 414–415, 416.

Discusses *Salome, Tenebrae Super Gesualdo, Worldes Blis, Taverner*, and *Eight Songs for a Mad King*.

B966. Watkins, Glenn. *Soundings: Music in the Twentieth Century*. New York: Schirmer Books, 1987.

pp. 610–613, 626, 629, 642, 652, 663, 667–668.

Includes mention or discussion of *Ave Maris Stella, Miss Donnithorne's Maggot, Eight Songs for a Mad King, From Stone to Thorn, Hymn to St. Magnus, Hymnos, Leopardi Fragments, The Martyrdom of St. Magnus, The Medium, The No. 11 Bus, Renaissance Scottish Dances, Resurrection, Revelation and Fall, Salome, Sinfonia, St. Thomas Wake, Stedman Doubles, String Quartet, Symphony No. 1, Symphony No. 2, Symphony No. 3, Taverner, Tenebrae Super Gesualdo, Turris Campanarum Sonantium*, and *Worldes Blis*.

A Note on the Orcadian *and the St. Magnus Festival*

Anyone pursing research on the history of the St. Magnus Festival in Kirkwall or on performances of Peter Maxwell Davies's works in the Orkney Islands will find a wealth of reviews, interviews, and other material in Kirkwall's weekly newspaper, the *Orcadian*. Though there are abundant critical reviews of Orkney performances in the *Scotsman*, the *Glasgow Herald*, and other mainland Scottish newspapers, the *Orcadian* often supplies unique information on local events and local perceptions of the Festival. As of this writing, access to back issues is only available to users calling in person at the Kirkwall Public Library or the newspaper offices in Kirkwall (contact the Chief Librarian, The Orkney Library, Laing Street, Kirkwall, Orkney).

Films and Videotapes

Films with Scores by Peter Maxwell Davies

F1. *The Boyfriend*. Directed by Ken Russell. MGM, 1971.

F2. *The Boyfriend*. Directed by Ken Russell. Culver City, California: MGM/UA Home Video, 1990. Videocassette (VHS), 137 minutes; two 12-in. videodiscs, 135 minutes.
This is a 'Director's Cut' including material not in the motion picture version released in 1971, which ran for 110 minutes.

F3. *The Devils*. Directed by Ken Russell. Warner Brothers, 1971.

F4. *The Devils*. Produced by Robert H. Solo and Ken Russell; screenplay by Ken Russell. Directed by Ken Russell. New York: Warner Home Video, 1980?, 1984. Videocassette (VHS), 105 minutes.

F5. *The Devils*. Produced by Robert H. Solo and Ken Russell; screenplay by Ken Russell. Directed by Ken Russell. New York: Warner Home Video, 1991. Videocassette (VHS), 103 minutes.

Chronological List of Works, with First Performances

Works are listed in order of year of *composition*, which generally means the year in which a work was *completed*. A range of years in parentheses following a title indicates that the composition of that work spanned those years (such indications are necessarily very approximate). Dates of first performances, where known, follow *without* parentheses. Works having parts that were premiered in different years are usually listed in more than one place, sometimes under the titles of those parts (see for instance *Eram Quasi Agnus, Ut Re Mi*); these are cross-referenced here and in the *List of Works and First Performances*. I have also omitted some untitled manuscripts.

Each entry is prefaced with the 'J' number (in boldface type) for the work in question, if it has one. These represent the most recent revision of Judy Arnold's catalog, and in some instances they differ from the J numbers that appear in Bayliss's catalog (see, e.g., *Farewell-A Fancye*, now **J214A**). Because of revisions, there are also gaps (e.g., there is no **J204**). For the most part, my chronological list of works is in J-number order.

1942

J1   *'Moderato' in E Flat.*

1944

J4   *The Cloud* (1943–44). May 20, 1948

1947

J2   *Incantations.*
J3   *Birds.* Dec., 1947

1948

J5   *The River.*
J7   *Funeral March in B Major for a Pig.* (ca. 1950)

1949

J6   *Prelude.*
      Parade. 1949

1950

J8   *Stehn am Fuß des Gebirgs.*
J9   *Five Songs.*
J10   *Andante in E Major.*
J16   *[Unidentified Sketches/Drafts* from 1950s–1960s: see **W267**)

1952

J11   *Allegretto, con Moto.*
J12   *Quartet Movement.* May 23, 1983

1954

J13   *Sonata for Piano.*
J14   *Woodwind Octet.*

1955

J15   *Illa Autem Arbor.*
J17   *Burchiello.* (possibly 1960s)
J18   *Sonata for Trumpet and Piano.* 1955
J20   *Stedman Doubles* (revised 1968). Apr. 23, 1968

1956

J19   *Five Pieces for Piano.* Dec., 1956
J21   *Sonata for Clarinet and Piano.* July 20, 1957

1957

J22   *Alma Redemptoris Mater* (instrumental version). May 7, 1957
J23   *St. Michael Sonata.* July 13, 1959

1958

J24   *Sextet.* (revised 1972) May 17, 1972 (revised as *Septet*)
J25   *Prolation.* (1957–58) July, 1959
J26   *Carol at Christmastime '58 for Julian.*
J76   *Stedman Caters.* (revised, 1968) May 30, 1968

1959

J28   *Ricercar and Doubles on 'To Many A Well'.* 1959
J29   *Five Motets.* (1959; 1964; 1965) Mar. 1, 1965
J30   *Five Klee Pictures.* (revised 1976) Oct. 16, 1976
J31   *Three Dances by William Byrd.*
J32   *Four Canons.* Feb. 3, 1960
J33   *Pavan and Galliard from the Mulliner Book.* Feb. 3, 1960

1959-61 (at Cirencester)

There Is No Rose of Such Virtue.
Lord, Thy Word Abideth.
Amor Jesu.
Andantino and Allegro from 'Les Cinq Doigts' by Igor Stravinsky.
[Unidentified Arrangement: see **W266**].
Hodie Christus Natus Est.
Oggi È Nato un Bel Bambino.
'O Haupt Voll Blut und Wunden' by J. S. Bach.
Plainsong Melodies: Ave Verum Corpus; Ave Maria; Plangiamo [sic] Quel
        Crudel Basciare; Tantum Ergo.
Canzona 14 from Canzone e Sonate, 1615 (Giovanni Gabrieli).

1960

           Pavan by Newman from the Mulliner Book.
J34   *Prelude from 'Jack-in-the-Box' by Eric Satie.*
J35   *Romance from 'Trois Rag-Caprices' by Milhaud.*
           Three German Folksongs.
J36   *Mouvement Perpetuel No. I by Poulenc.*
J37   *Watkins Ale.*
J38   *'Benedicam Dominum' by Johnson from the Mulliner Book.*
J39   *O Magnum Mysterium.*   Dec. 8, 1960 (includes **J40**)
J40   *Organ Fantasia on 'O Magnum Mysterium'.* Nov. 30, 1960
J41   *Five Voluntaries.* 1960
J42   *Movement from 'Il Ballo delle Ingrate' by Monteverdi.*
J43   *Ritornello from 'L'Incoronazione di Poppea' of Monteverdi.*
J44   *String Quartet.* Nov. 9, 1961

1961

J45   *Ave Maria, Hail Blessed Flower.*
J46   *Te Lucis Ante Terminum.*   Nov. 30, 1961
J47   *Richard II.*
J48   *National Anthem.*
J52   *Four Carols.*   Nov. 26, 1962

J53   *Leopardi Fragments*.   July 19, 1962

1962

J50   *Four Movements from 'Vespers of 1610' by Monteverdi*.
J51   *First Fantasia on an 'In Nomine' of John Taverner*.   Sept. 13, 1962
J54   *The Lord's Prayer*.   July 1, 1962
J55   *Sinfonia*.   May 9, 1962

1963

J56   *Veni Sancte Spiritus*.   July 10, 1964

1964

J57   *Second Fantasia on John Taverner's 'In Nomine'*.   Apr. 30, 1965
J58   *Realisation of a Canon by Michael Praetorius*.
J59   *Shakespeare Music*.   Dec. 8, 1964
J60   *Ave Plena Gracia*.
J61   *Five Little Pieces* (1960–64). Aug. 1964
J64   *In Illo Tempore* (see *Ecce Manus Tradentis*). Aug. 20, 1965

1965

J62   *Pagoda Fugue*.
J63   *Seven In Nomine* (1962–65). partial Aug. 20, 1965; complete Dec. 3,
         1965
J65   *Revelation and Fall* (1965–1966; revised 1980). Feb. 26, 1968
J66   *Shall I Die for Mannis Sake?* 1965
J67   *I Can't Compose Today*.
J68   *The Shepherds' Calendar*.   May 20, 1965

1966

J69   *Notre Dame des Fleurs*.   Mar. 17, 1973
J70   *Five Carols*.   Dec. 11, 1966
         Illuxit Leticia.

1967

J27   *Songs to Words by Dante*.
J71   *Canon ad Honorem Igor Stravinsky*.   July 15, 1967
J72   *Antechrist*.   May 30, 1967
J73   *Hymnos*.   July 17, 1967

1968

J74   *Epistrophe*.

J75   *Missa Super L'Homme Armé.* Feb. 26, 1968
J77   *Fantasia and Two Pavans after Henry Purcell.* Jan. 13, 1969
J87   *Songs.*

1969

J78   *St. Thomas Wake: Foxtrot for Orchestra* (1966–69). June 2, 1969
J79   *Worldes Blis* (1966–69). Aug. 28, 1969
J80   *Eight Songs for a Mad King.* Apr. 22, 1969
J81   *Cauda Pavonis.* Jan. 3, 1970
J82   *Solita* (revised 1972). June 25, 1969
J83   *Canzona by Giovanni Gabrieli.* Apr. 11, 1969
J84   *Eram Quasi Agnus* (see *Ecce Manus Tradentis*). June 19, 1969
J86   *Sub Tuam Protectionem* (see *Two Piano Pieces*). Jan. 13, 1970
J85   *Vesalii Icones.* Dec. 9, 1969

1970

J88   *Nocturnal Dances* (1969–70). June 1970
J89   *Four Quartets: Incidental Music.*
J92   *Taverner* (begun 1962–1968, completed 1970). July 12, 1972
J93   *Taverner: Points and Dances From the Opera.* Feb. 20, 1971
J95   *'Also Hat Gott Die Welt Geliebet' by Dietrich Buxtehude.* Aug. 10, 1970

1971

J94   *Ut Re Mi* (see *Two Piano Pieces*) (1970-71). Jan. 19, 1971
J96   *From Stone to Thorn.* June 30, 1971
J97   *Turris Campanarum Sonantium – The Bell Tower.* Mar. 12, 1971
J98   *The Devils.* (film premiere 1971)
J98A   *Suite from 'The Devils.'* Dec. 11, 1971
J99   *The Boyfriend.* (film premiere 1971)
J99A   *Concert Suite from 'The Boyfriend.'* Dec. 11, 1971
J100   *Pussycat.*
J101   *'Hoquetus David' by Machaut.*
J102   *'Ma Fin Est Mon Commencement' by Machaut.*
J111   *Canon in Memoriam Igor Stravinsky.* June 17, 1972

1972

J103   *Song.*
J104   *[Untitled Work* for alto flute and marimba: see **W269**].
J105   *Walton Tribute.* Mar., 1972
J106   *Blind Man's Buff.* May 29, 1972
J107   *Fool's Fanfare.* Apr. 23, 1972

J108   *Hymn to St. Magnus.* Oct. 13, 1972
J109   *Tenebrae Super Gesualdo.* Aug. 25, 1972
J110   *Tenebrae Super Gesualdo (choral version).* June 28, 1984
J112   *Lullabye for Ilian Rainbow.* Sept. 18, 1972
J113   *Prelude and Fugue in C♯ Minor by J. S. Bach.* Oct. 13, 1972
J114   *Veni Sancte–Veni Creator Spiritus.* May 6, 1972

1973

J115   *Stone Litany: Runes From a House of the Dead* (1973-75). Sept. 22, 1973
J116   *Renaissance Scottish Dances.* July 29, 1973
J117   *Four Instrumental Motets: Si Quis Diliget Me.* July 29, 1973
J118   *Fantasia Upon One Note.* July 24, 1973
J119   *Fiddlers at the Wedding.* May 3, 1974
J122   *Four Instrumental Motets: All Sons of Adam.* Feb. 20, 1974

1974

J120   *Dark Angels* (1973–74). July 31, 1974
J121   *Miss Donnithorne's Maggot.* Mar. 9, 1974
J123   *Four Instrumental Motets: Psalm 124.* July 28, 1974
J124   *Nach Bergamo–Zur Heimat.* Sept. 14, 1974
J125   *Prelude and Fugue in C♯ Major by J. S. Bach.* Nov. 27, 1974
J126   *Song for Jenny and Her New Baby.*
J127   *Black Furrow, Gray Furrow.*
J128   *Wedding Telegram for Gary Kettel.*
J129   *Christmas Card for Judith and Roger.*
J130   *Yesterday: Lennon and McCartney.*

1975

J131   *Ave Maris Stella.* May 27, 1975
J132   *The Door of the Sun.* Mar. 9, 1976
J133   *The Kestrel Paced Round the Sun* (1974–75). Mar. 9, 1976
J134   *The Seven Brightnesses.* Oct. 12, 1975
J135   *Three Studies for Percussion.* Oct. 15, 1975
J136   *My Lady Lothian's Lilt.* Aug. 20, 1975
J137   *Stevie's Ferry to Hoy.*
J139   *Kinloche his Fantassie.* Aug. 19, 1976
            Der Heiße Ofen. Mar. 18, 1989 (composite work)

1976

J138   *Three Organ Voluntaries.* July 31, 1979
J140   *Anakreontika.* Sept. 17, 1976

J141 *The Blind Fiddler.* Feb. 16, 1976
J142 *Symphony No. 1* (1975–76). Feb. 2, 1978
J143 *The Martyrdom of St. Magnus.* June 18, 1977
J144 [*Untitled Piece* for piano: see **W268**].
J150 *Ave Rex Angelorum.* Dec. 18, 1976

1977
J149 *A Mirror of Whitening Light* (1976–77). Mar. 23, 1977
J146 *Westerlings.* May 25, 1977
          Ice Walk in Sheldon's [Borrowed] Boots.
J148 *Runes from a Holy Island.* Nov. 6, 1977
J151 *Four Instrumental Motets: Our Father Whiche in Heaven Art.* Aug. 18, 1977
J152 *Cantata Profunda op. 2002.*
J177 *Two Little Quartets: Quartet No. 2* (revised 1987). Nov. 12, 1987

1978
J153 *The Two Fiddlers.* June 16, 1978
J154 *Dances from 'The Two Fiddlers'.* Oct. 6, 1978
J155 *Le Jongleur de Notre Dame* (1977–78). June 18, 1978
J156 *Salome.* Nov. 10, 1978
J157 *Four Lessons for Two Keyboards.* Aug. 23, 1978
J159 *Solstice of Light* (1976–79). June 18, 1979

1979
J145 *Orkney Strathspey and Reel Society's Silver Jubilee Salute.* June 17, 1979
J158 *Black Pentecost.* May 11, 1982
J160 *Nocturne.* Jan. 28, 1983
J161 *Kirkwall Shopping Songs.* June 16, 1979
J162 *The Lighthouse.* Sept. 2, 1980
J163 *Quiet Memory of Bob Jennings.*

1980
J164 *Cinderella.* June 21, 1980
J165 *Yellow Cake Revue.* June 21, 1980
J166 *Farewell to Stromness.* June 21, 1980
J167 *Yesnaby Ground.* June 21, 1980
J168 *A Welcome to Orkney.* June 30, 1980
J169 *Two Little Quartets: Quartet No. 1.* July 26, 1982
J170 *Symphony No. 2.* Feb. 26, 1981

1981

J168A	*The Well – Incidental Music*. June 20, 1981
J172	*The Medium*. June 21, 1981
J173	*Sonata for Piano*. May 23, 1981
J174	*The Rainbow*. June 20, 1981
J175	*Hill Runes*. July 25, 1981
J176	*The Bairns of Brugh*. May 30, 1981
J178	*Sonatina for Trumpet*.
J179	*Lullabye for Lucy*. June 19, 1981
J180	*Brass Quintet*. Mar. 19, 1982
J181	*Seven Songs Home*. Dec. 13, 1982
J182	*Songs of Hoy*. June 21, 1982
J192	*March: The Pole Star* (for brass band). June 17, 1983
J191	*March: The Pole Star* (for brass quintet). Aug. 18, 1983

1982

J182A	*'Take a Pair of Sparkling Eyes' by Arthur Sullivan*.
J183	*Sea Eagle*. Aug. 16, 1982
J183A	*Bessie Millie's Wind Shop*. June 19, 1982
J184	*Image, Reflection, Shadow*. Aug. 22, 1982
J185	*Sinfonia Concertante*. Aug. 12, 1983
J186	*Sonata for Organ*. June 23, 1982
J187	*Four Voluntaries by Thomas Tallis*. (1982–1983). Dec. 9, 1983
J189	*Two Motets by Gesualdo*. Aug. 18, 1983

1983

J193	*Birthday Music for John*. Oct. 13, 1983
J194	*Into the Labyrinth*. June 22, 1983
J195	*Sinfonietta Accademica*. Oct. 6, 1983
J230	*Island of the Saints – Incidental Music*. June 18, 1983

1984

J197	*Agnus Dei*. June 23, 1986
J198	*Sonatine for Violin and Cimbalon*. June 3, 1984
J199	*Unbroken Circle*. June 1, 1984
J200	*The No. 11 Bus* (1983–84). Mar. 20, 1984
J201	*Sonata for Guitar* (1983–84). June 20, 1987
J202	*One Star at Last*. Dec. 24, 1984
J203	*Symphony No. 3*. Feb. 19, 1985
	Veni Sancte Spiritus on a Plainsong. 1984–1991

1985

J196   *We Met in St. Louis: A Birthday Card.* Nov. 19, 1985
J205   *An Orkney Wedding, With Sunrise.* May 10, 1985
J206   *First Ferry to Hoy.* Nov. 12, 1985
J207   *The Peat Cutters.* Aug. 18, 1985
J208   *Concerto for Violin and Orchestra.* June 21, 1986

1986

J209   *Jimmack the Postie.* June 22, 1986
J210   *House of Winter.* June 23, 1986
J211   *Sea Runes.* Nov. 16, 1986
J212   *Excuse Me.* Feb. 26, 1986
         Schools Music Association Grace.
J214   *Winterfold.* Jan. 20, 1987
J214A *Farewell—a Fancye.* Jan. 20, 1987
J215   *Strathclyde Concerto No. 1 for Oboe and Orchestra.* Apr. 29, 1988
J215A *Veni Sancte Spiritus on a Plainsong* (theme for *Music in Camera*).

1987

J216   *Resurrection* (1986–87; conception from 1963). Sept. 18, 1988
J218   *Strathclyde Concerto No. 2 for Cello and Orchestra.* Feb. 1, 1989

1988

J217   *Mishkenot.* May 3, 1988
J219   *Concerto for Trumpet and Orchestra.* Sept. 21, 1988
J220   *Dances from 'The Two Fiddlers'* (violin and piano). June 19, 1988
J221   *Six Songs for St. Andrew's.* June 18, 1988

1989

J222   *The Great Bank Robbery.* June 16, 1989
J222A *Alma Redemptoris Mater* (for mezzo-soprano and oboe).
J223   *Hircus Quando Bibit.* June 20, 1989
J224   *Symphony No. 4* (1988–89). Sept. 10, 1989
J225   *Hallelujah! The Lord God Almichtie.* June 11, 1989
J226   *Jupiter Landing.* Apr. 3, 1990
J227   *Strathclyde Concerto No. 3 for Horn, Trumpet and Orchestra.* Jan. 19, 1990
J228   *Dinosaur at Large.* July 4, 1990
J229   *Threnody on a Plainsong for Michael Vyner.* Oct. 25, 1989

1990

J231   *Tractus Clausum et Reconditum.* May 20, 1990
J232   *Dangerous Errand.* June 25, 1990
J233   *Strathclyde Concerto No. 4 for Clarinet and Orchestra.* Nov. 21, 1990
J234   *Caroline Mathilde: Ballet in Two Acts.* Mar. 14, 1991
J235   *Highbury Fling.*
J236   *Concerto No. 27.*
J237   *A Little Christmas Music.*
J238   *Apple Basket, Apple Blossom.*
J239   *Hymn to the Word of God.* Mar. 6, 1991

1991

J240   *Ojai Festival Overture.* June 1, 1991
J241   *The Spiders' Revenge.* June 25, 1991
J242   *The Road to Colonnus.* June 21, 1991
J243   *Witch.* June 21, 1991
J244   *Caroline Mathilde: Concert Suite I.* (1990–91) July 12, 1991
J245   *Strathclyde Concerto No. 5 for Violin, Viola and String Orchestra.* Mar. 13, 1992
J246   *'Vanitas' by Jan Albert Ban.*
J247   *Strathclyde Concerto No. 6 for Flute and Orchestra.* Mar. 13, 1992
J248   *First Grace of Light.* Nov. 7, 1991
J249   *Caroline Mathilde: Concert Suite II.* Oct. 5, 1992

1992

J250   *A Selkie Tale.* June 19, 1992
J251   *Judica Me.*
J252   *Omnibus Voluptatem.*
J253   *The Turn of the Tide.* Feb. 12, 1993
J254   *Strathclyde Concerto No. 7 for Double Bass and Orchestra.* Nov. 25, 1992
J255   *Sir Charles his Pavan.* Sept. 22, 1992

1993

J256   *Souvenir de Strathclyde.*
J257   *Seven Summer Songs.* June 18, 1993
J258   *Strathclyde Concerto No. 8 for Bassoon and Orchestra.* Nov. 24, 1993
J259   *Two Dances From Caroline Mathilde.* Sept. 24, 1993
J260   *Corpus Christi, with Cat and Mouse.* Nov. 30, 1993
J261   *A Spell for Green Corn: The MacDonald Dances.* Nov. 24, 1993
J262   *Six Secret Songs.*
J263   *Shepherds of Hoy.* May 25, 1994

1994

J264   *Chat Moss.* Mar. 15, 1994
J265   *A Hoy Calendar.* Mar. 15, 1994
J266   *Symphony No. 5.* Aug. 9, 1994
J267   *Cross Lane Fair.* June 18, 1994
J268   *Sunday Morning.* Sept. 18, 1994
J269   *Carolísima – Serenade.* Aug. 30, 1994
J270   *Birthday Greeting.* Oct. 1, 1994
J271   *Mercurius.* Nov. 6, 1994
J272   *Strathclyde Concerto No. 9 for Six Wind Instruments.* Feb. 9, 1995
J273   *Drummond's Dumpe.*
J274   *Coleran's Currant.*

1995

J275   *The Beltane Fire: Choreographic Poem for Orchestra.* Apr. 3, 1995

Index

Since the Bibliography is itself an annotated index, the authors cited in it are included here only if they are mentioned in references of which they are not the authors. For references to Peter Maxwell Davies's works, consult the *SEE* references in the List of Works and First Performances.

About the Author

CAROLYN J. SMITH is a humanities bibliographer at the Sterling C. Evans Library Collection Development Department, Texas A & M University Library. Her previous publications include *William Walton: A Bio-Bibliography* (Greenwood Press, 1988). She is currently continuing work on Sir Peter Maxwell Davies and his music.

ISBN 0-313-26831-2

EAN

9 780313 268311

90000>

HARDCOVER BAR CODE